Pro Sports in 1993

Pro Sports in 1993
A Signature Season in Football, Basketball, Hockey and Baseball

David Ostrowsky

McFarland & Company, Inc., Publishers
Jefferson, North Carolina

LIBRARY OF CONGRESS CATALOGUING-IN-PUBLICATION DATA

Names: Ostrowsky, David, 1984– author.
Title: Pro sports in 1993 : a signature season in football, basketball, hockey and baseball / David Ostrowsky.
Description: Jefferson, North Carolina : McFarland & Company, Inc., Publishers, 2020 | Includes bibliographical references and index.
Identifiers: LCCN 2020038874 | ISBN 9781476680262 (paperback : acid free paper) ♾
ISBN 9781476641676 (ebook)
Subjects: LCSH: Professional sports—United States—History—20th century. | Professional sports—Canada—History—20th century. | Nineteen ninety-three, A.D.
Classification: LCC GV583 .O78 2020 | DDC 796.04/2—dc23
LC record available at https://lccn.loc.gov/2020038874

BRITISH LIBRARY CATALOGUING DATA ARE AVAILABLE

ISBN (print) 978-1-4766-8026-2
ISBN (ebook) 978-1-4766-4167-6

© 2020 David Ostrowsky. All rights reserved

No part of this book may be reproduced or transmitted in any form or by any means, electronic or mechanical, including photocopying or recording, or by any information storage and retrieval system, without permission in writing from the publisher.

Front cover (clockwise, from top left): Troy Aikman (John Fuller/Shutterstock), Michael Jordan *(El Gráfico)*, Patrick Roy (Canadian Press), Barry Bonds (Jim Accordino)

Printed in the United States of America

McFarland & Company, Inc., Publishers
Box 611, Jefferson, North Carolina 28640
www.mcfarlandpub.com

To Dad,
for making me an all-star
"athletic supporter"

Table of Contents

Acknowledgments ix

Introduction 1

1. Montana's Last Stand   5
2. "An Old-Fashioned Ballpark with Modern Amenities"   34
3. When Michael Jordan (and the Chicago Bulls) Owned the NBA   62
4. Canada's Last Stanley Cup   110
5. Shot Heard 'Round North America   139
6. How 'Bout Them Cowboys?   171
7. The Comeback Game   212

Epilogue 231

Chapter Notes 233

Bibliography 243

Index 249

Acknowledgments

I must say there is a very good chance that you would not be reading this look back at the phenomenal year in sports that was 1993 had it not been for Gary Mitchem and Rhonda Herman at McFarland.

Back in winter of 2019, I was about to give up on finding a publisher. Like many authors, I was tired of opening one email after another in which the first sentence included the word "unfortunately." Then one rejection seemed just a bit different from the others when I received an email from Kimberly Guinta, editorial director at Rutgers, who admired my writing, but just didn't feel that my work was the right fit for Rutgers University Press. So rather than sending the obligatory "thank you for your consideration" email, I asked her for some direction. She said try McFarland. I had never heard of McFarland. This was the last publisher I would try. If it didn't work out, I decided I would self-publish this book and move on with my life. After submitting my proposal, I waited a few weeks, and then on a lazy Saturday afternoon in March 2019, I got the response I had been waiting for since March 2018.

Thank you so very much, Gary and Rhonda.

Writing even a non-fiction book is largely a solitary pursuit. That is, except for getting to interview folks who can provide personal insight from which you can develop a compelling narrative outside the box scores. I had the privilege of speaking with dozens of people who made 1993 a momentous sports year, an opportunity for which I will be forever grateful.

Smiling emojis to the following people who took the time to reflect on the events I chronicled: Penny Hardaway, Jeff Dellenbach, Steve Christie, John Jett, Rob Awalt, Ed Ronan, Pat Conacher, Jimmy Carson, Tony Granato, Kirk Muller, Kerry Huffman, Kevin Glover, Brian Bellows, Stacey Augmon, Greg Foster, Dennis Awtrey, Clarence Weatherspoon, Alan Mills, Jay Bell, Jack McDowell, John Burkett, Andy Benes, Devon White, Mickey Morandini, Alfredo Griffin, Bob Milacki, Mike Trombley, Jason Bere, Crawford Ker, Scott Williams, James Washington, Jim Jeffcoat, Don Beebe, Darrell Walker, Andre Reed, B.J. Surhoff, Matt Blundin, Joe Valerio, Larry

Drew, Bill Cartwright, Ken Dayley, Dick Schofield, Woody Williams, Bryan Barker, Herm Edwards, Butch Davis, Erik Helland, Richie Whitt, Jackie MacMullan, Jack McCallum, Bill Stetka, Janet Marie Smith, J.J. Birden, and Jay Horwitz.

My sincere gratitude to the following ladies and gentlemen who helped facilitate those interviews: Dominick Saillant, Paul Capobianco, Andy Zilch, Dan Fremuth, Mark Rosenberg, Brian Olive, David Cohen, Matthew Chmura, Kristen Hudak, Abby Murphy, Nick Flammia, Phylicia Short, Bill Vint, Chris Ware, Ben Wagner, Matthew Birch, Eric Kay, Kevin Brown, Bart Swain, Eric Gallanty, Curtis Danburg, David Weber, Michael Hogan, Emily Walthouse, Charles Hampton, Samantha Pujol, David Plati, Brent Harner, Add Seymour, Chip Hurd, Theresa Villano, Emily Metelski, B.J. Evans, Amanda Fenwick, Raina Birden, Alex Mayer, and Phil Stukenborg.

The beautiful images included throughout this book were courtesy of Bryan Barker, Jon Cram, Bill Frakes, Bobby Alworth, Matt Conti, Camron Ghorbi, Steve East, Kaleb Center, Steve Lipofsky, Ron Vesely, Cody Voga, and Jeff Moeller.

Perhaps the hardest part of spending more. than three years working on a book is that it takes you away from the people you care about the most.

A tip of the cap to the in-laws, Jim, Judi, and Jill, for their continuous support of my writing career and this recent endeavor. Even if they weren't exactly sure what kind of book I was writing (or, if they did, why I was writing it).

Thank you, Sharon, for being a sibling with whom I can share my love of sports. Maybe it all started for you in 1993 as well?

Back in 2017, when I was credentialed for Red Sox, Celtics, and Bruins games for doing book-related interviews, it was a treat to be able to have post-interview/pregame dinners with my younger brother Jonathan on four separate occasions. Especially considering that in the following months, Jonathan would move across the country to attend law school at UCLA. In hindsight, our dinners added an extra layer of meaning to what were naturally the most exciting days of my book journey.

Growing up, I had a lot more room in my closet than I do today. The Boston teams weren't winning championships, which meant my mom wasn't buying commemorative t-shirts, sweatshirts, and hats. There were hardly any Boston-related sports feats worthy of honorary garb in the early to mid-nineties, but that didn't stop Mom from getting me meaningful sports gifts, whether it was a Steve Young replica uniform or Charlotte Hornets hat (the teal was irresistible). But as the nineties rolled on, it was, of course, so much more than the gifts. It was coming to Little League games, buying tickets for Red Sox games, learning about Red Sox games, and simply getting more interested in sports because she knew it meant so much to me.

Acknowledgments

Mom, if you are reading this, it means that you are about to read nearly 300 pages about sports not involving David Ortiz or Paul Pierce. It is appreciated.

I'm back in 1993.

Sunday, August 15, 1993, to be more precise.

My dad and I are walking by the putting greens of Chatham Bars Inn. We are headed to the Sunday night buffet, which is the non-sports highlight of the summer. The Boston Red Sox have just dropped two out of three to the visiting Toronto Blue Jays, including this afternoon's 9–1 loss in which Roger Clemens got lit up. The Sox appear to be going nowhere and the Blue Jays look destined for more October glory. I remember two things about our talk: my dad explaining to me how Joe Carter, as a dead-pull right-handed slugger, has always hit well at Fenway Park (he hit a two-run homer off the Rocket this day) and that Devon White is probably the best outfielder in baseball.

Something tells me that Dad wasn't thinking that (a) I would remember this chat more than a quarter-century later or that (b) I would one day be writing a book chronicling the 1993 Blue Jays, whereby I would have the opportunity to sit down for a personal interview with Devon White to gather his reflections.

This was one of many sports talks with my dad in 1993, whether it was along the greens of Chatham, dunes of Truro, or slopes of Gunstock Mountain. With three young kids and a full-time job, he had his hands full … but always had time to answer a question about Mo Vaughn or Bill Parcells.

Decades later, it seems safe to say these talks weren't a bad investment of his time.

Meanwhile, the sports year of 1993 wouldn't have been recreated in a book without my wife, Lauren.

Well, that's not entirely true. More like without the blessing of my wife, Lauren.

It is Thanksgiving weekend 2016 and we are out strolling our daughter Colby. I broach the subject of publishing my second book to Lauren. I have been thinking about starting this project for months (I plan to hit the phone and books right after the holiday season), but I won't get very far if Lauren is not on board.

Clearly, she was.

There are many emotions when you spend years working on a book: elation, frustration, exhaustion, dejection, nervousness, amusement, and fulfillment, to name several. Lauren had a front-row seat as I experienced them all.

Was she always mesmerized by the book's topic(s)? Perhaps not.

Was she able to realize how much joy the book ultimately brought me? Absolutely.

Lauren, there is no one I would rather have shared the highs and lows of this (or any other) experience with than you.

You are loved.

If I am going to be completely honest, it is quite ironic that I am mentioning Colby in the Acknowledgments. Certainly, constantly noisy living rooms and occasional sleep deprivation are not conducive to authoring a book.

But on the other hand, there is also no one who is more deserving of being mentioned in this section than Colby.

When I became committed to writing this book in summer of 2016, it became apparent to my wife and me that Colby would be facing significant developmental challenges in the years ahead. And so, as I soon embarked on this project, and faced challenges such as acquiring sources, gaining access to interviewees, and, most significantly, being accepted by a publisher, I was able to draw a parallel to Colby and her journey. Colby's perseverance provided great inspiration as I continued to get turned down by dozens of former pro athletes for interviews and hundreds of publishers for contracts. But, like Colby, I don't like hearing "NO" for an answer, even if I'm a little less vocal.

Thank you, Colby.

And by the time you are taking in these final words of the Acknowledgments, Colby will have gone to more than 50 sporting events (everywhere from Miami's American Airlines Arena to East Rutherford's MetLife Stadium) with her father. It's clear that the sports bug has successfully been passed down three generations … and it's hard to imagine a better way to start a book than that.

Introduction

It is December 1993 and I am sitting in Mr. Holland's third-grade classroom during lunchtime.

And I feel terribly left out.

A substitute teacher is trying to kill time by asking us to raise our hands if we watch any of the following television shows:

Saved by the Bell?

Full House?

Beverly Hills 90210?

My hand stays glued to the desk.

A classmate asks me if I own a television.

I do. Except I don't watch any shows. In fact, I don't watch anything on television unless it involves ... sports.

I am hooked. My life-long obsession with the four major North American professional sports has begun this year.

Over the course of this three-year book project that entailed more than 300 emails, 50 phone calls, 120,000 words, and 7,000 miles, I thought back to that day in third grade, but more importantly, how I got there:

Snacking on Lay's Sour Cream & Onion potato chips at a Memorial Day weekend barbecue while anticipating another Eastern Conference Finals showdown between the Bulls and Knicks; sitting in the doctor's office waiting room following a freak baseball injury on July 13, 1993, frustrated as hell that I would be missing the All-Star Game (no YouTube or DVR back then) but still soaking up the *Sports Illustrated* cover story on rookie phenom Mike Piazza; playing wiffle ball during a family summer vacation on Cape Cod while pretending to be Braves outfielder Ron Gant, who was on an absolute tear in the final months of the 1993 season; being told by Dad on Labor Day weekend that it's okay to root for the New York Yankees when their one-handed pitcher, Jim Abbott, was tossing a no-no; sitting in the Fenway Park bleachers the following afternoon as the Boston Red Sox were getting shelled by the Kansas City Royals—while wondering how Bill Parcells and Drew Bledsoe were faring in their New England Patriots debut against the Buffalo Bills in Western New York; walking home from Mason-Rice Elementary School on a brilliant early October afternoon, overjoyed that the ALCS game at Comiskey Park was slated for a 4 p.m. start, meaning I could actually watch all nine innings; blissfully watching the Dallas Cowboys–Miami Dolphins game on Thanksgiving Day in my Uncle Steve and Aunt Kathy's cozy finished basement … while looking forward to the next day's slate of college football rivalry games.

My wife doesn't understand how I can remember such random things from decades ago yet forget her request to unpack a bag of holiday gifts on a given evening.

Priorities, I guess.

In all seriousness, I feel blessed to have spent hundreds of hours reliving such memories and recreating moments that, let's be honest, probably wouldn't have comprised an entire book if it weren't for me. Or, as Toni Morrison once said, "If there is a book that you want to read, but it hasn't been written yet, you must be the one to write it."

So, from the perspective of a sports fan, one not named David Ostrowsky, what made 1993 any different from 1992 or 1994?

Nineteen ninety-three was the year of the greatest comeback in NFL history; the last time a Canadian-based team would win the Stanley Cup in more than a quarter of a century—and beat arguably the world's most gifted player in doing so; the final hurrah for Joe Montana—at the time the greatest quarterback to have ever played; the pinnacle of the Chicago Bulls dynasty and the career of Michael Jordan; the emergence of the Dallas Cowboys dynasty during an era in which the NFL was trying to facilitate parity; a World Series–winning walk-off home run; and an All-Star Game that introduced us to the new retro-style ballpark.

As the United States and Canada were undergoing transformative political changes in transitioning from conservative-leaning governments to more liberal-minded leadership, with President Bill Clinton and Prime Minister Jean Chrétien entering office, both nations were witnessing momentous sporting events. These 12 months not only encapsulated transcendent feats by some of the greatest participants in the history of North American sports but also coincided with team accomplishments that have proven perpetually inimitable.

However, for many of the year's protagonists, it was not a year without strife. When they weren't performing awe-inspiring athletic feats, some were burdened by harrowing pain, both physical and emotional, leaving indelible scars on their living legacies.

But above all else, it was a year for the most important people in professional sports—the fans.

Introduction

For sports fans living in Dallas, Buffalo, Kansas City, Montreal, Toronto, Baltimore, and Chicago, 1993 was a glorious year.

For sports fans throughout North America, 1993 was a historic year, one whose influences continue to reverberate.

In the sporting world, 1993 was no ordinary year.

1

Montana's Last Stand

Alex Gibbs felt he had to be brutally honest.

It was a searing late July morning and the Kansas City Chiefs were starting training camp at the University of Wisconsin–River Falls. The new offensive line coach for the Kansas City Chiefs knew that his linemen were taken aback as they were leaving the hockey rink (which served as a makeshift dressing area) and turning the corner toward the Division III school's football stadium, which was essentially a glorified high school stadium. With each step the burly linemen took, the crowd's roar magnified, perhaps accounting for the most deafening noise to ever penetrate the sleepy town of River Falls. After all, in past summers, the Chiefs opened camp to a throng of several hundred fans.

Not in 1993.

Before entering the stadium, Gibbs stopped the offensive linemen and said, "Hey boys, look at that crowd. Let me tell you something, they ain't here to see you."[1]

The crowd, easily several thousand by this point, was there to see the new quarterback, the one with four Super Bowl rings, three Super Bowl MVP trophies, two regular season MVP awards.

Indeed, the masses were there to lay eyes on a 37-year-old Joe Montana, the erstwhile San Francisco 49er legend who had thrown 21 passes over the past two years due to elbow surgery (after battling myriad injuries in the 1980s) and was now finishing a brilliant three-decade NFL career—while being considered the savior to a franchise that had one playoff victory since winning Super Bowl IX in 1970.

The divorce between Joe Montana and the San Francisco 49ers became official on April 20, 1993, when the 49ers dealt Montana along with safety David Whitmore and a 1994 third-round draft pick to the Chiefs for a first-round pick in the upcoming draft. However, the roots of the eventual schism were laid on April 3, 1987, when the Tampa Bay Buccaneers signed University of Miami quarterback Vinny Testaverde to a six-year,

$8.2 million contract, a few weeks before officially selecting him with the No. 1 overall pick in the 1987 NFL Draft. While the much-hyped Testaverde became the richest rookie in NFL history, the deal spoke volumes for how Tampa viewed incumbent quarterback Steve Young, a Heisman finalist while at BYU who was having an underwhelming early NFL career (3–16 record as starter) after a brief stint in the USFL. Clearly, Tampa was ready to move on from Young. Meanwhile, San Francisco now needed a backup to Montana after Mike Moroski retired and Jeff Kemp joined the Seattle Seahawks. Therefore, on April 24, 1987, Tampa Bay traded Steve Young to San Francisco for a second-round and fourth-round pick in the upcoming draft and $1 million.

Heading into the 1987 season, Montana was only 31 years old but coming off a subpar 1986 season that was truncated due to a severe back injury. Still, he wasn't anticipating that the team was acquiring his heir apparent, as he was only a couple seasons removed from quarterbacking the San Francisco 49ers to their second Super Bowl title of the decade. (The 49ers had won Super Bowl XVI in 1982 and Super Bowl XIX in 1985.) Presumably, in Young, the Niners were acquiring Montana's backup, not eventual replacement.

Only problem, for Montana, was that Steve Young would prove to be the furthest thing from a backup quarterback.

In fact, it didn't take long for Young to emerge as a legitimate threat to Montana. Late in the 1987 strike-shortened season, when Montana suffered a couple relatively minor injuries, including a sprained index finger, Young got three starts, of which the most impressive was his four-touchdown performance in a 41–0 drubbing of the Chicago Bears on "Monday Night Football."

As the postseason dawned, San Francisco head coach Bill Walsh was faced with the dreaded quarterback controversy. Montana or Young? Who would start in the Divisional Round against the Minnesota Vikings on January 9 at Candlestick Park? During the final three regular season games with Young playing, the 49ers had obliterated opponents 124–7. But statistically speaking, the 1987 season was Montana's finest, as he tossed 31 TD passes and finished as the highest-rated passer in the NFL.

(Two days before the regular season finale against the Los Angeles Rams, the 49ers held a practice on Christmas. For the first time, Montana invited Young, who was single at the time, over to his house for dinner afterward. According to Young, in his 2016 book, *QB: My Life Behind the Spiral*, when everyone sat down to break bread, Montana's three-year-old daughter asked her dad, "Is this the guy we hate?"[2] Young tried his best not to cackle. Montana was not so amused, responding, "No. That was someone else.")

1. Montana's Last Stand

Montana was eventually tabbed the starter against Minnesota. Joe Cool slogged through one of his worst postseason performances (12–26, one INT, four sacks) and was spelled by Young midway through the third quarter with his team trailing 27–10. In his first postseason appearance, Young passed for 158 yards and one touchdown, but the effort went for naught. The heavily favored 49ers would lose to the Vikings, 36–24, rendering the 1987 season a colossal disappointment.

While Montana entered the 1988 regular season as the starter, Young, increasingly adept at confounding opponents with his alacrity as a scrambler and ability to quickly hit the open receiver, took advantage of sporadic starting opportunities over this season and the following one when Montana suffered a rash of ailments. But it was never enough to make Walsh seriously contemplate a change—or for Young to ingratiate himself with the Niners' fans. Irrespective of Young's flashes of brilliance, Montana, when healthy, was still playing some of the best football of his career in the late eighties, leading the 49ers to victories in Super Bowl XXIII and Super Bowl XXIV, the latter in which he received Super Bowl MVP honors for a third time.

After the 1990 regular season in which Montana, who was now healthy enough to start 15 games, threw for 3,944 yards and 26 touchdowns, the 49ers fell to the eventual champion New York Giants 15–13 in the NFC Championship Game on January 20, 1991. The game was decided by Matt Bahr's last-second field goal but is most remembered for Giants defensive end Leonard Marshall's ferocious hit on Montana with less than 10 minutes remaining in the game.

The sequence was full of irony—and foreshadowing. All-time great linebacker Lawrence Taylor initially whiffed on Montana, which left Marshall to go in for the kill. And Steve Young, of all people, was the first teammate to rush over to a downed Montana after the vicious blow, one that left Montana writhing in pain with a wounded sternum, bruised stomach, cracked ribs, and broken hand.

The moment provided a glimpse into what would transpire over the ensuing months: Montana was out; Young was in.

During summer of 1991, Montana entered training camp no longer feeling the residual effects from the Marshall hit. Oddly, however, he started experiencing a gimpy elbow. On August 27, he went on injured reserve with what was described as a torn pronator teres tendon. Which meant he was due for a season-ending (if not career-ending) surgery. In fact, another all-time great quarterback, Terry Bradshaw of the Pittsburgh Steelers, had ended his career at age 35 after a similar surgery proved unsuccessful. San Fran head coach George Seifert, who had taken over for Walsh in 1989, even acknowledged the possibility that Montana had taken his final snap.

However, after Young failed to lead San Francisco to the playoffs during the 1991 season, the starting quarterback issue resurfaced when Montana came to training camp in July 1992 feeling considerably healthier after a successful surgery and threatening to assume a role on which Young presumably had a stranglehold.

As training camp got underway in 1992, Steve Young confided to Peter King of *Sports Illustrated*, "My situation is like running in the Kentucky Derby and then going back and running with the trotters at Yonkers. Forget it."[3]

Once the 1992 season began, Young backed up his words with spectacular play. The Niners got off to a 6–1 start behind Young, who would ultimately lead the NFL in completion percentage, touchdown passes, and quarterback rating. Meanwhile Montana was feeling great physically … and thus incredibly frustrated. By November, Montana, who had resumed throwing, told reporters he was 98 to 99 percent healthy. However, the 49ers' decision to keep him on injured reserve rendered him unable to practice with the team. Finally, in late November Montana was placed on San Francisco's practice squad and in December, joined the team's active game day roster. Despite the team's magnificent year (they would finish 14–2 and Young was named NFL MVP), the sight of Montana once again donning a 49ers uniform only stirred up further controversy. Now, arguably the most high-profile positional battle in the history of the NFL was dividing the entire city of San Francisco—from Fisherman's Wharf to Golden Gate Park.

The ironic thing was that Montana and Young did *not* despise each other. In fact, they even liked each other, at least at times. They weren't exactly close friends, but certainly not bitter enemies either. They were, as author Adam Lazarus coined them, "the best of rivals."

They were, however, *so* different, both on and off the field. Montana was a classic pocket passer, while the intrepid Young was impatient in the pocket, inclined to scramble amid menacing linebackers and explosive defensive backs. Whereas Montana had his trademark cool, laid-back demeanor, Young was uptight, often a nervous wreck in the huddle. By 1990, Montana had a stable of sports cars to choose from when he felt like coasting around the Bay Area: Corvette, BMW, Mercedes-Benz 500 SEC, Porsche 928, Ferrari 308, and Ferrari Testarossa. Young, despite being a millionaire several times over, drove a dingy 1965 Oldsmobile Cutless until it died with over 270,000 miles on the odometer.[4] For years, rumors had existed that Montana was using cocaine (a very common extracurricular activity for professional athletes in the late eighties). Young was a devout Mormon whose reputation was never sullied by accusations of illicit behavior.

One commonality between the two ultra-competitive quarterbacks was that, naturally, they both had zero interest in holding a clipboard on the sidelines. Now that Young was an established All-Pro, there was no way he was going back to second-stringer. Montana, despite his age (36) and suspect elbow, was not going to end his iconic career in a backup capacity. At one point in the 1992 season, Montana even publicly stated, "Losing every game of the year is better than sitting on the bench."[5]

The Montana-Young rift was awkwardness personified and eventually, the tension left an indelible mark on the locker room, where many players had no interest in exuding impartiality. Offensive tackle Harris Barton, himself a former roommate of Young's, remarked, "I don't think this team will ever be anybody's team like it was for Joe Montana."[6] Remarkably, the 49ers remained atop the NFC throughout the season, despite the ceaseless drama permeating the franchise.

The 49ers entered the final week of the 1992 regular season in an enviable, but not unfamiliar, position—having already secured the No. 1 seed (and home-field advantage) in the NFC playoffs. What was unfamiliar this year was that this otherwise meaningless regular season finale was going to give Montana, not the typical backup Young, a chance for some reps.

After a 23-month layoff, Montana was inserted in the second half against the Detroit Lions on "Monday Night Football." On a characteristically windy, drizzly early winter night at Candlestick Park, Montana (15–21 for 126 yards, two touchdowns) showed the NFL that he was not done. (The night was a win-win for the 49ers: Young got to rest while Montana's performance served as an audition to boost his upcoming trade value.) Nevertheless, in his press conference the day after San Francisco's 24–6 win over Detroit, George Seifert told reporters that, barring any significant injuries, Young was still his guy.

As would be evident a couple weeks later though, Young's brilliant regular season did not translate to postseason success. While he played serviceably well in a 20–13 Divisional Round win over the Washington Redskins, Young faltered in the 1992 NFC Championship Game (two costly interceptions in a 30–20 loss to the Dallas Cowboys) prompting fans sitting behind the San Francisco bench to serenade head coach George Seifert with homophobic obscenities for not giving Montana one last chance to spearhead another comeback before his looming departure.

Not only did Young's performance lead to an outcome marking the end of San Francisco's decade-long dominance of Dallas, but questions arose as to whether Seifert and 49ers team president Carmen Policy were acting rashly in (presumably) parting ways with Montana.

Was Young really capable of quarterbacking San Francisco to another world championship?

Apparently, from all media reports, Seifert and Policy had made up their minds. This one deflating loss was not going to change the long-term plan.

A reality of which Montana was aware.

Minutes after the loss, Montana trotted off the field, nestled into the training room, and removed his 49ers uniform one final time before changing into civvies and ducking out of a back entrance, never to return—as a member of the San Francisco 49ers.

One of the relatively few people in the 49ers organization who struggled to accept the inevitability of Joe Montana's departure was … the most influential person in the 49ers organization.

San Francisco 49ers owner Eddie DeBartolo, Jr., simply couldn't let go of Montana. Even though doctors advised the club that, given his age and condition, it would be lucky to get 10 games out of Montana in 1993. Even though Steve Young had emerged as one of the most prolific quarterbacks in the NFL. Even though San Francisco general manager Carmen Policy was committed to dealing Montana.

And most critically, even though keeping Montana was now undeniably impractical from a financial standpoint.

A new collective bargaining agreement reached in 1993 translated to drastic changes across the NFL landscape—including an impending salary cap, which meant that San Francisco could no longer spend so extravagantly. So, when the 49ers re-signed unrestricted free agent quarterback Steve Bono (third-stringer in 1992) to a three-year, $5.15 million pact on April 7, Montana's fate was sealed as no team could bankroll three quarterbacks making seven figures. Several franchises, most notably the Kansas City Chiefs, Phoenix Cardinals, Minnesota Vikings, New Orleans Saints, and Los Angeles Raiders, pounced on the opportunity—especially because they had cap space after losing out on Reggie White, the immensely talented defensive end and most highly coveted free agent who eventually signed with the Green Bay Packers.

Of all these teams, Phoenix was most aggressive in recruiting Montana, but Kansas City soon emerged as the front-runner. In Kansas City, he could play for a Super Bowl contending team coached by Marty Schottenheimer, who was committed to adopting the West Coast Offense—a system which Montana knew intimately. His offensive coordinator would be his former positional coach Paul Hackett (a football lifer from Burlington, Vermont, of all places). Kansas City not only offered Montana unrivaled comfort and zero ambiguity about his starting status but soon a three-year, $10 million pact to boot.

Montana was in and so was the San Francisco front office.

While Policy was initially inclined to deal Montana to Phoenix, which was offering more—the No. 3 overall pick in the upcoming draft—he ultimately granted Montana's wish and dealt him to his preferred destination in Kansas City, even though it meant reneging on his commitment to get max compensation for dealing Montana. San Francisco settled for Kansas City's offer of the No. 18 overall pick in the upcoming draft in exchange for Montana, David Whitmore, and a future third-round pick. (Montana, after all, was approaching his late thirties and KC wanted more in return for parting with a first-rounder.)

Still, DeBartolo persisted.

He, along with a reluctant George Seifert, met with Montana in-person in San Francisco to tell Montana that he would be the "designated starter" if he stayed. Two months earlier, Seifert had unequivocally declared Young his starter and was now employing this ambiguously coined term. The dubious move reeked of DeBartolo's influence and Montana saw through the farce. Lacking the intestinal fortitude to tell DeBartolo in-person he was leaving, Montana simply acknowledged his appreciation of the gesture. Ultimately, it didn't matter. Policy had worked out a deal amenable to all three parties—Montana, San Francisco, Kansas City—that was now coming to fruition. When Montana flew back home to San Francisco, the 49ers brass (which awkwardly included Montana's former teammate Dwight Clark, who was coordinator of football operations) met with Montana and his wife to confirm the decision.

Finally, DeBartolo accepted the fact that Montana would not retire as a San Francisco 49er.

The official press release was soon issued, followed by a fifty-minute press conference at the team's Santa Clara facility the following day. Montana, flanked by his wife and parents, cracked that his knowledge of Kansas City was limited to its legendary barbecues. He expressed relief that this episode was over. Meanwhile, the other half of the dais appeared less buoyant. The seemingly interminable negotiations had taxed Policy and Seifert; DeBartolo remained crestfallen.

"I don't have the relationship with anyone on this team I have with Joe Montana," DeBartolo told reporters. "It transcends football. I feel a deep sadness. This is a personal loss for me."[7]

(It wasn't as personal of a loss as his turning over control of the 49ers to his sister in 2000 after pleading guilty to failing to report a felony when he paid former Louisiana Governor Edwin Edwards $400,000 to help secure a casino license.)

Most of the Bay Area was crushed.

All of Kansas City was exuberant.

And Steve Young? He had hardly been following this series of events. "Mr. Hyperactivity" was busy studying for final exams to earn his law degree from BYU's J. Reuben Clark Law School, where he had matriculated as a part-time student in summer of 1988. Despite having earned millions starring in the NFL, Young remained steadfast in his commitment to earn a law degree, annually spending off-seasons in Provo, Utah, studying constitutional law. Shortly after losing to Dallas in the NFC Championship Game in January, Young resumed his legal studies. By April, he was either studying or sleeping—in the library.

It wasn't until he finished his last final that Young took a call from a friend informing him of the trade.

One that was now two days old.[8]

Steve Young wasn't the only affected stakeholder to get the news as if it were transmitted in 1793, not 1993.

The trade went down early in the off-season, weeks before minicamp, when many players were vacationing in locales perhaps interested in fútbol, but not football.

"I was actually on vacation, on a cruise," recalls former Kansas City wideout J.J. Birden. "And I remember how the *USA Today* would come later on in the day, and I remember picking up the *USA Today* and reading an article that said Joe Montana might become the Kansas City Chiefs' next quarterback. And I was like, 'No way in the world is that going to happen.' And I just kind of wrote it off because I'm thinking, 'OK, here's a guy I used to watch play in the eighth grade, one of the greatest quarterbacks. You're telling me he's going to be my quarterback? No way.'

"The very next day, the headline said: 'JOE MONTANA IS THE KANSAS CITY CHIEFS' NEW QUARTERBACK.' I just couldn't believe it. I could not believe it until I saw Joe walk into the meeting room."[9]

"I will never forget the day that I walked into the locker room in the off-season and sitting at a table in the middle of the locker room was [offensive coordinator] Paul Hackett and Joe Montana," recalls Bryan Barker, a young punter for the Kansas City Chiefs in 1993. "I literally said, 'What the heck is going on here?' Paul was like, 'I just want to introduce you to your new teammate.' So that was my personal introduction to Joe."[10]

"He [Montana] had some prior connections to some of the players but also with Paul Hackett," remembers Matt Blundin. "So that made it a really good transition as well because Paul didn't treat him any differently than he treated the other guys."[11]

Fans of the Chiefs were also shocked. Was one of the game's legendary quarterbacks really interested in ending his career for the Kansas City Chiefs? When he could have played for a West Coast team in a more temperate climate? Or at least for a team in a bigger market? Or when he could have retired and landed a cushy broadcasting gig?

1. Montana's Last Stand

For Montana, joining Kansas City was a new challenge, one which he relished.

When Marty Schottenheimer became head coach in 1989, the Chiefs had qualified once for the playoffs in seventeen years as the Oakland/Los Angeles Raiders and Denver Broncos owned the AFC West. Under Schottenheimer, the Chiefs made the postseason in three consecutive years from 1990 to 1992, but they never advanced past the second round. The primary culprit behind the team's inability to contend for a Super Bowl title was the quarterbacking. Ever since Len Dawson (who wore Montana's No. 16, which is why Montana wore No. 19 as a Chief) retired, the quarterback position was a black hole. Over a seventeen-year period, the Chiefs had drafted ten prospects, none of whom proved to be the long-term solution. When the club acquired longtime Seattle Seahawk Dave Krieg prior to the 1992 season, he was the presumptive starter for the foreseeable future.

That was, until Montana came aboard.

For the Kansas City fans, landing Montana was more than an answer to their unsettled quarterback situation. It was as if Christmas, Hanukkah, Kwanzaa, Cinco de Mayo, and Chinese New Year all converged. A billboard leading into River Falls declared: "WELCOME JOE MONTANA AND THE KANSAS CITY CHIEFS." The Chiefs had to hire six additional security guards to help navigate Montana through the crush of fans hovering around the team's facilities. Sales of tickets and merchandise skyrocketed— and not just in Western Missouri, but across wide swaths of the American heartland that now comprised the team's broadened market.

Meanwhile, most San Franciscans who had even a passing interest in sports were not so giddy. When Montana was traded, the *San Francisco Examiner* published a poll in which 85 percent of fans in San Francisco overwhelmingly favored Montana over Young; many season ticket holders promised to shred their tickets; "I MISS JOE" bumper stickers whizzed up and down Interstate 280.[12]

Even though the reigning MVP was their team's quarterback.

At the onset of his 15th NFL season, Joe Montana acted more like a fringe player trying to crack the roster than the most accomplished quarterback in league history, who, after choosing the Kansas City Chiefs over a passel of other teams, was now being idolized by a fan base longing to see its team advance past the second round of the playoffs. River Falls was abuzz as the Chiefs, now armed with an elite quarterback, appeared poised to compete with Jim Kelly's Buffalo Bills, Dan Marino's Miami Dolphins, and Warren Moon's Houston Oilers for conference supremacy. The hoopla was intense, perhaps even suffocating, but it hardly fazed Montana.

"The first day of practice, I'm sitting back there with the secondary and

I'm watching seven-on-seven and there wasn't a ball that hit the ground," remembers Herm Edwards, who was cutting his teeth in the NFL as Kansas City's defensive backs coach at the time. "I had never seen a practice like that where a quarterback went for 15, 16 balls in a row, never hit the ground. Joe was one of those guys that had the 'it' factor. It was amazing when you watched him in practice, how accurate he was. The guys in the huddle, because he was Joe Montana entering the huddle, they felt this presence of like, 'We're really good.'"[13]

"The very first practice we were inside the facility and it was our first practice with Montana, and I remember we get into the huddle," recalls J.J. Birden. "I'm looking to my left, and I see Joe Montana. I'm looking to my right, and I see Marcus Allen. The very first play they call is 'X-Hook.' I'm an X, so I'm literally thinking I get to catch Joe's very first pass as a Kansas City Chief. I could run this route in my sleep. I remember running the route and about 10 yards, I got hit in the back of the head with the ball. Joe calls me over and he goes, 'Come here, kid. I don't wait for you to get open. I've already read the defense. I know where the hole is. I'm expecting you to get your head around faster because I throw it before you get there.' And that statement alone instantly changed my game as a wide receiver because I had never had a quarterback who had anticipated the throw like Joe. It let me know that you're playing with a whole different level of a professional quarterback who instantly made my game better."[14]

Montana could make an even more profound impression when he didn't have a football but simply a pencil in his hand.

"It's mini-camp and we're learning this new offense, so it's all hands on deck," recalls Kansas City offensive lineman Joe Valerio. "And we show up for the first minicamp meeting as an offense and Paul Hackett, new offensive coordinator, goes, 'Alright guys look. It's still football, it's not rocket science, but we've got some work to do as far as transitioning into this whole new West Coast Offense. We're going to learn a couple plays this minicamp, we're going to learn a couple plays next minicamp, and then training camp we're going to fine-tune it all.'

"So, we were sitting down, and we were getting ready to put in a play called '38–39 Whack' which was basically quarterback under center. He takes the snap, he takes a reverse pivot, and he pitches it out to the tailback. It doesn't get any simpler as a play. The blocking scheme was pretty simple. It was straight ahead man, point of attack, pulling guard goes out and blocks second level to the play side. It was the kind of stuff you drew up in the sand when you were a kid. It was a good old-fashioned football play.

"I'm watching Joe Montana, a guy with four Super Bowl rings, three-time [Super Bowl] MVP and he took like three pages of notes. He had his pencil sharpened, he was there, he was engaged, he asked questions. If there was ever a guy who could have checked it in at that particular time in his life it was Joe Montana. And he didn't. He was the first guy in the weight room at the facility, and he was the last guy to leave. When somebody needed help with their job, it was 'Hey, how can we be better together? What can we work on together to improve?' He never pointed at anybody. He never scowled at anybody. To me, that's how he integrated so quickly.

"He [Montana] made it fun. He got to know everybody. I wasn't sure what to expect because I had never been around a player like that who had hit that ultimate superstar pinnacle. He was just one of the guys. But at the same time, he was also not one of the guys, from the way that he treated the game. He treated it special. He wasn't a screaming, yelling captain type leader. He was absolutely not that. He led exactly how his personality was— to outwork you, to stay calm under pressure, and to make you feel comfortable about what you were doing."[15]

In a sense, teammates respected Montana for many of the same reasons that fans adored him. He was not standoffish. He was not above joining the offensive linemen for a midweek steak dinner. They could relate to him. Whether they had 102 career receiving touchdowns or two career receiving touchdowns. (Joe Valerio recalls one particular situation during an early October game versus the Los Angeles Raiders when he hauled in a one-yard touchdown pass from Montana: "It was 4th-and-1 and he [Montana] gets in the huddle and he called the play like I was Jerry Rice. I couldn't have been further from Jerry Rice as far as my skills in the open field. He called the play like I had been a wide receiver my entire career.")

"I was just trying to learn all I could from him [Montana]," recalls Kansas City's third-string quarterback Matt Blundin. "And that was kind of what I was charged with from Carl Peterson. He said, 'Hey, we're bringing this guy in and learn all you can.' And certainly, that's what I tried to do. Joe was just more than willing at any turn to answer a question or explain something or explain what he was doing out there. It wasn't at all like I was bothering him as a young guy trying to take his job. He just wanted to share about the game and what he knew. Maybe it was a product of where he was in his career and I was no real threat to him at that time or moment, but I really don't think he would act any way differently if I was because as quarterbacks we all got along.

"Joe's not a rah-rah guy. He's definitely one of those 'lead by example' type guys. He's not so introverted in a way that he's not approachable and doesn't reach out to you. He's one of those guys that if he's going to say something in the locker room or in the huddle or on the field, people are going to listen. I think that was probably a product of where he was in his career. Having so much success, he came with that credibility. I can't imagine him being anything different earlier in his career because he was authentic in who he was. There wasn't any kind of show or anything like that. He spoke up when he had to, but he wasn't the boisterous leader."[16]

Nevertheless Montana knew how to leverage his status as a global celebrity and NFL legend toward leaving an indelible impression on some of his teammates. Especially those who left an indelible impression on him—such as the exceptionally affable and compassionate Joe Valerio, who, in only his third year in Kansas City, had emerged as a fan favorite

Told by high school coaches he was too nice to play football, Valerio enjoyed a standout career at the University of Pennsylvania before getting drafted by Kansas City, where he was now establishing himself as a valuable NFL offensive lineman. Aware that Valerio, who would be nominated for the Walter Payton NFL Man of the Year Award later in his career, was the furthest thing from an Average Joe, Montana waited for an opportunity to perform an unsolicited act of kindness.

And so, one day Valerio was hanging out in the locker room with his father, who, naturally, was interested in meeting the star quarterback.

"We're in the locker room and Joe comes up and he says, 'Joe, is this your dad?'" remembers Valerio. "He came up to me and my dad. I didn't have to drag my dad over to him and say, 'Hey Joe, would you mind meeting my dad?'"[17]

It went beyond taking the initiative. There were a lot of people who wanted to spend time with Montana. He could have shaken Mr. Valerio's hand, made small talk for a minute, and parted ways. But Montana was very fond of Valerio and was genuinely interested in learning more about his teammate's father.

At one point the elder Valerio, a former professional boxer who grew up in South Philly during the Great Depression, said to Montana, "Joe, you are my favorite Italian football player. But I've got to tell you, you're not my favorite Italian athlete."[18]

Valerio was starting to get a tad uneasy. Was his father really giving Joe Montana a hard time?

Montana was intrigued, however, wondering who exactly the father's favorite Italian athlete was.

Going into "South Philly Italian storytelling mode," the elder Valerio explained how back in the early fifties, there were a couple weeks when he got to practice with Rocky Marciano, the world heavyweight champ, who was in town to fight Jersey Joe Walcott. After Valerio's father finished telling the story of Marciano, his favorite Italian athlete, Montana acknowledged, "You got a chance to spar with Rocky Marciano, that beats hanging out with a schlump like me any day of the week."[19]

His bit of tongue-in-cheek humor aside, Montana realized how meaningful this story was to his teammate's father, and he expressed such appreciation.

As Valerio recalls, "He [Montana] was so engaging and he took the time. He made my dad feel like he was the most important person in the world at that moment. My dad used to talk about that moment all the time. He gave my dad something that he took with him for the rest of his life."[20]

Valerio's father passed away in the early 2000s.

To this day, this conversation remains one of Valerio's favorite memories from his football career.

In the weeks leading up to the season opener against the Tampa Bay Buccaneers, the public craze for all things Joe Montana was at a fever pitch. His age (37) and recent spate of ailments were of little concern to an ardent, championship-deprived, at times maniacal, fan base.

Montana had yet to throw a meaningful spiral for his new team, but that did not stop a woman from asking him to sign the urn containing her late husband's ashes before they were interred. One night, Montana and friends were drinking brews at Steve's Pizza in River Falls, and after getting up to leave, the quarterback spotted a woman snagging his empties before stuffing them in her purse. Another day, Montana almost ran over a young boy who had camped out under his car in hopes of securing an autograph. When the team traveled for preseason games, a crush of autograph-seeking fans was camped out in the hotel lobby; in years past, the only people who awaited the Kansas City Chiefs in hotel lobbies were typically visiting relatives.[21]

There were other times when the public attention could be overwhelming, even borderline distracting. Such as when a throng of fans would hang on his every move at training camp, constantly beseeching him for an autograph and/or photo.

"Our training camp was up in River Falls, Wisconsin, just a tiny town," says Bryan Barker, who, having grown up in the East Bay of San Francisco and later attending Santa Clara University, followed Montana's heyday closely. "They obviously were extremely excited about Joe Montana, and just the Chiefs overall, because [of] three playoff seasons in a row. Well, the crowds were larger than usual every day and Joe was an absolute competitor. I think he would try and race you to sleep for a dollar, to somehow prove that he fell asleep before you. A group of us would go play golf in between practices during training camp. We would all run off the practice field, head out to the golf course, have a little skins game, eat a chicken sandwich, and then rush back to get to practice without being late. One particular day, Joe and I were the last two in the locker room trying to hurry up and get out there, and there was a huge gauntlet of people outside that locker room in River Falls. Joe looked at me and said, 'Hey, give me your jersey.' We both wore white mesh jerseys for practice, mine was Number 4 and his was obviously 19. So, I gave him my Number 4 and he said, 'Watch this.' He went over to the door where everybody was waiting. He put my jersey on. He sort of trotted with his head down for a little bit. He kept his helmet on. When they saw the Number 4, they just assumed it was me and they sort of had this, 'Ohhhhh, it's not Joe.' So, I was the last guy in the locker room, wearing Number 19. They went crazy until I took two steps, took my helmet off and showed them all that I was actually the punter. So, he escaped the gauntlet that day, got to practice without being late."[22]

This was classic Montana. Being a practical jokester, not taking himself too seriously—despite being a global celebrity who was now married to well-known model Jennifer Wallace and often escorted around team facilities by a cadre of security guards.

"With him [Montana] coming over, he had the celebrity status and he wasn't that at all," says Herm Edwards. "He was just a football guy. He got along with everybody and was just one of the guys. If anything else, him leaving San Francisco, the Bay Area, where you get a lot of notoriety, and all of a sudden coming to a Midwest town, people were excited, but it was the Midwest. It wasn't like he was on the West Coast with all the media members or even the East Coast. It was kind of Joe's deal coming back."[23]

"He [Montana] definitely had a major impact right away on our program from the very first time he was there," says Blundin. "I just remember specifically how easy it was for him to come into that team and just be one of the guys and not be someone who was coming in with any kind of expected special treatment or anything like that.

"I think everyone on the team would say the exact same thing. There was no sense of 'I'm this guy.'"[24]

"He was an absolute professional," says Barker. "He just was so talented. You would look at him and think, 'How can this guy continue to play at this level?'"[25]

On the night of Saturday, September 4, Kansas City's new quarterback was feeling miserable.

Joe Montana was trying to pass not a football, but a kidney stone.

Merely hours from starting his first regular season game since 1990, Montana writhed in excruciating pain in his Tampa hotel room.

"First game of the season, when we went to play Tampa, he [Montana] passed a kidney stone the night before the game," recalls Herm Edwards. "And he didn't get any sleep and we were playing Tampa in Tampa, that's a twelve o'clock game. [The game began at 1:00 EST, but the Kansas City Chiefs were accustomed to playing in CST.] He came out and played. I was like, 'Are you kidding me?' It happened that night when he was going to bed. He was rushed to the hospital that night. He was in the hospital half the night and came out and played."[26]

And played like Joe Montana circa 1984, completing his first nine passes and throwing three touchdowns while earning AFC Offensive Player of the Week honors.

"I'll never forget that day, it was hot," recalls Bryan Barker. "That's always a tough place to play and it started off with Joe doing what Joe did for the 49ers for so long."[27]

After the game, running back Marcus Allen, the other all-important off-season acquisition for KC, told reporters, "To me, he looks like the same old Joe. He hasn't changed a bit."[28]

Indeed, Joe Cool shredded a Buccaneers team, one coached by Sam Wyche, his former position coach in San Fran. On a sun-splashed late summer afternoon, the Chiefs' resounding 27–3 victory did have a dark cloud: Halfway through the third quarter, Montana misfired a pass intended for wideout Willie Davis in the end zone. On the follow-through, he whacked his right wrist into linebacker Broderick Thomas' helmet. Montana played the next snap (connecting with Allen for a 12-yard touchdown pass, essentially sealing the Chiefs victory), but was later relieved by backup Dave Krieg.

The following morning, Montana's wrist was noticeably swollen. He sat out several days of practice, prompting Schottenheimer to go with Krieg in the Week 2 matchup against the Houston Oilers. In the hostile Astrodome, the Chiefs were blown out 30–0 as Krieg threw two picks and was sacked four times.

The season was only two weeks old, but it was evident that for Kansas City to be considered one of the AFC's elite teams, it needed Joe Montana starting.

As the regular season unfolded, the Kansas City offensive linemen evaluated their performance by answering one question: Could Joe Montana play golf the next day? That was the litmus test. If the answer was "yes" then the line had done its job; a "no" meant the QB was let down.

After his Week 2 absence, Montana was back for a much-hyped "Monday Night Football" showdown with AFC West rival Denver Broncos and quarterback John Elway. In one of the most highly anticipated events in KC sports history (and his first regular season home game at Arrowhead), Montana finished 21–36 for 273 yards, engineering five drives ending in field goals. The Chiefs won 15–7, but perhaps more importantly, despite being sacked three times, Montana felt good enough to hit the links the next morning ... and start in the next game following the bye week against yet another divisional opponent, the Los Angeles Raiders.

With a similarly boisterous home crowd returning to Arrowhead for the Raiders matchup, Montana dazzled in the first half—he had as many touchdown passes (two) as incompletions—until he showed why San Francisco had been reluctant to name him the starter over Steve Young. While sprinting toward the sidelines before halftime, the now 37-year-old quarterback was taken down by Los Angeles Raiders linebacker Aaron Wallace—an arguable cheap shot that forced Montana to limp out of the game with a strained hamstring.

Kansas City won easily, 24–9, to improve to 3–1, but it was painfully obvious to the 77,395 fans in attendance that, when it came to taking health precautions, Joe Montana of the 1990s, while still incredibly effective, was quite different from Joe Montana of the 1980s.

The most significant (and overlooked) side effect of Joe Montana signing with the Kansas City Chiefs in April was that fellow future Hall of Famer Marcus Allen came aboard as a free agent two months later. The promise of sharing the backfield with Montana proved to be the perfect recruiting pitch for the star running back.

While at times he was relegated to the sidelines in 1993, Joe Montana quickly became one of the most celebrated pro athletes in the history of Kansas City (courtesy Bryan Barker family).

But, of course, it was not as if Allen needed any incentive to leave the Los Angeles Raiders—it was just a matter of where he would land.

Simply put, by the early nineties, Marcus Allen grew to *loathe* all things Silver and Black.

This was rather ironic, considering Allen's background. A versatile halfback who excelled in both the running and passing game, Allen, a native Southern Californian who went to USC (ironically, a bitter rival of Montana's Notre Dame), was selected by the Los Angeles Raiders with the 10th overall pick in the 1982 NFL Draft. He soon emerged as one of the premier playmakers in the 1980s, being named MVP of Super Bowl

XVIII (a 38–9 Raiders win) and then receiving MVP honors during the 1985 regular season.

But shortly thereafter, Bo Jackson happened.

Jackson, of course, was a freakish, once-in-a-lifetime athletic marvel who, despite splitting his time between baseball and football, had phased Allen out of the Raiders' offense. Even after Jackson left the NFL after the 1990 season, Allen found himself competing with over-the-hill former superstars such as Roger Craig and Eric Dickerson for carries. The coaching decision seemingly inexplicable, Allen believed the situation stemmed from the icy relationship he had with team owner Al Davis. At the tail end of the 1992 regular season (Allen's last under contract in Los Angeles), he made the following comments to Al Michaels in a taped interview aired during halftime of a "Monday Night Football" game: "What do you think of a guy who has attempted to ruin your career? When someone messes with your livelihood—this is what I've wanted to do since I was eight-years-old, and this very thing has been taken away from me and not, I don't think, for a business reason, but for a personal reason."[29] Months later, the spiteful executive Davis fired a parting shot, referring to Allen as an "asterisk" in Raiders history. It was a ridiculously petty comment considering Allen departed the Raiders as the franchise's all-time leading rusher.

Naturally, during the 1993 off-season, Allen was interested in joining the Raiders' hated rival (the Kansas City Chiefs) yet teams such as the Miami Dolphins and Washington Redskins were reportedly interested in offering Allen more guaranteed money. Signing with Kansas City would mean taking a below market value. Which he was inclined to do once Montana, another veteran out to prove the naysayers wrong, inked his pact earlier in the spring.

At the time of his signing with Kansas City, Allen acknowledged that over the past couple years, he hadn't always been playing through the whistle on every play. In the same breath, Allen exclaimed that he still had a lot of football left in him.

In a Week 6 matchup against the Cincinnati Bengals, Montana was shelved with the injured hamstring (the passing game was in the hands of Dave Krieg) and running back Harvey Williams was scuffling. The offense needed a spark—and got one with Allen, who scored one of Kansas City's two touchdowns (a third quarter nine-yard run) to boost the Chiefs (4–1) to a 17–15 win over the Bengals. The next week at San Diego, with a less-than-hundred percent Joe Montana back starting, Allen again carried the offense with a rushing and receiving touchdown as Kansas City escaped with a 17–14 win, upping their division-leading record to 5–1.

Four touchdowns in the past three games. Not bad for Allen, whose off-season signing was somewhat of an afterthought given the mileage

Montana wasn't the only future Hall of Famer who was happy to call Kansas City home in 1993. Running back Marcus Allen was delighted to be joining his former team's AFC West rival (courtesy Bryan Barker family).

on his 33-year-old legs and expected backup role. By the end of the 1993 regular season, Allen would score 15 touchdowns and rack up over 1,000 all-purpose yards, effectively reviving his career. In fact, Allen would end up being named NFL Comeback Player of the Year upon conclusion of the regular season.

For a bonus, Allen's lighthearted demeanor was perfectly in line with Montana's penchant for clownery.

"Marcus is one of those guys that had a sense of humor," says Herm Edwards. "Playing with the Raiders all those years, they were one of those teams that had fun anyway. Knowing Marcus from him growing up in San Diego, going to Lincoln High School and recruiting him, and then going to USC, it was just fun to watch him toward the end when a lot of people thought he was done, and he really wasn't done at all. He was just starting as far as I was concerned."[30]

"Marcus [Allen] was unbelievable," remarks Matt Blundin. "He was an amazing professional, but he had a lot of fun. He really, really made a point to have fun. He just wasn't so caught up in the seriousness of the game.

1. Montana's Last Stand

Obviously at that level, it's a business, but he really kept it fun and enjoyed what he did."[31]

For the entirety of the 1993 regular season, Joe Montana would really need *his own* good-humoredness. Whether it was unleashing stink bombs in meetings. Or messing up assistant coaches' offices. Whatever it took to grind through his penultimate NFL season, yet another one marked by injuries and frustration. It wasn't just, at times, being relegated to the sidelines (he only played in 11 regular season games), while watching a far less accomplished quarterback in his stead. It was playing at 80 percent, 70 percent, 60 percent of his late 1980s self—while knowing that in the Bay Area, Steve Young was having yet another phenomenal regular season.

"We drilled Montana because we were trying to find out the scoop. 'What's the scoop between you and Steve [Young]? What really happened?'" recalls J.J. Birden. "Joe was the ultimate professional. Whatever he was feeling, he was not sharing with us. I really believe that at the end of the day that Joe did want to prove that he still had the ability to play, that he still had the ability to lead a team to the Super Bowl and that he wasn't washed up. And I believe that was certainly at the back of his mind."[32]

As well as pulling the aforementioned pranks.

"It was fun because we had Joe [Montana] and David Krieg. They were practical jokers," says Herm Edwards. "I was one of those kind of neat guys. Quarterbacks used to meet up on the coaches' floors in their meetings and they would be in the quarterback room and everyone else would be meeting downstairs. They would go by my office periodically and just ransack my office, just turn things over and misplace stuff. It took about three weeks for me to finally figure out who was doing it."[33]

No one was spared from the buffoonery. Particularly during team meetings following a loss when Montana felt inclined to unleash a room-clearing, potent stink bomb.

"It kind of broke up the monotony of what was going on and let us know you can be one of the best athletes out there, but you can still have fun and relax a little bit," says Birden.[34]

This was a rare instance in which Joe Montana would exploit his elevated status (he was not into excessively yelling at receivers à la Dan Marino). Because besides Marcus Allen, Montana was probably the only Chief who could stand in the corner cackling without drawing the wrath of head coach Marty Schottenheimer.

For good reason. Montana had recently suffered debilitating injuries, but he was still willing to subject himself to more violence—not for his first Super Bowl ring (he had four of those) or for financial security (he had millions in the bank), but for the chance to continue pursuing a passion that had started in the early 1960s, when he was growing up in the coal mining city of Monongahela, Pennsylvania.

However, on the late afternoon of October 31, Montana was in no mood to treat teammates and coaches with tricks.

After quarterbacking Kansas City to the win over San Diego two weeks earlier, Montana led the Chiefs into Joe Robbie Stadium for a Week 9 matchup versus the Miami Dolphins. As halftime neared, Montana was scrambling to elude pressure when he jammed his leg into the ground, re-aggravating his injured hamstring. Already trailing by two touchdowns, the Chiefs could not compensate for Montana's absence and lost 30–10. Meanwhile, Montana exited Joe Robbie Stadium, the location of his legendary Super Bowl XXIII win nearly five years earlier, hobbling around on crutches.

With Montana sidelined the next three weeks, Krieg and the Chiefs went 2–1. Still, the understanding was that when reasonably healthy, Montana would be the starter.

There was no quarterback controversy this year.

By Thanksgiving, Montana was preparing to return for a pivotal Week 13 matchup versus the Buffalo Bills and their imposing defense. A few days later, in one of the most impressive performances of this comeback season, Montana (18–32, 208 yards) connected with eight different receivers while tossing a pair of touchdowns as his Chiefs thrashed the visiting Bills, 23–7. The win over Buffalo marked the beginning of the Chiefs' 4–2 run to close out the regular season. It was a stretch in which Montana and the Chiefs swept the Seattle Seahawks by scoring a combined 65 points in the two games. During Week 16, the Chiefs' offense outgunned the San Diego Chargers, 28–24. But the Buffalo game was the biggest confidence-booster, for Montana proved once again that he could shake off injuries and produce results against a nasty defense.

The kind of defense he could encounter in January.

For Montana, the 1993 postseason was the best of times … and the most distressful of times. Indeed, it was a month of glorious comebacks alternating with more vicious assaults on his already battered body.

The playoffs opened with Kansas City, having clinched its first AFC West title since the early 1970s, hosting the Pittsburgh Steelers in the Wild Card Game. Under ebullient head coach Bill Cowher, formerly KC's defensive coordinator, the Steelers defense had developed a reputation for relentlessly pressuring quarterbacks, earning the moniker "Blitzburgh Steelers," one that sparked memories of the Steel Curtain dynasty of the seventies.

And at the beginning of the opening game of the 1993 NFL Playoffs, they came as advertised.

1. Montana's Last Stand

Montana, smothered by a black and gold haze, got off to a slow start, throwing seven straight incompletions to open the game. With temperatures well below freezing, he started the contest wearing a glove on his throwing hand for the first time in his career. On his first attempt barehanded, Montana connected with wideout Willie Davis for a 25-yard completion, but not before Pittsburgh defensive end Donald Evans leveled him to the artificial turf. Bruised ribs forced Montana to the sidelines for three plays—one of which was a 23-yard touchdown pass from Dave Krieg to J.J. Birden that knotted the game at 7–7 in the first quarter.

While Montana would return on the following drive, for the remainder of the first half he was outplayed by Steelers quarterback Neil O'Donnell, who tossed a pair of touchdown passes to give the visitors a 17–7 edge heading into halftime. After Kansas City tied the game at 17 early in the fourth quarter, O'Donnell threw his third touchdown pass of the afternoon to give the underdog Steelers a 24–17 lead with less than five minutes remaining in regulation. Both teams were forced to punt on their next possessions, however when the Steelers tried to execute their punt, tight end Keith Cash sliced through the Steelers' protection, stuffing the punt, which allowed for teammate Fred Jones to return it to Pittsburgh's nine-yard line. After three plays yielded two yards, KC faced a 4th-and-goal at the seven with 1:48 remaining.

With the season on the line, the history of the franchise in limbo, and millions of football fans watching nationwide, Montana went into the huddle and cracked a joke to his teammates.

This was vintage Montana. When everyone was panicking, he was relaxed. When everyone's heart rate was speeding up, his was slowing down. This was just another of the dozens, if not hundreds, of times during Montana's career in which he worked his magic of defusing tension at a climactic moment.

Seconds after a more relaxed huddle of teammates broke, Joe Cool dropped back in the pocket, looked off the safety, and rifled a bullet that wide receiver Tim Barnett, likely Montana's third or fourth option, hauled in at the back of the end zone for the game-tying score.

"I had watched Joe Montana do this more times than I could probably count," says Joe Valerio. "There was a lot of drama around that game. Bill Cowher, Marty Schottenheimer, the student versus the teacher. Coach Cowher had been our coach in years past in Kansas City. So, there were a lot of emotional undertones to that game. Some of the feelings that we had watching him [Montana] and being in the huddle with him during that drive when he hit Tim Barnett in the back of the end zone for that game-tying touchdown, it was Joe Montana 2.0 at that point."[35]

In the waning seconds of the fourth quarter, Pittsburgh went three-and-out, giving Kansas City a chance to break the 24–24 tie in regulation. While the Chiefs put kicker Nick Lowery in good field position, he missed a 43-yarder on a rushed attempt.

Which meant Montana had the chance to be the hero.

For the millionth time.

In overtime, Montana engineered a methodical 66-yard drive (5–5, 46 yards passing) that set up another game-winning field goal attempt for Lowery. This time, the veteran kicker did not miss, converting the 32-yard field goal 11:03 into OT to capture the 27–24 win.

This was a special day for a city that had seen its NBA franchise (the Kings) leave for Sacramento less than a decade ago and the face of the baseball franchise (George Brett) retire months earlier. For the rest of the country, a throwback Joe Montana comeback was a nice respite from the 24/7 news coverage of the kneecapping of Nancy Kerrigan that had occurred earlier in the week during a pre–Olympic trial practice session.

Looming the upcoming weekend was an AFC Divisional Round matchup against the Houston Oilers in the Astrodome, a.k.a. defensive coordinator Buddy Ryan's House of Pain. The cocky Oilers played off the nickname. Several players from Houston's blitz-happy defense, a unit that had tormented quarterbacks all season, were talking about how they were going to inflict violence on Montana. (Before kickoff, cameras caught a smiling Oilers linebacker promising Montana would be KO'd in the first quarter.) Montana, of course, was already in a precarious physical state. The right elbow was so swollen it appeared a tennis ball was implanted on it; the purple-hued left hand could have belonged to the newly popular television character Barney the Dinosaur; the ribs were so sore that breathing became a laborious task; the back required a pregame injection. Houston was hell-bent on capitalizing.[36]

The past two Januaries, the Oilers had been eliminated from the postseason after blowing significant leads on the road. Now, they were playing in the Astrodome behind a raucous indoor crowd, one intent on providing decisive home-field advantage. Embarrassingly, however, at the end of the National Anthem, when it got to "Home of the…" a booming roar of "CHIEFS!" came echoing down from brave Kansas City fans occupying the stadium's upper level. With the stadium naturally hushed, everyone heard. Including the players. As if they needed any more motivation to assault Montana, the Oilers grew even more incensed that their fans were being shown up by the Midwestern road trippers.

"Maybe that's why they got a jump on us, they were totally ticked off," recalls Bryan Barker.[37]

The Oilers, armed with their run and shoot offense, did jump out to a 10–0 first half lead, courtesy of an Al Del Greco 49-yard field goal and a

1. Montana's Last Stand

two-yard rushing touchdown from Gary Brown, an NFL minimum-wage replacement for injured starting running back Lorenzo White.

"I remember the first half was not a very good half for us," recalls Birden. "We were not playing well. There were a lot of mistakes. I remember Joe [Montana] was just getting beat up."[38]

In the first 30 minutes, Houston certainly played like the NFL's hottest team, one that was riding an 11-game win streak into the Divisional Round, where they were now 7-point favorites. The Chiefs only totaled 12 yards rushing and five first downs. Montana was constantly being harassed by an onslaught of Oilers and entered halftime with 87 passing yards, having underthrown receivers multiple times—although there were several dropped balls, including one by wideout Willie Davis that surely would have been a touchdown.

(It is worth noting that for the Oilers, 1993 was a bizarre, tumultuous season. Perhaps the residual effect of having blown the 32-point lead in last January's Wild Card Game, they started 1-4. However, as the Oilers faced adversity as the season developed—offensive tackle David Williams' controversial decision to skip a game after his wife gave birth, the suicide of defensive tackle Jeff Alm, who shot himself after killing his best friend in a car accident, the violent clash between Buddy Ryan and offensive coordinator Kevin Gilbride on the sidelines—the team proved immune to such turmoil, as evidenced by their 11-game win streak to close out the season.)

However, the second half was a different tale. By the final whistle, Warren Moon appeared to be the 37-year-old quarterback to whom duress proved inescapable, getting sacked nine times for 68 yards and fumbling five times (he lost two).

"We had played them earlier in Kansas City and they had their way with us a little bit [the Oilers had defeated the Chiefs 30-0 in Week 2]," says Herm Edwards. "They [Oilers] were a really good football team. We did some things a little bit different coverage wise to make him [Warren Moon] hold the ball where he couldn't get it out. We were predominantly a man-to-man team because we had those great corners and those two big pass rushers. We gave him [Warren Moon] a look of like we were playing man and fell off into some zones that made him hold the ball and our rushers got to him.

"It was a marvelous ride when you think about our team back then. It was built defensively very, very good. We had an outstanding defense with Derrick Thomas and Neil Smith and Albert Lewis. It was kind of a who's who of defensive players."[39]

Meanwhile, Montana, perhaps no longer capable of hurting defenses deep like he used to, channeled his impeccable vision and uncanniness for picking apart secondaries toward firing three second half touchdown passes in rallying Kansas City to a come-from-behind 28–20 win.

"Joe always had this aura about him," says J.J. Birden. "When you looked at his eyes, it was like, 'OK, he's been there, done that.' Nothing's fazing him. We've just got to go do our thing."[40]

The rally started when tight end Keith Cash hauled in a seven-yard touchdown pass less than five minutes into the second half, slicing Houston's lead to 10–7. Seconds after crossing the goal line, Cash looked up, saw a poster prominently featuring Buddy Ryan's face, and chucked the ball smack in the middle of the image. Cash's cockiness mirrored some of his teammates' attitude toward Ryan, a grizzled NFL veteran who wasn't used to being ridiculed. (Decades before serving as an NFL defensive coordinator Ryan had been an Army sergeant during the Korean War and supposedly punched his soldiers in the face to keep them in line.) But now, he was graying, in his early sixties, and during pregame, when he had stood near midfield, arms crossed over his pot belly, presumably as a sign of intimidation, a few Chiefs giggled like high school seniors in a study hall.[41]

The score remained 10–7 heading into the fourth quarter before another Al Del Greco mid-range field goal gave Houston a 13–7 advantage with less than 10 minutes remaining. No problem. Montana coolly drove the Chiefs down to the Houston 11-yard line before dropping back in the pocket, shaking off a half dozen Oilers, and finding Birden in the end zone. The extra-point gave Kansas City its first lead of the evening, 14–13. After a rejuvenated Kansas City defense forced a Houston turnover, Montana was facing a 3rd-and-16 when he darted a textbook back-shoulder pass to Willie Davis in the right corner of the end zone. The second touchdown in less than 60 seconds upped KC's lead to 21–13. On this 18-yard strike, it wasn't just the impeccable execution (Cris Dishman was blanketing Davis). Arguably more important was that Montana shrugged off Davis' first half drop and adhered to Paul Hackett's play-call that tabbed Davis as his first option.

To their credit, the Oilers didn't fold. On his team's next possession, Moon made it a one-point game (21–20) when he hit Ernest Givins from seven yards out with less than four minutes remaining. On their next drive, the Chiefs faced a 3rd-and-1 from their own 30-yard line. Presumably, time to run and pray for a defensive lapse. But head coach Marty Schottenheimer, confident that Montana could find some way to move the ball across 36 inches of turf, was inclined to buck convention. The Chiefs broke huddle in a passing formation. They weren't bluffing. Montana dropped back and tossed a pass just as defensive end William Fuller whacked his right arm. Keith Cash yanked the fluttering football out of the air and dashed forty-one yards to Houston's 29-yard line. Three plays later, on 3rd-and-2, Montana handed off to Marcus Allen. Before Allen even took his second step on the way to a 21-yard score that would secure his team's instant classic victory, Montana had signaled touchdown. Swollen right fist pumping, spindly legs high-stepping, Montana was one of the first Chiefs to rejoice with Allen in the end zone.

Understandably.

The two men destined for Canton had been considered damaged goods by many pundits around the league for the last few years. Before the 1993 season began, there was great uncertainty surrounding Montana's ability to stay under center for consecutive games while Allen was essentially signed to be rookie Harvey Williams' backup. But now they had jointly engineered Kansas City's second consecutive 10-point comeback, this time against an even more punishing defense.

"These two guys [Montana and Allen] were celebrity football players that some will say maybe were at the twilight of their careers," remembers Herm Edwards. "Well, that was not the case when they showed up for us. And when you got those two guys, it enhanced our offense tremendously."[42]

The following PAT gave Kansas City a 28–20 lead, one that would stand as the Oilers' ensuing drive went nowhere.

This Divisional Round win over the favored Oilers served as not only a highlight of the Chiefs' 1993 season, but also as an iconic moment in the history of the franchise.

"I think the game against Houston was just an absolute phenomenal game," says Bryan Barker. "They had an incredible defense. That was a stadium that had really hard turf, like we did at Arrowhead. Every time they could get Joe on the ground hard, it was tough. If you watch the highlights, he got beat up pretty good in that game. It didn't look good for us, and then he just marched us down the field. We pulled it off in classic Joe Montana fist-pumping fashion. It was an incredible win."[43]

"We knew that Joe was peaking at that point," recalls Joe Valerio. "After that big win against the Steelers, we knew that if there was one guy that was a quarterback in the NFL at that time that was going to be able to go and beat a team on an 11-game winning streak at their place with Buddy Ryan at the helm of the defense, we literally knew it was Joe Montana. It was almost destiny.

"That run through the playoffs, I don't think I will ever have an emotional high like I had for those three to five weeks, going from that overtime with Pittsburgh, beating Houston in Houston, the House of Pain, and getting the privilege of getting to the AFC Championship."[44]

"When I look at my career, I played nine years and I never made it to the Super Bowl, but I will never forget the moment after that game and how excited we were in the locker room and how when we got home [we] saw a huge crowd at Arrowhead," recalls Birden. "I remember talking to Willie

Davis and some of the other players and I said, 'Guys, look at this feeling. What do you think it's going to be like next week when we beat Buffalo?'"[45]

Others in Kansas City weren't looking ahead.

Not with Montana's precarious health.

In the days leading up to the AFC Championship Game versus the Buffalo Bills, Marty Schottenheimer, when informing reporters of Joe Montana's injury status, said: "He'll be on the injury list with ribs, wrist, elbow … one of the above. But the elbow thing looks worse than it actually is. It's just a [bursa] sac that's got some fluid in it. It doesn't inhibit him in any way from doing what he needs to do."[46]

Unfortunately, another part of the body would spell doom for the quarterback as his team was one win from its first Super Bowl appearance in nearly a quarter-century.

Going into the 1993 AFC Championship Game, most fans around the country were rooting for Joe Montana—not just because it was a great comeback story about legendary player chasing a record-setting fifth Super Bowl ring. For good measure, if the San Francisco 49ers could beat the Dallas Cowboys in the late afternoon NFC Championship Game, an epic Joe Montana–Steve Young matchup would headline Super Bowl XXVIII.

They were also happy to be watching this conference championship game from home.

This AFC Championship Game was to be played in typical late–January weather for Western New York (wind chill at kickoff was 12° Fahrenheit), conditions to which Montana was no stranger. After all, Joe Cool had won the 1979 Cotton Bowl while battling hypothermia and the 1988 NFC Championship Game at Chicago's Soldier Field while battling Lake Michigan-induced sub-zero wind chill conditions. Even the Wild Card Game versus Pittsburgh two weeks ago was played in rather frosty weather.

Naturally, the Buffalo Bills, a franchise that owned the AFC in the early nineties, an era of dominance essentially sandwiched between Saddam Hussein's invasion of Kuwait and the infamous attack on Nancy Kerrigan, were in their element, too.

In the first half, Montana twice marched the Chiefs deep into Buffalo territory, before settling for a pair of Nick Lowery 31-yard field goals. Just before halftime, with his team trailing 20–6, Montana was leading another promising drive until, on 2nd-and-goal, fullback Kimble Anders bobbled a pass inches from the goal line. The sputtering football fell softly into the hands of defensive back Henry Jones and Buffalo went into the half with a comfortable 14-point advantage.

On the Chiefs' opening drive of the second half, Montana, facing a

1. Montana's Last Stand

3rd-and-14 from his team's 12-yard line, hooked up with tight end Keith Cash downfield for a first down conversion.

However, on the tail end of the play, Montana, who had hung in the collapsing pocket to uncork the spiral, was leveled by a trio of Bills, including future Hall of Fame defensive end Bruce Smith. The jarring collision jolted the quarterback's head against the frozen, unforgiving AstroTurf. Seconds after the thud, Smith, upon hearing Montana's moans, asked the quarterback if he were OK, only to realize Montana couldn't comprehend the question. (After the game, Montana would tell reporters, "As soon as I landed, everything went white.")[47]

As Montana lay on Kansas City's 14-yard line, attended to by a collection of team trainers, coaches, and teammates, it was (correctly) assumed by the tens of thousands watching in attendance and the millions viewing at home that he was concussed. Yet in the late 20th century, concussions were still considered more of a nuisance than the league-wide epidemic that they became during the early 21st century. Few people worried that the career was in jeopardy. And, indeed, a grounded Montana clutching his hot red Riddell helmet with two hands would not mark the encore moment of his football life, but it would be the lasting image of his 1993 career-revitalizing season.

"I think it [concussion] was just something that happened and that was it," says Matt Blundin. "Gosh, if we had known then what we know now, guys would have maybe had a different take on it all—right away, immediately. It was just something that happened."[48]

"I don't think we really worried about concussions back then," says Bryan Barker. "You crawl off a fence and get a concussion as a kid. I don't know that we were concerned about his future."[49]

In the present, however, Montana had some inkling of the gravity of his situation.

"I don't remember feeling anything when I got hit," Montana told reporters afterward. "I just remember right after that grabbing my head. I had a real severe pain in my head. I don't remember what had even happened, let alone what was going on. I was trying to pay attention, but I couldn't even remember what the score was."[50]

Of course, Montana was familiar with this situation—left sprawling on the ground late in a conference championship game, unable to return. Now, while his career was perhaps not in jeopardy, the team's chances of winning the AFC were.

"I think we were still in the game with Dave Krieg at quarterback. We still had a chance. It just wasn't the same, obviously," says Barker. "We all to this day feel that if Joe doesn't slam his head on the turf in Buffalo in the championship game, we probably beat Buffalo and go on to win the Super Bowl."[51]

"We became a different team," says J.J. Birden. "I still believe we would have beat Buffalo if Joe hadn't got hurt."[52]

Dave Krieg relieved Montana and filled in admirably. But Buffalo's suffocating defense and running back Thurman Thomas' performance (three touchdowns) were too much as Kansas City fell, 30–13.

After the final whistle, the disparity between the teams' reactions was borderline indiscernible. Buffalo's postgame "celebration" was perhaps the most subdued in NFL playoff history. Virtue of their fourth consecutive AFC crown, the mostly stone-faced Bills realized they were now tasked with avoiding a fourth consecutive Super Bowl loss. Meanwhile, the Chiefs were not overly despondent. This was their first appearance in the AFC Championship Game since 1970. Which meant the 1993 season was an exceedingly good (if not legendary) one for the franchise.

Still, this was little consolation to Montana, who was accustomed to playing in (and winning) Super Bowls.

"I'm not sure how satisfying it is when you almost make it," Montana told the press corps afterward. "It hurts more when you almost make it than when you go home early. You know you're out of it then. But when you almost get there..."[53]

(In his postgame remarks, Montana also cited the fact that virtue of the Chiefs losing to inferior opponents at the end of the regular season, the game was played in such an inhospitable environment—and not in front of their exuberant fans in far milder weather.)

Meanwhile, as darkness descended on Rich Stadium, all indications were that Joe Montana still burned for a Super Bowl ring on every digit of his right hand.

In 1994 (Joe Montana's final NFL season), the Kansas City Chiefs were like the prior year's edition—very good, but not Super Bowl-bound. They finished 9–7, falling to the Miami Dolphins (27–17) in the AFC Wild Card Game. The loss was not on Montana as his departing performance (314 yards passing, two touchdowns) was a fitting, albeit not memorable, send-off.

So, Joe Montana did not end his career with one final confetti shower—the way John Elway and Peyton Manning exited. But his final act was not reminiscent of those of Johnny Unitas and Joe Namath. After a legendary career with the Baltimore Colts, Unitas went to the San Diego Chargers, where he threw more interceptions (seven) than touchdown passes (three) during his final NFL campaign; four years later during the 1977 season, Namath ended his Hall of Fame career with one of his least productive years ever for the Los Angeles Rams.

By going to Kansas City in 1993, Joe Montana did not foolishly prolong his career.

Certainly not from the perspective of anyone affiliated with the Kansas City Chiefs organization that year.

"I played 16 seasons and I've said many times that the '93 Chiefs were probably the best overall team I played on," says Bryan Barker. "What a fantastic year '93 was for sure."[54]

2

"An Old-Fashioned Ballpark with Modern Amenities"

Concrete. Turf. Efficiency. Uniformity.

Such were the features of the behemoth multi-sport "cookie-cutter" stadiums opening in the fervent baseball cities of Philadelphia, Pittsburgh, and Cincinnati in the early 1970s. Philadelphia's Veterans Stadium, Pittsburgh's Three Rivers Stadium, and Cincinnati's Riverfront Stadium, with their massive seating capacities, were primarily built to maximize revenue. Baseball and football teams would play on the same unforgiving artificial turf. The dimensions were consistently uniform, hence the moniker "cookie-cutter" stadium. There was no creativity, no character, and certainly no aesthetic beauty to these stadiums, which such legends as Mike Schmidt, Willie Stargell, and Johnny Bench called home. In building such bland, monolithic stadiums during the post–World War II era, Major League Baseball forgot what had attracted so many fans at the dawn of the 20th century: quirky, fan-friendly parks used exclusively for baseball that were naturally embedded in downtown urban neighborhoods.

The early 1970s cookie-cutter stadiums, while particularly emblematic of the movement, were not the first of their kind. Their breaking ground was the continuation of a disturbing trend that had been developing across the country for years. Houston's Astrodome, the planet's first multi-purpose indoor stadium, was built in 1965. Some marveled at this novel feat of engineering. Others were impressed by the chandeliers illuminating the field. It soon became known as the "Eighth Wonder of the World." But it grew famous for hosting a slew of events that had nothing to do with baseball. It was the site, for example, of college basketball's "Game of the Century," when Houston's Elvin Hayes outdueled UCLA's Lew Alcindor (Kareem Abdul-Jabbar). And it is where the tennis match known as "Battle of the Sexes" took place, when Billie Jean King soundly defeated Bobby Riggs. In the end, the Houston Astros were just one of the stadium's many occupants.

Years earlier, when the Brooklyn Dodgers bolted to the West Coast,

2. "An Old-Fashioned Ballpark with Modern Amenities"   35

they moved into Dodger Stadium (after a brief stay at the Los Angeles Memorial Coliseum). But aside from the mountains and palm trees in the picturesque background, there were hardly any unique features intrinsic to the stadium. Several hundred miles north, Oakland Coliseum broke ground on April 15, 1964. Co-tenancy of the stadium left Bay Area sports fans accustomed to seeing their football team (the Raiders) ravage the infield dirt of their baseball team (the A's). The 1960s also saw multi-purpose, uniformly-shaped stadiums opening in St. Louis, Atlanta, and Queens, New York.

These cities were forgetting that baseball is a sport whose facilities are uniquely suited to creative architecture: unlike football, basketball, and hockey, in which the playing surfaces are of uniform lengths, the baseball field is open to interpretation. Baseball (and perhaps most importantly, their fans) deserved better than the concrete donut stadiums of the '60s and '70s—and, as the 20th century was drawing to a close—the visionary Baltimore Orioles organization knew it.

When many baseball fans, particularly those in National League cities, turned on their television sets the night of July 13, 1993, to watch the All-Star Game, they laid eyes on Oriole Park at Camden Yards for the first time. And in doing so, they saw the past—and future—of Major League Baseball. Ivy. Brick. Steel. Iron. Lush green grass. Different-sized walls. Urban buildings. The dullness and homogeneity of the cookie-cutter stadiums had been supplanted by the innovation and eccentricities of this groundbreaking new retro style ballpark, one that would jumpstart a trend and forever change the setting of America's most storied recreational activity.

Oriole Park at Camden Yards, known as simply "Camden Yards," was the freshly minted home of the Baltimore Orioles, a team that at the time was not a perennial World Series contender. It would take several years before Camden Yards would host any primetime postseason game. In the early 1990s, regular season baseball games were not frequently broadcast on national television. The evening of Tuesday, July 13, 1993, would be the first opportunity for this cathedral of a ballpark to garner the national spotlight. The 64th edition of the Midsummer Classic would be Major League Baseball's version of the World's Fair. The rest of America could finally see a modern fan-friendly ballpark built with exquisite detail that paid homage to the game's metropolitan roots simply by virtue of its location in downtown Baltimore, a few blocks west of the Inner Harbor area.

Perhaps baseball came to existence in the pastures but the sport's nascent popularity in the early 1900s coincided with America's exploding urbanization. The legendary ballparks such as Ebbets Field (Brooklyn), Polo Grounds (Upper Manhattan), Shibe Park (Philadelphia), Crosley Field

(Cincinnati), Fenway Park (Boston), and Wrigley Field (Chicago) were purposely designed to have very distinct characteristics, with one major exception: their location. Constructed in the heart of their respective cities, these parks were a short stroll (or trolley ride) from many fans' homes. They were just as much a part of the fabric of city life as were skyscrapers, department stores, and tenement buildings. Sadly, in the post–World War II era, a seemingly endless succession of franchises started transplanting their ballparks in the suburbs or on the outskirts of their respective home cities.

Now, this trend was about to be reversed.

"An old-fashioned ballpark with modern amenities."[1]

When it came to blueprinting the Baltimore Orioles' new ballpark, this was the mantra that team president Larry Lucchino invoked. Lucchino grew up in Pittsburgh in the mid–1900s, which meant that he spent a considerable amount of time in and around Forbes Field, an old-timey ballpark with its ivy-covered outfield wall back dropped by a tree-lined park. Like many Steel City natives, Lucchino was devastated in 1971 when Forbes Field, one of the last legendary old-time ball yards left standing, was demolished in order to make room for new dormitories at the University of Pittsburgh. In Baltimore during the late 1980s, there was the perfect confluence of circumstances that allowed Lucchino, the former Princeton basketball star and protégé of famed litigator Edward Bennett Williams, who owned the Orioles until his death in 1988, to revitalize the institution of the old-fashioned ballpark.

"The stars really aligned when William Donald Schaefer, who had been the Mayor of Baltimore before he became Governor of Maryland, selected a downtown site for the new baseball park," explains Janet Marie Smith, who served as the Orioles' vice president of planning and development in the midst of the design and development stages of Camden Yards.[2]

Since the mid–1900s, the Orioles (and Baltimore Colts) had been playing in Memorial Stadium, another multi-purpose facility with uniform dimensions, one that was several miles north of downtown Baltimore. By the mid–1980s, baseball was the only pro sport in town and the Orioles insisted on signing a long-term lease only if a new facility was exclusively for baseball, and not for a hypothetical football team that could someday land in Baltimore.

"The fact that it was baseball-only was a big decision," acknowledges Smith. "It probably wouldn't have happened had the Colts not already left for Indianapolis. He [William Donald Schaefer] wasn't going to see another team leave on his watch. He was very invested in downtown Baltimore. He was the godfather of the aquarium, the science center. His instincts were if we put a ballpark downtown, it would reshape the definition of downtown. It would help populate the hotels, the restaurants, the infrastructure already in place and would allow that to be a far less costly investment by the public sector."[3]

The promise of a downtown location was the real clincher, however, as the ballpark could naturally mesh within the urban ambience.

"Had Larry gotten his baseball-only park, but it had been out in the cornfields, it simply would have never had the kind of architectural parameters that we were able to give it, working with that existing inner city location. Our goal was to try and make it a contextual park, one that really fit with downtown Baltimore," recalls Smith, who toiled tirelessly in the late 1980s to ensure that the scale for Camden Yards would compete favorably with the city's signature three-story brick row houses—and its most famous warehouse.[4]

From Smith's perspective, a retro style ballpark authentic to downtown Baltimore had to reflect the city's rich industrial history. And no element was more reflective of such history than the Baltimore & Ohio Warehouse, which above all else, would be the ballpark's defining feature in supporting its asymmetrical layout.

Stretching over 1,100 feet long across Eutaw Street, the imposing B&O Warehouse had not been used since 1976 when the B&O Railroad ceased making stops in Baltimore. From America's bicentennial to 1988, the edifice sat vacant, deemed a dilapidated, godforsaken eyesore by most. By the late 1980s, all 983 windows were broken, floorboards were creaking, and the roof was leaking. The interior was infested with thousands of rats and blanketed with decades' worth of rail yard soot.[5] The B&O Warehouse had been built a few months after the Spanish American War, and now, at the end of the Cold War, it was painfully apparent that the building had been neglected for years.

It wouldn't be neglected for much longer, however. After some deliberation, the three parties involved in the construction of Camden Yards— the Maryland Stadium Authority, representatives from the architectural firm HOK, and the Orioles representation, which included new owner Eli Jacobs, Lucchino, and Smith—concluded that the new ballpark would be built in a manner that could accommodate the soon-to-be refurbished warehouse. (The process of sanitizing this relic of Baltimore's industrial past would ultimately last 33 months. Initially, the plan was to use power washers to spray the century-old bricks. Once the bricks started crumbling and mortar seeped out, it became apparent that more harm than good was being done to the building. So, armed with a concoction of very mild acid and water, contracted workers got up on scaffolds and used scrub brushes to wash millions of bricks—by hand.)[6]

While many people were skeptical of the Baltimore & Ohio Warehouse being adjacent to Camden Yards, the ancient building soon emerged as the ballpark's defining feature (author's photograph).

Once the blueprint for Camden Yards—and the inclusion of the B&O Warehouse—became public knowledge, a storm of criticism ensued.

There were skeptics all over the Chesapeake Region, and beyond, who questioned why anyone would want to revert to unflattering Prohibition Era design elements plagued with incongruous dimensions, when constructing a new ballpark. Many questioned the rationale behind preserving the iconic, yet rundown Baltimore & Ohio Warehouse just so there could be another historical landmark flanking this new ballpark. After all, the center field bleachers were to be constructed adjacent to Camden Station, a 19th century passenger and freight station that already served as a reminder of the B&O Railroad. Even if the warehouse's interior were thoroughly cleansed, wouldn't the exterior still be an eyesore? Not to mention, this would be a publicly funded project that would benefit an already profitable sports franchise. (The ballpark ended up costing roughly $110 million to build and was primarily financed with bonds supported by the proceeds of the Maryland Lottery.)

Fearing that Camden Yards would merely be an extension of aging Memorial Stadium, *Baltimore Sun* columnist John Steadman opined, "Now the official blueprints have been drawn, and it's downright ugly. The public deserves to be forewarned. As incredulous as it seems, Baltimore is the only city in America that is actually trying to create an old stadium. If it's being built to look old and rundown, we already have one of those."[7]

Many citizens of Baltimore had initially rejoiced upon hearing in the spring of 1988 that their team would get a new home in downtown Baltimore. But, by the early 1990s, some fans had grown skeptical; indeed, the backlash to Smith's radical plans grew harsh, and, in some cases, quite offensive.

On June 20, 1991, the *Baltimore Sun* published a letter to the editor that stated: "I became ill when I saw the design of Baltimore's new stadium. Who told these designers we wanted to go back to the old days?"[8]

The newspaper published another letter with a more vitriolic message: "Now we know why this stadium is such a hokey, screwed-up mess. It's being done by women from Mississippi who know nothing about baseball. Great job, Lucchino. You really know how to pick 'em."[9]

Actually, Lucchino really did know how to pick 'em. The daughter of a Jackson, Mississippi, architect, Janet Marie Smith would blaze a trail on many levels as she shepherded Oriole Park from conception through completion—an undertaking that would forever change both what MLB teams built and where they built it. And, perhaps more importantly, she, along with Lucchino, had the fortitude to withstand the fierce criticism and to persevere in thinking (and executing) outside the box. Smith did not dwell on the rampant calls to raze the industrial landmark that was the B&O Warehouse. She knew there was something behind the decaying facade of brick and glass. She also knew that the warehouse would naturally force right field to be shallower than left, thus facilitating a ballpark with the kind of uneven dimensions that would give it character. And so did Lucchino, the innovative baseball lifer who hired her because the two shared a similar belief: this new ballpark could be resplendent with modern-day amenities yet still reflect the brick-skinned texture of Baltimore's industrial past.

Decades later, with Camden Yards firmly established as a national treasure, Smith can look back and rationalize the skepticism.

"Their questions were valid questions," acknowledges Smith. "There was one group that viewed it as not worthy of preservation. It was a warehouse. It wasn't like it was the Capitol [Building] with big beautiful, ornate columns. There was another group that questioned whether or not it was going to force such irregularities to the ballpark as to make it not workable or not flexible enough, and that was a valid criticism too because this was before everybody got on the bandwagon of quirky, asymmetrical parks. The older parks like Ebbets and Fenway were quirky and asymmetrical because their sites forced them to be. We relished the chance for the warehouse to play that role so that our asymmetry and irregularities were borne [out] of the context just as Ebbets and Fenway were. But I can see where at the time, people were thinking symmetry is the thing—we were coming out of the round park era, and even though Kansas City [Kauffman Stadium] was there for all to see, it was still a perfectly symmetrical park with a lot of space around it. And then the third criticism came from a smaller camp, but still a vocal one, and that was the champions of the Baltimore Inner Harbor itself. The city was so proud then, as they are 25 years later, of the Inner Harbor. They felt if we took the warehouse down, you would have that view down the right field line and 'Isn't that worth taking the building down?'

"Our reaction to all of those probably speaks for itself so many years later."[10]

As the 1992 season approached, Camden Yards was no longer an abstract concept, but rather a brick-and-mortar reality, the aforementioned skepticism now began to give way to excitement, and as more and more people saw the finished product, the buzz increased. Finally, there were well-deserved five-star reviews from the press. The fans couldn't burst through the ballpark's wrought iron gates quickly enough while the ballplayers couldn't help but realize that Monday, April 6, 1992, would be no ordinary home opener for the Baltimore Orioles.

"The hype was unbelievable," recalls Bob Milacki, who pitched for the Orioles in 1992. "We got a chance to go down there and look at it before it was done. When we came back after spring training in '92, you walk in there and you're just kind of in awe of how beautiful it was. All the green seats. In Memorial Stadium they had different color seats, they had some yellow, some orange, but [in Camden Yards] all green, just looked so clean, looked so state-of-the-art. It was just awesome. Going from old Memorial

2. "An Old-Fashioned Ballpark with Modern Amenities"

Stadium to Camden Yards was a big change. It's just a beautiful stadium—the way they did it."[11]

(Currently, all but two of the ballpark's 45,971 seats remain green: in left field, an orange seat marks the landing of Cal Ripken, Jr.'s 278th home run that set a career record for a shortstop, and in right field another orange bleacher commemorates Eddie Murray's 500th career homer.)

April 6 was the first regular season game played at Camden Yards. On an early spring afternoon with postcard weather, Baltimore's Rick Sutcliffe tossed a five-hit complete game shutout in leading the O's to a 2–0 win over the Cleveland Indians. The season opener was played in just over two hours in front of 44,568 fans, an event regarded by many as the opening of the new ballpark at 333 West Camden Street. Official opening that is—because during the celebratory events in the days leading up to Opening Day, many fans had already gotten the opportunity to sit down in the Camden green seats and acquaint themselves with the new ballfield.

"So, they opened that stadium, they had an open workout for the fans, and there was a parade downtown. It was really a special time," says Bob Milacki's former bullpen mate, Alan Mills.

Baltimore sports fans needed a reason to rejoice. It had been nearly eight years since the once-beloved Baltimore Colts had unceremoniously left for Indianapolis. Of the four major North American professional sports, only baseball was alive in Charm City—and now there was no doubt it would be staying. The parade, open workout, private tours for well-connected fans, and ballyhooed preseason exhibition game only intensified the hype for the ballpark's official unveiling on April 6.

Technically, Rick Sutcliffe did not throw out the first pitch at Camden Yards. That honor was bestowed upon Bob Milacki days before in a preseason tilt against the New York Mets. Let the record show that April 3, 1992, was the date of the first actual competition at Camden Yards.

"We had an exhibition game against the Mets three days before Opening Day," explains Bob Milacki. "I was fortunate to be able to throw the first pitch off the mound there in an exhibition game actually against the Mets."[12]

In the *Washington Post*'s account of the actual inaugural game (a 5–3 Baltimore win), commissioner Fay Vincent, upon getting a tour of the facility, was quoted as saying:

> It's just terrific. This is the day we've looked forward to for a long time and it has been well worth the wait. This is going to be the prototype. Texas is following. Cleveland will. People will try to improve on this, but this is nice. It's intended to be asymmetrical and different and a reminder of the old parks. The grass is always the first thing that hits you. It's so rich and powerful. It's just so nice.[13]

Vincent wasn't the only luminary to wax poetic about stepping foot in Camden Yards during its early days of operation. Renowned journalist and author George Will would later comment, "Every fan has a kind of memory of how a baseball park is supposed to look. This is a park that is bound to generate memories."[14]

For older fans, Camden Yards rekindled fond memories of ballparks from their childhoods. Prominent billboards along the park's right field wall recall Ebbets Field's famed right field advertisements. The ivy-covered green backdrop to center field was designed to honor both Fenway Park and Wrigley Field. The park's modest complementary use of red brick and steel is meant to reflect the understated dignity of the Polo Grounds.

"It [Camden Yards] was meant to learn from those older parks and try and identify what made them resonate even after they were long gone. Ebbets had been gone for a full generation by the time we did Camden Yards and yet it served as a reference point," adds Janet Marie Smith.[15]

The Orioles finished the '92 campaign with a respectable 89–73 record, but because they failed to make the postseason that year, Camden Yards received scant primetime coverage. That all changed the next year during a few scorching days in mid–July. At long last, Camden Yards would be at the epicenter of the baseball universe as the ballpark would play host to the 1993 All-Star Game.

"I think knowing when we opened in '92 that we were going to be home to the '93 Game gave us almost like a second opening," says Smith. "It was like the April 6, 1992, debut was a local opening, a chance to showcase what we got to all of the Orioles fans in the region. But the 1993 All-Star Game would be our spotlight from the national perspective, so it gave us a full year and a half to kind of clean up our act. We were ready for that moment and for the convergence of all of baseball on Baltimore."[16]

Such painstaking preparation and meticulous attention to detail were not lost on the national media. Throughout the pages of the '93 All-Star Game program, gushing praise was heaped on Lucchino's and Smith's trailblazing creation.

Acclaimed author James Dodson remarked, "The design of Oriole Park at Camden Yards pays homage, right down to the very last rivet, to the history and traditions of the national pastime."[17]

Longtime baseball scribe Peter Gammons observed, "For a time baseball was so involved in so many other things that they forgot about the people coming to the ballpark. But it's fitting that the trend was reversed in Baltimore, because this is a town that worships the Orioles, and this is a park that welcomes fans."[18]

(Gammons was downright prophetic when, in the very same article, he boldly predicted, "The more time you spend here, noticing all the little details, the more you realize this ballpark represents a turning point in the game of baseball. From now on, Oriole Park is the standard by which new ballparks will be judged. All new baseball parks will be built like this—or baseball fans will demand to know why."[19])

New York Times architecture critic Paul Goldberger succinctly referred to Camden Yards as having "a design that enriches baseball, the city and the region."[20]

A concept that was widely criticized just a few years earlier was now being celebrated as a national treasure.

And while the game itself would be the grand showcase of Camden Yards, the annual home run derby held the day before provided a moment that rekindled local history while nearly defying the laws of physics.

With hundreds of glass windows dotting the renovated B&O Warehouse, the right field concourses along Eutaw Street were designed to create a wind tunnel to keep balls from shattering glass. Thus, it would take a prodigious shot for a left-handed slugger to make contact with the warehouse. And that's exactly what Ken Griffey, Jr., did on the afternoon of July 12, 1993. With one sweet left-handed swing, baseball's most celebrated star of the 1990s became the only player to ever knock a ball off the B&O Warehouse when his 465-foot shot nailed a stone pillar at its base. In over a quarter-century, dozens of fly balls have bounced off Eutaw Street, but no lefty basher has ever pulled off Griffey's trick—even with performance-enhancing drugs or juiced balls. (As the park was celebrating its 25th anniversary during the 2017 season, only 93 balls had ever plopped down on Eutaw Street.)

"Everyone was wondering who was going to be the guy to do it," recalls fellow '93 American League All-Star Jack McDowell. "That [right field warehouse] was there for that. Everyone was looking, 'who's going to pop this, who's going to get it?' To be able to see that, everyone went a little bit nuts. No one better than Griffey to be able to do it, too.

"Just having the wall out there for guys to shoot for was always fun. The overall look of it was just real cool and I'm glad that they kind of stuck with it over the years."[21]

(Before the home run derby, when asked if he thought he could hit the warehouse, Griffey responded, "I won't get a chance, unless I'm standing on first base with a fungo bat."[22])

In surprising himself, Griffey, who later in July would tie an MLB record by hitting a home run in eight straight games, provided baseball and its fans with one of the final joyful moments before the impending labor-management strife that would culminate in the 1994 strike and jeopardize the sport's future. And the 430,000 square foot building that railroad historian Herbert H. Harwood once referred to as "a truly classic turn-of-the-century railroad warehouse"[23] figured prominently in one of the great moments in the history of MLB All-Star festivities while building the new ballpark's mystique.

From the right-side, Juan González of the Texas Rangers at one point hit a missile that reached the upper deck in left field, a feat that hardly ever happens in an actual game. González would go on to edge Griffey in a play-off round for the derby title, but the latter's warehouse shot was the talk of baseball in the hours leading up to Tuesday night's starfest.

As Griffey and González hit their majestic moonshots, their fellow All-Stars soaked up the blistering sun—and the sparkling new ballpark. For the National Leaguers, most of whom were accustomed to playing in the multiplex behemoth stadiums, this afternoon was their first time seeing the retro style ballpark in-person.

San Francisco Giants All-Star John Burkett, familiar with pitching in the multi-purpose cookie-cutter Candlestick Park, says, "Camden Yards was in the American League, so I hadn't seen it yet. I was definitely looking forward to that because probably all of the stadiums we played in to that point were the 1970's cookie-cutter stadiums. It was kind of neat to see that retro idea come to life at Camden Yards. It was really something I looked forward to. I know a lot of the guys enjoyed it.

"The 1970's cookie cutter stadiums, Riverfront Stadium, Three Rivers Stadium, even like Montreal [Olympic Stadium] even though it was an indoor stadium, they all had the same basic dimensions and there was really no character to the stadiums. But Camden Yards breaking ground on the new outlook and the new feel, it was kind of neat how people started using their imagination and coming up with different types of things. I think everybody was excited to see that ballpark."[24]

While watching Griffey's and González's performances, Burkett, along with his fellow All-Stars, didn't sit on artificial turf, but rather on natural grass—the game's original playing surface.

"The other good thing was they went back to natural grass, which I think is best for baseball. I just love natural grass and it seemed like all the new stadiums at that point started bringing in natural grass," says Burkett.[25]

At Camden Yards, baseball, and only baseball, is played on a field of Kentucky bluegrass, one that is protected by a 2,000-pound tarp that can be deployed in 90 seconds. The drainage system is the best in the business. (In September 2003, as Hurricane Isabel barreled toward Baltimore, Camden Yards' drainage system was able to withstand the drenching rains and maintain a playable surface for at least two hours.) A sod farm sits near the outfield bullpen, supplying rolls of fresh green grass that is then manicured to create a pleasing checkered pattern that better reflects the light.[26]

As the All-Stars lounged on the emerald carpet and watched the

Not only did the urban setting of Camden Yards enhance the charm of the ballpark, it also inspired teams across the country to bring the game back to the city (author's photograph).

barrage of long balls, they also enjoyed a panoramic view of downtown buildings—a backdrop that was not dissimilar to what the game's early stars had played under.

"It was such a pretty place with all the buildings in the background. They did such a wonderful job implementing the ballpark in the city," remarks Jay Bell, the bespectacled infielder who was representing the

Pittsburgh Pirates at the 1993 All-Star Game. "What I enjoyed most was the practice before the game the day before. When you go to Camden, everything was brand new and it was just such a thrill to be there. You add the beauty of the stadium to the event itself and it's hard to beat, it's hard to replicate."[27]

"I think probably the first thing that comes to mind is that it was a brand new stadium," recalls San Diego Padres pitcher Andy Benes, who to this day still raves about Camden Yards despite acknowledging it is one of the great parks for hitters. "Just everything about it was obviously new but kind of setting the stage for what was to come, and maybe a blueprint for a lot of the other organizations that were going to be building stadiums. It just looks good. And then you look out, you see beyond it, you see the buildings. It's just a neat view. What a beautiful stadium."[28]

Beautiful, yes. Stadium, well, that was the word for describing Jack Murphy, where Benes' Padres played their home games. Indeed, "stadium" was a forbidden word in the Orioles organization when construction for Camden Yards was underway. If you said the "S word," you were fined five dollars. Baseball was played in a *ballpark*.[29]

Having previously played for the American League's Cleveland Indians, Jay Bell had played many games at Baltimore's old Memorial Stadium in the late 1980s. It didn't take long for Bell to realize that Memorial Stadium was a stadium whereas Camden Yards was a ballpark.

"It's such a unique place, compared to Memorial Stadium," says Bell. "It just is overwhelming. To have had the opportunity to play in that ballpark and see the transition between one to the other was extraordinary. It is such a great atmosphere and of course as a hitter, it was a nice place to hit also. Having been a kid coming up in the American League, seeing the old stadium compared to the new one was extraordinary."[30]

Even for those American League All-Stars who had already set foot in Camden Yards, this multi-day celebration of the ballpark reminded some of what their home stadiums lacked. This was particularly true for All-Stars from the Chicago White Sox, a franchise that had moved into the new Comiskey Park in 1991. Comiskey had modern amenities to be sure, but certainly not the character or the defining quirks that permeated Camden Yards.

"A few new stadiums had gone up. After playing in Chicago, we were kind of the first of the new stadiums to come up," recalls former White Sox ace Jack McDowell. "Being in Camden, we were really jealous of the cool unique look of that stadium compared to what we had in Chicago for sure. Camden Yards was still fairly new, so it was kind of a special place."[31]

Particularly, on this day.

Monday's festive lineup of events also included a celebrity home run contest that involved quite possibly the most famous person in America at that time not named Bill Clinton. Weeks removed from leading the Chicago Bulls to a third straight title and months before he would play in the Minor Leagues for the Birmingham Barons, Michael Jordan took some hacks in front of the top big leaguers. (Jordan won the contest by launching the deepest drive to the outfield.) These were the best baseball players on the planet but when MJ graced the All-Stars with his presence that afternoon, it was hard not to be in awe of a fellow professional athlete.

Andy Benes, pitching in his first and only All-Star Game, still relishes the memory of shaking hands with the legend.

"As far as stuff on the field, the first thing I remember is the practice day, the day before when they had the home run derby and the celebrity hitting contest," says Benes, who, ironically, unlike Jordan, was the number one overall pick in his sport's draft. "I grew up in southern Indiana and was an avid basketball player and basketball fan and I had the chance to meet Michael Jordan in the dugout and that was a really cool thing for me. I loved watching him play and compete so to have the opportunity to meet him in-person was really cool. To hang out with some of the other celebrities that were very talented in different ways was fun. All of the events surrounding the All-Star Game with the gala, the events that they had us going to were all just phenomenal. They were very well done by Major League Baseball."[32]

Jordan had established himself as arguably the greatest basketball player ever, but his unprecedented talents and level of fame didn't preclude him from soliciting an autograph from Ken Griffey, Jr., this afternoon. In the AL clubhouse, Jordan, who, at the time, was a seven-time scoring champion and three-time MVP, navigated his way through a media scrum so Junior Griffey, the 23-year-old prodigy, could sign a bat for him. On this day, Griffey was the Michael Jordan of baseball.

The actual game was still a day away, but Monday's festivities would provide Baltimoreans with another indelible memory of their city's storied baseball history.

On the morning of Tuesday, July 13, Dan Shaughnessy, covering the All-Star Game for the *Boston Globe*, began his column by writing, "It's hot. I'm hot, you're hot, and the All-Star Game in Baltimore is very, very hot. Oriole Park at Camden Yards is the hot ballpark in the hot baseball city and we hear that $60 tickets are getting four figures on the open market."[33]

The 1993 MLB All-Star Game was the hottest ticket in Baltimore for some time. For not only was it an exhibition game with baseball's greatest stars, it was the coming-out party for a transformative architectural achievement that would finally be showcased to the rest of America in living color.

Baltimoreans wanted to be there in-person when Camden Yards was spotlighted on the national stage. (In order to do so, most fans made their way into the ballpark via the unconventional center field-located entrance while breezing past adjacent Camden Station, the very same train depot in which Abraham Lincoln stopped on the route to Gettysburg in 1863.) These lucky ticket holders knew that on this night, the baseball universe was converging on their city's stunning new ballpark. Monday afternoon's home run derby and celebrity home run contest, which also featured the likes of Tom Selleck, Reggie Jackson, and Patrick Ewing among others, provided great live entertainment—for tens of thousands of fans. In fact, most of America was only able to see snippets of Camden Yards in the form of home run derby highlights on Monday night's newscasts. On Tuesday night, tens of millions of baseball enthusiasts could tune into CBS and watch nearly three hours of game competition at Camden Yards in real time—for the first time.

And they would do so while watching an American League All-Star roster that boasted Roberto Alomar, Cal Ripken, Jr., Kirby Puckett, Wade Boggs, Iván "Pudge" Rodríguez, Frank Thomas, and Ken Griffey, Jr., compete against a National League squad stacked with Barry Bonds, Tony Gwynn, Barry Larkin, Mike Piazza, Gary Sheffield, and Ryne Sandberg. The lineups may have been loaded with future Hall of Famers (and controversial superstars) but the two lefty starting pitchers (Terry Mulholland and Mark Langston) were notable for their relative lack of star power. Perhaps realizing the promise he showed in 1990 when he threw a no-hitter, Mulholland was having a career year for the 1993 pennant-winning Philadelphia Phillies when he got the starting nod for the National League. The journeyman lefty would finish his career with more losses (142) than wins (124), but in 1993 he had submitted a very strong first half in helping the surprising Phillies stay atop the NL East.

"He [Mulholland] was a leader on that pitching staff, always took the ball, always gave us innings," says Mickey Morandini, who was a teammate of Mulholland's during the 1993 season. "He didn't have the best stuff, but he was a big competitor. He threw strikes, was great at holding runners, picked off a lot of guys. Just a guy you need on your staff, a guy who can give you innings, go deep into games, pitch a lot."[34]

Mulholland was opposed by Langston, another southpaw who was a more than serviceable starter for a passel of clubs throughout a lengthy career. He would be participating in his fourth and final All-Star Game. However, it would not be a memorable night for the skinny lefty. Minutes after the National Anthem, Florida Marlins third baseman Gary Sheffield took him deep for a two-run homer as the NL jumped out to a 2–0 lead in the top half of the first.

After not allowing a hit in the bottom of the first inning (and retiring

Roberto Alomar and Ken Griffey, Jr., in doing so), Mulholland gave up a solo home run to Minnesota Twins outfielder Kirby Puckett with one out in the second inning that would cut the NL lead to 2–1. Puckett, one of the most popular ballplayers in the late 20th century, would finish the night with a pair of RBI on the way to being named the game's MVP following the AL's 9–3 triumph. For Puckett, it would be the last major highlight of a Hall of Fame career that was truncated due to glaucoma in 1996. But that Puckett even had a career in Major League Baseball was perhaps even more remarkable.

Traditionally, game day programs, particularly those for All-Star Games, include only fun facts about the participants. Nothing remotely serious or deep. So those who picked up a copy of the 1993 All-Star Game Official Major League Baseball Program must have been slightly surprised to read the following excerpt from Kirby Puckett's mini bio tucked inside Page 13:

"Puckett was the youngest of nine children growing up in Chicago's tough South Side, in the even tougher Robert Taylor Homes housing projects. When Puckett was 12, the family moved out of the projects, to the city's southern suburbs."[35]

"Tough" was the family-friendly way to describe Puckett's childhood. His was an upbringing that included frequent walks past drug dealers and gangbangers. Young Puckett was accustomed to seeing public displays of fatal violence. There's a reason why South Chicago's Robert Taylor Homes were stigmatized as the "place where hope dies." Yet Puckett did have hope because he had the sport of baseball, even if a balled-up scrap of aluminum foil or tightly rolled-up socks wrapped in tape passed for the baseball itself.

The youngest of the nine Puckett children would attend college (he started at Bradley University before transferring to Triton Junior College) and later sign with the Minnesota Twins with whom he would have a spectacular career, one that included two World Series rings, six Gold Glove awards, and 10 All-Star selections. The man known by many of his teammates and opponents simply as "Puck" always had a smile on his face, whether it was in center field or in the hospital room of a sick child whom he was visiting. By 1993, Puckett was worshipped in the Twin Cities as well as beloved by fans on both sides of the Mississippi River. If hometown hero Cal Ripken, Jr., was not going to take home MVP honors on this special night for the city of Baltimore, Puckett was the next best thing.

"Kirby Puckett was never a player to be booed by another city. Every city he went to, he was always cheered. They just loved him," recalls former Minnesota teammate Mike Trombley. "Especially in an All-Star Game situation, I've heard that the stars among the stars would just gravitate to him.

Obviously, you'd see that day to day when we would play another team, the good players, the stars on the other team wanted to come over and talk to Kirby. They would always want to talk to Kirby.

"Not so much he was a great baseball player and made a lot of money, but how he handled it and how he handled the fame. I guess he really didn't change. He was always a great guy before. He was a great guy after. He never got too big for his britches. I think he understood it's a fan's game and we're entertainers and Puck was great about that. I think the All-Star Game is just a perfect example of how much he was loved by the fans."[36]

At this point in Puckett's life, the fans only had reason to love him. He took the game seriously but didn't take himself too seriously—even on the very rare occasion in which a stray fan tried to have some fun at his expense.

"Puck was such a great ambassador of the game. He was just so good for the game," says Trombley, the former relief pitcher. "I remember one of the times we went back to Chicago and played the White Sox. We were in Comiskey and Puckett grew up in the projects right across the way. He was in the outfield and we were in the bullpen watching the game and a fan was kind of getting on Puckett. He's a hometown guy, but the guy was getting on him. Puckett was getting ready for the pitch to be thrown and the guy in the stands yelled, 'Puckett, you're fat! Man, look at the size of your butt!' Well Puckett very calmly turned around with a big smile on his face and said, 'That's not my butt. That's my wallet!' He just had a great way of winning the fans over and saying things in a way—he was funny, he was quick with it, he was just great for the game."[37]

Opponents respected Puckett because he respected the game so much. Puckett was the rare star player who treated every at-bat like it was his last and did not jog but sprinted out of the box.

"Puck was such a hard-nosed player, yet he had so much fun, too," recalls longtime American League foe Jack McDowell. "He was one of those guys that when he stepped into the batter's box, you knew it was on. You knew that you were going to bring it, he was going to bring it. Someone was going to have to go down, but it was going to be a fight. But then the next day, he had a smile on his face, saying, 'Hey, let's go on' and then you would go and compete another day. He was a great guy overall."[38]

Unfortunately, Puckett's life was bookended with trouble. The 1993 All-Star Game was not only one of the last highlights of his career, but also of his life. Several years after glaucoma forced him into retiring prematurely, Puckett was first accused by his wife of threatening to kill her and then charged with criminal sexual conduct, false imprisonment, and assault after another woman accused him of forcing her into the men's room at a restaurant in Eden Prairie, Minnesota. (In the first case no criminal charges were filed, in the second a jury ruled him not guilty.) Puckett would continue to battle serious weight issues and in March 2006, succumbed to a massive hemorrhagic stroke at 45 years old.

But on the night of July 13, 1993, at a splendid new ballpark built for the fans, one of their most prized ballplayers delivered an encore performance.

Kirby Puckett was batting in the sixth spot, behind and in front of three Hall of Famers. The American League roster was stacked with Hall of Famers as well as Blue Jays, who, in 1993, were putting up gaudier numbers than those of many enshrinees. In the bottom half of the third, Andy Benes came in to relieve Terry Mulholland and had the unenviable task of facing the top of the ferocious AL lineup.

"I was hoping that I would get to start the All-Star Game, since I was the ERA leader," says Benes. "My record wasn't great because our team was average in San Diego, but I had pitched really well and was excited that I got to share that opportunity with Tony Gwynn. We got to fly from Montreal to Baltimore and all of my family was there.

"I came in second and I faced eight guys, and six of them are Hall of Famers. The opportunity to compete against greatness—you don't really think about it as much when you are playing during the regular season or playoffs because teams are really good but they're not like the All-Star team. And when you have one of the best at every position, it's pretty exciting to compete against those guys."[39]

Leading off the inning was Blue Jays second baseman Roberto Alomar, one of the best all-around ballplayers of the early 1990s. Fourth pitch into the at-bat, the score was tied 2–2.

"Robbie Alomar hit a home run. He was the first guy that I faced. It probably took the pressure off," recalls Benes. "Back then it was an exhibition game and there wasn't a whole lot on the line except pride. But I remember jogging in from center field and Tommy Lasorda [the famed Dodger manager] was on the mound waiting for me with the ball and he said, 'Have some fun big fella.' It was hard to breathe in the beginning just because there was so much excitement with being in the game. I ended up striking out Ken Griffey Jr. and Cal Ripken Jr., so I pitched well.

"I was typically a second half pitcher. In 14 years, I would have made the second half All-Star team a lot of times. I was usually a little bit more of a slow starter so to have the privilege to be there and represent the National League was amazing."[40]

Before calling it a night after the fourth inning, Benes would retire three more Hall of Famers, Paul Molitor, Kirby Puckett, and Wade Boggs, as well as John Olerud, the eventual AL batting champ that season.

Unfortunately, for the National League, their next young right-hander from the West Coast, John Burkett of the San Francisco Giants, who started the bottom of the fifth, didn't fare as well.

"Ninety-three was my first All-Star Game. It was only my fourth year in the big leagues. I got off to such a great start that year," recalls Burkett, who, a few days prior, had matched up against Curt Schilling and the Philadelphia Phillies in triple digit temperatures at Veterans Stadium. (This brutal heat wave smothering the East Coast ultimately contributed to at least 12 deaths in Philadelphia.) "That's something you always want to do, is play in the All-Star Game and be recognized as one of the star players in your league. I was in the National League at the time so that was a great feeling and I just remember being really excited about every part of it—playing against and pitching against the best guys in the other league."[41]

The relentless AL attack was simply too overwhelming—starting with the bottom of the order. Catcher Iván "Pudge" Rodríguez of the Texas Rangers greeted his future teammate with a deep fly to left field that landed in the most bizarre fashion.

"Pudge Rodríguez hit a double off of me off the left field wall and it stuck in the wall," Burkett remembers. "So that was an interesting thing. The ball stuck right in between the pad handles for a double. I've never seen that in my whole life so that was interesting."[42]

Cleveland's Albert Belle would plate Rodríguez on a single to right field, before Griffey Jr., and Puckett drove in a run each to give the American League a 5–2 lead.

Burkett would end up being the losing pitcher this evening, yielding the three earned runs before getting pulled mid-inning for Steve Avery. Fittingly, the winning pitcher was the year's eventual AL Cy Young winner, Jack McDowell, who now admits, "Looking back on it, I wouldn't have had a chance in these days to actually pitch in the game because I had thrown that Sunday. I kind of got lucky to be in the right era for that one."[43]

Before the AL's three-run rally, manager Cito Gaston had made his first non-pitching substitution of the evening. During the top half of the fifth, Cecil Fielder, one of the game's premier African American sluggers who was putting up Ruthian numbers at the time, had jogged over to first base, spelling John Olerud.

Less than two centuries ago, slave quarters had existed where first base was now stationed at Camden Yards.

For all the old timey nostalgia and storied hardball (and American) history that circulated through the veins of Camden Yards, the specter of the city's, the region's, the country's ugly history still lingered.

By the late 1900s, Baltimore had emerged as a vibrant hub for black culture and possessed one of the largest African American populations of any major U.S. city. But the city's tragic history was undeniable. For a half-century prior to the Civil War, over a dozen slave traders had operated from harborside storefronts along Pratt Street and adjacent roads. The dreary procession of black men, women, and children in chains along Pratt Street to Fells Point, where ships waited to transport them to New Orleans for auction, was a routine sight.[44] Similar to baseball's history, one marred by decades of racial segregation, Baltimore's was indelibly associated with racial injustice.

But over time, similar to Baltimore, baseball had experienced generations of drastic change regarding race relations. Indisputably, the sport's most significant development post–World War II was Jackie Robinson's shattering of the color barrier. As the latter half of the century progressed, baseball became fully integrated. The 1990s, in particular, was one of the most celebrated eras for African American sluggers. The 64th MLB All-Star Game included some of the greatest African American hitters in the game's storied history: Ken Griffey, Jr., Frank Thomas, Tony Gwynn, Gary Sheffield, Kirby Puckett, Albert Belle, Barry Bonds, and Cecil Fielder.

Yet not all of America's regions and professions were so racially harmonious. With the previous year's Los Angeles riots (the Rodney King incident) still fresh in the minds of a shaken country, it was evident that racial tension still simmered throughout early nineties America. It was only fitting for an All-Star Game hosted in a vibrant African American community to serve as a celebration of African Americans' grand cultural and athletic contributions and an acknowledgment of the struggles they had endured in making them.

Minutes before the first pitch, distinguished actor James Earl Jones (*Field of Dreams*), accompanied by the choir from Baltimore's historically black college, Morgan State University, delivered a beautiful rendition of the National Anthem. But the celebration had actually started days before when a college intern for the Baltimore Orioles' PR department orchestrated a commemoration of the Negro Leagues. In the early 1990s, Theo Epstein was in the nascent stages of what has become a brilliant career in Major League Baseball. While an undergraduate at Yale University, Epstein started with the O's as an intern in 1992 and came into his own during the 1993 All-Star Game festivities, where he channeled his baseball acumen and creative flair to create a novel and overdue tribute to Negro League stars who were aging, and in some cases, forgotten. What ensued during All-Star Week at Camden Yards was a five-day celebration of the Stars of Early Black Baseball. In effect, it was more than a reunion of long-neglected former ballplayers. It was a means for establishing a central theme throughout the festivities.

Years later, Dr. Charles Steinberg, a public affairs executive with the

Baltimore Orioles in 1993, still had fond memories of Epstein's impressive work. In Dan Shaughnessy's book *Reversing the Curse: Inside the 2004 Boston Red Sox*, published in 2005, Steinberg reflected, "It was one of the most thoughtful, well-written proposals I had ever seen. He took the idea to a new level. He was impatient to get it done that summer [1992], but we suggested taking an extra year and making it part of our All-Star celebration in 1993. And that's what he did. It was stupendous. And it resulted in Leon Day's getting elected to the Baseball Hall of Fame."[45]

(In March 1995, Leon Day, the legendary Negro League pitcher, was elected to the Hall of Fame, less than a week before his death.)

After the Orioles were sold in 1993, Larry Lucchino moved on to the San Diego Padres, for whom he served as president/CEO, while bringing Charles Steinberg and Theo Epstein along with him. Epstein would serve in the Padres front office and then come back east to join the Red Sox after Lucchino became president/CEO in 2001. In 2002, the Boston Red Sox made then 28-year-old Theo Epstein the youngest general manager in baseball history. Through serving as general manager of the 2004 Boston Red Sox and president of the 2016 Chicago Cubs, the former Baltimore Orioles PR intern helped put together rosters that succeeded in breaking decades-long world championship droughts.

Yet to this day, some might say the celebration of Negro League stars during the 1993 All-Star Week remains Theo Epstein's breakthrough moment in Major League Baseball.

After the American League jumped out to a 5–2 lead in the aforementioned fifth inning rally, AL manager Cito Gaston (representing the Toronto Blue Jays) made the customary mid-game lineup changes. Among the seven new All-Stars taking the field for the American League in the top of the sixth was Toronto's Devon White, the inimitable center fielder. Yet many fans at the time thought Kenny Lofton of the Cleveland Indians was a more deserving choice to be the reserve center fielder for the AL All-Stars. More than a few fans, perhaps still bitter that Toronto had edged Baltimore for the AL East title on multiple occasions, thought that Gaston selected White because he was a fellow Blue Jay.

"A lot of people were pretty upset," recalls Devon White. "They booed us because the year before we were battling with Baltimore for the race to the title in our division. I was one of the guys that day they thought knocked out Kenny Lofton. He had better numbers from what I heard. I never really looked back. Coming off the year of the World Series, I think I deserved it too, plus it was my manager."[46]

Surely, some of the 48,147 fans must have rolled their eyes as White jogged across shallow center field to get in position for taking his warmup tosses. And as many of those fans were beginning to learn more about their ballpark, they came to understand this shallow center field area was no ordinary patch of grass. It had been the site of a tavern owned by Babe Ruth's father.

Approximately 20 paces into center field, on the shortstop side, is where George Ruth Senior owned and operated a saloon in the early 1900s. While his mischievous son was off carousing around Baltimore's Inner Harbor (behavior that would get him shipped off to St. Mary's Industrial School for Boys), the elder Ruth was making a living as a barkeep.

Embedded in a hardscrabble community of shipyards and industrial factories, Ruth Senior's tavern was a rollicking establishment, frequented by drunkards and vagabonds hell-bent on settling disputes with their fists. Certainly no place for the already rambunctious and impressionable son to live—until he was older. Indeed, after the 1914 season, a newlywed Babe did live there on a temporary basis. Ruth Senior owned and operated the saloon until he died in 1918—a year before his son was sold to the New York Yankees.

Knowing that they were building a ballpark on such hallowed ground, the Baltimore Orioles and HOK Sports had taken great pains not to bulldoze over any bygone relics. In the early 1990s, architectural preservationists familiar with the saloon's location were called in and they soon discovered bottles and dishes that presumably were used to serve hungry and thirsty saloon customers.[47] Perhaps those artifacts would never have been uncovered if it weren't for the new ballpark.

While Babe Ruth will forever be associated with Boston and New York, it is fitting that his family's legacy remains firmly entrenched in the center of his hometown's ballpark.

In the home half of the sixth, Devon White vindicated his manager by sparking the AL's second three-run rally in as many innings with an RBI double. (The AL would score two more sixth inning runs on a pair of wild pitches by Atlanta's John Smoltz.) After American League reserve catcher Terry Steinbach smacked a two-out RBI double in the seventh, the home team held a commanding 9–3 lead, one that would remain intact by night's end.

Oddly, however, the top of the ninth unfolded as an uncomfortable ending to an otherwise glorious evening. When Toronto closer Duane Ward took the hill to close out the American League's easy 9–3 win, a chorus of boos rained down on the diamond.

Hosting this All-Star Game was supposed to be one of Baltimore's proudest sports moments in a decade. The city's next generation ballfield had been the hub of festivities over the past several days. The American

League was comfortably ahead and Cal Ripken, Jr., had been the starting shortstop—despite entering the game with a .215 average. So why were so many Baltimore baseball fans upset during what, for all intents and purposes, was merely an exhibition game? Because for his last pitching change of the night, AL manager Cito Gaston had opted to go with his own team's pitcher over Baltimore's only other All-Star, Mike Mussina, a young, slim right-hander with impeccable control. (Leading up to the game, Gaston, having selected seven Blue Jays for the AL squad, was accused of practicing nepotism.)

Amid a volley of jeers and chants of "We Want Mike!" Duane Ward proved effective, if not dominant. The inning started with Ward getting pinch-hitter Gregg Jefferies to flail on a pitch out of the zone for strike three. Nevertheless, the booing grew even more rancorous.

CBS broadcaster Tim McCarver had opined during the Jefferies at-bat, "It's a comfortable situation for Cito Gaston with his team up by six runs and I think we're going to see [Mike] Mussina before this inning is over."[48]

McCarver was wrong on two counts. The ninth inning proved to be anything but a comfortable situation for Gaston and the only sight of Mussina would be his warming up in the home bullpen, one located several feet below that of the visiting team (a feature of the cutting-edge ballpark design).

With one out, future Hall of Famer Tony Gwynn stepped up to the plate, and CBS play-by-play man Sean McDonough wondered if Gaston was going to use Mussina for the final out. "If he [Mussina] doesn't come in, they may boo when the final out is made when the American League wins in an American League park."[49]

When Ward uncorked a pitch in the dirt to Gwynn, the jeers only intensified. CBS panned over to Gaston who was shaking his head in disbelief.

McDonough commented, "Cito just shaking his head in amusement, perhaps amusement. That probably isn't the word that applies. In matter of fact, it's not even close."[50]

After Gwynn grounded out weakly to Travis Fryman at shortstop, the national TV audience caught a glimpse of Mussina warming-up in the Baltimore bullpen—minutes after many fans had become aware. The calls for Mussina to enter reached a crescendo. Yet unbeknownst to the crowd, the bullpen phone had never rung. Mussina had taken matters into own hands and Gaston now looked like the villain.

"Mike Mussina went to warm up and the American League had a big lead and Cito Gaston wasn't going to use him," recalls decades-long Baltimore Orioles employee Bill Stetka. "What really happened was Mike warmed up on his own, but the crowd thought he had been made to get up and then didn't get in the game. It might have been a little bit of Mike showing up Cito."[51]

Presuming that Gaston had called for Mussina to get up, the CBS announcers were incredulous as to why Gaston wasn't lifting his reliever for the sake of the hometown guy.

McCarver went on to say, "I'll tell you, it would take a lot of courage for him [Gaston] not to make the move right now."[52]

He could barely finish his point before McDonough, leaving all objectivity behind for the moment, chimed in, "Why wouldn't you bring him in? The game is for the fans. And if he is doing this to spite the 48,000 people plus that are here, it's a lousy decision. Why wouldn't you bring him in? If Mussina is unable to pitch in the game, why bother even having him warm up?"[53]

The inning (and game) mercifully ended with Ward painting the outside corner with a fastball to freeze rookie sensation Mike Piazza. McDonough continued to empathize with the frustrated Baltimoreans whose jeers still resonated at a fever pitch. An unfortunate ending to a star-studded night that showcased the game's future setting while evoking its nostalgic past.

Even decades later, this ugly finish (along with Randy Johnson notoriously airmailing a fastball over John Kruk's head in the third inning) would be one of many fans' lasting memories from the game. But whether or not they ever learned the truth, Gaston had never asked Mussina to warm up, and the veteran Toronto skipper would remain annoyed at the pitcher known as "Moose" for years.

After 1993, cities across America would break ground on sparkling ballparks that adopted retro style designs inspired by Camden Yards. Many of these ballparks would have more bells and whistles in comparison to the original "old-fashioned ballpark with modern amenities." Yet Camden Yards, with its understated elegance and natural ability to mesh with a metropolitan setting, would remain the standard by which all future ballparks were measured. A ballpark built after 1993 was one largely constructed of steel, with teams finally realizing that concrete was dull and uninviting. Asymmetrical dimensions in the outfield became standard, as did walls of different sizes. Upper deck bleachers no longer sloped at such at an acute angle. A brick facade was not an uncommon sight. In a sense, there is a little bit of Camden Yards in every ballpark that opened after the 1993 season.

"Every ballpark that has been built since this one owes its existence to Camden Yards," claims Bill Stetka, who became the Director of Orioles Alumni in 2008. "We've had teams come in here that were building new ballparks. The Angels modeled their press box totally after ours. [The Angels did not build a new ballpark but have performed major renovations to their original ballpark.] San Diego uses the left field corner there with their version of the warehouse because of this building. It's not quite as dominant, not nearly as dominant, but that's what they tried to do and it's all because of this warehouse."[54]

The legacy of Camden Yards is not lost on the players either. Longtime Baltimore reliever and coach Alan Mills acknowledges, "From what I understand, after the ballpark came into existence, a lot of people kind of copied the design of it. I guess the brick of the warehouse, you see that around in different parks nowadays or after that one was built. It kind of stands out."[55]

The B&O Warehouse is not just a 51-foot wide building that is almost as long (horizontally) as the Empire State Building. With its rusty crimson color, the warehouse represents the brick-skinned texture of Baltimore's (and America's) Machine Age. And that's just the exterior.

"A lot of people don't understand you can take a tour of the warehouse," says Mills. "There are so many things in that warehouse that aren't visible to everyday fans or the guy at home or girl watching the game. There are a lot of things inside the warehouse."[56]

An eight-story building that was once used for rail storage is now home to the box office, team store, eateries, art gallery, team administrative offices, kitchen space, television studio, and conference rooms. During games, as fans slip in and out of the ground floor souvenir store and Dempsey's Brew Pub & Restaurant or linger around the flag court, they are enjoying Camden Yards' intimacy, one of the features Lucchino most strongly desired to establish.

"A lot of people that have seats in the upper deck will come and hang out down here [Eutaw Street] and just stand and they're closer to the action," says Bill Stetka. "They're down lower, they've got a chance of getting a home run. I think that openness, even with the warehouse kind of looming behind them, gives the ballpark a much more open feel than it really appears to."[57]

It's probably Baltimore relief pitchers who can most appreciate the eccentricities and intimacy of Camden Yards. Not only are they a stone's throw from the warehouse, but, with the co-located bullpens in center field, fans are literally right on top of them.

"I think it is designed wonderfully," says Alan Mills, who has probably spent more time around Camden Yards than anyone in baseball. "I like the warehouse. I like Eutaw Street. I like everything about it. Where I became established as a major league player was there. I came up with the Yankees, but I spent the majority of my career in Baltimore in Camden Yards. I love the stadium. I love to have the opportunity to coach for the organization and now the opportunity to coach there. It's like being home for me."[58]

2. "An Old-Fashioned Ballpark with Modern Amenities"

And many relievers still have fond memories of the ballpark, even if it only measures 318 feet down the right field line and 364 feet to left center.

"I love baseball history. I'm kind of a nostalgic baseball guy. So, going to Camden and seeing the new ballpark in the old look was great," says Mike Trombley, who had previously pitched in the Metrodome with the Twins before coming over to Baltimore late in his career. "I loved that stadium. The only thing I don't like about that stadium is pitching there. It's not a very friendly place to pitch but it's a great atmosphere. It [Baltimore] is a great baseball city. I really liked the look of it. You've really got to be there to appreciate how nice it is."[59]

Bob Milacki hasn't pitched in Camden Yards for over a quarter-century but still recalls, "Just the way they left the big building in right field was tremendous and you have Eutaw Street. People can walk around. You have Boog Powell out there in Eutaw Street selling his food out there. It's just a tremendous atmosphere and the backdrop of that stadium is outstanding. The way the field is, the way it drains, I mean it could pour there and the field just drains completely.

"Camden Yards was a tremendous facility and still is. Probably state-of-the-art back then. Going from old Memorial Stadium to Camden Yards was a big change. It's just a beautiful stadium—the way they did it. I enjoyed pitching there when I played there for the '92 season."[60]

Of course, Camden Yards is more than just a beautiful ballpark; it is an establishment with a foundation built for sustainability. The original cookie-cutter parks in Philadelphia, Pittsburgh, and Cincinnati barely lasted 30 years. Camden Yards could last 130 years.

"If you look back over the course of time and you see different stadiums, there are the ones that are around quite a bit," notes Jay Bell. "You go back to Three Rivers Stadium, Riverfront, the Vet [Veterans Stadium] or Royals Stadium in Kansas City, they are places that stand out. The first three that I mentioned didn't [last] because they were multi-purpose stadiums—they were built for a purpose, but they weren't really pretty. But when you look back, you look at what they did to Kansas City and that stadium was built around the same time as Three Rivers, Riverfront, and the Vet were built, and yet that one [Kansas City] is still standing and the other ones aren't. That's how Baltimore is. With Camden Yards, that stadium will last a long, long time just because of the thought process that they put into the stadium. Camden Yards is going to be a ballpark that is ageless, that is going to continue to [withstand] the elements and just allow guys to go in there to enjoy it for a long, long time. I don't know about the nooks and crannies underneath and how that will date itself. As far as the aesthetics of looking at the ballpark from a fan's viewpoint or a player's viewpoint, man, there's not many of them that stand there like that one does. It still stands out to me as one of my top five places to play."[61]

For some baseball fans, Camden Yards remains their top place to watch a game.

While the seating capacity of now-defunct Memorial Stadium (53,371) eclipsed that of Camden Yards (45,971), the latter drew over three-million fans per year from 1992 through 2001, with the exception of the strike-shortened 1994 season. Memorial Stadium yearly attendance figures never approached the three-million mark, even during world championship seasons. It was former team president Larry Lucchino who believed that if you build it smaller, they will come.

"He [Larry Lucchino] had observed as an executive in sports that the two smallest parks in baseball, Wrigley and Fenway, had consistently the highest attendance," recalls Janet Marie Smith. "It was something about the atmosphere being played in that had all of that cachet in spite of the team's performance."[62]

Given that Baltimore's World Series drought dates back to 1983, the franchise ultimately could have found itself in a dire financial situation had it not given its fan base a reason to buy tickets.

"It's interesting, because I think for the longtime Baltimoreans, the feeling was kind of 'Why do we need a new ballpark? Just accept Memorial Stadium.' But once you came here, you realized what Memorial Stadium lacked," remarks Bill Stetka. "You cherish the memories of the old place but you sure as hell wouldn't want to move back there. I think people realize once they got here kind of what was missing at Memorial Stadium. It [Memorial Stadium] had its old character, but it didn't have the legroom it has here. It didn't have the concourses we have here. You just couldn't have fixed it up."[63]

Ironically, during winter of 2012, Camden Yards was given a facelift. The ballpark underwent considerable renovations as the Orioles brightened up the concourses, inserted new headings on food concession stands, posted new posters and photos (some of which commemorate the 1993 All-Star Game), and rebranded club lounges with thematic signage. Also in 2012, as part of the year-long commemoration of Camden Yards' 20th anniversary, the six Orioles who are enshrined in the Baseball Hall of Fame (Frank Robinson, Brooks Robinson, Eddie Murray, Jim Palmer, Cal Ripken, Jr., and Earl Weaver) were immortalized with bronze sculptures in the renovated center field picnic area that has become accessible to morning joggers and dog walkers as an inner city promenade. In the early 21st century, other former O's have been honored at Camden Yards during reunions of Baltimore's 1966, 1970, and 1983 world championship teams.

2. "An Old-Fashioned Ballpark with Modern Amenities" 61

It is hardly a coincidence that from 1994 to 2012, a total of 20 new ballparks opened across Major League Baseball. Hardly any bear even the slightest resemblance to the infamous cookie-cutter stadiums. "The Camden Effect" has been one of the most welcomed developments in baseball's history. In 2017, as the 25th anniversary season of Camden Yards was getting underway, MLB commissioner Rob Manfred was quoted in an *Associated Press* report as saying, "The wave of new ballparks has dramatically improved the fan experience in terms of access, sight lines, food options and a variety of other issues. These new ballparks have allowed baseball to ride a wave of record attendance that has improved the economics of all 30 clubs."[64]

It is not just baseball that has benefited from the birth of Camden Yards. On a macro level, the revitalization of the game's urban setting has been a boon for some of America's grand metropolises, including San Diego, whose ballpark, Petco Park, was also the brainchild of Janet Marie Smith and Larry Lucchino.

"I think the real victory here is for America's cities," says Smith. "I love seeing teams from Cleveland, Pittsburgh, San Diego, and San Francisco all move into their urban settings and really try hard to be a part of that. I never worried about the validity or the longevity of those venues because I felt that they took seriously their roles in urban environment, used the city to shape their park, and have really played a role in the development of the neighborhoods around them. I have worried more about some of those that have used the architectural vocabulary, but without the urban setting, and whether or not that really translates as well."[65]

Although the Orioles failed to make the postseason in 1993 and the strike truncated the 1994 season, Baltimore baseball once again became newsworthy when Camden Yards returned to the national spotlight in 1995. On the night of September 6, 1995, the ballpark was the setting as Cal Ripken, Jr., broke Lou Gehrig's consecutive games played record. And for the next two autumns, Camden Yards would play co-host to the American League Championship Series (ALCS). But during the 1993 All-Star Game, before all the other new ballparks and stadiums began opening across the country, no star shone brighter than Baltimore's crown jewel of a ballpark—the one that inspired them all.

3

When Michael Jordan (and the Chicago Bulls) Owned the NBA

James Jordan's youthful appearance often belied his age.
Even when he was around his son.
Always in great shape and often in casual attire, James could have passed as Michael's big brother when the two were hanging out.
This was never truer than during the night of June 20, 1993, when Michael Jordan had just led the Chicago Bulls to a 99–98 win over the Phoenix Suns in Game 6 of the NBA Finals, securing the franchise's third consecutive world championship and establishing it as the team of the decade. As the two embraced in a private NBC network room in Phoenix's America West Arena, the son looked drained, having been burdened by pressures to which most 30-year-olds would never be accustomed while the 56-year-old father exuded more vitality.[1]

In truth, for Michael Jordan, perhaps the most famous athlete on the planet, or at least in North America, this was a moment of relief, more so than one of elation—even though, during this series, he had bested league MVP Charles Barkley on the way to his third straight Finals MVP. Since MJ had gone from a star basketball player in the eighties to a global icon in the nineties, moments of privacy were virtually non-existent. On the road, he was a prisoner of his hotel room, for dozens, if not hundreds, of gawkers awaited in the downstairs lobby. At home, he couldn't leave his gated residence—unless he wanted to sign autographs ad nauseam before inevitably having to deny some long-awaiting children's requests. And this spring, the public scrutiny had intensified, when it was revealed that he had spent the night before Game 2 of the Eastern Conference Finals at Bally's Grand Casino in Atlantic City. This, after his most physically taxing season ever, one that essentially had no preceding off-season. (Chicago's 1992 season culminated in mid-June when they defeated the Portland Trail Blazers in the NBA Finals, and shortly thereafter, Jordan began participating in USA Basketball activities for the upcoming Summer Olympics.)

But now Michael Jordan had a couple minutes with his best friend—his father. Before satisfying the gaggle of media members awaiting outside; lighting up his trademark cigar at the upcoming victory celebration in Chicago; fulfilling more commitments to corporate America—by this point he was pitching his countrymen everything but reverse mortgages. In this room, he was not MJ, Air Jordan, or His Airness. He was just the son of James Raymond Jordan, Sr.

And now the two were celebrating not just another NBA championship, but something far more meaningful—what would turn out to be their last Father's Day together.

For five weeks later, James Jordan's murdered corpse would be draped over a tree limb in a South Carolina swamp and his mega celebrity son, still dealing with the aftermath of his gambling scandal, would start contemplating his career beyond basketball—the sport in which, by summer 1993, he had established himself as the all-time greatest participant.

Months after defeating Clyde Drexler and the Portland Trail Blazers in the 1992 Finals, the Chicago Bulls embarked on the 1992–93 season vying to pull off the three-peat, something that hadn't been accomplished since the Boston Celtics won eight straight titles from 1959 to 1966. The Showtime Lakers, Larry Bird–led Celtics, and Bad Boy Pistons teams were able to repeat, but never capture that elusive third consecutive title. And as far as the rest of the NBA was concerned, this year's Chicago Bulls sure as hell weren't going to either.

"I remember the difficulty of trying to win a third championship," recalls Chicago center Scott Williams. "There were a lot of outside distractions with the club. It's hard to keep your focus. Even though when you think you're working as hard as you were the year before, two years before, it's human nature to give into some of the accolades and praise that you receive. It takes away some of your hunger when people are patting you on the back and buying you dinner and drinks in town and everywhere you go. It's like being on stage with the Beatles or the Rolling Stones. You kind of fall into a sense of self-achievement that you haven't quite earned the way you had the previous years. And on top of that, I think it motivates your opponents to get up and raise their game to another level. So, if you're not ready to meet that level, it makes it extremely difficult. It was harder."[2]

That Michael Jordan and Scottie Pippen were not getting their customary rest and relaxation during summer of 1992, but instead playing on the Dream Team in the Olympics, made things exponentially harder. Just over a week after leading the Bulls to a second consecutive world title, the star duo began practicing for the Olympics and several weeks later, they were competing in Barcelona.

(Previously, the U.S. Men's Olympic Basketball Team had consisted of amateurs, however by the 1980s, the team struggled to compete against professionals, specifically those playing for the Soviet Union. Naturally, the 1992 team became open to NBA players, resulting in a roster with 11 future Hall of Famers, including not just Jordan and Pippen, but also Larry Bird, Magic Johnson, Charles Barkley, Patrick Ewing, Karl Malone, and David Robinson. Never before in the game's history had there been a collection of such otherworldly talent in the same gymnasium—a fact not lost on even the team of college standouts handpicked to scrimmage against the Dream Team at the University of California, San Diego. As Penny Hardaway, one of the nation's top collegiate players in the early nineties who headlined this amateur squad, says, "All of our idols in one building. To be selected to that team was a huge honor because we knew we were going to play against our idols. We were just in awe and really wanted to go and not embarrass ourselves. The one thing that I remember is just walking in the gym every day and just seeing these guys and going, 'Wow! I'm actually playing against my idols.'"[3])

The Dream Team's eventual utter dominance in Spain was *the* sports story of 1992, but, understandably, for the Bulls and their rabid fan base, there was concern that Olympic competition was going to compromise the team's ability to win a third straight title. With the franchise's fortunes resting on the two superstars, head coach Phil Jackson made the call early on in training camp to ensure Jordan's and Pippen's workouts were not as grueling as those assigned to the supporting cast. Given the circumstances, the star treatment was understandable ... but not without controversy.

"Scottie and Michael coming off the Dream Team experience was a big deal because they just didn't get away from the game for any length of time," recalls Erik Helland, Chicago's assistant strength and conditioning coach. "If you look at how quickly they had to turn around and start practicing, the reality is they weren't getting their normal off-season type of experience. The Olympics end, and a couple weeks later we're starting training camp.

"There's probably a couple that had some issues with it [the star treatment]. It's like any other family. I think if kids are treated a little bit differently at times, it can probably create a little bit of animosity."[4]

Perhaps the most notable gripes came from veteran forward Horace Grant, who, annoyed that Jordan and Pippen could basically train on their own terms, stormed out of a preseason practice, later venting over the "double standards" and "preferential treatment" that existed in Chicago.[5] This was a particularly sensitive issue for the begoggled Grant. When it came to training, the brawny power forward was a workaholic, the guy who turned the lights on and off in the weight room. He thought the truncated off-season robbed players of critical training time ... not R&R.

Grant, as had been well-documented from earlier seasons, was not afraid to stand up to Jordan. As chronicled in Sam Smith's 1992 runaway bestseller/bombshell work, *The Jordan Rules*, the most notable incident occurred on a plane ride home following a playoff loss against the Detroit Pistons a few years back. Jordan was in a sour mood coming off a down night in which he had been held to 18 points. He also had long enjoyed disparaging Grant, whom he believed had a rather limited intellect. Now Jordan was using Grant (one rebound during this game) as a scapegoat for the loss. Grant retorted by shouting, "Screw you, M.J. All you care about is your points and everyone knows it. You don't care about anything but yourself." Jordan fired back, "You're an idiot. You've screwed up every play we ever ran. You're too stupid to even remember the plays. We ought to get rid of you." After more verbal assaults were slung back-and-forth, the two were finally separated.[6] (As Grant was the first Bull who really challenged Jordan, most of the team sat on the plane stunned. However, Grant's stand did inspire teammates as evidenced by an incident in March 1991 when power forward/center Stacey King also built up the courage to shout "Fuck You!" at Jordan when MJ was poking fun of his rotund physique.[7])

And then there was veteran center Bill Cartwright, who, since the late 1980s, had disapproved of Jordan's approach to running the offense (lots of isolation plays designed for His Airness). Cartwright had to grow accustomed to getting fewer shot opportunities than almost any of the starting centers in the NBA, despite the fact that Phil Jackson constantly exhorted players to push the ball inside and get everyone involved via the triangle offense system, famously devised by assistant Tex Winter. Cartwright, the most famous big man from the University of San Francisco not named Bill Russell, not only couldn't stand how Jordan would seemingly ignore Jackson's offensive concepts but also didn't care for Jordan berating, even humiliating, teammates. Cartwright, who battled a litany of injuries throughout his career, despised how Jordan condescendingly nicknamed him "Medical Bill."[8] (Jordan held a personal grudge against Cartwright because the Bulls had traded rebounding machine Charles Oakley to the Knicks for Cartwright back in 1988.)

"He [Bill Cartwright] would get really disturbed sometimes by Jordan's hardline approach to some of the players," recalls Jackie MacMullan, longtime basketball writer for the *Boston Globe* and *Sports Illustrated*. "He didn't understand it. That wasn't his mindset. It wasn't the way he went about things. But I think if you ask Jordan, he would tell you that Cartwright was really, really important to that team because of the way he balanced Jordan's sort of ruthless personality."[9]

(While Jordan could be excessively demanding of and dismissive toward teammates, he certainly had a different persona off the court. Over the course of his NBA career, he was sincerely engaged in his exemplary charitable work, which included supporting such organizations as the United Negro College Fund, Special Olympics, Ronald McDonald House Charities, and Starlight Children's Foundation, which helps terminally ill children. Jordan was particularly generous with his time when it came to providing companionship to special needs youngsters.)

But in his workplace, Jordan did indeed have this ruthless persona, while constantly not getting reprimanded for hazing and degrading teammates. Simply put, the Chicago Bulls had rules for Jordan ... and those for everyone else.

Still, Jackson had to tread carefully at this juncture. By fall of 1992, chemistry between Jordan and his fellow Bulls (including even Grant and Cartwright) had improved from that of past seasons, ones pockmarked by acrimonious relations between star and teammates. Allowing Jordan (and Pippen) to sit while the rest of the team was grinding out a torturous Indian Run exercise posed the risk of mild resentment resurfacing. Which, on occasion, it did. After all, playing deep into the prior June had meant an abbreviated off-season for the entire roster. But, for the most part, by October 1992, Jordan was co-existing relatively peacefully with his colleagues.

(This was in large part because shooting guard Craig Hodges would not be returning this year. Hodges may have been, as Cartwright says, "one of the better shooters on the planet,"[10] but he was not a Jordan favorite as he would openly criticize MJ for his silence on sociopolitical issues, namely those involving racial injustice. Waiving Hodges before the 1992–93 season was an easy decision for Chicago as it could no longer justify tolerating the off-court distractions given his declining skill set. In particular, some Bulls resented how Hodges had drawn excessive attention to himself when the team was honored for its first championship at the White House in October 1991—he dressed in a dashiki and gave George H.W. Bush a hand-written note that articulated his discontent with the administration's treatment of African Americans.[11] Two months later, Hodges' private life proved rather messy when his estranged wife tried to light him on fire. So, in other words, the Bulls had no problem placating Jordan via this personnel move.)

Aside from ensuring that Jordan's and Pippen's strained bodies weren't overtaxed, the coaching staff was ever mindful of Cartwright and John Paxson, who came into training camp sporting almost identical scars on their left knees, the products of off-season knee surgeries to remove painful bone spurs and clean up the meniscuses—fairly common maintenance work for aging veterans who had logged significant mileage over the years. Cartwright and Paxson soldiered on—despite the public perception that because of their ages, 35 and 32 respectively, and lower production levels, they soon could be relegated to the bench. Eventually, Paxson grew tired of people dwelling on his diminished scoring output.[12] Meanwhile, Cartwright would hear how the team went 18–2 in his absence the prior year (couple years) and reminded them (folks) he was the starting center on two championship teams. That both vets were nearing the end of their contracts with Chicago only compounded matters.[13]

A couple weeks before the regular season started, Paxson, who had such a prominent role on the 1991 title team that he appeared on *Saturday Night Live* months later, told the *Chicago Tribune*, "I've never felt an inferiority complex, but I think there are a lot of people who I don't think understand the roles Bill and I play for this team."[14]

Nevertheless, this situation proved to be nothing more than a mini red flag. Neither Cartwright nor Paxson allowed his personal agenda to be a teamwide distraction. Truly, any teammate of Michael Jordan's, from established veteran to rookie, had to accept that, at one point or another, he would be overshadowed by the magnitude of MJ's stardom.

"By '93 Michael was just so beyond popular in the sports world," says former *Sports Illustrated* basketball scribe Jack McCallum, who had enjoyed unrivaled access to Jordan throughout the early nineties. "The Dream Team had made him clearly the most popular athlete in the world had he not been [already]. Jordan was in this class into himself. He almost owned the whole league."[15]

And much of America, as well.

The great-grandson of a sharecropper, Jordan was making millions through endorsing McDonald's, Hanes, Gatorade, Chevrolet, Wheaties, and Nike; he was gracing the covers of *GQ*, *Esquire*, and *Newsweek*; he was a guest visitor on *The Arsenio Hall Show*; he was a guest host on *Saturday Night Live*; he was responsible for bringing in hundreds of millions of dollars for television networks and the NBA.

As Steve Nidetz in the *Chicago Tribune* would write after the 1992–93 season, "Jordan not only became the star during the games, but the star during the commercials as well. Michael, indeed, became *the* cool dude in *the* hot medium. Jordan was made for television, and television made Jordan a millionaire many times over."[16]

The Jordan brand sold globally, too. Given Nike's significant foothold in China, the soaring MJ logo grew nearly as prominent as the Red Dragon. Dutch teenagers donned all types of Jordan paraphernalia. In Germany, teenage boys sported shaved heads, with only the initials "MJ" standing out.[17]

(It was also good business for a foreign country when Jordan visited. Always looking to polish his corporate image, Jordan once purchased no fewer than 18 designer suits on a trip to Paris.[18])

"I don't think there was a person on the planet who didn't know the name Michael Jordan, what team he played for, and how he could fly through the air," says Scott Williams. "It was like traveling with a rock band. The most popular rock band at the time. We would be getting into hotels and there would be anywhere between 50 to 250 people waiting for us to arrive at the hotel just so they could get a picture or a glimpse of Michael Jordan. It's one thing if you're arriving at four o'clock in the afternoon and there are a couple of kids there who have finished their homework and trying to get a picture with Jordan or an autograph. It's another thing when you're in Detroit or Cleveland and you just played earlier that night in Chicago and the plane doesn't arrive until two o'clock in the morning and you've got grown men, women, and children standing in a snowstorm and it's 25 degrees outside, trying to get an autograph or a picture. Sometimes MJ was gracious enough to sign a few and other times he was just so exhausted from the game and the travel that it was just a quick rush from the bus right into the lobby of the hotel to grab your key packet and up to your room and go to sleep. It was bizarre to see people losing their minds and screaming 'Michael! Michael!' and things of that nature in the early hours of the morning."[19]

In the world of North American professional sports, Jordan's celebrity status was incomparable. Megastar athletes such as Troy Aikman, Wayne Gretzky, and Ken Griffey, Jr., weren't even in the same discussion. Neither were pop culture stars such as Tom Cruise, Arnold Schwarzenegger, Paula Abdul, and Phil Collins. It was only the most iconic entertainers (Madonna, Michael Jackson) and powerful statesmen (Bill Clinton, Princess Diana) whose renown was comparable to that of Jordan's.

It made sense. Jordan was the two-time defending regular season and Finals MVP who had led the NBA in scoring each year since the 1986–87 season, one in which he averaged a ridiculous 37.1 points per game. Jordan was also a truly great two-way player. Many NBA superstars don't want to exert themselves on defense, so they can be fresh for their crowd-pleasing shooting performances. Not Jordan. By the late eighties, as MJ was emerging into an excellent perimeter shooter, he was also developing into one of the most tenacious defensive guards in league history, becoming a perennial selectee for the NBA All-Defensive First Team.

"He [Jordan] affected both ends of the floor," recalls longtime opponent Larry Drew, who, as a point guard for the Los Angeles Lakers, lost to Jordan and the Bulls in the 1991 NBA Finals. "I remember when he came in as a rookie, a lot of people just talked about him offensively, but as he spent more time in the league, he started affecting both ends of the floor and that was one thing that really stands out to me particularly in that first year he won a championship. He was just a nuisance on both ends."[20]

For aspiring NBA stars, their level of success against Jordan became the ultimate measuring stick.

"If I could compete against him and be successful against him then there wasn't anybody else in the league that I felt like I wouldn't have any confidence against," recalls former NBA All-Star point guard Penny Hardaway, whose first exposure to Jordan came in the scrimmage held in San Diego before the '92 Summer Olympics. "If you play against Michael Jordan, who's one of the best two-way players the game has ever seen, and make him uncomfortable, then you knew that the rest of the league would be a much simpler chore because he was the highest of the high."[21]

A trademark Jordan look was the tongue wagging as he soared through the air. Another was the "I can't explain why I'm so unbelievable" shrug. And then there was the scowl. The seemingly interminable, cold-blooded scowl that unmistakably conveyed one simple truth: losing was anathema to him. Any teammate who wasn't executing a high pick-n-roll to perfection or busting his buttocks to get back on defense was a personal enemy.

"The way he went about his business, how competitive he was on and off the court, it just kind of rubbed off on his teammates," says guard Darrell Walker, whom the Bulls acquired in a mid-season trade during the 1992–93 campaign.[22]

Jordan's entire career was marked by such uber-competitiveness and it wasn't just on the basketball court. Perhaps the most telling example occurred the 1992 Olympics. On the Dream Team, Duke legend Christian Laettner was the least accomplished basketball player but the most talented ping-pong player, schooling many of his teammates at table tennis. After Jordan lost to Laettner one night, supposedly MJ arranged for a ping-pong table to be delivered to his Barcelona hotel room. How dare a rookie beat him at anything. However, despite practicing for God knows how long, Jordan was never able to defeat young Laettner.

(Even when Jordan returned to the NBA a second time, as a middle-aged man with the Washington Wizards in the early 2000s, he would not tolerate losing in pick-up games against stronger and faster teammates, some of whom were young enough to be his offspring. It didn't matter that he had six titles to his name and the scrimmage was utterly meaningless. He needed to take the last shot—and always did. His relentless drive for greatness compensating for his diminished skills and athleticism, Jordan was an effective scorer up until his final games in April 2003 for Washington.[23])

In high school and college, Jordan's obsession with winning was quite apparent but his otherworldly talents were not. Coming out of Emsley A. Laney High School in Wilmington, North Carolina, Jordan was not the nation's most highly touted prospect. Even after leading the University of North Carolina Tar Heels to a national championship in 1982 and being honored with the Naismith College Player of the Year award in 1984, Jordan was not the top pick of the 1984 NBA Draft. In fact, with the No. 1 selection, the Houston Rockets, in need of a center, drafted Hakeem Olajuwon. Next up were the Portland Trail Blazers, who didn't see a need to draft Jordan as they already had a shooting guard in Clyde Drexler. So, they went with Sam Bowie. When the Chicago Bulls deemed Jordan worthy of the No. 3 pick, hardly anyone was foreseeing a transformative, once-in-a-generation talent overtaking the league.

"I remember when I first saw him [Jordan], I was in Kansas City, playing for the Kings and got a call from my GM about putting together a team to play against the Junior Olympic team," says Larry Drew. "And I had never heard of him. I remember after the game calling my brother and I said, 'I don't know who this kid is, but there's a kid on that Junior Olympic team. He's about 6'5", 6'6". You're going to hear *a lot* about him. His last name is Jordan. I think they called him Mike Jordan or Michael Jordan. You're going to hear a lot about this kid.' He was so special then, from an athletic standpoint."[24]

While it was inconceivable in fall of 1992, if Jordan were to step away from basketball after this upcoming 1992–93 season, he would still go down as arguably the greatest player ever.

At 30 years old.

On November 7, one night after defeating the Cleveland Cavaliers in the regular season opener, the Bulls returned home to Chicago Stadium, an arena that had been constructed during the Great Depression and was soon to be demolished. Prior to this home opener, the Bulls received their rings commemorating the 1991–92 title. Naturally, noise surrounding the three-peat narrative only escalated further.

In the Bulls' locker room, moments before the ring ceremony, Phil Jackson told his team:

> There's a couple things that I want to say about the season. For us to win a third championship is not even worth talking about at this time because it's a journey that begins with a single step. It's a thousand-mile journey. We've got to remember that each game is that step that you take along the way. And for us to do this again, we're going to have to take each one of these steps and match them and meet the challenge that each one brings.[25]

Despite a combined 63 points from Jordan and Pippen, the Bulls fell to an inferior Atlanta Hawks team, 100–99. With the much-anticipated home opener on the second night of a back-to-back, Jackson turned to his bench early and often to manage the workload of his starters.

The early season loss foreshadowed an important theme for the season. Jackson was going to prioritize keeping guys healthy at the expense of winning regular season games. He not only had an aging roster that needed downtime whenever possible, but also the most talented one in the entire league. It was a foregone conclusion that by April, the Bulls would be nestled into one of the top playoff seeds in the Eastern Conference; thus, the focus was on remaining healthy for an inevitable conference final showdown with the (considerably improved) New York Knicks and an NBA Finals matchup with the cream of the Western Conference crop (likely the Phoenix Suns, Seattle SuperSonics, or Houston Rockets).

"There was not that kind of sense of urgency in terms of the regular season," recalls Chicago assistant coach Erik Helland about a Bulls team that would go 57–25, a record otherwise considered stellar if not for their own heightened standards. (In 1991–92, the Bulls finished 67–15.)

"I think Phil [Jackson], rightly so, made that the priority by de-emphasizing that, 'Hey we've got to win every game.' He understood that. He had a very big picture view of the season.

"In terms of practicing and things of that nature, that ['92–'93 season] was an interesting year because as we aged a little bit, we were going through that cycle three times. One of the things that happened is just the cumulative number of games that you play. Not only are you stressing the athlete more, but your preparation time is less. The whole season took on a different approach to it. Really, nobody was concerned about the regular season. It was more so maintaining the chemistry and keeping guys healthy so we could make a successful run at the end of the year. Honestly, I believe it was probably the first time in NBA history where a coaching staff, an organization looked at the season in that light and deliberately limited minutes, limited practice exposure, and limited games for certain individuals."[26]

Jackson's macro perspective was pragmatic, but surely not one grounded in any semblance of softness. While Jackson didn't overwork certain players, he did expect a professional athlete who was reasonably healthy to play. With the exception of Bill Cartwright and John Paxson, who registered a fair number of DNP's, and Michael Jordan, who got the occasional day off because he was Michael Jordan, guys were expected to ice their achy limbs in the locker room, and then take the floor minutes later. (As this season progressed, Scott Williams would assume a more prominent role in coming off the bench earlier to give Cartwright a breather. Meanwhile, B.J. Armstrong would eventually supplant Paxson as the starting point guard.)

After all, before becoming a head coach, Phil Jackson had been a power forward on New York Knicks teams of the late 1960s/early 1970s that did not take sitting out lightly. Not when they had several players serving in the National Guard during the Vietnam War. One evening, Bill Bradley, upon his return from reserve duty, started at forward (even though he was a guard) and played an entire game amid three different vomiting episodes. Jackson's mentality also stemmed from his all-work, no-play childhood. In the 1950s, amidst a fervent Pentecostal wave sweeping over large swaths of the upper Midwest, he grew up in a puritanical household in Williston, North Dakota. Jackson's father was a Pentecostal preacher, his mother an Evangelist preparing for the apocalypse. He was barred from dancing, listening to rock 'n' roll tunes, watching TV, reading comics, or playing cards. While he couldn't instill such stringent rules in a late 20th century NBA locker room full of millionaires (and multi-millionaires), a resounding Protestant work ethic pervaded the franchise.

However, as this season progressed, Jackson still had to deal with rumblings of veterans' discontent once again surfacing. In early January, longtime center Will Perdue acknowledged, "This year is really confusing and frustrating…. Last year at this time, I felt like I settled into a role a little bit. If someone asked me now what my role was, I couldn't answer the question."[27]

While personal gripes over playing time are par for the course over an NBA season, this situation was a bit peculiar. Perdue was strictly a bench player, a guy who rarely scored in double figures in his career with the Bulls, but now seemed to be focused on his goals rather than those of a team gunning for a third straight title. (Jordan never had much use for Perdue, and, in fact, was very open about how he felt Perdue had, to put it nicely, rather marginal talent.)

Perdue's issues marked the beginning of a long, trying month of January. From January 5 to January 22, the Bulls dropped home games to the mediocre Los Angeles Lakers, Orlando Magic, and Charlotte Hornets. After the 128–124 OT loss to the Magic and rookie sensation Shaquille O'Neal, Scottie Pippen publicly questioned if Jordan had taken too many shots (49) to tally 64 points. Meanwhile, Grant, formerly a close friend of Pippen's, would later be quoted in an *Inside Sports* article as saying, "To be honest, Scottie has become arrogant and cocky, but that's to be expected of people who can't handle fame and fortune."[28] Reports would come out that some veterans were upset that B.J. Armstrong had taken playing time away from John Paxson at the point. Others were offended that general manager Jerry Krause was becoming so obsessed with recruiting Croatian star Toni Kukoč. (Kukoč would become an integral member of the Bulls the following season.)

But while the Bulls were losing to such teams they had normally dominated, they were still remarkably consistent, never enduring a three-game losing streak in the regular season. It certainly helped that Jackson was adept at preventing such issues from mushrooming.

"You have to be a people person when you are a coach and Phil [Jackson] was pretty good just like Chuck Daly whom I played for," recalls guard Darrell Walker. "They knew how to deal with people. Phil was very good at that, very good at pulling the right strings, pulling certain guys' chords, and leaving certain guys alone. He doesn't get enough credit for how he dealt with people, how he dealt with a bunch of egos."[29]

"His best skill as a coach was being able to assess his player's strengths and learn how to maximize those within the confines of his system while also minimizing their deficiencies and making those not affect how he could use different pieces to be successful for the collective good," says Scott Williams. "Being a young undrafted player, I don't think I always recognized that at the time. It wasn't until I had a few more coaches and a few more experiences after those Chicago Bulls days were over that I understood that some coaches have a system and they just put the player into that system and if he does great, 'Good,' and if he doesn't, they will ship him off. And I think that was one thing with [Phil] Jackson, that he knew that Stacey King was different from Will Perdue who was different from Scott Williams. And we all had our strengths that we could add to the success of the ball club, but he didn't put us in situations, whether it was matchups or plays or defensive assignments, [where] we couldn't perform as well as we would like."[30]

Adds Cartwright, "When Michael [Jordan] first got in the league before I got to the Bulls, Michael was unstoppable. It was really up to the coaches and up to the players to figure out how to best benefit from that. When I got there in '88, Doug Collins was still the head coach. I believe that when Phil [Jackson] took over the next year, we were able to really have a system developed, offensively and defensively, that allowed all of us to be able to play together. That was really a benefit of Phil having coached with the likes of Johnny Bach, a defensive coach, and Tex Winter, an offensive coach."[31]

(Johnny Bach, who died in 2016, led a remarkable life both on and off the court. A World War II vet who was one of the first military occupiers of Nagasaki after the atomic bombing, Bach was known for sprinkling film sessions and speeches with war references.)

Jackson's historic success has often been dismissed as the result of cherry-picking immensely talented rosters to coach. (Joins the Bulls once Jordan hits his prime, retires from the Bulls when Jordan retires a second time, then joins a Los Angeles Lakers team headlined by Shaq and Kobe.) Often overlooked, however, has been Jackson's ability to placate superstars (for the most part) while not alienating their teammates. While coming across as pompous at times, Jackson, a psychology major at the University of North Dakota, knew how to push the Bulls teams of the early to mid-nineties as they started acquiring younger replacements for the aging and departed veterans of the late eighties squads.

As longtime NBA center Greg Foster recalls, "I played for him [Phil Jackson] a couple times. Playing for Phil when he was in Chicago was a lot different than playing with him when he was in Los Angeles. In Chicago, I think he was a little bit more demonstrative. He was a newer coach. Obviously, he had a lot of success there. He was a lot more demonstrative in his coaching style, a lot more yelling, getting on guys. When I played for him in L.A., we had a veteran team there. He had seemed to kind of back off and let us play."[32]

Jackson fancied himself as a highly cerebral practitioner of the game. He urged his players to think of basketball as not just the greatest game in the world, but as a metaphor for the world. The NBA season can be a grind, but, per Jackson's beliefs, it also can be perceived as an enlightening journey, a belief very much aligned with his adherence to Zen Buddhism.

Whatever he preached to his team in winter of 1993 worked. The Bulls finished February with a 10–2 mark before going 10–4 the following month. The latter feat was no small accomplishment considering that for NBA players, the month of March represents 31 days of boredom, restlessness, and exhaustion that don't culminate with the onset of the postseason ... but instead lead into more regular season play—all while the rest of basketball fans in America are focused on the NCAA's March Madness. This March was especially taxing for NBA teams as the "Storm of the Century"—one of the deadliest and costliest weather events of the 20th century with its hurricane-force winds and staggering snowfall totals—caused excessive travel delays midmonth. Nevertheless, travel-weariness and sleep-deprivation didn't prevent the Bulls from playing well down the stretch while staying relatively healthy.

Meanwhile, for Jordan, the homestretch of this season's journey was particularly enjoyable. During the last two weeks of March, Jordan had nights when he scored 47, 43, and 44 points. (Perhaps Jordan's most satisfying regular season performance this year came on March 20, when, on the second night of a back-to-back against the Washington Bullets, he scored 36 points in the first half on the way to his 47-point outburst. It was sweet revenge as the prior night, Jordan was humiliated by allowing the immortal LaBradford Smith to drop 37 on him. Jordan had pledged to match Smith's total by halftime in the rematch, and obviously came pretty darn close.) After sitting out some games earlier in the month, Jordan was refreshed and playing some of his best basketball all season as the playoffs loomed. Not to mention, as March bled into April, his University of North Carolina Tar Heels rolled into the NCAA Final Four, where they would eventually be crowned national champs.

Virtue of their very good, but not spectacular, 57–25 record, the Bulls earned the No. 2 seed in the Eastern Conference playoff bracket and a first-round matchup with the Atlanta Hawks. Meanwhile, the New York Knicks, having prioritized gaining postseason home court advantage over resting veterans, finished 60–22, securing a No. 1 seed and Eastern Conference Quarterfinal date with the very mediocre Indiana Pacers (41–41 record). Certainly, the Bulls went into their best-of-five series as heavy favorites, but their opponent, Atlanta, with whom they had split the season series, wasn't quite the layup that was the Indy .500 team. The Chicago-Atlanta series had an additional sliver of intrigue as it showcased the league's top two leading scorers, Michael Jordan and Dominique Wilkins.

"We were playing well at that time," recalls former Hawks swingman Stacey Augmon. "Dominique Wilkins was there, Mookie [Blaylock] was distributing the ball, Kevin Willis was rebounding with the best of them at the time, and they all were playing at a high level. And I was coming in fresh off my first year almost winning Rookie of the Year. We were gelling at that time."[33]

But ultimately, not enough to dethrone Chicago.

Less than two weeks after the Waco Siege ended, the Bulls started their postseason run with a tone-setting 114–90 win in Game 1. MJ paced Chicago with 35 points while Bill Cartwright had 14 points and six rebounds in only 15 minutes.

"Cartwright, they would use early in games and he was a veteran presence, which they needed—a guy like that who could control the locker room and bring a level of toughness to the game," recalls Greg Foster, who was a backup center on this Atlanta Hawks team.[34]

"Cartwright was such an important part of that team," says Jackie Mac-Mullan. "People like to forget about him. He was gangly looking. He didn't look particularly athletic, but he was in many ways the soul of that team."[35]

(By this point in his long and distinguished NBA career, Cartwright had sustained a fractured larynx from taking so many shots to the throat while dueling mammoth centers. With Cartwright's actions always speaking the loudest, a hoarse voice didn't hinder his effective leadership skills.)

From the jump, Chicago emerged with a heightened sense of purpose, and ultimately sealed the series opener with a 13–2 run to start the second half that ballooned to a 30-point lead after three quarters. Finally, Chicago looked like the class of the Eastern Conference, outrebounding the Hawks 62–28 and forcing them into settling for one low-percentage shot after another.

Judging by postgame chatter, Chicago was the energized, rightfully uber-confident team while Atlanta was sorely lacking leadership and accountability. Rather than accepting responsibility for his team's dismal performance on the boards, Hawks veteran center Kevin Willis implicitly blamed his teammates, pointing out that he was forced to leave the post to assist when Jordan and Armstrong penetrated the Hawks' perimeter defense. ("I'm usually the focal point to keep teams from getting second and third shots," Willis said. "But once I had to go out of there, it was tough.")[36]

Two nights later, Chicago again waxed Atlanta (117–102) as Jordan and Pippen combined for 54 points. With the series shifting to the Omni Coliseum in Atlanta for Game 3, Chicago got a brief scare when Jordan rolled his previously sprained ankle (April 6 at Miami) while heading up court after a basket late in the third quarter. Yet he returned a few minutes later on one good leg to score 14 of his game-high 39 points, propelling the Bulls to a series-clinching 98–88 win, ensuring that his team (and gimpy ankle) would have optimal rest for the Eastern Conference Semis.

"My second year, it was very interesting. I was just getting used to the speed of the NBA, the strength of the guys. I remember guarding him [Jordan]," says Augmon, who was only two years removed from playing at UNLV and now assigned this mission impossible task. "He was very difficult to guard because he had a little bit of everything along with strength and also the will to win. It was difficult—I tried to take away his right and when I did, he crossed me over. I can remember definitely in the post where he just put his body on me, hesitate, baseline jumper. I remember like it was yesterday."[37]

Some pundits had predicted that the Hawks could push this series to a fourth or even fifth game virtue of having scoring machine Dominique Wilkins and the superior center in Kevin Willis. It was not to be as the snoozer of a series demonstrated that, at least in the Eastern Conference, there was still an insurmountable gap between the clutch postseason play of Jordan and that of its other stars.

Chicago's opponent in the Eastern Conference Semis was a familiar (and very welcomed) one in the Cleveland Cavaliers.

The Bulls' postseason dominance of the Cavs started in the late eighties, with the iconic moment occurring on May 7, 1989. On this day, during a winner-take-all Game 5 of the Eastern Conference Quarterfinals, Cavaliers shooting guard Craig Ehlo got posterized in the most humiliating fashion, courtesy of Michael Jordan. In one of MJ's defining early career moments, his Bulls were down 100–99 with three ticks left when he received the inbounds pass and subsequently sank a jumper from the top of the key with time expiring to give Chicago a 101–100 win. As the shot fell, a celebratory Jordan leapt into the air, legs outstretched, nearly kicking Ehlo in the

3. When Michael Jordan Owned the NBA   77

head as he crumpled to the floor in despair. The play known as "The Shot" became instant NBA highlight reel material but also served as yet another dramatic sports moment to come at a Cleveland team's expense. This was the second consecutive postseason in which the Bulls had ousted the Cavs as the Bulls also had won a decisive Game 5 in the 1988 Eastern Conference Quarterfinals. Years later, the 1992 Eastern Conference Finals matchup versus Cleveland was a stepping-stone for the Bulls on the road to their second straight title as they won the series, 4–2.

Just before the 1992–93 season got underway, Cleveland, growing tired of being dismantled by Chicago seemingly every May, signed free agent Gerald Wilkins, a 6'6" shooting guard known for being a rugged defender. After signing with the Cavs, Wilkins proclaimed, "I'm not afraid to guard Michael Jordan. I earned Michael's respect for the first time since I've been in the league. I made Michael think, and not many players can do that."[38]

Viewed by some as a potential difference maker for Cleveland, Wilkins was soon billed as the "Jordan Stopper."

During the 1993 Eastern Conference Semifinals, Wilkins was more like the Jordan Igniter: despite battling a sprained ligament in his right wrist, MJ averaged over 30 points per game this round while leading the Bulls in scoring every game but one.

While last year's series against Cleveland stretched to six games, this year's edition was hardly competitive. The Bulls swept the vastly overmatched Cavs, who found it impossible to contain Jordan and challenging to limit Scottie Pippen. (Prior to the 1992–93 season, Cleveland also had acquired bruising forward Jerome Lane, he of a very limited offensive skill set, primarily to intimidate Pippen, who by now had a reputation for wilting against brawny competition, especially come springtime. It was, however, another signing that didn't pan out. Pippen averaged over 18 points per game in the series while Lane didn't get a whiff of floor time.)

The series mercifully ended on May 17 at the now-defunct Richfield Coliseum (the same gym where Jordan not only had embarrassed Craig Ehlo but also had scored a career-high 69 points in 1990). Trying hard not to dwell on their repeated failures to challenge Chicago for supremacy in the Eastern Conference, the Cavs hung tough with the Bulls until the end—the game was tied 101–101 with 18 seconds left in regulation. Naturally, Jordan got the ball following the timeout. Guarded by Gerald Wilkins, Jordan posted up, pivoted, and faded, releasing a 17-foot shot (a dribble away from where he had nailed the previously mentioned buzzer-beater in the 1989 playoffs) that settled into the net as time expired.

The Bulls' 103–101 series-clinching win improved the team's 1993 postseason record to 7–0.

With each passing day, the three-peat seemed more likely.

Minutes after the Bulls had ruined the Cavs' spring for the fourth time in six years, Wilkins told reporters, "He [Jordan] just knew it was going in, and he had ended our season. He ruled."[39]

Cleveland wasn't the only team that had spent the prior off-season trying to knock off Michael Jordan and the Chicago Bulls. Prior to the 1992–93 regular season, the New York Knicks had acquired free agents Rolando Blackman, Doc Rivers, and Charles Smith, all veterans who had plenty of zeroes in their bank accounts ... and zero championship rings on their fingers.

And the moves seemingly worked, as the Knicks had steamrolled through the regular season and dispatched the Indiana Pacers and Charlotte Hornets in the first two playoff rounds. And when the Knicks left Madison Square Garden with a 98–90 win in Game 1 of the Eastern Conference Finals, former Showtime Lakers and current Knicks head coach Pat Riley, who with his slicked-back hair bore a slight resemblance to actor Michael Douglas, felt justified for having placed a premium on postseason home court advantage, even though he also had a veteran-laden roster needing rest.

"They [the Knicks] were a physical team led by a very aggressive coach in Pat Riley who realized that his team was built to play a style of ball," says Scott Williams. "He could always motivate his troops to do what was in their best interest to try to win a basketball game. He had big power forwards and centers who were very muscular. He basically sent them out there to be his front line of attack defensively with aggressive play. It was just a matter of whether or not we were going to get the same sort of play off of our bench, myself included, Stacey King, Will Perdue, and some of the other power players. It became known as a real bruising, black and blue, hips, elbows, forearm shiver type of a series. I had no problem with that because it better suited my game. I relished that."[40]

During this series opener, the Knicks' burliness most prominently manifested itself on the boards, as they outrebounded the Bulls by a 48–28 margin. On both ends of the floor, Chicago had no answer for Knicks perennial all-star center Patrick Ewing (25 points, 17 rebounds) who limited Bill Cartwright to four points. Perhaps more importantly, Jordan appeared mortal, going 10-for-27 from the field while missing 10 of his last 12 shots. Checking Jordan was Knicks shooting guard John Starks who, on both ends of the floor, was very much MJ's equal. When he wasn't playing airtight defense on Jordan, Starks (25 points) was nailing jumpers coming off picks and pulling up on fast breaks. Somebody could be in his face or he could be all alone. It didn't matter. This was his day. The overachieving Starks, an undrafted, former independent league member, embodied the

1990s Knicks' "we take crap from nobody" reputation—particularly when the Jordan-led Bulls were the adversary.

After the game Jordan acknowledged, "I had a tough shooting night. But you have to give credit to Starks. He was making me take shots I didn't really want to."[41]

However, in the early part of this series, it was what Jordan would do off the court, rather than on it, that made all the headlines.

On the night of Monday, May 24, Michael Jordan did nothing illegal or even the least bit offensive to any human on the planet—least of all his teammates or coaches. He was not abusing substances, food, or, most importantly, women. He was not driving while intoxicated. Nor was he partying at a chic Midtown Manhattan nightclub—a seemingly irresistible temptation for many pro athletes visiting NYC.

But he was also not relaxing in bed, ordering room service, and getting a full night's sleep—activities that would be conducive for coming out fresh for a pivotal (and sure-to-be-exhausting) Game 2 the next evening.

And that is why his late afternoon/early evening/late night/early morning sojourn to Bally's Grand Casino in Atlantic City was above the fold news.

On May 27, it was reported by Dave Anderson in the *New York Times* that, according to a casino employee, Jordan checked into the hotel at 5:07 p.m., and checked out at 11:05 p.m. Bally's is an approximately 2-hour drive from the Midtown Manhattan hotel, meaning Jordan would have returned around a late, but certainly not ungodly, time of 1:00 a.m. However, Anderson quoted sources who reported seeing Jordan, already notorious for his compulsive gambling, (he was frequently sighted during summer of 1992 at Monte Carlo Casino in Monaco before Olympic practices and had supposedly lost over a million dollars in wagers over golf) playing blackjack in a private area of Bally's baccarat pit as late as 2:30 a.m. Tuesday. Jordan was on-time for the mid-morning shootaround, so, if such reports were true, it was concluded that Jordan settled for taking a brief cat nap before a crucial Game 2—all for satisfying a personal craving.[42]

(Jordan later swore that he departed the casino at 11:00 p.m. and was back at his room at The Plaza by 1 a.m. and threatened to "lay a lawsuit" on anyone who said otherwise.[43] Certainly from Jordan's perspective, the *New York Times* account in general was not news fit to print.)

The gambling jaunt was even more newsworthy because Jordan had another subpar performance during Game 2, shooting 12 for 32 from the field and dishing out only one assist as his team fell 96–91, and thus faced a 2–0 series deficit. It didn't matter that New York's suffocating defense had masterfully clogged the lanes, effectively challenged perimeter shots, or vigorously defended the high pick-and-roll. Once Anderson's report hit the newsstands, the main narrative was that the culprit behind Jordan's uncharacteristic struggles, and thus the team's, was his nocturnal behavior.

"That was another kind of distraction that we had to deal with while trying to come back and tie the series," admits Scott Williams.[44]

What really got under Jordan's skin was that the ever-prying media had clawed into his off-court life, sparking such intense scrutiny. His casino trip became a story on network news shows. New York tabloids took their weak shots (*HIT ME!* headlined an ensuing edition of the *New York Post*). Jordan's gambling exploits mushroomed into a full-blown ordeal, one fueled by the relentless machine that was late 20th century American media sensationalism. This resultant scandal was incredibly irksome to Jordan, who, as one of the league's marquee players and corporate America's most prominent pitchmen, had always toiled tirelessly to maintain his squeaky-clean image.

(Back in November 1990, when one of his collegiate teammates, highly respected Los Angeles Lakers star James Worthy, was arrested at a Houston hotel on two counts of soliciting prostitution and jailed hours before his team's game against the Rockets, Jordan was reminded of the repercussions inherent in a celebrity making poor judgment. As Jordan remarked in the immediate aftermath of the Worthy incident, "I know it's my greatest fear. I've spent a life building something positive, and I know any mistake I make could damage that for the rest of my life. People look to their role models to be almost flawless and I guess I'm the closest thing to being viewed positively, very little being flawed in my life."[45])

Now, Jordan had to do something to which he was unaccustomed—account for his behavior off the court.

On May 27, the penultimate off day before Game 3, Jordan explained his story when he held court with the press following a workout at the team's suburban practice facility. The impromptu press gathering involving over 50 members of the local and national media turned ugly when an intrepid/nagging TV reporter asked Jordan offensive questions (Is this the way you normally prepare for a playoff game? Do you go to Joliet [a legalized gambling institution outside Chicago] the day before games?) Then came a mentioning of James "Slim" Bouler, the convicted money launderer to whom MJ had admitted paying $57,000 in gambling debts last year and a question of whether the "gambling problem" was "escalating."[46]

Questions about his lifestyle and past behavior seemed like piling on. The media had crossed the line and Jordan had a perfect out for ending this aggravating session.

Instantaneously, he stormed away.

During this rapid-fire interrogation, Jordan had done his part, meticulously chronicling his itinerary—practicing from 10 a.m. to 1 p.m. Monday, taking a nap until 3:30 p.m., and then taking a limo to Bally's Grand Casino with his dad and a few pals, and returning to his hotel room by 1:00 a.m.—and once again reiterating his need to take a break from basketball. During this group interview, Jordan even acknowledged:

> I'm just trying to get away from the city of New York and relax, instead of listening to the media hype up the first game, our mistakes.... Scottie Pippen didn't play well, Michael Jordan didn't play well. I'm just trying to get away from it instead of staying in my room, which is four walls. I chose to take a ride in a limo, didn't drive, rested, sat there talking about all the different conversations my father and friends could talk about, got up there, gambled in a private area and was home by a respectable hour. That's the truth.[47]

Jordan was also getting peeved over the media badgering him because his feeling was that since his teammates were not upset (As Jack McCallum recalls, "All these guys, they had their own sins going on. You can bet that all of them were not in their beds at 1 o'clock")[48] then why should the media question how seriously he was taking his responsibility to the Bulls while also attacking his personal life—even if he was one of the most prominent public figures in America?

Phil Jackson certainly didn't come across as upset (at least not publicly). In fact, Jordan's coach rushed to his defense, telling reporters:

> What's wrong with it? It's better than him going out on Manhattan Monday night, isn't it? I have no problem with that at all. I have a lot of friends in New York who pick up the phone at 11 o'clock and get a car and go down to Atlantic City, too. He assured me he was back at an appropriate hour and he had plenty of rest for the game. I know Michael. He's not going to feel like sitting around the hotel room for 10 or 12 hours on a Monday. That's an awfully long time. He can't go anywhere in Manhattan. So if he went down there, I felt perfectly comfortable.[49]

Pippen echoed the sentiment of most, if not all, of Jordan's teammates when he said, "I haven't been distracted, not at all. Whatever Michael does is his prerogative. He's always going to come ready to play, and I think people should let him live his life."[50]

(Interestingly, some of Jordan's teammates who, at times, had resented the star treatment afforded to him, were now in his corner.)

That there was a ridiculously long four-day layoff between Games 2 and 3 only made life worse for the Bulls. Jordan's Atlantic City escapade was *the* story of the series and there was nothing Jordan (and his teammates) could do.

Except boycott the media for the rest of the Eastern Conference Finals. Which, for the most part, is exactly what they did.

Following Game 2, the Bulls had bigger problems than Jordan opting to play craps over ordering in a Pay-Per-View flick on his night off.

Never before in the Jordan era had the Bulls come back to win a series after going down 2–0. After two games in NYC, the Knicks looked like the tougher, more complete squad—and not just because Jordan was off his game. Bill Cartwright was getting grossly outplayed by Patrick Ewing. Now an established starter at the point, B.J. Armstrong (only seven points, two assists in Game 2) was a shell of his regular season self. A bench that had yielded significant production all year suddenly appeared thin. (Rodney McCray, once thought to be a necessary ingredient to get the Bulls a third championship, was now registering one DNP after another.)

In his press conference following Game 2, Phil Jackson had reasoned, "Well, we're concerned. There's no doubt about that. They're playing their style of game on their home floor. They're not going to play that style of ball game on our floor."[51]

His prophecy proved true. When the series resumed during Memorial Day weekend, the Bulls returned to their dominant form. Behind a balanced scoring attack in Game 3, Chicago routed New York, 103–83, to slice the series deficit to 2–1. Jordan had another off-night (3–18 from the field) but Pippen (29 points) delivered while Horace Grant, B.J. Armstrong, and John Paxson all scored in double figures.

The box score, however, didn't reflect what transpired on the floor during Game 3, another blood-and-thunder contest pitting two squads conditioned to despise one another. A couple nights earlier, Pat Riley had tweaked the Bulls, who already loathed all things Big Apple, by claiming they were "hung by their thumbs in the city square" while playing in Manhattan.[52] Riley's brashness reflected his team's penchant for trash talking and utter lack of respect for Jordan and Pippen. As if the Bulls needed more motivation, seconds before the opening tip, New York's Charles Smith dismissed Jordan's pass at a pregame handshake. Meanwhile, several Knicks—mindful of how the Detroit Pistons had successfully rattled Pippen in earlier postseasons—continued to sling barbs at Jordan's sidekick throughout the game.

Once the game mercifully ended, there were five technical fouls called—three on New York, two on Chicago. Scott Williams received a flagrant foul. John Starks was ejected. This came on the heels of Game 2 in which the refs had issued six technical fouls and ejected two players, one of whom was Knicks guard Greg Anthony for smacking a driving Jordan in the head.

Starks was magnificent at home in Games 1 and 2, but he was off this evening in Chicago (eight points, two assists) and vented his frustration via trash talking—and later tussling with Jordan in the fourth quarter, an altercation for which he earned his second technical foul and subsequent ejection. Starks' harassment of Jordan wasn't just about blowing steam. By trying to goad Jordan ("You wanna go, Mike? You wanna go?"),[53] the bulldog guard was trying to send his teammates a message: he wasn't going to melt in Jordan's presence, so they shouldn't either. (Of course, several of Starks teammates were already on the same page with him on that one.)

The bad blood spilled over to the postgame locker rooms.

Exclaimed the late Knicks forward Anthony Mason afterward, "That's the type of team they are, the Chicago Bulls. They talk when they're up, they don't talk when they're down."[54]

Chicago's Stacey King had his own theory: "It's been a physical series and we're just trying to match up with them and challenge them the way they're challenging us. I think sometimes they can dish it out, but they can't take it."[55]

While King articulated his honest thoughts, most of his teammates kept theirs private, seeing no reason to make reporters' lives any easier by providing electric sound bites, of which there could have been many given the acrimonious nature of the series. The Bulls weren't just angry over the *New York Times* prying into Jordan's private life. They resented the reporters ignoring their improved play while dwelling on the gambling story. They also knew that the media-induced distraction was, at the very least, a contributing factor toward Jordan's recent struggles.

The following day, with Jordan's teammates following his lead in (mostly) stonewalling the media, James Jordan gave his son the biggest assist of the year when he stood outside practice and told the scrum of reporters:

> Michael feels like if riding to Atlantic City and riding back impeded his performance the next day, then it would have been wrong. But we have sat at his house the night before he had a game and watched movies until 3:30 in the morning. He's up late all the time. He has a lot of energy. … He's a competitor. Losing $10,000 to him would be like me losing 10 cents.… If he was playing for matchsticks or straws, he'd have the same level of competition. … He certainly doesn't have a gambling problem. He wouldn't be doing that if he couldn't afford it. He isn't that stupid. He has a competition problem. He was born with that. And if he didn't have a competition problem, you guys wouldn't be writing about him. The person he tries to outdo most of the time is himself.[56]

He succeeded in doing so on Memorial Day. On this afternoon, Jordan, even by his lofty standards, had a phenomenal game. While Ewing, at this hour looking like the league's most dominant center, was overpowering Chicago's frontcourt, Jordan was finding holes in the Knicks' perimeter defense, pouring in 54 points while going six-for-nine from downtown. Jordan played a taxing 39 minutes and was in foul trouble near game's end, yet he still sank a 15-foot jumper with 1:36 remaining, giving the Bulls a 99–90 lead that effectively secured the series-tying 105–95 win. After enduring a shooting slump in Games 1–3, Jordan was lights-out from long-range this afternoon—of his 18 field goals, one was a layup, one was a 10-footer, two were from 15 feet, and the rest came from the perimeter.

(Even after the banner afternoon, Jordan continued his prolonged silence, this time refusing to be interviewed by NBC, which had a $600 million contract with his employer and its business partners.)

With the series now tied 2–2, Chicago was still going to have to win at least once at MSG. Which it did two days later, largely due to players of lesser renown.

After his statement game two nights earlier, Jordan banged quite a few balls off iron and glass in this pivotal Game 5 (particularly in the first half). However, Scottie Pippen had another monster game (28 points, 11 boards). An even more pleasant surprise was an offensive spurt from an inexplicably rejuvenated Bill Cartwright, who chipped in with 13 points. (Perhaps Jackson's decision to sit Cartwright for some games before the All-Star break in order to give him extended rest was paying dividends.) While he had a strong opening round performance against Atlanta on both ends of the floor, offense simply was not Cartwright's forte, especially at this late stage of his career against a tenacious rim protector such as Ewing, as evidenced earlier this round.

"My role was the same when I came over from New York," explains Cartwright. "I was the veteran guy on the team. When I came over to the Bulls, I was a defender. That was really the role that I played over there."[57]

Going into the series, Horace Grant had been assigned the unenviable task of leveraging his quickness and agility to counter Charles Oakley's brute strength in the paint. By this point, Grant was no longer getting overwhelmed by Oakley in the low post, as was the case when Grant only scored a total of 13 points in Games 1 and 2. After incremental improvements over the next couple games, Grant posted a double-double while holding Oakley to 6 points in Game 5. (While it was a matchup of sheer brutality, the two never tussled, à la Jordan and Starks. As Grant would comment during this series, "He [Oakley] pushes me, shoves me, scratches me, hits me and bites me, but never an elbow or a cheap shot.")[58]

Despite the balanced scoring attack, the Bulls found themselves down 93–92 with over a minute remaining after the Knicks went on a late fourth quarter run. On the ensuing Chicago possession, it was neither Jordan nor Pippen who attempted the three-pointer. It was B.J. Armstrong, the slender, baby-faced University of Iowa product. Armstrong's swished three-ball, which gave Chicago a 95–93 lead, proved to be the eventual game-winner and most pivotal shot of the series.

Jordan was okay not being the hero this time as he proudly watched his kid brother Armstrong deliver in the clutch.

"Michael liked B.J. and that's all that mattered," says Jackie MacMullan. "If Michael likes you, just imagine the amount of confidence that injects into you, into your game and to the decisions you make. I can remember a bunch of times during that season where Jordan had an open shot but had the presence of mind that B.J. was open too, knowing that was going to pay dividends down the line. It's like Larry Bird used to do it with Dennis Johnson. He used to tell everybody DJ was the greatest player he ever played with. Well he played with Robert Parish and Kevin McHale and Bill Walton, so that probably wasn't true, but DJ thought it was true and that's all that mattered. I think that's kind of how Jordan was with B.J."[59]

Nevertheless, the indelible moment of Game 5 (if not the entire series) was on the Knicks' final possession with Chicago clinging to a one-point lead with 12 seconds remaining. With the ball under the hoop, power forward Charles Smith had his shot blocked by Grant. Smith corralled the rebound, only to be stripped by Jordan. Smith scooped up the loose ball, tried to heave up a shot, but was blocked from behind by Pippen. Smith rebounded the ball again, tried to get off a shot again, but was blocked by Pippen again. Chicago's block party ended with Grant coming away with the loose ball, passing it to Jordan, who then assisted on Armstrong's fast break layup right before the buzzer sounded.

The 97–94 win would go down as one of the most exhilarating games in Chicago sports history.

More importantly, it all but buried the Knicks, whose 27-game home winning streak ended.

After the game, Patrick Ewing remarked to the postgame media scrum, "There's no sense crying over spilled milk, but we thought [Smith] was fouled. It wasn't called. That's it."[60]

Meanwhile, after beating the Knicks in three consecutive games, Chicago regained its trademark bravado. Especially considering this victory was at MSG where the Knicks had grown accustomed to manhandling the Bulls.

"We won because we're a much better team than them," Pippen matter-of-factly said afterward.[61]

Armed with a 3–2 lead and homecourt for Game 6, the Bulls ensured the series would not return to Manhattan for a Game 7. Ewing had another rock-steady performance (26 points, 13 rebounds) but the Knicks, as a team, had no answer for Pippen as he made an assortment of clutch shots, including the final dagger of a three-pointer with 1:01 remaining that put the Bulls ahead by eight on the way to the 96–88 win.

With Jordan not having an overly dominant game, the spotlight was on his sidekick. This gutsy crunch time performance (seven of his 24 points came in the final five minutes) was sweet redemption for Pippen, who, only a year earlier, was maligned for a supposed languid approach against the Knicks in the Eastern Conference Semis. The storyline going into this series was that Pippen lacked the mental fortitude to withstand a torrent of verbal jabs from the Knicks (and their fans).

In his postgame press conference, Phil Jackson remarked, "Is there anything else to be said about him? He had just a terrific series against the Knicks after being portrayed as somewhat of a pussyfooter, as a guy who couldn't take a beating, last year. He came back."[62]

In certain respects, it was unfair that the stigma of meekness was tethered to Pippen at times in his career. He was the youngest of 12 kids, whose father Preston had toiled tirelessly in local paper mills for years before a major stroke left him wheelchair-bound. A native of Hamburg, Arkansas, Pippen enrolled at the University of Central Arkansas as a walk-on hopeful who would be expected to moonlight as team manager. Pippen's raw talent was undeniable, but his 6'1", 150-pound frame made college coaches hesitant to recruit him, which is why he settled for University of Central Arkansas coach Don Dyer's offer to come aboard as manager (a role that provided tuition assistance) and earn his roster spot during tryouts, which he did. During his first year, Pippen grew two inches and played in 20 games; by sophomore year, he had sprouted to 6'7" and was scoring 18.5 points per contest. As this upward trajectory continued each winter, Pippen was spending his summers laboring as a welder attaching the arms of school desks to the legs, which left his own arms scarred.

But not permanently damaged.

By his senior year, one in which he averaged 23.6 PPG and 10.0 RPG, Pippen and his now long, brawny arms were attracting the attention of NBA scouts. A small forward by trade, Pippen could direct the offense like a point guard, rebound like a power forward, score like a shooting guard, and defend on the perimeter like precious few others.

After being selected with the fifth pick in the 1987 NBA Draft by the Seattle SuperSonics, Pippen was traded to Chicago for a package headlined by Olden Polynice, a 6'11" center from the University of Virginia. Within a few years, Pippen would emerge as one of the most versatile players in the league and the second-best player on the Bulls—while, at least for the early part of his career, not being paid commensurate with his level of production. (In the team's glory years, Pippen became one of the league's most notorious skinflints, known to Chicago restaurant workers as "No Tippin' Pippen." Ironically, in retirement, Pippen, like so many former star athletes, was rather careless with his funds, and would face significant financial troubles.)

Even if Chicago Bulls principal owner Jerry Reinsdorf never fully appreciated Pippen, Ewing and the Knicks sure did.

3. When Michael Jordan Owned the NBA

Back in January 2010, Scottie Pippen, the school's most recognized alumnus, had his No. 33 jersey retired in a halftime ceremony during a men's basketball game. When Pippen joined the school's basketball team as a scrawny freshman, it was hard to imagine that he would one day help lead the last great NBA dynasty of the 20th century (courtesy University of Central Arkansas).

Commented Ewing after the Bulls' close-out win, "Scottie Pippen's play was really the key to the series. When we shut him down in New York, we won the first two. We just couldn't do it the rest of the way."[63]

There was no denying the Bulls' resiliency. After falling behind 2–0, the Bulls had advanced to their third consecutive NBA Finals by winning four straight games against a Knicks team that hadn't lost four straight games all season.

Even more impressive was that they had done so while dealing with a tabloid-fueled distraction, hostile New Yorkers, and truly dirty opponent.

The next evening, June 5, the Phoenix Suns, behind a monster game from league MVP Charles Barkley (44 points, 24 rebounds), defeated the Seattle SuperSonics 123–110 in Game 7 of the Western Conference Finals. (In the best-of-five Western Conference Quarterfinals, the Suns had found themselves down 2–0 to the Lakers, before winning three straight, narrowly avoiding a historic upset.)

Certainly, the Suns, with their regular season best 62–20 record, would be a formidable NBA Finals opponent.

This was new territory for the Chicago Bulls.

Two years earlier, the 1991 NBA Finals matchup of Los Angeles Lakers-Chicago Bulls was a spectacle. Magic vs. Michael. Converse vs. Nike—a battle of corporate titans. The last vestige of the eighties vs. what lay ahead in the nineties. "That was so special," says Larry Drew, who was a backup point guard for that Lakers team. "I know everybody wanted to see that matchup, that particular year. That was such a special time for the NBA. You're getting Magic, who was the player that he was, and then Michael trying to get his first ring."[64]

But the series was also a mere formality (Chicago went in heavily favored and won in five games) given that during the prior series, the Eastern Conference Finals, the Bulls had finally knocked off the Detroit Pistons, their perennial roadblock to the NBA Finals. The next spring, once the Bulls got past New York and Cleveland, they defeated the Portland Trail Blazers in six games, but the outcome was never really in doubt considering that the Bulls' average margin of victory was 15 points.

In this upcoming Finals, the Bulls were better than the Suns, but not *that much* better.

Led by first-year head coach Paul Westphal, the 1992–93 Phoenix Suns were the most balanced team the Bulls would face in a postseason series during the early nineties. Not only was Phoenix less one-dimensional than superstar-reliant teams like Los Angeles and Portland, but Westphal's squad was grittier than the Cleveland teams and more talented offensively than the New York squads of this era. The roster spoke for itself. Phoenix had a relatively young superstar in Barkley, who, in his first year in the desert, had established himself as one of the league's top five players. Phoenix point guard Kevin Johnson was a ball handling wizard, far superior to Chicago's B.J. Armstrong. Tough guy Dan Majerle was an all-time great three-point marksman, perhaps even deadlier than Chicago's John Paxson. Barkley, Johnson, and Majerle were in their prime and the bench included proven veterans such as Danny Ainge and Tom Chambers. (Phil Jackson also didn't do his team any favors when he provided the Suns with prime bulletin board material. When his team was awaiting the winner of the Western Conference Finals, Jackson even admitted to reporters, "I don't pay attention too often to the Western Conference, at least in the scholarly aspect of basketball." Whatever that meant.)[65]

"I think they [the Suns] had a good combination of guard play and guys who could stretch the floor and shoot three-ball with Dan Majerle. Once you had that type of team and had a guy [Barkley] playing at a player of the year level, that Phoenix team really took to him," says Clarence Weatherspoon, who was a much-hyped rookie forward for the Philadelphia 76ers, Barkley's former team, during the 1992–93 season.[66]

While the matchup of teams was quite intriguing, the spotlight was on the Michael Jordan-Charles Barkley showdown, one that dominated sports discussions across America, if not the world, in the second week of June 1993. (In the years ahead, hype surrounding the NBA would often gravitate toward young hotshot prospects, but in the mid–1990s, the league's marquee matchups still involved established legacy players, à la Jordan and Barkley. "In '93 it was still a veteran-based league where veterans were still respected," says Penny Hardaway, who broke into the NBA as a rookie for the Orlando Magic in 1993 and left the NBA in 2007, when a 22-year-old LeBron James was all the rage.)[67]

Jordan finally had a worthy star opponent whom he would compete against in the NBA Finals. After all, in June 1991, Earvin "Magic" Johnson was in the twilight of his career (he would retire for the first time several months later after contracting HIV) and in June 1992, Portland's best player was shooting guard Clyde Drexler, a future Hall of Famer, but not one of the all-time greats. Certainly not Charles Barkley on top of his game.

"Earvin couldn't have stopped Jordan if Jordan had two broken legs," says Jack McCallum. "The Portland Trail Blazers never scared them [the Bulls] for one single second. Michael never thought two shits about Clyde Drexler, never did throughout his whole career."[68]

In summer of 1992, Jordan and Barkley had spent significant time together in Spain while playing for the Dream Team. From Barkley's perspective, the two were friends first, opponents second.

The feelings weren't exactly mutual.

"Jordan had done such an amazing psychological job on Barkley," recalls Jackie MacMullan. "He was playing golf with him. They were paling together during the Finals. Jordan was doing it willfully and Barkley was just like, 'Well, this guy's my friend. This is what we do.' Jordan was so locked in."[69]

(For what it's worth, Barkley would later deny the widespread reports that he had golfed with Jordan during the early part of the NBA Finals.)

There were also reports that MJ would try to soften up Barkley by treating him to a $20,000 diamond earring during the Finals. Jordan felt that there was no better use of his exorbitant financial resources and scant free time than to make Barkley continue believing they were good friends. Perhaps Barkley would not push the boundaries of his imposing physicality. Essentially, MJ knew he needed every advantage possible against Barkley, who had become an unstoppable force playing isolation ball on the wing while still proving compatible with his new team's game plan.

"It was a clichéd perfect storm," says McCallum. "Number one, Charles wanted out of Philadelphia, so he got out. Number two, Charles was at the top of his game. I remember talking about it then and because Magic and Larry were older, we concluded right then that the number one player in the world was Michael Jordan and number two was Charles Barkley. Number three, he went to the perfect team. This was Charles' time."[70]

Which meant Barkley was now a national celebrity whose fame transcended the realm of sports.

While Jordan had his gambling saga, Barkley had his own tabloidesque sideshow. Heading into the Finals, there were rumors aplenty linking Barkley with Madonna after the two were spotted together at a Phoenix restaurant that spring. Barkley vehemently denied that he was sleeping with the Material Girl. In fact, Barkley was not the least bit amused by such celebrity gossip as he had recently separated from his wife, Maureen, and three-year-old daughter, Christiana. In 1993, Barkley may have been thriving professionally, but his personal life was in tatters.

Barkley was also a season removed from his ignominious departure from Philadelphia. Fans of the 76ers had little brotherly love for a guy who was constantly berating teammates, accusing management of making racist-fueled roster decisions, and referring to general manager Gene Shue as a "clown" and a "caddie" for owner Harold Katz. Barkley even publicly (and falsely) predicted that the 76ers would be better off without his services.[71]

Several weeks before the 1992 Summer Olympics, the desperate 76ers front office dealt the disgruntled star to the Suns for guard Jeff Hornacek and a couple role players. Once they lost Barkley, the

Don't let the smile fool you. Charles Barkley wanted nothing to do with the Philadelphia 76ers in the early 1990s. The Phoenix Suns came to the rescue and Barkley's career took off (courtesy Auburn Athletics).

3. When Michael Jordan Owned the NBA 91

76ers tried to find his "replacement" by selecting Clarence Weatherspoon out of Southern Miss with the ninth overall pick in the NBA Draft. Weatherspoon was quickly dubbed "Baby Barkley" because, like Barkley, he was a wide-bodied forward whose limited verticality didn't hinder his rebounding skills.

But it was soon apparent that the Barkley comparisons were unfair to Weatherspoon.

"Coming out of college and all through my college career there were a lot of comparisons, but I was just trying to come in and establish myself as a quality NBA player," says Clarence Weatherspoon. "Charles [Barkley] was a perennial all-star, was one of the guys that already had a name brand, and everything in the NBA. Now playing against him that first time, it was like playing against one of your heroes. I was in awe of the moment. He was in Phoenix and having an all-star year. It was a learning experience because I think Charles really played well that game. He had a tremendous year overall, MVP of the league and everything. It was definitely a learning experience."[72]

But in his first two matchups against Barkley, Weatherspoon was not schooled (he scored in double digits both games) and ended up having an impressive rookie season (15.6 PPG). Nevertheless, there was—and always would be—a gaping disparity between his skills and Barkley's.

(In the '92–'93 season, with Weatherspoon in lieu of Barkley, the 76ers had fewer PR issues as well as wins, finishing with one of the league's worst records at 26–56.)

Of course, it wasn't just Philadelphia that had tired of Sir Charles' antics. Barkley was one of the most polarizing pro athletes in the world. Whereas Jordan graciously embraced his role model status, Barkley had no interest in such a role. Barkley once screamed at an elderly female fan in Boston, "Shut up, you bitch!" During the 1991 NBA All-Star Game in Charlotte (played weeks after America had entered the Gulf War), he donned a cap that read "FUCK IRAQ." That was nothing, though, compared to what happened several weeks later, on the night of March 26, 1991, in New Jersey, when he turned to spit at a fan who was yelling derogatory comments at him. The spittle ended up falling on an eight-year-old girl who was attending the game with her parents. (Barkley did apologize profusely afterward and later befriended the girl and her family.)[73]

Even though Barkley was considered one of the top players in the world in 1991, serious debate began swirling over whether his character, or lack thereof, should prevent him from playing in the Olympics. Ultimately, Barkley was selected, however, during the United States' first game, a 116–48 win over Angola, he didn't exactly represent the Stars and Stripes with dignity when he delivered a vicious elbow into the chest of Herlander

Coimbra, a 176-pound guard/economics scholar from this war-torn nation, who was simply running back up court following a Barkley layup. Postgame, Barkley justified his bullying assault as retaliation for Coimbra roughing him up earlier. No one was buying, including teammates such as Jordan, who said after the game, "If Charles would quit doing what he's doing, we'd get the cheers instead of the whistles."[74]

Understandably, Barkley didn't get many cheers in Barcelona over the next couple weeks.

Back home, around the NBA, Barkley didn't always get the respect shown to other superstars. Even when he was having a career year, positioning Phoenix as a bona fide contender for dethroning Jordan's Bulls.

David Robinson, he was not.

"That year [1992–93] I don't think he [Charles Barkley] should have gotten it [MVP award]," says Stacey Augmon. "I think Mike should have won it that year also."[75]

Nevertheless, come June, of greater significance was the upcoming battle for the more coveted trophy.

Finally, Michael Jordan's nearly two-week long boycott of the media ended.

It was on the evening of June 9, when he spoke to reporters following the Chicago Bulls' 100–92 defeat of the Phoenix Suns in Game 1 of the 1993 NBA Finals. (Technically, it was earlier during a taped interview with NBC reporter/good friend Ahmad Rashad that aired at the half in which Jordan basically denied being a compulsive gambler.)

Now, there was a good reason for Jordan to talk. Nary a mention of his gambling was whispered by the press. Not on this evening, anyway. The predominant storyline was how he and his teammates stormed into America West Arena, raced out to a 20-point second quarter lead, and fended off the onrushing Suns in the second half. Jordan once again dazzled, scoring 14 of his game-high 31 points in the first quarter—an early outburst that deflated the Suns faithful.

"We stunned them with our movement and execution offensively, and then we were able to hold them off at the end," said Jordan after the Game 1 100–92 win.[76]

Game 2 followed a similar script.

Jordan (42 points, 12 rebounds) was even more dominant this night while Scottie Pippen had a triple-double (15 points, 12 assists, 12 boards). On defense, the Bulls had no answer for Charles Barkley (42 points, 13 rebounds) but held Dan Majerle to 13 points and ensured Kevin Johnson (four points, four turnovers) was a non-factor.

And while Jordan and Barkley had identical scoring totals, the disparity between their respective defensive skill sets was glaring: Barkley allowed Horace Grant to score 24 points while Jordan played lockdown defense on Majerle, one of the best perimeter shooters of his generation. This dynamic alone virtually allowed the Bulls to become the first team to win the opening two Finals games on the opponent's court.

"Well, we're a team trying to make history and that goes along with it," reasoned Scottie Pippen in the locker room following the 111–108 win.[77]

Far more fascinating history, however, would be made two nights later when the series shifted to Chicago Stadium for a must-win Game 3 for Phoenix.

For Paul Westphal, Game 3 must have felt like he was back in the Bicentennial.

On June 13, 1993, at Chicago Stadium, Westphal and the Phoenix Suns were sweating out a triple-overtime NBA Finals game—just as they had been 17 years earlier, when he was holding down the backcourt for Phoenix. Only this time, of course, he was a coach.

And on the winning side.

On June 4, 1976, the Boston Celtics hosted the upstart Phoenix Suns in Game 5 of the NBA Finals with the series knotted 2–2. By the second quarter, the Celtics held a commanding 22-point lead as the Suns appeared to be overmatched against future Hall of Famers Jo Jo White and Dave Cowens along with the rest of the battle-tested Celtics roster.

This wasn't exactly shaping up to be the greatest NBA game ever.

"People all over Phoenix were probably turning the game off halfway through the second quarter because we were getting killed," says Dennis Awtrey, backup center for the 1976 Phoenix Suns team, who, later in his career would gain notoriety for punching Kareem Abdul-Jabbar in the jaw during an on-court skirmish.[78]

But the "Sunderella Suns" stormed back in the second half to force the first of three overtime periods. In the second OT, Phoenix was clinging to a one-point lead with four seconds remaining when Celtics legend John Havlicek darted the length of the parquet and banked home a 15-foot shot. Hundreds of Boston fans stormed the fabled court. The only problem was that time hadn't expired—the referees promptly convened and correctly put one second back on the game clock. (Sheer chaos ensued when one deranged Celtics fan darted over to head referee Richie Powers and thumped him in the chest before being escorted away by security.) When order on the court was finally restored, the intrepid refs prepared to give the Suns the ball—underneath their basket. And that was when Westphal (who used to call Boston Garden home) asked for, and was granted, a timeout he knew his team didn't possess. By design, the Suns were assessed a technical and the Celtics were granted a foul shot, which Jo Jo White converted, upping their lead to two points. But the Suns were now able to inbound the ball from midcourt. Subsequently, Phoenix forward Gar Heard caught the inbounds pass, spun around, and sank a jump shot (no three-pointers until 1979) at the buzzer that sent the marathon contest into a third OT.

"Stupidest thing I have ever seen," cracks Awtrey about Westphal's ploy. "We were sitting there talking, and Paul said, 'Hey, let's just call a timeout. It doesn't matter if we lose by one or by two.' We were down one. I think we asked the officials where we get the ball and they said, 'Well, you get it where you would after an illegal timeout.' So that kind of clinched it for us."[79]

While Boston ultimately prevailed, 128–126, in triple-OT and went on to win Game 6, securing its 13th championship in team history, it was Westphal's gutsy, brainy call that prolonged this game, securing its place in the annals of NBA history.

"He [Westphal] was always looking at games," remembers Awtrey. "He's very big on games. In those days we had roommates typically, and Alvan Adams was his roommate, and they're very close. They used to do kind of some crazy things. Everything was a game to Paul, and he wanted to win the game, so that's how he did things in his life. He became very creative and I guess that would be part of the gamesmanship that he had was his creativity. He was always thinking about a way to beat you. It wasn't necessarily the way you think he was going to try to beat you. The creativity he had, along with his talent, was one of his best attributes."[80]

Now, nearly two decades later, in the Suns' only other NBA Finals appearance, Westphal was employing his craftiness as a head coach tasked with outmaneuvering a more talented Chicago team. Indeed, three hours and 20 minutes after tip-off, the final buzzer sounded on Phoenix's 129–121 Game 3 win—the only other triple-OT Finals game in NBA history. As the Suns were celebrating one of the most glorious nights in franchise history, the Bulls trudged off their home floor in front of bummed fans left wondering if their team had considered Phoenix merely an afterthought in pursuit of a third straight title.

"This will go down in history as one of the greatest games," Westphal said afterward. "Up there with the one I played in. But this one was better because we won."[81]

The history was not lost on the current players, either. In fact, during one of the many timeouts, Phoenix forward Cedric Ceballos wondered, "Is this '76 all over again, or what?"[82]

Never short of a colorful sound bite, Charles Barkley told the postgame media scrum, "This was the greatest basketball game I ever played in today. I actually didn't even care who won or lost."[83]

The Bulls sure did. They knew they blew it. There was no way Phoenix could have come back from a 3–0 deficit. (From the balcony, one Chicago fan hoisted a sign: "Final Sunset Wednesday Chicago Stadium.") Such talk of an impending Chicago sweep was foolish. At this juncture, it was very much a series, and a loss in Game 4 would mean that Phoenix would reclaim home court advantage.

How exactly did the Bulls let the Suns back into the series? While playing on their home court? Against Barkley, who had badly bruised his shooting elbow when he had hit the deck hard in Game 2? (Throughout this game, Barkley was nursing a gimpy right elbow that had been drained of fluid only a half-hour prior to tip-off. When team physician Dr. Richard Emerson had asked Barkley if he was OK to play, Barkley responded, "Unless I have a heart attack and die before six [p.m.]."[84] Barkley clanked his first nine shots in pregame warmup, but apparently made the right call to play as he finished with 24 points and 19 boards.) When Phoenix had led for a total of just 3:54 entering Game 3?

The primary culprits were Jordan and Pippen, who combined to shoot just 26.5 percent from the field after the third period. Pippen, whose left thigh started cramping at the end of the first OT session, scored just two points in the three overtime periods combined; Jordan, meanwhile, misfired on 14 of his final 20 shots.

While in his postgame comments Phil Jackson attributed his stars' subpar performances to fatigue, it was obvious that Paul Westphal's gutsy decision-making was a momentous factor in the Suns one-upping their opponent—just as it had been in 1976. The young coach made the pregame decision to change every single matchup, the most pivotal being swapping out a 6'6" Dan Majerle in favor of point guard Kevin Johnson for the Jordan assignment. Bold move. Jordan had nearly a half-foot on the 6'1" Johnson (who ended up playing an NBA Finals record 62 minutes this evening), but KJ's lightning-quickness proved capable of inhibiting Jordan's initial moves to the rim. When Jordan wasn't settling for perimeter jumpers, he was posting up inside—the area where Westphal knew the Suns could most effectively double-team him. Meanwhile, Majerle, no longer burdened with guarding Jordan, was able to exert more energy on offense, scoring 28 points and nailing six of eight shots from behind the arc, with the final trey sparking Phoenix's game-sealing 13–4 run in the third OT.

Following the next morning shootaround, a very forthright Scott Williams told reporters, "This is a team that has always needed a lot of motivation to play its best, and we had almost none of that going into Game 3. But we have it now. Everybody was frustrated and disappointed after the loss, and now we're going to show the fire that has gotten us where we are."[85]

Hearing Williams refer to his team as lacking motivation was a tad disconcerting. So, too, was Will Perdue once again stewing over a lack of floor time. The annoyed center, who had yet to play in the Finals, told the media, "I'm really surprised. I thought I'd get a little time against [Oliver] Miller or [Mark] West. But it hasn't happened, so it's getting pretty frustrating just sitting there watching, especially in a game like Sunday night when we go into the third overtime and it looks like a couple of guys are tired."[86]

Jackson, however, could live with an eyebrow-raising comment here, a personal gripe there. More disturbing than words were the actions (or inactions) of Jordan's supporting cast. In Game 3, Jordan took a whopping 43 shots—which meant that nearly a third of the Bulls' possessions ended with the ball in his hands. With such an imbalanced offensive attack, questions resurfaced about whether the Bulls were actually a great team, or an operation fueled by one transcendent individual. And if the latter proved true, were the Bulls' chances of the three-peat in jeopardy?

Three nights later, Michael Jordan's Game 4 performance served as a stark reminder as to why he was the most highly endorsed pro athlete in history and the recipient of preferential treatment from essentially every authoritative figure (and institution) in his life.

In the most important game of the most important season in club history, Jordan was simply indomitable. Rebounding from an "off-night" in Game 3 in which he finished 19 of 43 from the field, MJ scored 55 points (22 in the third) to tie Rick Barry for the second-highest Finals scoring effort in league history. On this evening, no one on the Suns, not Dan Majerle, not Kevin Johnson, could contain Jordan, who got most of his buckets by driving through the lane, rather than settling for the outside jumper—as was his wont in Games 1–3.

But Jordan's masterpiece almost wasn't enough. Charles Barkley capped off his own sparkling performance (32-point, 12-rebound, 10-assist triple-double) with a basket with 1:01 remaining to slice the Chicago lead to 106–104. Ultimately, to avoid coughing up the 2–0 series lead, it took a Jordan three-point play with 13.3 seconds left to give Chicago an insurmountable 109–104 lead. Chicago prevailed, 111–105, which meant that, finally, the home team won a game.

Minutes after his team had secured a 3–1 series lead, Jordan told the press:

> I think every big game, you try to play your best basketball. And it's been many times where when a big game comes, I try to do too much or maybe I'm a little bit more hyped than I need to be and I get out of rhythm the first part of the game and somehow I seem to get it back in the fourth quarter. This game, I was just more or less trying to carry the load for the team, go to the hole, get some fouls if we could get some fouls. Whenever we needed a big basket, I was always there to get that big basket for

them. As my role for this team, that's what I have to do and I'm willing to do that—whatever it takes to get us over that hump.[87]

In retrospect, it was probably not the best idea for Chicago city officials to brace for a title party on the morning of Friday, June 18. Precautions had to be taken to counter any unruliness, but the city's presumption that the Bulls would clinch the three-peat at Chicago Stadium served as prime bulletin board material.

"Rude. It's like selling the estate before the person's dead," remarked Charles Barkley about the premature planning.[88]

A fired-up Suns team came out blazing in Game 5, torching the Bulls for 33 first quarter points on their way to a 54–49 halftime lead. Ultimately, while Michael Jordan (41 points) and Scottie Pippen (22 points) came through, it was a highly imbalanced scoring attack as Pippen's starting frontcourt mates Horace Grant and Bill Cartwright had three points combined. Phoenix withstood Chicago's late surge and pulled away with a 108–98 win, sending the series back to the desert. There would be no victory party at the Madhouse on Madison.

But that mattered little to a Bulls team that knew this third title was rightfully theirs—even though they were facing their stiffest postseason competition in years.

"I think the big thing was that we felt like we were in control of the series, and we were," recalls Cartwright. "In Game 5, when we lost at home, this was the situation where it came down to the last minute of the game and the score was tied and Michael [Jordan] had the ball at the elbow. So, we felt pretty good. Normally when we're in that situation, we're going to win that game pretty much 98 percent or 99 percent of the time. Kevin Johnson made a quick play on Michael and just took the ball from him, which never happens. I can remember thinking, 'Holy Smokes, you've got to be kidding me!' We ended up losing that game at home and then something interesting happened on the plane. I kind of felt like the guys were even more confident. Guys were pretty loose. Michael was smoking a cigar. It was kind of like, 'OK, we didn't get it done, but we're going to get it done now.'"[89]

The lighthearted cockiness largely stemmed from Phil Jackson, who, at the time, tongue-in-cheek bemoaned the fact that the return trip would force him to forfeit front-row tickets to a Grateful Dead concert in Chicago and, of course, Jordan, who had quipped that he wouldn't fly back with his teammates if they failed him in Game 5.[90] (As Cartwright noted, Jordan and his ubiquitous cigar were on the team jet.)

However, as would be apparent less than 48 hours later, Game 6 in Phoenix would be no joking matter—or mere formality preceding the coronation.

It was only fitting that the final game of the 1992–93 season was a grind.

Virtually nothing about this season had been easy. Horace Grant's resentment over star treatment of Michael Jordan and Scottie Pippen. Bill Cartwright's and John Paxson's recoveries from off-season knee injuries. Will Perdue's nagging complaints. An improved and nastier Knicks team. The gambling scandal. The pressure of the three-peat.

And on the evening of June 20, the Bulls were struggling mightily as Game 6 of the Finals unfolded.

In the first quarter, Chicago wasn't executing well. Grant and Cartwright were continued offensive liabilities. Pippen was maddeningly inconsistent from the field. A Game 7 seemed like a distinct possibility. However, by the second quarter, the Bulls got hot, even vaulting ahead by 11 at one point, before the Suns trimmed the deficit to five at the half. Heading into the fourth quarter, Chicago, which held three 10-point leads in the third quarter, clung to an eight-point advantage (87–79). Then Chicago played some of its worst basketball of the season at the least opportune moment. Chicago didn't even score until *more than six minutes* into the final quarter when Jordan sank a free throw. Buoyed by a crazed sea of purple-and-orange-clad fans who stood for most of the fourth quarter, the Suns dominated, forcing three 24-second violations (two in the final 3:19), while preventing the Bulls from scoring on eight straight possessions. With less than a minute remaining, the two-time-defending champs found themselves down by four before Jordan's coast-to-coast layup cut the Suns' lead to 98–96 with 38.1 seconds remaining. On Phoenix's ensuing possession, Dan Majerle airballed a potential game-sealing open jumper from the right side. Pippen corralled the loose ball and called a timeout with 14.4 ticks on the clock.

In Chicago's huddle, Jackson opted to play for overtime, which meant clear the lane for Jordan to get a driving layup. However, once the play unfolded, Jordan was getting smothered on defense, and had no choice but to dish to Pippen at the top of the key. Pippen found a cutting Grant, who subsequently whipped the ball out to John Paxson for an open three-point attempt. The veteran marksman calmly converted Chicago's 10th trey of the game, a then-Finals record, which gave Chicago a 99–98 lead with 3.9 seconds remaining.

After the subsequent timeout, Grant, who, having registered a single point for the second consecutive game, had the defensive play of the series, blocking Kevin Johnson's last-second runner to preserve the Bulls' 99–98 victory that made them the first team in 27 years, and only the third ever, along with the Minneapolis Lakers and Boston Celtics, to win a third consecutive title.

"That was the longest four seconds," says Darrell Walker. "It took forever for the four seconds to get off the clock. Big shot by Paxson. Great block that people keep forgetting about. Horace Grant made a great block on Kevin Johnson at the end to seal the victory."

"I had been on a bunch of bad teams and a few good teams. For me to sit there and be a world champion, I just broke down and started crying. I couldn't believe it."[91]

Ironically, Jordan, who, prior to Paxson's three-pointer, had scored all nine of Chicago's fourth quarter points, was virtually a non-factor in the final two plays. It made no difference. With a third title to his name, Jordan's legacy as a living legend was now secure. After the clock hit zeroes, MJ leapt into the air before navigating his way through the crush of teammates and photogs to secure the basketball.

This was one of the most magnificent moments in his legendary life.

For the third consecutive spring, Jordan demonstrated that his individual brilliance could synchronize with the timely contributions of teammates.

But this spring was different. The spotlight had been on him during every waking breath for the past couple months. Now, Jordan could exhale while knowing he just proved the naysayers wrong.

Again.

Given the road setting, the celebration was soon ushered into the locker room where NBC was set to televise the trophy presentation to Jordan's Bulls. For all the talk of selfishness surrounding Jordan, he was remarkably appreciative of his entire supporting cast in his comments that initiated NBC's series of postgame interviews. In fact, one of his first remarks to reporter Bob Costas was "From Corey Williams to Ed Nealy to all the guys that were on the injured reserve, this was a hard-fought three-peat."[92]

During the 1992–93 season, Corey Williams averaged 2.3 PPG and didn't see a sniff of postseason action; Ed Nealy, who wasn't even on the postseason roster, played 11 games for the Bulls that winter before retiring from the NBA and later embarking on a career as a car salesman in Texas. Nevertheless, from Jordan's perspective, Williams and Nealy were two scrappy, diligent teammates whose contributions warranted a mention.

(Apparently, such comments were not out of character as Jordan could be very supportive of lesser heralded teammates. According to Scott Williams, "We both played for a legendary coach, Dean Smith, at North Carolina. I wasn't drafted by the Chicago Bulls so MJ, I think, looked at me as a younger brother or a younger North Carolina basketball fraternity member. And he wanted to make sure things went well for me. I don't think he had anything to do with me earning the spot on the team, but I think he gave me an opportunity to be judged on my merits and not let any of the NBA political garbage affect my opportunity to make the team. I always appreciated him for that."[93])

A couple minutes after MJ's thoughtful comments, Paxson told NBC's Bob Costas, "This is a dream, what can I say? Maybe we were the ones destined to win after all. What a great feeling. I can't describe what I feel."[94]

"I can't think of a more dramatic finish for us," Bulls coach Phil Jackson told the press corps afterward. "Three games on the road to win certainly typifies the emotional swings that went on in these playoffs."[95]

Years later, in his 2013 memoir, *Eleven Rings: The Soul of Success*, Jackson would wax poetic on this trying season as he wrote, "This season had been a hard ride. The pressure kept building and building until it felt like it might never stop. But the players turned to one another for strength, and then ended it all with a moment of pure basketball poetry that made all the pain and ugliness melt away."[96]

The 1992–93 Chicago Bulls would not go down as the most dominant of the six championship squads of the nineties. But it can be argued that this was the most impressive edition, at least regarding the dynamic Jordan/Pippen duo. The two franchise cornerstones had returned from overseas exhausted, both physically and mentally. (For Pippen, the truncated 1992 off-season was particularly aggravating as he didn't have ample time to recover from tendinitis in his right foot.) For Jordan, his ever-increasing global celebrity status was proving, at times, burdensome. As was the pressure to excel in every game. The gambling scandal was a distraction that occurred at the worst possible time. And yet, the end result was supremacy: The Bulls were popping corks for the third consecutive June while Jordan had earned his third consecutive NBA Finals MVP, averaging 41 PPG in the series.

While there was little question that Jordan, perhaps only at the midpoint of his career, had already established himself as the greatest player in league history, debates started ensuing over where the early 1990s Bulls sat atop the pantheon of all-time NBA teams, which included the octa-peat Celtics dynasty during the Bill Russell-Red Auerbach era.

As Jordan remarked in his postgame press conference, "I know there's going to be a lot of opinions about who is the greatest team forever. When you look at the Celtics, they got 16, 18, I don't know how many championships they've got, but they never won the championship when they had 28 teams and so much parity in the league at this era."[97]

Jordan may have forgotten the exact number of Celtics titles (16) but he didn't forget to mention in this presser that Bird's Celtics and Magic's Lakers never won three in a row.

As *Chicago Sun-Times* columnist Jay Mariotti claimed in the next day's paper, "A three-peat simply isn't supposed to happen in this era, not with free agency and wealthy athletes who often prioritize winning no higher than having a clean Mercedes."[98]

"It hit me fairly quickly after we accomplished it [three-peat] because it had been about 27 years since it had been done," recalls Scott Williams, who, by this point, had won a title in each of his first three years in the league, a true feel-good story considering not only that he went undrafted but also that he experienced unspeakable tragedy as a teenager when his father murdered his mother before turning the gun on himself. "I understood the magnitude of doing that while playing with the best player on the planet. The knowledge that all of us received from that, except for a couple of guys who were toward the real twilight of their careers, the rest of us went on to use those experiences and that knowledge to help ourselves become better basketball players, help other coaches become better coaches, and certainly to help younger players, which was my forte. It prolonged my career in the NBA for sure because I had the talent to play a few years in the league, but having gotten that experience in my first few years in the league allowed me to play 15 years in the league."[99]

At the moment, though, the Bulls were just content knowing that an inferior team didn't steal what was rightfully theirs.

"Honestly, I think it was just relief," remembers Erik Helland, when asked about the prevailing emotion in the locker room. "The anticipation was always that was where you were going to end up. I think at that point, you had already done it twice. The third time, to me, it oddly took on a sense of normality in a lot of ways. And I think when you have a new person on the roster, you see that reaction of 'Oh My God, I just won a championship!' But I think for the veterans, there was a sense of normality and I think a sense of relief and certainly a sense of accomplishment, but the difference in the locker room from '91 to '93 was obviously really, really significant. When you expect to do something, it's just human nature that your reaction is not the same."[100]

No one was more relieved than Horace Grant, who made up for his recent shooting slump by having the most important assist and block of the season. Normally a guy who could consistently sink the open 17-foot jump shot while working in the triangle offense, Grant had all but disappeared in the final two games as the Suns had made adjustments to their perimeter defense. But, just as he had so many times earlier in his NBA career, Grant found other ways to contribute down the stretch.

For the Bulls, it wasn't just about the stars and other starters. The team's depth chart was continuously replenished with good system players, intelligent guys who could run the triangle offense, get their touches, but ultimately accept that even if they had a career night, they would be overshadowed by Jordan.

"They [the Bulls] had great complementary players, guys that a lot of people probably don't even recognize their names," says Greg Foster, who played for seven NBA teams throughout the nineties.[101] (During the second three-peat later in the decade, such unsung players included Jud Buechler, Jason Caffey, Bison Dele, and Luc Longley.)

Certainly, this year's supporting cast was more capable than that of the mid-eighties (many pundits had correctly predicted that Jordan could never win a title playing alongside Sidney Green and Quintin Dailey, role players who were now long since departed) and, for the most part, Jordan had grown comfortable with them.

As Cartwright recalls, "We felt like we had not only a great starting unit. We had a great second group of starters to come in. Some people liked to call them our bench. I would call them second group of starters. We felt pretty confident that our whole team was better than anybody else's. Seemingly every year, every championship year, we were able to have great role players."[102]

Of course, the most vital member of the supporting cast was Pippen. Generally content being Robin to Jordan's Batman, Pippen truly believed that Jordan had advocated for him to be a member of the Dream Team. He was forever indebted to Jordan for the opportunity but was also worn out after this 11-month commitment to basketball. And like Jordan, Pippen had vindicated Jackson's decision to let him chill during the preseason by proving that when it was game time, he would exert maximum effort.

Few people could appreciate this evening more so than Darrell Walker, a now sparsely used journeyman guard who, ironically, only had been playing for the Bulls a few months since coming over from the Detroit Pistons mid-season. However, Walker was nearing the end of his decade-long career and had never won a title. More importantly, though, he was the only Bulls player who actually hailed from Chicago. As a student attending the South Side's Corliss High in the seventies, Walker knew that for many years the Bulls were either playing in the shadow of the cross-town Bears and Cubs or, when relevant, ultimately disappointing the sports-frenzied city. No longer. Now, NBA fans worldwide were envious of the Windy City.

"The locker room was great," recalls Darrell Walker, who retired following the 1993 NBA Finals, a decision that received slightly less fanfare than that of a certain teammate.[103]

"Everybody was jumping around. Champagne was flowing. People talk about the rings. It's not the ring you get—it's the rush that you get that you are the champions of the world. People don't understand that. That's just a special feeling. The locker room was just full of joy and I'm sure Michael [Jordan] had some relief off of his chest."

As the ensuing months would prove, however, not nearly enough.

3. When Michael Jordan Owned the NBA

On July 22, 1993, James Jordan attended the funeral of a former colleague in Wilmington, North Carolina. Afterward, he hit the road shortly after midnight, coasting into the summer darkness in his red Lexus. It was a 3.5-hour drive to his Charlotte home. The plan was to get some brief shut-eye before flying out to Chicago for a charity golf tournament his son was hosting.

On the same muggy evening, Daniel Green and Larry Demery were hanging out at a cookout in Lumberton, North Carolina, before hitting the road themselves.

The most widely accepted version of the story is that a little over an hour into his drive, Jordan had stopped to nap in his Lexus on the shoulder of US Highway 74 and while asleep, was shot in the chest by Green and Demery before they pilfered through his jewelry and wallet among other belongings. Green and Demery then cruised into South Carolina and tossed Jordan's body off Pea Bridge, before spending the next 72 hours joy-riding in the Lexus to impress girlfriends and pals (while also using Jordan's car phone to dial a sex line). Meanwhile, the Jordan family went a few weeks without reporting James' absence. Eventually, a corpse was later found by a construction worker as he was fishing in Gum Swamp. The body was so severely decomposed that it was impossible to identify (and was soon cremated), however, when police eventually learned that Jordan was missing, his dental records were rushed from Charlotte across a trio of counties and one state line. Subsequently, it was confirmed the identity of the victim was one James Jordan.

The murder of James Jordan was a bizarre, multi-faceted crime, loaded with ambiguity. There is still not one hundred percent certainty that the vandalization of Jordan's car can be linked to the murder. In fact, it was postulated that the car thieves and murderers were two distinct sets of perpetrators, who may, or may not, have crossed paths. There was also a theory that no one initially intended to murder Jordan, that he was a victim of a crime that may have begun as a car theft and escalated to murder. Another account was that the teens sought to murder Jordan because he had observed their involvement in a drug deal. No one will ever know what exactly transpired in the Carolinas during the long, hot summer of 1993. By all accounts, James Jordan was not targeted because of his relation to a celebrity; it was simply happenstance. The nearly three-week lag between James' abduction and the Jordan family's public notification further muddled the story. However, documented records indicate this much (or little) is known about the chronology of events:

1. On July 23, Jordan's whereabouts became unknown.
2. On August 3, nearly two weeks after Jordan went missing, his

severely decayed corpse (the race was even indiscernible) was discovered not in his vandalized Lexus, but rather in a swamp in McColl, South Carolina. It was concluded that Jordan was shot once in the chest with a .38 pistol.

3. On August 5, Jordan's 1992 Lexus was discovered—not on the side of the road where he had supposedly slept but rather in abandoned woods near Fayetteville, North Carolina, 60 miles from where his body would eventually be found. Four men were charged with the theft and vandalism of Jordan's $45,000 car. Police believed that the murder may not have been directly linked to the vehicle theft, although Cumberland County (N.C.) Sheriff's Department Capt. Art Binder said the thieves may have "crossed paths" with the killer or killers.

4. On August 11, law enforcement authorities announced that the vandalized car belonged to Jordan.

5. On August 13, the confirmed identity of Jordan's corpse was announced.

6. On August 15, funeral services for James Jordan were held in Wallace, North Carolina.

In the months and years ahead, there were significant questions regarding the shared culpability of Green and Demery as well as their modus operandi, but for the public, arguably the two most confounding aspects of the case were that (a) James Jordan had opted to park and sleep roadside when he was a few hundred yards away from a Quality Inn offering rooms for less than $30 per night and (b) the family had waited until August 12 to report that James was missing.[104]

(There were never definitive answers to such questions.)

The ghastly murder of Jordan's father marked a horrific summer for the NBA. During this sliver of calendar time, Boston Celtics swingman Reggie Lewis died of a sudden heart attack while practicing at Brandeis University; New Jersey Nets star guard Dražen Petrović was killed in a car accident in Germany; Miami Heat guard Brian Shaw's parents and sister also died in an auto accident.

But the slaying of Michael Jordan's father was the tragedy that rocked the sports world at this time. And not just because of the magnitude of Jordan's stardom. Theirs was no ordinary father-son relationship. In a world of jealous teammates, bitter rivals, greedy corporate executives, intrusive reporters, and pestering fanboys, James Jordan was Michael's best friend, most devout supporter, and closest confidant.

"I always just wondered if he dealt with that [father's death] the way that he should have," recalls Jack McCallum. "I remember asking Michael when I was interviewing him for the *Dream Team* book if he ever considered counseling. He looked at me basically like, 'Get the fuck out of here.'"[105]

In the immediate aftermath of his father's death, the general assumption was that returning to the basketball court would prove most therapeutic.

On the morning of Wednesday, October 7, 1993, Michael Jordan, sporting a pale olive suit, white shirt, green and black tie, and white pocket handkerchief, prepared to hold court with reporters at the Berto Center in Deerfield, Illinois, which served as his team's practice facility.

Err, now his *former* team's practice facility.

Everyone was bracing for the official announcement. The *Chicago Sun-Times* had already published a report confirming rumors of Jordan's retirement—rumors that had been swirling for days. Today's press conference was a formality ... but still an event that, like Jordan, transcended the world of sports.

In the Berto Center parking lot, satellite trucks were parked to air Jordan's comments live on network television as people kept streaming into the facility. Passersby couldn't help but gawk at the hubbub. Inside, there were well over 100 journalists, including NBC's Tom Brokaw, hovering around the podium. Major dailies across America had dispatched reporters to this press conference. Former teammates such as Scottie Pippen, John Paxson, B.J. Armstrong, Bill Cartwright, and Scott Williams were in attendance. (No Horace Grant though.) So were Phil Jackson and team owner Jerry Reinsdorf.

Sitting beside wife Juanita, *a 30-year-old* Jordan told the world that he was done playing basketball:

> It's not because I don't love the game. I love the game of basketball, I always will. I just feel that I don't have anything else for myself to prove. ... When I get to the pinnacle and I feel that my skills are still good—I'm not starting on the downside of my career—I want to walk away from the game. And it's been very fortunate that I'm on top. And coming off three championship seasons, it's the perfect timing for me to walk away ... I know the kids are going to be disappointed, but [hopefully they learn that] basketball is great to play, it's enjoyment, it's fun, it's a hobby. But there's a lot to life other than sports.[106]

For Jordan, by October 1993, there certainly was.

His continuous stream of corporate commitments. Mounting criticism from the African American community for his silence on socio-political issues. The lingering effects of the shocking reports in *The Jordan Rules*. The high stakes gambling allegations. The association with Slim Bouler. The relentless scrutiny from the media. And, of course, the sudden and tragic death of his father.

Perhaps still bitter at the *New York Times* for publishing the account of his gambling, he took some parting shots at the media during this farewell conference. (By fall of 1993, it was quite apparent how Jordan had become far more antagonistic toward the press in general since the Bulls' first title in spring of 1991.) While Jordan made a point of telling reporters that they did not drive him away from the game, he slang a barb at the fourth estate when he cracked, "This is probably the first time I've met [with] this many people without a scandal around."[107]

Truthfully, however, this premature retirement *was* a scandal. One popular rumor was that NBA commissioner David Stern had asked Jordan to step down because of the gambling issue—something Stern vehemently denied. It was hard to believe that Stern would have nudged Jordan out when the superstar was generating untold millions for the league. But this narrative gained slight currency as it was so unfathomable how a perfectly healthy Jordan in his prime would walk away.

Irrespective of the impetus, this was horrible for the NBA. This was the third straight off-season in which a legend retired. In November 1991, Magic Johnson retired (for the first time) due to contracting HIV. Nine months later, in August 1992, Larry Bird made it official: His excruciating back ailments would spell the end of his career. But Jordan's departure was bigger. Not only because his legacy was unrivaled (Johnson and Bird played with superior supporting casts yet neither was able to capture the three-peat) but also because of the mysteriousness surrounding his exit. Unlike Jordan, Magic and Larry had documented physical conditions that were not compatible with professional athletic competition. But Jordan? Why would he turn down more potential MVP titles, championship rings, and multi-million-dollar contracts?

The most baffling part of this day was Jordan sending mixed signals regarding a potential return. When asked if he would consider a comeback after a year or two, Jordan responded, "I never say never. I don't close the door to any possibilities."[108] But then two minutes later, he remarked, "My father saw my last basketball game, and that means a lot."[109]

What was next for Jordan? Smart money was on him playing golf (lots of golf), spending more time with family, expanding his corporate brand globally.

No one foresaw him pursuing a craft that he hadn't practiced in over a decade.

On February 7, 1994, Michael Jordan signed a Minor League deal with the Chicago White Sox. Despite not having played organized baseball since high school, Jordan wanted to honor his recently slain father, whose favorite sport was baseball.

Jordan's heart was in the right place.

Unfortunately, the rest of his body wasn't, as his supreme gracefulness on the basketball court did not translate to the diamond.

Spring Training was brutal. Jordan hit below .200 in Grapefruit League action, struggling mightily against curveballs. He once referred to an umpire as "ref." White Sox hitting coach Walt Hriniak grew so aggravated with Jordan's ineptitude at the plate that he complained to team owner Jerry Reinsdorf, the same Jerry Reinsdorf who owned the Bulls, about how this "publicity stunt" was preventing him from coaching guys who were actually serious prospects.[110] An already skeptical press readily scrutinized Jordan's mistakes. The cover of *Sports Illustrated*'s March 14 issue showcased an image of Jordan whiffing at the plate, accompanied by a headline reading, "Bag it, Michael!" The subtitle ("Jordan and The White Sox Are Embarrassing Baseball") was even less flattering. (For a long time, Jordan would boycott speaking to reporters from the venerable magazine, one that had elevated his brand throughout the early 1990s.)

Nevertheless, on March 31, 1994, Jordan was assigned/flown by private jet to the Double-A Birmingham Barons, whose manager, Terry Francona, would later credit the Jordan experience as valuable preparation for handling the pressure inherent in leading the Boston Red Sox to a curse-busting World Series title in 2004.

Jordan finished the season batting .202 and totaled 51 RBI and 30 stolen bases. He had seven game-winning hits, but his greatest moment occurred during his 354th at-bat of the season, when he hit a deep fly that sailed over the left field fence for his first home run. As a sold-out crowd of 13,279 at Hoover Metropolitan Stadium erupted, Jordan, upon crossing home plate, kissed his fingers and pointed to the heavens in a fitting homage to his late father.

For Jordan, notwithstanding the seemingly interminable bus rides through swampy, humid outposts in the Deep South, there were worse ways to spend a year away from basketball. When MJ wasn't chasing down fly balls for the Barons, he was hanging out at A.J.'s, a sports bar in Five Points South owned by former NFL running back Alonzo Highsmith; going to the movies in Hoover and at the Colonnade; playing golf at Greystone, Shoal Creek, Country Club of Birmingham, Oxmoor Valley, Inverness, and Old Overton; patronizing Sammy's, a strip club on Valley Avenue. ("About half of the audience is watching the girls, the other half is watching him," club manager Little Sammy would say in 1994.)[111]

Eventually, baseball's doomsday hit on August 11, 1994, when the MLB players went on strike and the rest of the season was cancelled. Any glimmer of hope Jordan had of making it to the big leagues in the foreseeable future was gone.

As Jordan was growing increasingly restless, it became painfully obvious that the Chicago Bulls had become a so-so operation in his absence. During the 1994 playoffs, Chicago finally fell to the New York Knicks when Pat Riley's guys defeated the Jordan-less Bulls in Game 7 of the Eastern Conference Semifinals. The Knicks and Indiana Pacers were now the class of the Eastern Conference.

No one was hoping for an MJ re-entry into the NBA more than Scottie Pippen.

"I remember [Scottie] Pippen leading the team in every category and how tired he was," says Greg Foster, who played for the Bulls during the early portion of the 1994–95 season. "He was missing Michael Jordan. He found out how hard it was to actually lead a team, but he did a great job."[112]

(With the glaring exception of when Pippen refused to play in the final seconds of Game 3 of the 1994 Eastern Conference Semis because Phil Jackson didn't call the final play for him. The Bulls won anyway, but it was a selfish act that tarnished Pippen's reputation.)

As the 1994–95 season got underway, buzz surrounding a potential Michael Jordan return amplified. By late winter, the Jordan watch began in earnest when he attended a couple Bulls' practices after partaking in an informal video session. The sightings of Jordan at the Bulls' practice facilities ignited an international form of Michael Mania that spread from the Midwest to Las Vegas gambling parlors to world capitals. Throughout *Europe*, sports and political dailies alike devoted two to three pages a day to the subject, with foreign reporters flying to Chicago and calling their American counterparts for any tidbits of information.

Finally, on March 18, 1995, Jordan faxed a six-letter message to the NBA league offices: "I'm Back."

It was official. Michael Jordan would be in uniform for the Bulls' matinee game against the Indiana Pacers the following day.

However, on the morning of March 19, Jordan simply couldn't get off the private nine-seat jet that touched down in Indianapolis, where later that afternoon, he would see his first NBA action in 21 months. (Understandably rusty, he would have a disappointing performance, scoring 19 points while shooting 25 percent from the field, as the struggling Chicago Bulls fell to the Indiana Pacers 103–96.) But at this moment he was a bundle of emotions as the plane sat on the tarmac: anxious, exhilarated, uncertain, lonely.

Immediately upon landing, he asked his entourage (security guards and NBC's Ahmad Rashad) to exit, which normally would have meant having time alone with the man he called "Pops."[113]

Today, of course, he would have to deplane alone.

It took almost an hour for Michael Jordan to step into the brisk

Midwestern air.[114] The tears wouldn't stop. After all, James had been there for the critical milestones of Michael's basketball career: UNC's victory in the 1982 NCAA Championship Game; the string of postseason disappointments against Detroit; Chicago's first NBA title in 1991 against the Lakers; Game 7 of the 1992 Eastern Conference Semifinals against the Knicks; the night of June 20, 1993, in Phoenix when the Bulls clinched the three-peat. But now, as Michael was embarking on the second half of his career, one that would eventually include another three-peat (1996–1998), James wasn't there to reassure Michael that he wasn't returning to basketball too late or hadn't left baseball too early. Ironically, Michael Jordan, a role model to so many, had lost his. How could he return without his father watching from the stands at Market Square Arena this afternoon?

With each passing minute, morning shootaround crept closer. The basketball world couldn't wait much longer. Eventually, it became time. Time once more to pay tribute to his father, in this case by returning to his destined craft while revitalizing a country's sports landscape, one remaining scarred by ongoing labor strife.

By mid-morning, Jordan was ready to get off the plane.

The Second Coming of Air Jordan would commence.

4

Canada's Last Stanley Cup

With just under half a period remaining in Game 5 of the 1993 Stanley Cup Finals, Montreal wing Brian Bellows turned to his linemates John LeClair and Kirk Muller, and said, "How great is this? We just get to play the next ten minutes knowing we are going to win the Stanley Cup."[1]

Now, at the conclusion of a postseason run that included 10 consecutive overtime wins, the Canadiens could finally enjoy the sweet anticipation of victory. With a comfortable 4–1 lead, Bellows was confident the game and the series (Montreal was up 3–1) were secure—especially given how utterly dominant goaltender Patrick Roy had been this spring. And indeed, the 4–1 advantage remained intact by the final horn, as the Montreal Canadiens dusted off Wayne Gretzky and the Los Angeles Kings in the decisive game of the championship series.

But it couldn't have dawned on Bellows, or any of the crazed fans in attendance at the Montreal Forum, that this would be the last time a Canadian team would win the Stanley Cup for at least a quarter-century.

The story of Montreal's run to a Stanley Cup title in 1993 began in the most improbable manner, when, on June 11, 1992, the team hired Jacques Demers as its new head coach.

Two weeks before the signing, Demers had declared himself done with coaching when he inked a five-year contract extension to continue serving as the Quebec Nordiques' radio color commentator. In 1990, Demers was canned by the Detroit Red Wings and had since been passed over for coaching gigs to the point that he had given up. Demers wondered if he was being blackballed. Despite a solid, though certainly not spectacular, track record as a head coach, Demers had never made the Stanley Cup Finals, falling just short in 1986 when his St. Louis Blues team lost to the Calgary Flames in the seventh game of the Clarence Campbell Conference Finals.

When Pat Burns stepped down as Montreal's head coach in late May 1992 (a few weeks after his team got swept by the rival Boston Bruins in the Adams Division Finals), Demers did not regret signing the broadcasting extension. Especially considering the Montreal job was reportedly longtime NHL coach Michel Bergeron's to lose. However, Montreal general manager Serge Savard ultimately balked at offering Bergeron the pressure-packed role, fearing that Bergeron's history of heart ailments could prove hazardous.

The Quebec Nordiques would need to find a new radio broadcaster.

Ironically, Demers, himself, did not personify a clean bill of health. Significantly overweight, the hockey lifer was a binge eater who was inclined to nervously overeat at restaurants. The postgame locker room scene often involved Demers finishing nearly an entire pizza ... before dining with his wife. He was still relatively young, in his late forties, but there were significant concerns about his physique, and in effect, long-term well-being.

In truth, food was an escape from Demers' personal demons, many of which stemmed from childhood as he was raised in an abusive and dysfunctional household in working-class Montreal. For years, no one in the Demers household could escape the wrath of the alcoholic father Emile, a butcher who moonlighted as a janitor. Even though Emile, certainly no flyweight, constantly beat Jacques' mother, Mignonne, who was barely 100 pounds, the couple didn't divorce, a function of the stringent moral code pervading French Canada in the mid–20th century.[2] Not only a belt-wielding terror, Emile was also verbally abusive toward Jacques, often calling him "a son-of-a-bitch who wouldn't do anything right in life."[3]

Ultimately, Emile never lived to see his son do a lot of things right. The oldest of four children, Jacques became an orphan and the de facto sole provider of the family—in his early twenties—when his father died of a heart attack, only a few years after his poor mother had succumbed to leukemia. Demers had long left academics to join the workforce full-time (he had dropped out of school in the eighth grade due to an inability to focus stemming from uncontrollable anxiety). He never learned to read or write, and once he became the family breadwinner, there was scant time for intellectual pursuits. Thus, Demers entered adulthood as a functionally illiterate man and would (secretly) maintain that status even after establishing himself as an NHL coach. When the flamboyant Demers was asked to read an article or sign an autograph, he would pat his chest, claiming he had forgotten his glasses. Which were usually in his pocket. Even the rink wasn't a safe harbor from his embarrassing disability. Demers was a coach who was reluctant to draw up plays, telling his guys he wasn't much into X's and O's; who had his trainer fill out the lineup card; who, when coaching in the United States, used his French-Canadian heritage as an excuse for being unable to write letters in fluent English. Such awkward moments served as painful reminders of his nightmarish past … and lifelong struggles to cope.

And even now as a middle-aged man, Demers remained deeply troubled while living a highly unhealthy lifestyle.[4]

He also happened to be the perfect guy to serve as the next head coach of the Montreal Canadiens.

Whereas his predecessor Pat Burns was rigid, intense, and, perhaps too domineering, Demers was upbeat, sensitive, avuncular. The kind of coach for whom most players dream of playing.

Demers was inheriting a Habs team coming off a 93-point regular season, but also one with an aging core. Demers was hired to lead Montreal to a title in the mid—not late—1990s. He even acknowledged the transient nature of the coaching profession in his opening press conference: "If I think I'm going to coach the Montreal Canadiens for ten years, I'm foolish."[5]

Once the regular season got underway, it seemed Demers would be lucky to last ten games.

A rather underwhelming five-game start included an embarrassing 5–3 defeat to the expansion Ottawa Senators and an even more humiliating 8–2 loss to the Buffalo Sabres. The season was not even two weeks old, yet the high-pressure crucible of Montreal hockey began sizzling with the locals posting just one victory.

"We weren't a team expected to win the Cup that year," acknowledges Ed Ronan, who played right wing for Montreal in 1993. "There were certainly times during that season when we were underperforming, and we heard it and felt it. Can make for a difficult environment, but that's what sports is. Sports is about winning and in Montreal that's all that really ever mattered. If you didn't play well or play hard, it didn't take long for the fans and media to get on you.

"I kind of relate a lot of things to what I'm familiar with. I grew up in Massachusetts, obviously being a Boston fan in every sense for every sport. I guess I would compare how the team was treated in Montreal much like back in those days what the Red Sox would be like in Boston—where the first two, three, or four pages of the sports page was the Montreal Canadiens. And that wasn't just after a game. It was every day. The storied history there was still very much the fabric of the city and who they identified with as a city. That was part of it. When you did well, you knew and when you didn't, you knew. They didn't give us a lot of room for underperformance."[6]

Ever a players' coach, Demers had prioritized establishing a relaxed atmosphere after many guys had tired of the uptight coaching style employed by Burns. But Demers soon realized it was too lax. On an off day following the Buffalo debacle, locker room talk prior to practice revolved around everything except hockey: playing 18 holes, buying a pet dog, shopping in downtown Montreal. Twenty minutes into the ensuing sloppy and lethargic practice, the coach grew apoplectic. He ordered his players off the ice, mandating they return for a 2:00 p.m. practice, one that promised to burn many calories. He also announced that the next session would be at the Forum at 6:00 a.m. the following morning. For many of the shocked Canadiens, this was their earliest ice time since they were peewees.[7] As Demers told the press, "Some of these guys have to learn that they're blue-collar workers and that starts with blue-collar hours."[8]

Things didn't get much better when the Habs dropped a 5–2 decision to the Pittsburgh Penguins to fall to 1–3–1 on the young season. But two nights later, the early skid ended with an 8–1 thrashing of the Minnesota North Stars to kick off a three-game home stand in which Montreal walloped opponents by an aggregate 22–7 margin.

It was now late October, and as the weather started cooling, Montreal got hot. Scalding hot. The win over Minnesota sparked a 12-game unbeaten streak in which its resurgent and increasingly balanced offense potted 64 goals. On many nights, the penalty killing work and goaltending were unspectacular, but such deficiencies were often offset by a potent, perhaps trailblazing offensive system that morphed Montreal into one of the most feared teams in the NHL.

"I think we had very good puck moving and puck skating defensemen," says Ronan. "I think at the time the style that they played was a lot different than what was the norm in the league. It's probably more normal now to have defensemen, more than one or two, that are really good with the puck, handling the puck, skating backwards, trying to draw the other team toward them so they can create openings for their teammates, their forwards when they advance the puck in a transition. Those type of things weren't as common back then. Back then it was more big strong tough defensemen, physical, can really hit, maybe they had a hard shot."[9]

As Ronan's former teammate Brian Bellows explains, "Overall, I think it's rare we had three complete lines to throw up against teams and we had legitimately seven top-line defensemen. So that's pretty incredible. You don't see that in most teams. Normally there's a bigger drop-off."[10]

Such depth would prove invaluable as the long winter soon took its toll on a veteran-laden roster.

Following a loss to the Philadelphia Flyers that broke up the point streak, the Canadiens hosted the Boston Bruins for the first time since last year's playoff sweep. After a scoreless first period, the next twenty minutes was a flurry of offense. During one span of 93 seconds, the Bruins tagged Patrick Roy for three goals. While Montreal responded with five goals against Bruins netminder Andy Moog to take a 5–3 lead heading into the third period (the Habs would win this wild affair by a 6–3 final), Roy's dismal second period performance rekindled memories that had haunted him since Mother's Day. (During the 1992 Adams Division Finals, Roy had one of his worst postseason showings as the Bruins blitzed him for 13 goals over four miserable games.)

In the intermission following the second period, Boston's GM Harry Sinden ran into a Montreal scribe and blurted out, "That was Andy Moog's impression of Patrick Roy in the playoffs."[11]

Ouch.

His confidence already shaken, Roy got word of the slight from the opposition, but, to his credit, made no retaliatory comment.

He had bigger concerns.

Like his job.

And his sanity.

The brilliance (and madness) of Patrick Roy was introduced to the world in spring of 1986. On the eve of the 1986 Stanley Cup playoffs, Roy was named Montreal's starting goalie—as a 20-year-old rookie. Less than two months later, on May 24, he hoisted the Stanley Cup and the Conn Smythe Trophy (awarded to the MVP of the NHL playoffs) in front of a shell-shocked crowd at the Olympic Saddledome where the host Calgary Flames had fallen to the Montreal Canadiens in the Cup Finals.

Clearly, Roy was a once-in-a-generation talent. Rare is the rookie goaltender who can take over not just a playoff game, or a playoff round, but an entire playoff tournament the way Roy did in 1986. But there was more to Roy than the breathtaking saves in the clutch. The more they watched, fans started noticing his striking histrionics—namely his bizarre conversations with the goalposts. As the spotlight shone brighter on Roy with one dazzling performance after another, the fans realized this "dialogue" was not just a superstition. As media coverage intensified during the 1986 Cup Finals, reporters felt compelled to ask Roy about his ritual. Roy explained that during a regular season game against the Hartford Whalers, he had begun talking to the goalposts "by accident" during the anthem, a conversation for which he credited his strong performance that evening.

And as the years went by, Roy would forge an intimate relationship with the red steel tubes, talking to them in his native French tongue—and, according to him, hearing them reply. Many NHL goalies had eccentric superstitions, but Roy took it to another level. His routine was more than eccentric. It was downright disturbing.

And in the latter half of the 1980s no one in hockey-crazed Montreal cared, because they had the best goalie on the planet.

However, as the 1992–93 season unfolded, Roy clearly wasn't on top of his game. After the disastrous middle period against Boston in mid-November, Roy started playing some of the worst hockey in his career. A couple weeks after the Boston game, the Vancouver Canucks torched him for six goals. A few weeks later, the Quebec Nordiques potted a combined eight goals over two consecutive evenings. The following week, two middling franchises, the Hartford Whalers and New York Islanders, scored five goals and four goals respectively on his watch.

By January 1993, a fan base that used to deify Roy was growing restless while the local press was pinning much of the blame for the team's up-and-down play on his broad shoulders.

On January 13, 1993, the French-language daily *Le Journal de Montréal* conducted a poll as to whether Montreal should trade Roy. Fifty-seven percent of respondents were in favor of a deal.[12]

While public support waned, the goaltender found unwavering loyalty and solace inside the locker room. A standoffish veteran star Roy was not. As far as the levity he brought to the locker room, little had changed from his early years, when teammates would poke fun of his ill-fitting wardrobe, calling him "humpty dumpty." He also had acquired the nickname "Casseau" (which means french fry container in French) because of his fixation on junk food. Even in 1993, nearly a decade later, as a celebrity, he still didn't take himself too seriously. Which, perhaps ironically, made it easier for teammates to follow his lead and provide support during this bout of uncharacteristically sloppy play.

"I think Patrick was certainly the brains or the backbone of the team," says Ed Ronan.[13]

In the frosty days of the new year, as over half of Montreal was calling for Roy's head, this was a team that knew it was far from seeing the best, and last, of Roy in a Montreal uniform.

Despite Roy playing inconsistently throughout the winter months, his squad had an astounding run from January 10–March 1 (a period during which the Montreal Forum hosted the All-Star Game), posting a 17–4–1 record and becoming the first team to clinch a postseason berth—while defying the conventional wisdom that defensemen had to be stout and burly. The Habs' physically unimposing yet nimble blue-liners who could move the puck and skate forward and backward with considerable grace and fluidity, thereby drawing defenders toward them and creating openings for linemates in transition, provided Demers with a plethora of scoring options. Four different defensemen (Patrice Brisebois, Éric Desjardins, Mathieu Schneider, and Kevin Haller) would reach double figures in goals scored. There was also balanced scoring along the frontline. By season's end, five different players would score at least 20 goals while 10 would eclipse the 40-point mark. Newly acquired veterans Vincent Damphousse and Brian Bellows were having career years. As was Kirk Muller, a longtime New Jersey Devil who was thriving in his second year in Montreal. The club had third-year wing John LeClair finally showing signs of potential and even though his best days were behind him, future Hall of Fame center Denis Savard was still good for 50 points by season's end.

"I'm having the time of my life," declared Demers after the postseason-clinching win on February 27.[14]

Less than two weeks later, while preparing for a practice at the Forum, Demers feared he was having a heart attack. Upon experiencing chest pains, Demers checked into the Montreal General Hospital, where he underwent a battery of tests over the next two days while missing a couple games. Thankfully, the results turned up normal and the medical staff gave Demers the green light to return to the rink—but not before exhorting him to make significant dietary changes.

Soon, things got a bit scary on the ice, too, when the Canadiens dropped three of five, getting soundly defeated by the Boston Bruins, Quebec Nordiques, and Buffalo Sabres—all possible postseason opponents. Montreal was going to battle with tired skaters and the offensive attack was having too many quiet evenings.

As the home stretch of the regular season loomed, questions resurfaced over whether Montreal could be a serious threat in the Stanley Cup playoffs.

As Roy and the Canadiens were grinding through the regular season, Wayne Gretzky, now in his fifth year with the Los Angeles Kings, was enduring one of the most trying campaigns of his Hall of Fame career.

It started early in training camp, when The Great One, still in shipshape condition, awoke one night with excruciating chest pain. During the ensuing week-long hospital stay, doctors discovered the culprit: a herniated thoracic disk.

Since the start of his NHL career in the late 1970s, Gretzky's back had taken a beating as he had been pummeled from behind hundreds, if not thousands, of times. And during recent years, the violence directed toward Gretzky had escalated. Now he faced the scary prospect of suffering a lifelong debilitation and the even more frightening one that he had skated his last shift.

On November 7, only days after he was discharged from the hospital, a despondent Gretzky sat down for an interview on *Hockey Night in Canada* in which he acknowledged the end was near. (He would later remark, "You have to understand, this has been my life since I was six.... I was scared by how much I missed it. I was scared by how much I wanted to play.")[15]

A crippling back affliction had forced basketball legend Larry Bird into a premature retirement back in August. Naturally, the hockey community wondered if Gretzky, the most prolific scorer in league history, would follow the same path. Meanwhile, in November 1991, Magic Johnson also had retired early, leaving Los Angeles virtually starless on the athletic front. Was L.A.'s lone iconic pro athlete preparing for departure?

Eventually, the worries from hockey enthusiasts and Californians were put to rest.

By mid–November, the pain from the aggravated disk was subsiding. Shortly after Thanksgiving, Gretzky was skating, and it became a question of when, not if, he would return.

The answer was January 6, 1993, against the Tampa Bay Lightning. Gretzky, who couldn't even lift his children months earlier, dished out two assists in the Kings' 6–3 loss. Two nights later, the Kings once again lost 6–3, this time to the Winnipeg Jets, despite Gretzky potting his first two goals of the year.

The most unbelievable part of Gretzky's second game back? When the puck dropped in Winnipeg, the thermometer read -28° Fahrenheit, even brisk for Canada in mid-winter. It was, in all seriousness, life-threateningly frigid, yet Gretzky's return to action in his home country drew over 14,000 fans to Winnipeg Arena.

Suddenly, wherever the Kings went, the visiting locker room was more cramped with reporters while the stands were invariably packed.

As a nine-time league MVP and four-time Stanley Cup champion, Gretzky was a legend, not just among the general public, but also among his colleagues who were considered world-class athletes themselves.

"For me, it was amazing because growing up you idolize Gretzky and suddenly you're in a locker room with him," says former Kings teammate Jimmy Carson, who, back in 1988, was dealt to the Edmonton Oilers in the blockbuster trade that sent Gretzky to the Kings. Carson had no interest in living in Western Canada and within a year demanded a trade to an American club. After playing for his hometown Detroit Red Wings for a few years, Carson was traded back to L.A. as the centerpiece of a deal that netted Detroit All-Star defenseman Paul Coffey. Carson would rejoin the Kings in late–January, shortly after Gretzky made his big return.[16]

Not that Gretzky, himself, made a big deal out of the return, or anything involving his greatness, for that matter.

When Gretzky was spearheading the Edmonton Oilers to Stanley Cup titles in the 1980s, the organizational culture was less hierarchical than that of most professional sports franchises. Whereas many NHL teams would provide stars with private hotel rooms on the road, the Oilers assigned a roommate to every skater. For Gretzky, a night's stay at the Renaissance

Center in Detroit meant an opportunity to share pizza and family stories with a guy praying to crack the opening night roster. Even a decade later, as arguably the all-time most famous Canadian athlete, Gretzky was still the lanky, unassuming kid who came of age in Alberta.

"I always say this—as great a player as he was on the ice, he was a greater person off," says Pat Conacher, who had been Gretzky's teammate in Edmonton during the 1983–84 championship season before rejoining him in Los Angeles for the 1992–93 campaign. "That guy never changed. If you're the 23rd, 24th, or 25th player on the roster, he always made you feel like the first player on the roster. He had time for everybody. It was just that calming influence that he brought each and every day."[17]

"He [Gretzky]'s just kind of a regular guy, kind of quiet," says Carson. "You have this vision of a person whom you idolize and is a legend and all of a sudden he's kind of a regular guy."[18]

By the early nineties, Gretzky was perhaps no longer the greatest player on the planet, but he was still a perennial MVP candidate, a dynamic goal scorer, the bedrock upon which you could build a championship-caliber team. However, given the severity of the recent back injury, people around the NHL started wondering if Gretzky could return to such elite form. While Gretzky showed flashes of brilliance in his first couple games back, it soon became apparent that he was not himself. In fact, Gretzky didn't even register a point over the final three games before the All-Star break and started wondering if he, ironically, was the culprit behind the team's mid-season swoon. In his 2016 autobiography *99: Stories of the Game*, Gretzky would reflect on his return in 1993: "I made the team worse for about fifteen games. We were forty-five games into the season and near the top of the division. I wasn't playing well—and you reward players for how they're playing now, not for their past history."[19]

"He [Gretzky] struggled early because he had to get back in shape and everything," acknowledges Conacher.[20]

For the Kings, it may have been a blessing in disguise that Gretzky was out until January. A highly focused team that had gotten off to a hot start (19–7–2 record) without Gretzky realized that it was a playoff contender with or without the superstar.

"I think the turning point was when we didn't have him [Gretzky]," reflects Kings left wing Tony Granato. "Barry [Melrose] pulled us together to believe if we could play well without Wayne, when he came back it would make us a pretty special team. I think that was kind of the tone for the whole year because at that point when we knew we were missing him, we weren't sure when he was coming back or if he was coming back. I think the message all year wasn't 'OK, we are missing Wayne, what are we going to do?'"[21]

4. Canada's Last Stanley Cup

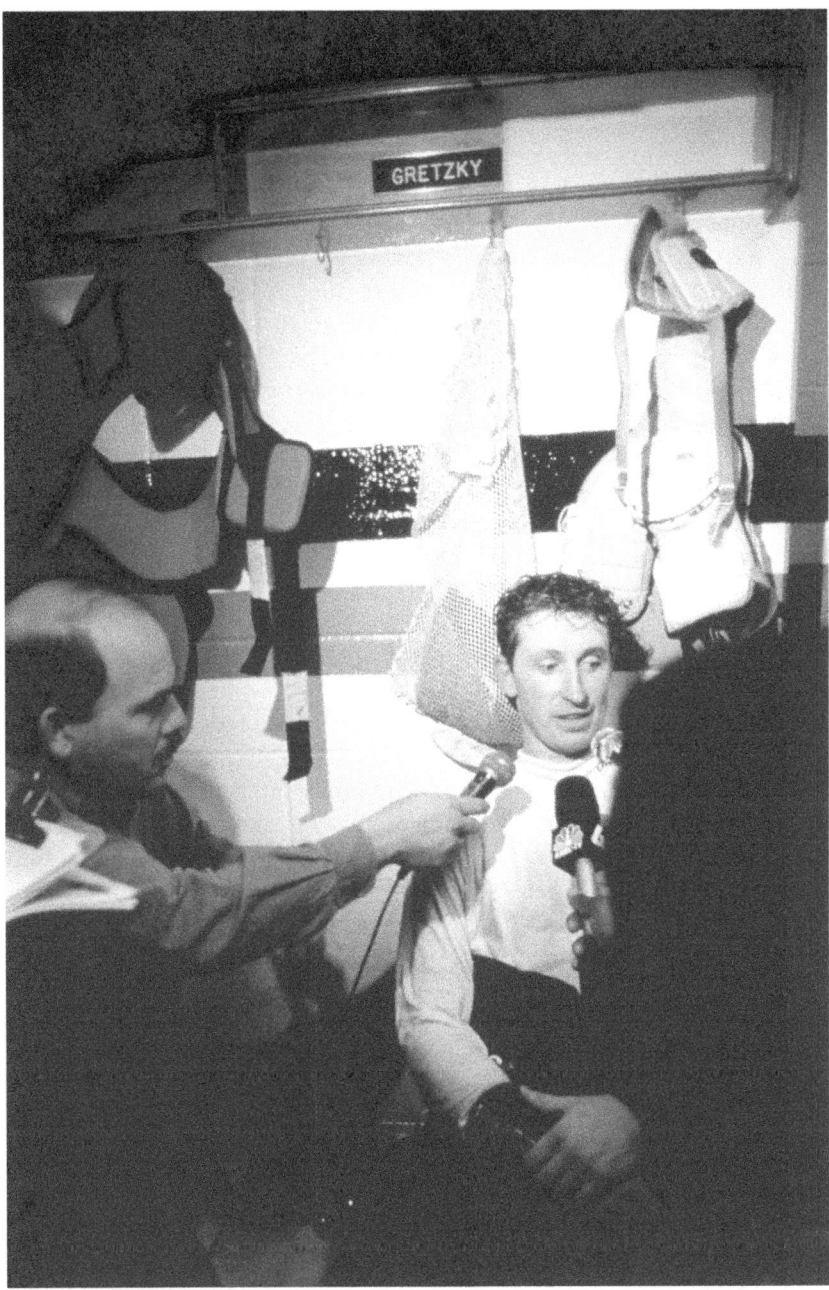

Wayne Gretzky may have been just one of the guys around his teammates, but he was still the biggest celebrity to ever play in the NHL (courtesy Los Angeles Kings).

"In that year he only played about 30 something games for us," remembers Pat Conacher. "I think that it was probably good for our team because we had to learn to win without Wayne. Sometimes when you play with a guy like that, you're sitting on the bench and he jumps on the edge and you think he's going to win it for you. Barry Melrose did a great job coaching us and pulling us together when Wayne was injured."[22]

Come early March, however, Gretzky's production levels improved and the Kings remained a lurking threat to derail the Toronto Maple Leafs in their quest for a Campbell Conference title … and crush the hopes of millions of Canadians who were praying for an all–Canadian/Original Six Cup Finals matchup between the Leafs and Habs.

Montreal began the postseason the same way it had begun (and finished) the regular season: poorly.

A Habs team that came into the 1992–93 season looking like one still hung-over from the debacle against Boston months earlier finished the regular season slate with a 2–5 record.

And now, as the playoffs were underway, the Habs faced a 2–0 opening series deficit to their interprovincial rivals, the Quebec Nordiques.

The opening round, the Adams Division Semi-Finals, was billed as the "Battle of Quebec," featuring one of Canada's newest teams, Quebec Nordiques, versus one of its most legendary franchises, Montreal Canadiens. It also featured a hot Quebec team (7–3 in its final ten regular season games) versus a Montreal team that had limped to the April finish line with uninspired, lackadaisical play that had apparently carried over to the playoffs.

"Honestly, the biggest thing for me was that we struggled going into the playoffs," recalls Montreal left wing Kirk Muller. "And our last ten games, I think we might have won two or maybe three. So, we weren't going in with a lot of momentum."[23]

Quebec squeaked out a 3–2 OT victory in Game 1 before embarrassing Montreal, 4–1, in Game 2.

The primary target for the team's early struggles was Roy, the mercurial goaltender, who, after helping stake Montreal to a 2–0 Game 1 lead, allowed a pair of goals in the final three minutes of regulation before giving up the game-winner in OT. Two nights later, the 1986 Conn Smythe Trophy winner never gave his team a chance, yielding three unremarkable first period goals as Quebec built a 3–0 lead and never looked back. For Montreal, the saving grace was that those contests had been played in the Colisée Pepsi. Now the series was shifting 250 kilometers southwest to the Montreal Forum, an arena with a considerably greater seating capacity to accommodate its notoriously raucous fans.

"Everyone picked Quebec to beat us in four or five," says Muller. "Then we lose the first two games in there and now we're going home, and I still remember Serge Savard as the general manager going to eat after the game. And I remember him standing up and saying, 'Guys listen, if you play the way you are [playing] right now, you will win this series.' Whether he believed it or not I don't know, but he was really calm about it."[24]

Savard's comments may have been reassuring but the truth was undeniable: Montreal wasn't going anywhere unless its goaltender found his mojo.

Which he soon did.

"Patrick's play really was a mirror image of what the team did as the season went along and certainly into the playoffs," says Ed Ronan. "Early in the playoffs, it wasn't that clean. We lost the first two games in Quebec against the Nordiques. We didn't go in on a roll. The roll actually started in the playoffs and [with] Patrick's play as well. The team just kind of carried on along with Patrick. As Patrick played better and got more focused and serious and competitive, the team also took that same persona where we got more in the zone so to speak, more focused. I think that's why we went so far."[25]

"I don't think Patrick Roy had his greatest nights those couple of games," recalls Quebec defenseman Kerry Huffman. "It seemed like all of a sudden he found himself during that series. I do remember Patrick playing like Patrick and just really turned it on. I do know that his play was sort of the difference in how that series was going."[26]

Indeed, Game 3 was vintage, mid-1980s Patrick Roy. Over 70:30 of competition, Quebec fired 35 shots on goal, only netting one. Unfortunately, for Roy and the Habs, Quebec's goalie, Ron Hextall, was every bit as dominant, also allowing a single goal in regulation.

As the game headed into overtime knotted 1-1, Roy, knowing that his next goal allowed would virtually end his team's season, was flawless.

Just as he would be for the next nine overtime sessions this spring.

Halfway through this game's first OT period, a loose puck careened off the skate of Quebec defenseman Alexei Gusarov, gently sliding to a rest millimeters over the goal line. This sudden death goal that gave the Canadiens a 2-1 OT win propelled them back into the series and jump-started a string of fortuitous events

"That really triggered it where we got momentum from Quebec," says Muller. "We came home, we won a huge Game 3 and then Game 4 and now Patrick was starting to heat up. His first few games were a little rough. That series really united our team because of the rivalry with Quebec City, the fans got all of a sudden really excited, and we took that momentum into Buffalo."[27]

After winning the next three games to take the series 4-2, Montreal geared up for the Buffalo Sabres, who, in the first round, had upset the Adams Division No. 1 seed Boston Bruins. Montreal was not happy about the upset. Maybe on paper, Boston posed more of a threat, but on ice, Buffalo was the gritty, onrushing underdog that no one wanted any part of.

"They [Buffalo Sabres] had a hell of a team," says Muller.[28]

But not a healthy one.

In the Adams Division Finals, Buffalo linchpins Pat LaFontaine (95 assists and 148 points in the regular season), Alexander Mogilny, Keith Carney, and Doug Bodger were a shell of their regular season selves as they continued battling a litany of ailments. Nevertheless, the stubborn Sabres didn't go down easily, losing all four games—three of which were OT affairs—by the same 4–3 margin.

After sweeping Buffalo, Montreal readied for the Pittsburgh Penguins, the heavy favorite to defeat the New York Islanders in the conference semis.

Mario Lemieux and the two-time defending Stanley Cup champion Pittsburgh Penguins were one of the great stories of the 1992–93 NHL season. Since starting his career in Pittsburgh in 1984, Lemieux emerged as one of the NHL's legendary players and single-handedly established the Steel City as one of the hubs of North American hockey. And then on January 12, 1993, the Penguins announced that their 27-year-old franchise center had cancer. He was diagnosed with Hodgkin's Disease after an enlarged lymph node was extracted from his neck. Less than two months later, Lemieux, after having gone through weeks of radiation treatment, was back on the ice. The only thing more impressive than his swift recovery was that he was out for over a quarter of the season, yet he still finished with 160 points while sparking his team's late season 17-game win streak, an NHL record at the time. Lemieux's dominant play continued in the postseason. In the first round, he tallied nine points as the Pens knocked off the New Jersey Devils in five games. As Round 2 (Patrick Division Finals) approached, the prospect of the Penguins pulling off the three-peat still seemed conceivable, but the New York Islanders, down 3–2, held serve at home in Game 6 to force a Game 7, one in which they would ultimately triumph 4–3 in OT.

Now, all that stood between Montreal and a chance to return to the Cup Finals for the first time in four years were the not-so-terrifying yet inexplicably arrogant New York Islanders.

Cheers erupted from the Montreal camp.

"They [Adams Division Finals vs. Buffalo] were four hard games and to win them in four straight, now you're sitting there waiting for probably Pittsburgh, and the Islanders kicked them out," says Muller. "The Islanders knock off Pitt, now everyone is sitting there going, 'Now it's wide open.' They [Islanders] are not really looking too much toward us. I think we caught them a little off guard at how well we were playing, and we were able to finish that series."[29]

But not without a few heart attacks.

Following a 4–3 double-OT win in Game 2 to go up 2–0, Montreal survived yet another OT thriller in Game 3 when captain Guy Carbonneau lit the lamp 12:34 into the first OT period. Less than an hour after the Habs' 2–1 victory, one that gave them a commanding 3–0 series lead, a heretofore ho-hum series grew more intriguing. In the bowels of Nassau Veterans Memorial Coliseum, New York's legendary coach Al Arbour was seething. Arbour thought referee Kerry Fraser (more on him later) missed a blatant tripping penalty on Montreal left wing Benoît Brunet against Brad Dalgarno on the winning goal. Additionally, Arbour was convinced that all three officials missed Montreal having too many men on the ice only seconds before this decisive sequence. He used his postgame presser to call out the referees, and, in effect, the NHL when he complained, "It's very apparent that there are two sets of rules. There's a rule regarding the Montreal Canadiens. There's a rule regarding everybody else. You know what it looks like to me: they're trying to get a final with two Canadian teams."[30]

Bitching about the Canadiens getting favorable officiating was a seemingly annual tradition around the league. Boston Bruins executive Harry Sinden once famously quipped that three certainties in life are death, taxes, and the first call in the Montreal Forum going in favor of the Canadiens. When Michel Bergeron coached the Quebec Nordiques, he would nearly break down in tears when discussing the linesmen turning a blind eye to Montreal penalties. Even Philadelphia's Broad Street Bullies of the seventies would rail against Montreal getting all the breaks. But Arbour's remarks were particularly newsworthy not only because he was one of the most successful coaches in league history (he was behind the bench during the Islanders dynasty of the eighties) but also because during the 1984 Wales Conference Finals, he had griped over Montreal receiving preferential treatment.

The morning following Game 3, Montreal GM Serge Savard exclaimed, "It's too bad Arbour's destroying his own product—the league. The referees are part of our league, too."

A ticked-off Islanders team, refusing to let Montreal party on its home rink, won Game 4 soundly, 4–1. Two nights later, with the series back in Montreal, the Canadiens coasted by the Islanders (a breezy 5–2 win) and into the Stanley Cup Finals.

In the past two rounds, Montreal was a combined 8–1.

Even the most biased hockey fans in the Northeast couldn't dismiss the run as a serious of fortuitous events.

By Memorial Day weekend, the only suspense remaining for Montreal was who would be their opponent in the Stanley Cup Finals. Would it be Canada's other storied franchise, the Toronto Maple Leafs, or the poster boys for the NHL's Southern Strategy, the Los Angeles Kings?

The answer largely hinged on Wayne Gretzky's new ailment—his battered ribcage.

As far as Gretzky's health concerns, an aggravating regular season had given way to an agonizing postseason. During the first round against the Calgary Flames, Gretzky suffered a broken rib on a nasty cross-check from center Joel Otto. Every night thereafter, he suited up with a rubber flak jacket before getting injected with freezing in the upper thigh minutes before the puck dropped. Ever the gamer, Gretzky was a contributor for L.A. in its dismissal of the Calgary Flames and Vancouver Canucks in the first two rounds. However, the interminable postseason eventually took its toll. Over the first five games of the Campbell Conference Finals against Toronto, The Great One was off his game, potting only one goal. There wasn't the trademark flash and dash to his game. Gretzky looked like a player who had been playing professional hockey since the Jimmy Carter administration.

(A fun subplot to the series that shifted a little attention away from the Gretzky angle was that the two coaches, Los Angeles' Barry Melrose and Toronto's Pat Burns, were tweaking each other publicly. Melrose poked fun of Burns' plump physique while Burns referred to Melrose as sporting a Billy Ray Cyrus haircut.)

Following Game 5, a 3–2 Toronto win that sent L.A. to the brink of elimination, *Toronto Star* hockey scribe Bob McKenzie wrote "Last night, Gretzky looked as though he were skating with a piano on his back … never have his efforts to sidestep a hit been so blatant."[31]

With newfound motivation, Gretzky answered the call in Game 6, scoring a power play goal in OT for the Kings' 5–4 win that forced a Game 7. (Earlier in Game 6, Gretzky had infamously cut Toronto star Doug Gilmour's chin on a high-stick. Remarkably, no penalty was issued.) Still, as the series shifted back to Toronto, the noise about Gretzky's potential demise grew louder. Puckheads across North America expected Toronto to prevail at the Maple Leaf Gardens and contain Gretzky.

"I think there were doubters maybe that [believed] Wayne was slowing down and that Toronto might be able to stop him," recalls Tony Granato. "I remember people started to question that a little bit, the media."[32]

The Kings knew better. They knew that Gretzky, even at 70 percent, was still the best offensive player still alive in the postseason. With that in mind, the Kings flew back to Toronto with an excessive amount of carry-on luggage. The post–Game 6 travel itinerary listed a flight to Toronto and a second flight to Montreal, scheduled to take off at 11 a.m. on Sunday, May 30. There was no mention of a backup flight returning to L.A. Subsequently, the Kings were already loose headed into Game 7, the culmination of one of the greatest postseason series in NHL history. And then literally minutes before face-off, Barry Melrose brought actor John Candy, ironically himself a Canadian, into the locker room to give a pep talk. The room erupted in laughter as Candy, who was in winter sports mode with his flick *Cool Runnings* due out in October, took his motivational duties very seriously.

Now, the Kings were ready for a contest that would mark the pinnacle of the Gretzky era in Los Angeles, one that elevated California hockey to another stratosphere.

In front of a sold-out Maple Leaf Gardens crowd, (the nearby SkyDome opened its doors to 30,856 fans to watch the game on the Jumbotron) Gretzky delivered a tour de force performance, one reminiscent of his glory years in Edmonton, when he notched a hat trick, scoring a goal in each period, with his final strike holding up as the eventual winner.

Following the Kings' 5-4 win, no one was making wisecracks that Gretzky (three goals, one assist) was carrying a piano on his back.

Because he looked like a man carrying a team on his shoulders.

"I just remember even before the game his [Gretzky's] demeanor, what he looked like in warmups, what he looked like in the dressing room," says Granato. "He didn't say it, but you could tell by the way he was carrying himself that he knew we were going to win the game and how we were going to win it."[33]

Gretzky may have been on the wrong side of 30 with a decaying musculoskeletal system, but he was still capable of taking over—especially when seemingly everyone in his native country, from British Columbia to Newfoundland, was watching ... and rooting against him for the sake of there being an all-Canadian Stanley Cup Final.

While Canadians may have been pulling for Toronto, the Canadiens were thrilled to see Los Angeles win as that meant playing against a team starting to get worn out from cross-continent plane rides. (Travel had been a sore topic for the coastal Kings this year. Late in the regular season, penny-pinching team president Roy Mlakar had issued a memo to his players to shut up about the team's travel policy, which included many day-of-game flights to avoid extra hotel expenses. At one point when he was surrounded by his incensed teammates, Gretzky uncharacteristically cursed and trashed the edict.)

As Montreal's Kirk Muller says, "L.A. had their time and Wayne was unbelievable and wins Game 7 in an unbelievable game that he played. And now it's us against L.A. And we go to that series and really I think we hit a team, with the travel they had to do and how hard it is to win three rounds in the West and then come out here, we were a rested team and we were young. I think we had the legs to outskate them. We were much more rested, and I think that really helped us in the final round."[34]

On the eve of the 1993 Stanley Cup Finals, Jacques Demers did his best to downplay the dominant storyline: The league's best team, Montreal, was going up against (arguably) the best hockey player ever. Montreal was more rested, deeper, and, most importantly, had the hottest goalie on the planet in Patrick Roy. But Los Angeles still had The Great One, and perhaps he alone could prevent the Habs from winning their 24th Stanley Cup title.

Before Game 1, Demers reiterated to a rapidly expanding press corps, "I'll say this over and over: I have an enormous amount of respect for Wayne Gretzky, but he's not the only guy on that team."[35]

On that very same day, the buzz surrounding Gretzky's return to the Cup Finals (his last appearance was in 1988 with Edmonton) only intensified when talk of his potentially impending retirement resurfaced. There wasn't an ink-stained or microphone-toting reporter who wasn't interested in what was going on in Wayne's world. At one point in his session with the media, Gretzky even admitted, "Honestly, next year, if I don't play the way I'm capable, I won't continue."[36]

The Game 7 performance against Toronto was one for the ages, but Gretzky was coming off a relatively unproductive regular season. And then there was the recent physical torment inflicted on his aging body. And his resentment toward skinflint management. Perhaps this series, win or lose, would be it.

However, once Game 1 got underway on the evening of Tuesday, June 1, the attention shifted toward the favored (and rested) Canadiens' surprisingly dispiriting performance. The Canadiens looked like the Kings—the team that didn't have home ice in any round; the team that, since the start of the playoffs, had flown almost the equivalent of once around the world (20,393 miles to be exact); the team that had just escaped a winner-take-all duel.

It was an inexplicably lackluster series-opening performance by the Habs, especially in the crease as Patrick Roy was vastly outplayed by his counterpart in Kings' goaltender Kelly Hrudey.

Montreal Gazette hockey writer Red Fisher opined in the next day's paper, "This wasn't merely a matter of one team finding a little more in the tank than the opposition. The reality is that except for the first half-dozen minutes of the second period, the Canadiens weren't in the Kings' class."[37]

Minutes after the bloodshed, Demers acknowledged that "Gretzky toyed with us."[38] (Gretzky finished with three assists and netted an insurance goal in the third period. Demers would make a subsequent lineup change for the next game, assigning veteran Guy Carbonneau to check Gretzky in lieu of Kirk Muller.)

Perhaps most disturbing was that Patrick Roy once again showed signs of his early season self. He wasn't bad, but he was far from dominant, allowing three goals on 37 shots.

"I think Patrick Roy doubted himself a little bit," recalls Pat Conacher.[39]

If he was also distracted, it was, at least on this night, understandable.

When his postgame media session wrapped, Roy bolted to the Lakeshore Hospital, where his pregnant wife, Michele Roy, was to be induced overnight. Mrs. Roy wanted her husband to be there for the birth, but knew he was about to go to California for four days and didn't want to risk going into labor with him over 3,000 miles away.

Jana Roy was born at 7:50 a.m. on June 2.

A sleep-deprived and overwhelmed Roy again was shaky two nights later in Game 2, allowing a couple goals, the latter being a Pat Conacher strike midway through the third, putting L.A. ahead, 2–1.

Then Roy tapped into the wayback machine and rediscovered his 1986 Stanley Cup Finals form.

From this point forward, Roy would shut out the high-flying Kings for the rest of the evening—and, ultimately, keep them in check for the rest of the series.

"He [Patrick Roy] is in the Hall of Fame for a reason," says Conacher. "You can't give those guys a chance. And that's what we did. I think we gave them a little breath of life and Roy got a second wind and like all great players, he did what he is supposed to do."[40]

As it would turn out, however, Roy's play down the stretch was not the main storyline of this evening.

With 1:45 remaining, Montreal still trailed Los Angeles 2–1. While Roy apparently had steadied himself, his offensive mates were still proving grossly inept, putting the team in a most precarious situation. For the Canadiens, the inconvenient truth was that since 1966, no NHL club had ever lost the first two games at home and bounced back to win the Stanley Cup.

E.M. Swift of *Sports Illustrated* wrote the following commentary regarding Montreal's status: "Dead. Dead on the frozen water. Dead as smelt. Lifeless, inanimate, without a snowball's chance in hell. That's where the Stanley Cup aspirations of the Montreal Canadiens stood."[41]

In danger of falling behind 2–0 before the series moved stateside, the Canadiens needed a miracle.

And they got one in the form of L.A. defenseman Marty McSorley's stick.

NHL rules stipulated that the width of a stick's curvature cannot exceed a half-inch. Coach Jacques Demers had a hunch that McSorley's stick was not in compliance and so he instructed Guy Carbonneau and Kirk Muller to ask ref Kerry Fraser for a measurement. Indeed, Fraser concluded that the curvature was over a quarter-inch in excess of the max half-inch width permitted. After L.A. was assessed a penalty, Demers pulled Roy to give the Habs a 6-on-4 advantage.

The Kings were dumbfounded. That Demers could recognize the illegality of the stick's curvature was borderline unfathomable. Was he really that confident in his ability to decipher a difference in millimeters that he was willing to risk a delay of game penalty, which would have sealed the win for the Kings? Gretzky and the Kings had their own theory—that Demers had inside information from a Montreal Forum employee who was tending to (and doctoring?) the visiting team's equipment before the game. On the Kings' bench, there was the feeling that Demers had to have known McSorley had an illegally warped stick at his disposal and now was the optimal time to catch him.

It didn't matter. It was impossible to prove that Demers was a weasel. Instead, the Kings were caught red-handed on the NHL's grandest stage.

Riding the two-man advantage, Montreal executed its simple power play to perfection. After Kirk Muller controlled the puck, Éric Desjardins and Mathieu Schneider shuffled the puck back-and-forth on the blue line before passing to forward Vincent Damphousse, who, upon corralling the puck near the face-off dot, found Desjardins perfectly positioned for a one-timer, which he fired past Hrudey.

With 1:13 left in regulation, the game was tied 2–2, the Canadiens were back in the series, the Kings were a mess, the Montreal Forum was the loudest building in North America, and Kerry Fraser knew he would never have to pay for his own dinner north of the border. At least not in Montreal.

The ensuing OT session was a short affair. Less than a minute in, Montreal broke out of its own end on a three-on-two. Desjardins retrieved the puck in the lower face-off circle but rocketed it over the L.A. net. The hockey gods smiled on Montreal, once again, when the puck bounced off the glass, landing on the stick of teammate Benoît Brunet, stationed alone behind the Kings' net. He zipped the puck to Desjardins, who slipped it past Hrudey, vaulting Montreal to the 3–2 win and tying the series at 1–1.

While the Canadiens rejoiced on the ice, the Kings' locker room was funereal. This was going to be a long eight-hour plane ride across the continent. Particularly for Marty McSorley, who got caught bending the rules (i.e. his blade) by the wily opposition.

"We all felt bad for Marty because he was such an important part of getting to that point," says L.A. center Jimmy Carson. "He was very intense and focused. If you look at it objectively, yes it did play a bit of a role. I wouldn't say it was the main part. It was a gutsy call by Jacques Demers on the other side. I would say it did play a role. There was a lot of other hockey that was played and bounces and overtime games, etc. Splitting the difference of saying it does not matter at all and was the only reason we lost."[42]

With the series tied 1–1 and headed to Los Angeles, the Kings had home ice for the next two games. But that provided little solace in the immediate aftermath of Game 2. In his 2016 memoir, Gretzky acknowledged, "That night in the locker room there was a tremendous mood swing."

While McSorley's doctored stick was the newsworthy story in the moment, Roy's insanely quick reflexes were starting to make history. For the first 100 minutes of these Stanley Cup Finals, Roy had cooled. But now he had regained his focus and was primed to continue his unbelievable postseason run.

"The second game I thought was one of the best games played by both teams," says Conacher. "It was a hard-fought game. But like all superstars, we let them back into the game and at the end of the day, I think he [Patrick Roy] was the difference maker."[43]

Perhaps so, but McSorley's doctored stick was a close second.

As the series shifted 4,500 kilometers diagonally across North America, the league's future was on sparkling display.

Game 3 marked the first Stanley Cup Finals game ever played in California—26 years to the day, June 5, 1967, that Los Angeles was officially awarded an NHL team. Now, on June 5, 1993, over 16,000 fans packed the Great Western Forum to watch their state's upstart, glitzy team battle Canada's legendary, pail and shovel team.

This new Southern Californian fan base marked a new generation of hockey enthusiasts, one that knew more about heat waves than blizzards. The SoCal fans were realizing a night by the ice nicely complemented a day in the sand. The NHL was rapidly expanding in the Sun Belt overall in the 1990s and the response was overwhelmingly positive as folks in California and Florida started coming out in droves to watch their newly adopted teams. While the Kings had been in Los Angeles since the 1960s, the franchise had never stirred such considerable buzz until Gretzky was acquired in the 1988 blockbuster trade.

As Tony Granato recalls, "The buzz about hockey and the Kings began before that [Gretzky arriving] and I think it was just building and building and building and all of a sudden you have a chance for a championship team. And that enthusiasm and that following just became that much louder and more prevalent."[44]

Sprinkled among the silver-and-black clad fanatics were the likes of Ronald and Nancy Reagan, Andre Agassi, Reggie Jackson, Goldie Hawn,

Michelle Pfeiffer, and John Candy. It was not uncommon for such celebrities to grace the Great Western Forum with their star-studded presence … for Lakers games. Traditionally, the celebs were a no-show for the Great Western Forum's other indoor tenant. But this spring, La La Land was now going gaga for hockey. (It certainly helped that the Showtime Lakers era was over and that the Lakers were currently mediocre, at best.)

"The fans in L.A. were great. I mean they were special," says Granato "That energy that they had and showed the rest of the hockey world that hockey is part of L.A. I think that was their staple as far as at least their center stage for being able to show that because I think hockey in California at that time, most of the people around the country really didn't think that was anything. To have your team get to the Finals, kind of to be able to show the rest of the hockey world that fans in California can be as good as the fans in Chicago and New York and Toronto and Montreal. I thought it was their stage, and they certainly supplied that energy and enthusiasm and support."[45]

However, as Game 3 unfolded, there wasn't much to cheer about. By the early second period, Montreal had raced out to a commanding 3–0 lead, and L.A. looked like it was still hung-over from the McSorley incident a couple nights earlier. Yet the second half of the middle period belonged to the hosts as L.A.'s top offensive weapons (Luc Robitaille, Tony Granato, Wayne Gretzky) scored to force a 3–3 tie and send this pivotal game to overtime.

That's when a 23-year-old kid from St. Albans, Vermont, took over Game 3.

Just as he would in Game 4, too.

Ironically, by the late 20th century, Vermont, a wintry state home to college hockey powerhouse University of Vermont and innumerable frozen ponds, had raised twice as many presidents (Chester Arthur, Calvin Coolidge) as NHL players. Indeed, the Green Mountain State's lone NHL player was Montreal Canadiens left wing John LeClair, known as Little Johnny around St. Albans, the site of the Civil War's northernmost skirmish and currently a farming community situated less than 20 miles from Canada, of course one of the predominant breeding grounds for NHL players.

When he was drafted by the Montreal Canadiens in 1987, the self-deprecating LeClair thought he would be fortunate to hang around in the minors as a third-line wing for several years after he was done playing for UVM. Following a solid, but injury-riddled collegiate career, LeClair made his NHL debut for Montreal in March 1991. While he was an imposing physical presence on the ice, LeClair not only struggled to score but also displayed weak balance and agility, often struggling to keep himself upright when cruising into the corners. At a practice during this past regular season, LeClair stumbled and knocked down a teammate, who subsequently slid and took out coach Jacques Demers. This was rather ironic considering at the time, Demers was one of the few people standing up for LeClair amidst the torrent of criticism spewing from fans and reporters (although supposedly he was very forthright in his criticism toward LeClair in private).[46] Demers stuck with LeClair throughout the 1992–93 regular season, one in which he tallied 19 goals and 44 points. The coach was further vindicated this past spring when LeClair had netted a couple timely goals in earlier playoff rounds.

As LeClair skated on a line with more prolific offensive players a la Brian Bellows and Kirk Muller, plays were seldom drawn up with him as the primary scoring option. But now in overtime of Game 3, LeClair, a native New Englander who grew up adoring the Canadiens and hating the Bruins, had a chance to fulfill a childhood dream. Montreal had the puck deep in Los Angeles' zone, and with tight coverage on Muller and Bellows, LeClair was able to get off a couple clean shots on L.A. goalie Kelly Hrudey. After the second misfire, LeClair cradled the deflected puck and flipped it over Hrudey's left shoulder thirty-four seconds into OT to give Montreal a 4–3 victory and 2–1 series advantage.

Two nights later, on June 7, Game 4 naturally went into overtime, but unlike the prior two contests, the Kings didn't fizzle within the first minute, as they mounted a furious attack on Roy in the extra session. Fortunately, though for the Canadiens, Roy was an impenetrable wall in the crease. (Perhaps the most iconic moment of the Finals was during this OT session when Roy thwarted Kings sniper Luc Robitaille. After making the save, Roy stared down and then winked at L.A.'s dejected Tomas Sandstrom, who was parked outside the crease, hoping to pounce on the deflected rubber. Television crews captured the gesture, one that perfectly embodied Roy's trademark swagger and instantaneously became part of his career highlight reel.) Meanwhile, on the other end of the ice, Roy's counterpart in Hrudey was similarly dominant at this juncture.

Just over five minutes into the OT session, LeClair moved the puck deep into L.A.'s zone down the left side on a 2-on-1 break. The only Kings defenseman back home was Darryl Sydor, who flung himself on the ice to seal off the passing lane. Realizing LeClair was going to shoot, Hrudey came out of the net to cut off LeClair's shooting angle. LeClair's shot went directly at Hrudey's chest, but the netminder couldn't hold on as the puck trickled behind the net where it found LeClair's stick. Now that Hrudey was out of position, LeClair easily converted the wraparound goal to give Montreal a 3–2 win and 3–1 series lead.

At this moment, perhaps the happiest place in Northern New England, if not the entire six-state region, was the Sherwin-Williams on North Main St. in St. Albans, managed by John's dad Robert, where a throng of townsfolk celebrated their most famous native being the Stanley Cup Finals hero for the second straight game.[47]

LeClair was an easy guy to root for. For one, he was exceedingly humble. (In a 1997 *Sports Illustrated* profile story, LeClair, by this point one of the league's better offensive players, looked back on the 1993 Stanley Cup Finals OT game-winners and admitted, "It's not as if I dominated the games and deserved to score. Did you see those goals? The first went off their guy [defenseman Darryl Sydor] into the net, and the other I took three swipes at.")[48] He also genuinely embraced his New England small town roots. Despite being away for months jetting from one major North American city to the next, LeClair, upon returning home to St. Albans each summer, never forgot that the general store was "Bill's Shop" and the gym was "Frank's workout place." And throughout his home state, LeClair performed exemplary charitable work, starting the John LeClair Foundation, coincidentally in 1993, which would raise hundreds of thousands of dollars for Vermont children's charities.[49]

In Montreal's locker room, the unassuming kid from St. Albans was everyone's new favorite teammate. For LeClair's Game 4 overtime heroics meant that an exhausted Canadiens team, one now coming off their 10th overtime game this postseason, was 60 minutes away from the greatest summer vacation ever.

After three consecutive OT thrillers, the decisive Game 5 back at the Montreal Forum was relatively anticlimactic.

But still bizarre.

In the biggest game of the season, Wayne Gretzky proved to be a non-factor. No goals. No assists. No points. No shots on net.

After leading all NHL scorers with 40 points in the postseason, Gretzky came up empty when his team needed him most. Their best player neutralized, the Kings were unable to generate much offense in the series' final showdown, an eventual 4–1 win for Montreal.

"There were lots of good players in the league," says Ed Ronan. "No one's going to argue that Wayne Gretzky wasn't the best player in the league as far as goals and assists. He certainly was. He was still very imposing at that time, even though it might have been just beyond his peak. He certainly had a great year that year.

"We did our job as far as stopping a very difficult player and just keeping him off the score sheet. I think it goes to guys saying, 'This is my job and this is my role, and I'm probably not going to get a lot of glory for this because it's not putting the puck in the net, but it's stopping another player.'

Maybe some of those things get overlooked a little bit. A lot of times you look at the goal scorers."[50]

Montreal was clinging to a 1–0 lead early in the second period when Marty McSorley wristed a puck from the slot that ricocheted off both posts before getting past Roy. No worries. Montreal quickly broke the tie on its next shift when Kirk Muller corralled the loose puck from an errant Vincent Damphousse wraparound attempt and banged it home from the top of the crease. (Decades later, Muller is still reminded that he was the last Canadian to score the go-ahead goal for a Canadian winning Cup team.) Minutes later, the Habs tacked on a power play goal and took a commanding 3–1 lead into the second intermission. After the break, light scoring forward Paul DiPietro, who had scored Montreal's first goal this evening, accounted for the final insurance goal with less than eight minutes remaining.

Clearly, Roy's glove and McSorley's stick were in the Kings' heads. They had endured three deflating OT losses in one week and on this evening rolled out a punchless offensive attack, from Gretzky on down. (The Kings fired only 19 shots on net the entire game. For comparison, a team getting off 19 shots in a period is not unheard of.)

"I can honestly tell you going into that game we were not just thinking about that [shutting down Wayne Gretzky]," says Brian Bellows. "I can tell you all we wanted to do was get out in front, stay in front. And when it's on your home ice, once you get a lead, you're just concentrating on playing the best defense you can. Because if you concentrate too much on Wayne then someone else would really catch you."[51]

The approach worked. Besides a Marty McSorley second period score, the Kings were silenced for the rest of a very frustrating evening as Roy remained indomitable in the crease.

Finally, for Montreal, a chance to exhale.

"What a great feeling. You're literally waiting for this your whole life," recalls Bellows. "At that time, we had a 4–1 lead—it just seemed insurmountable. At the time, you're just sitting on the bench going, 'This is fantastic.' You had a few shifts to reflect on it. You have a few minutes to reflect on the fact that you *are* going to win the Cup."[52]

Once Montreal skated away with the 4–1 series-clinching win, the primary narrative was now, rightfully, the marvelous performance by Roy, who once again snagged the Conn Smythe Trophy. Demers' audacity, LeClair's heroics, and Gretzky's disappearance in the decisive game were compelling storylines, but they all paled in comparison to Roy's otherworldly play in the three straight overtime sessions.

Of course, it was not just the final round in early June; it was (basically) all spring.

After dropping the postseason opener against the Nordiques in OT, the Canadiens didn't lose another one-goal game again. In the 10 consecutive overtime wins, Roy played 96 minutes and 39 seconds of sudden death hockey while turning away all 65 shots he faced. This after an underwhelming postseason performance in 1992, followed by an even more disappointing regular season. But he certainly atoned by mid-spring, and as the playoffs progressed, it almost seemed like the Canadiens were playing for overtime, as they would constantly dump the puck into their zone during the final minutes of regulation in a tied game. Once the puck dropped in overtime, a more rested Montreal offensive attack could let loose while knowing Roy had its back.

"When I think of the team, that's the reason I come up with [in] regards to how you can win 10 overtime games without somebody shooting it off somebody's pad in front of the net and the other team winning on a goal," says Ronan. "I don't think it was just luck. I think it was a lot about the individuals at that time maybe being somewhat underdogs, having the key component of Patrick Roy, and having a bunch of guys that knew that they couldn't afford to give a game away. We had to lay it on the line every day because we weren't maybe the most skilled team in the league at that time."[53]

"It [the ten consecutive overtime wins] wasn't really something we were aware of," reflects Kirk Muller. "At the time we were so into the moment of every game. I don't think it was till about halfway through later on that we were like, 'Oh boy, another overtime game.' I think Patrick had a big part in it, playing as well as he did. He was hard to beat. The way we played, we were all on a defensive kind of mode. All the games were tight and close so that gave it the opportunity that there were going to be one-goal type games. And just the way it all kind of transpired that we ended up with so many overtime games."[54]

Perhaps the most iconic postgame scene was when Guy Carbonneau, upon receiving the Cup from commissioner Gary Bettman, scanned the throng of revelers, league personnel, and media to locate veteran teammate Denis Savard. Montreal's hard-nosed captain handed Savard the trophy, believing there was no worthier recipient of hockey's most revered prize than the Quebec native who, despite being one of the most prolific goal scorers of the 1980s, spent the majority of his career toiling for non-contending Chicago Blackhawks teams. Savard, who couldn't stand Chicago head coach Mike Keenan, was traded to Montreal in 1990. At this point, Savard was nearing the end of a Hall of Fame career and while he was finally on a championship team, the Cup Finals were a bit of a letdown as a Game 1 knee injury relegated him to the bench for the remainder of the series. Carbonneau knew that wearing a suit and tie—rather than a hockey sweater and polyester shorts—during the on-ice celebration was maddening for Savard. Carbonneau's gesture beautifully symbolized the team's trademark qualities of selflessness and cohesion that had propelled them to this triumphant moment.

Meanwhile, this was not a Hollywood ending for the Kings. Los Angeles knew that these Montreal Canadiens were not the Pittsburgh Penguins of the early nineties nor the New York Islanders of the early eighties nor the Boston Bruins of the early seventies. Los Angeles knew that Montreal was a deep, but beatable squad, one that would have struggled to come back from a 2–0 deficit. Los Angeles knew that irrespective of Roy, Montreal was the beneficiary of a string of fortuitous events—just like nearly every other Stanley Cup champion.

"Even though we lost in five games, it was a lot closer of a series and very well could have gone the other way if a couple bounces had gone the other way in overtime," says Jimmy Carson.[55]

"Every game, they were so tight, so tight checking," says Pat Conacher. "It was great hockey. With the type of style that we played and the Montreal style, it was very entertaining. It was an exciting game for the people watching."[56]

The Kings would not return to the Stanley Cup Finals while Gretzky was onboard. (Immediately after this game, Gretzky, still bitter toward Kings management, again hinted at a possible retirement, which ultimately did not happen until years later. He would, however, briefly join the St. Louis Blues in 1996 before ending his career with the New York Rangers, never to return to the Stanley Cup Finals.) The Kings didn't just blow a chance to win a Stanley Cup. They blew a chance to win the first NHL title for Southern California, a region trying to establish itself in a sport dominated by frostier areas of North America. While nearly half the continent was tuned in.

Thus, memories of letting Roy and the Canadiens back into the series were impossible to forget.

"He [Roy] obviously was probably the main difference in that series, especially with the overtime games, and the saves he made in overtime to turn the game his team's way were pretty incredible," recalls Tony Granato. "He had the swagger that he showed in that series throughout his career and I think that's what made him so great and able to play and dominate for so long.

"I have a ton of respect for him [Roy] as a player and I had the opportunity to coach him in his last year of playing [for the Colorado Avalanche in 2003]. I looked at him and wanted to run him over a few times when I had flashbacks of the series."[57]

Seconds after the final horn, thousands of well-hydrated fans surged through the streets of downtown Montreal, looting and vandalizing businesses. It was sheer chaos. Forty-seven police cars were damaged, including eight that were demolished. Terrifying sounds of storefront window glass smashing and alarms blaring echoed through Ste.-Catherine Street. For hours. It took nearly a thousand law enforcement officers to subdue the riot, one that ultimately accounted for millions of dollars in damage and 115 arrests.[58]

Seven years earlier, the Montreal police had taken serious heat for not keeping things in order following the championship-clinching win against the Calgary Flames. Already skeptical of law enforcement's ability to control the masses, local shop owners vented frustration over the repeated Wild West atmosphere with one proprietor exclaiming, "The police are a bunch of idiots. Anyone else would have learned their lesson last time."[59]

(Members of the Los Angeles Kings had to stand in the aisles of the team bus, so they didn't get nailed by bricks thrown through the windows by fans.)

Of course, the raucous behavior was not only to glorify the Habs' title as many deranged "fans" exploited the celebratory atmosphere to steal high-end stereos and commit arson with minimal fear of adjudication. But a considerable number of Quebecers did engage in rather fanatical behavior, because they honestly believed they were celebrating the end of a drought as their Habs hadn't won the Cup since 1986 and the Great White North had been deprived of a title for two whole seasons. For Canadians, hockey was (and still is) more than a sport their ancestors had created. It was an institution ingrained in the daily fabric of their nation. After all, a hockey player is emblazoned on their currency and a puck is arguably a more iconic cultural symbol than is a maple leaf. An American team had no business hoisting Lord Stanley's Cup. One can only imagine the unruliness of the "revelry" if the Montreal fans knew what a real drought felt like. But at the time, conventional wisdom was that come June, Canadian teams would spray bubbly on the Stanley Cup trophy on a fairly regular basis. After the New York Islanders dynasty ended in 1984, the Edmonton Oilers and Calgary Flames had owned the balance of the 1980s, and the Montreal Canadiens and Toronto Maple Leafs appeared poised to continue representing Canada in the Stanley Cup Finals for years to come. None of the Original Six members from America (Boston Bruins, Chicago Blackhawks, Detroit Red Wings, and New York Rangers) appeared to be perennial title contenders. Meanwhile, the influx of fledgling franchises in milder climates that sported teal, turquoise, purple uniforms and tacky logos presumably would be an afterthought for many, many, many years.

Not exactly.

During the waning years of the 20th century and early years of the 21st, many NHL franchises either established roots in or relocated to warm climate cities (Dallas, Raleigh, Tampa Bay, Anaheim, Atlanta, Las Vegas, Sunrise, Phoenix), forever changing the game's landscape. In 1999, the Dallas Stars became the first Sun Belt team to win the Cup while the Tampa Bay Lightning, Carolina Hurricanes, and Anaheim Ducks would follow suit in the next century. The Kings ultimately rewarded their faithful by winning two Cups within three years, 2012–2014. This development, combined with the remarkable success of other American teams (namely the Detroit Red Wings, Chicago Blackhawks, and Pittsburgh Penguins) in the early 21st century, meant that the sport's original birthplace, Canada, with its classic NHL franchises and fervent fan bases, would be left out in the bone-chilling cold. Thus, the 1992–93 Montreal Canadiens would go down as the last Canadian team to capture a Stanley Cup in over a quarter-century.

"Not just the Montreal Canadiens, but the last Canadian hockey franchise [to win a Stanley Cup] is surprising and certainly when I was in the league at the time, we certainly wouldn't have thought that would have been possible," says Ed Ronan. "The Canadian franchises were very strong—certainly the days of Edmonton Oilers with Gretzky were not that long prior to my time there [Montreal]. We had very strong franchises in Montreal, Quebec. Definitely surprising to think that a Canadian team wouldn't win a Cup within this time frame. I feel fortunate just in general to have won the Stanley Cup and been a part of that team."[60]

In a sense, over the past few decades, the NHL's Southern Strategy has been a boon to hockey with expansion into new markets, many of which have become accustomed to postseason excitement every spring. No doubt, the extension of interest has been good for the league's coffers. But new American teams (and displaced Canadian ones) have shifted the game away from its Canadian roots, depriving its most devout fans of a chance to experience indescribable joy.

In retrospect, that the Montreal Canadiens won their 24th Stanley Cup on their hallowed home ice made the feat even more meaningful. The Montreal Forum opened its doors in 1924 and by the 1990s, like many other historic stadiums across North America, would soon be closing its doors. (The Montreal Canadiens would play their final game at the Montreal Forum in 1996.) Like other legacy franchises around the league, Montreal was now gearing up for not only a new wave of opponents but also a new home environment.

But on the night of June 9, 1993, the soon-to-be-defunct Montreal Forum, not the Great Western Forum nor one of the posh Sun Belt stadiums, was the setting for the last coronation of a Canadian team for a very, very long time.

"Looking back, Montreal has not won a Stanley Cup since and that Stanley Cup really cast off a glorious stadium with 24 Stanley Cups," says

Jimmy Carson, who even as an American playing for the LA Kings could acknowledge the magnitude of the moment. "The Forum was the church or the temple of hockey, etc. I played Junior Hockey in Montreal so to me the ultimate stadium was the Montreal Forum. The people there bleed hockey as their religion. When you went into the Forum, it was almost like sacred hockey grounds. I remember having lost the Stanley Cup and seeing their celebration, obviously very disappointed and upset. Then just thinking there for a moment, 'Well, this is pretty historic to be at the Forum.' I just remember looking around and you think about all the legends that were on that ice from [Jean] Béliveau to Maurice Richard. It was pretty amazing."[61]

5

Shot Heard 'Round North America

For the first time all year, Cito Gaston actually had to manage.

It happened on the afternoon of October 19, 1993, before Game 3 of the World Series.

After the Toronto Blue Jays and Philadelphia Phillies split the first two games in Toronto's SkyDome (playing under American League rules), the series shifted to the National League setting of Philadelphia's Veterans Stadium. With the pitcher hitting, either designated hitter Paul Molitor or first baseman John Olerud was going to sit. Both had stellar regular seasons; Olerud batting .363, Molitor .332. It was an embarrassment of riches—do you choose Olerud, the American League's leading hitter, or Molitor, the surefire Hall of Famer who was having a better postseason thus far?

As manager of the 1993 Toronto Blue Jays, Gaston had one of the easiest jobs in North American professional sports. He had one of the greatest, deepest lineups in baseball history with the top three hitters in the American League in Olerud, Molitor, and Roberto Alomar. And while the defending World Series champs were known for their prolific offense, they also had Gold Glove caliber defense at key positions and a serviceable pitching staff that had improved in the second half.

"Everybody knew exactly what he needed to do," says former Blue Jays middle infielder Alfredo Griffin. "Manager had to talk to nobody. Cito [Gaston] only had to get the pitchers out, that's it. Those guys hit-and-run on their own. They steal on their own. They do whatever they need to do. It was amazing.

"The '92 team, it wasn't that easy. I don't take anything away from '92. But inside I know the little things that happened, that didn't happen in '93."[1]

"Cito [Gaston] had a lot of talent there and I think he would be the first one to tell you, all he wanted to do was pencil them in and leave them alone and not screw it up," notes reliever Ken Dayley, who joined Toronto after having pitched for the Atlanta Braves and St. Louis Cardinals.

"Cito was pretty quiet. I think Cito pinch-hit 39 times that first year that we won the World Series and I'm like, 'Thirty-nine times? Whitey [Herzog] would do that in a month.'"[2]

This was an ideal scenario for any manager, particularly one like Gaston who had a natural inclination toward a laissez-faire approach. But as Game 3 neared, he had to make an executive decision. During this "dilemma," Gaston went with Molitor (without a peep from Olerud, ever the consummate teammate).

Despite acknowledging after the game that he was uncoordinated on a couple of plays in the field, Molitor led Toronto to a 10–3 romp in Game 3, going 3-for-4 with three RBI. For the rest of the week, Gaston wouldn't have to debate whether Molitor belonged in the starting lineup. The achy 37-year-old notched a pair of RBI in Game 4 and did so again during the title-clinching Game 6 win, finishing the series hitting .500 with two homers and eight RBI en route to being named the 1993 World Series MVP.

Even though Toronto right fielder Joe Carter, one of the game's premier right-handed sluggers, would hit the iconic walk-off home run in the bottom of the ninth inning of Game 6 to send Toronto to its second consecutive title.

At least in hindsight, Toronto's acquisition of Paul Molitor on December 7, 1992, was one of the most impactful free agent signings in the 1992–93 off-season. At the time, however, it was merely an afterthought.

Although Molitor was coming off an All-Star season in which he had batted .320, his signing was overshadowed by that of another free agent, two-time National League MVP Barry Bonds, who, a day earlier, had agreed to a six-year, $43.75 million pact with the San Francisco Giants, making him the highest-paid player in MLB history. (After the 1993 season, Bonds would be a three-time National League MVP.)

After the cash-strapped Milwaukee Brewers, for whom Molitor played 15 seasons, asked him to take a pay cut, Molitor went to the defending World Series champs, who were in need of another offensive threat when it became evident that slugger Dave Winfield was not going to re-sign. (Molitor didn't exactly cash in as a free agent, as his new contract with Toronto bumped up his prior year's salary less than $200,000.) Molitor was ticketed for Cooperstown but the transaction didn't even warrant its own article in the Sports section of most dailies. Meanwhile, the Bonds signing was the talk of the MLB off-season. Weeks of speculation over Bonds' destination ended with a massive press conference airing on networks across the country.

The contrast reflected the players' disparate personas—Bonds, the showboating egomaniac; Molitor, the game's most unheralded star. (After arriving in San Francisco later that spring, Bonds blasted an impressive home run during batting practice and reportedly turned to his new teammates and asked, "Am I not a special [expletive] person, or what?")[3] It also served as a strong reminder of the gaping disparity that continued to separate the haves and have-nots in baseball. A relatively big market team like San Francisco could spend lavishly on a prized free agent (at the time of the signing, Peter Magowan, the leader of the investment group that would soon purchase the Giants and prevent them from relocating to Tampa–St. Petersburg, remarked, "It's a lot of money, but there's only one Barry Bonds")[4] while a small market club like Milwaukee couldn't pony up a little more to re-sign the longtime face of the franchise who was still one of the top hitters in baseball and close friend of the club's owner, Bud Selig.

The significance of Paul Molitor switching AL teams was indisputable. With Molitor, the 1992 Brewers finished 92–70, four games behind first-place Toronto in the AL East. Without Molitor, the 1993 Brewers would finish 69–93, 26 games behind first-place Toronto in the AL East.

"Just going into that year ['93], we knew it was going to be that much more difficult to lose a guy that hits .300, 20 homers, and 40 doubles. You just don't replace someone like that," says B.J. Surhoff, Molitor's longtime friend and teammate in Milwaukee.

"He wasn't looking to leave Milwaukee. With the circumstances, he had no choice. I can't emphasize to you how much of a blow it was when the Blue Jays signed him [Molitor]."[5]

Blow.

A decade earlier for Molitor, that word had a far more profound meaning than a reference to his impact on the baseball diamond.

In the late 1970s/early 1980s, Major Leaguers were certainly not immune from the rampant popularity of cocaine in America. It was in the nascent, injury-riddled years of his illustrious career when Molitor started using cocaine, which became public in 1984, when drug dealer Tony Peters testified in court that he had sold cocaine to several Brewers players, including Molitor.

The low point was December 1980 when Molitor was house-sitting for his agent, Ron Simon. Simon later chronicled the episode in his book *The Game Behind the Game: Negotiating in the Big Leagues*.

> The police were called to my house on Christmas Day 1980. They had to break in to see if Paul Molitor was inside, dead or alive … [Molitor was] sleeping off a wild night of cocaine abuse.... On Christmas Eve, Paul invited some friends to my house for a cocaine party. After the revelers left, long after midnight, Paul was unable to sleep. High on cocaine, he stayed up all night. He unplugged all the telephones, then finally fell asleep somewhere between 6 and 7 a.m.

While he was sleeping, his parents, six sisters, and brother were gathering for a family Christmas dinner at his parents' St. Paul home. When Paul didn't show by 11:30 a.m., his family became concerned.[6]

No one was more concerned than his fiancée, Linda, who had threatened to leave Molitor if the substance abuse continued. Her future husband eventually awoke, realized the depths to which he had fallen, and beseeched God for help to overcome this addiction. While not seeking formal treatment, he resolved to make the new year one of sobriety.

Indeed, 1980 was the last year Paul Molitor snorted a line of cocaine.

But it was also the year in which he played only 111 games after pulling a muscle in his rib cage, the first of a litany of career-defining injuries. Between 1980 and 1986, Molitor was placed on the disabled list six times. A 1984 elbow injury nearly ended his career. His stellar 1987 season (39-game hitting streak) was tainted by missing 44 games due to a hamstring pull, groin pull, sore ankle, and puffy elbow. Yet he still finished atop the league leaders in doubles and runs scored. When he turned 30, Molitor estimated he had broken 10 different bones on the baseball diamond.

"How he got hurt for me explains the type of player he was," says Surhoff. "[In 1987] he tore his hamstring staying in a rundown. He was on third base, trying to go home, pulled up, stayed in a rundown for two, three, four throws, hopefully getting the runner on first to second.

"The way he played all-out, head-first, going home to second out of the box. I think the only guy I've ever seen score on a single from first. There weren't too many days when Paul was a hundred percent. He had his elbow reconstructed. I think one year he had three surgeries in one day at the end of the year.

"After my first couple years, I lived in Milwaukee and I worked out with him [Molitor] and I saw the effort and the work that he put in. I always wanted to be able to do some of the things he did. I spent a lot of days before the games playing cards with him, talking about the game. His instincts and his intelligence level were just tremendous. He's quieter. He and Robin [Yount] weren't real vocal guys. We all looked to them because of the way they played, the way they carried themselves, the way they showed up every single day and were professionals."[7]

There was one season that was not truncated due to injuries. And that was 1982, when the Brewers won the AL pennant and faced the St. Louis Cardinals in the World Series. As a 26-year-old third baseman, Molitor had five hits in his first World Series appearance (a 10–0 Game 1 win for Milwaukee). However, Milwaukee would lose the World Series in seven games, and never make it back. Now, approaching his late thirties and in the autumn years of his career, Molitor wanted another crack at the Fall

Classic. Joining Toronto represented his best and likely final chance to get a World Series ring.

"No disrespect to Paul Molitor, Hall of Famer, but he came to a team that was already pretty good," recalls Toronto's center fielder Devon White.[8]

But also, a team that stood to benefit from his hardball expertise.

"He [Molitor] was just very quiet, very calm, obviously very mature at that time," remembers pitcher Woody Williams, a rookie for Toronto during the 1993 season. "When he spoke, you listened. It's not that he commanded it, but his presence commanded it. Just incredible to be around. Incredible to learn how to be a professional ballplayer from him. I know that he dealt with a lot of injuries and a lot of setbacks in his life to get him to that point. Man, the Paul Molitor that I played with and got to see play on a daily basis was amazing."[9]

"Paul Molitor was always a favorite of mine when I was in high school, before I got drafted," says shortstop Dick Schofield, who was a reliable bench player for the 1993 Blue Jays.[10]

"I used to sit on the bench and just watch him because his hands through the strike zone were so quick," says Ken Dayley. "It was just incredible how quickly he could get his hands through the zone. I would watch him, trying to figure out how or why or what I would do to pitch to him if I had to. He was different from everybody else as far as his hands getting through the zone."[11]

"We did learn a lot from him [Molitor]," acknowledges White. "I think he learned a lot from us too, being a younger set of guys. The way he played blended in perfectly with how we were running the organization and what we were doing."[12]

Upon arriving at Toronto's spring training camp in February 1993, Paul Molitor said, "If you can't beat them, join them."[13]

No one could beat the Toronto Blue Jays in 1992. Not Molitor's former club, the Milwaukee Brewers. Not the Oakland Athletics, who lost in the ALCS. Not the Atlanta Braves, who lost in the World Series.

"The lineup we had was pretty impressive," says the gifted Jamaican-American center fielder Devon White. "Toronto at that time, from the late-Eighties to the mid–Nineties, was a team to be reckoned with. They had some good young ballplayers and they made some good decisions in bringing ballplayers there. As far as the lineup from top to bottom, it was awesome. The pitching staff we had, they were underrated. They carried us in a lot of ways, too."[14]

Yet there were questions as Spring Training commenced. Questions not just about replacing departing stars but about the team's cohesiveness and hunger to repeat as world champs.

Veteran pitcher Jack Morris was quoted in *Sports Illustrated*'s baseball preview issue as saying, "I've been on closer teams. We're good, but we have questions."[15]

Gracing the cover of that preview issue was ace pitcher David Cone. In a Kansas City Royals uniform. Cone had been a brilliant mid-season acquisition for the Jays in 1992 (2.55 ERA after coming over from the New York Mets), but he had defected to KC in free agency. The pitching staff was further attenuated when veteran lefty Jimmy Key signed with the divisional rival New York Yankees. And then, of course, there was outfielder Dave Winfield opting to return to his St. Paul roots by signing with the Minnesota Twins.

The skepticism was vindicated when Toronto finished April with an underwhelming 13–10 record and proceeded to drop seven of its first 10 games in May. The vaunted lineup was vastly underperforming ... with the exception of 24-year-old first baseman John Olerud, who was posing a serious threat to be the first hitter to eclipse the .400 mark since Ted Williams had hit .406 in 1941. By Mother's Day, as Toronto was mired in .500 land, Olerud was establishing himself as one of the best pure hitters in the game with a batting average hovering around .450. (First baseman Andrés Galarraga of the wildly popular expansion Colorado Rockies was tearing up the National League, hitting well over .400 in the early months. Like Olerud, Galarraga had previously enjoyed productive seasons, but never anything close to this breakthrough campaign.)

It was somewhat ironic that John Olerud was the most exciting part of the defending champs' early season. Whereas Molitor was often taciturn, perhaps a bit reserved, Olerud was borderline comatose. Olerud's resting heartbeat was once measured at 44 beats per minute. Longtime teammate Joe Carter would say that getting two sentences out of Olerud was a challenge. Former Toronto team president Paul Beeston once exclaimed, "John's so modest, if he hit a home run, he'd apologize for losing the ball."[16] Dick Schofield couldn't believe he found a teammate quieter than himself.

From a distance, Olerud was shy, soft-spoken, someone who didn't venture far from his locker. An avid reader, Olerud was perfectly content indulging in a political thriller like Robert Ludlum's *The Icarus Agenda* in the pregame clubhouse—while his teammates were playing video games and ping-pong. But once teammates got to know the man under the ubiquitous helmet, they realized he was a gentlemanly scholar who happened to play baseball for a living. The more they got to know him, the more they realized he was one of the most compassionate and calmest players to grace an MLB diamond. And as he became a breakout star during the 1993 season, baseball fans across North America learned about the secret behind the helmet.

5. Shot Heard 'Round North America

On January 11, 1989, as an undergrad at Washington State, Olerud was jogging with a teammate in the Hollingbery Fieldhouse, where he collapsed upon suffering a brain seizure. After vomiting through a 70-mile helicopter ride to a Spokane hospital, Olerud was diagnosed with having a subarachnoid hemorrhage, which triggered bleeding into the spinal column. *Baseball America*'s NCAA Player of the Year in 1988 (he was both a standout first baseman and pitcher) stayed in the hospital for approximately two weeks for further testing and, upon conclusion, was presumed ready for the 1989 season. At the time, Dr. Scott Carlson, one of the Pacific Northwest's most highly regarded neurologists, said, "He beat the odds tremendously. He's probably not going to have any problems at all."[17]

But a colleague of Olerud's father, Dr. John Olerud, a renowned dermatologist at the University of Washington Medical Center, was skeptical, suggesting that the son be X-rayed at additional angles. Upon further observation, doctors uncovered an aneurysm at the base of John Olerud's brain, which, if it re-bled, had a 70 percent chance of proving fatal. Olerud was scheduled to undergo six-hour surgery to remove the aneurysm on February 27, 1989. The surgery was not without peril. Doctors would be operating not only around the optic nerve but also around the brain's frontal lobe, which influences personality. It was also possible the operation could forever mar his hawkish eyesight and deft limberness.

Seven weeks after the surgery, a still even-keeled John Olerud rejoined the Washington State Cougars baseball team for his junior season.

"Once I made it through surgery, I could see clearly and move everything all right," Olerud told the *Los Angeles Times* in 1990. "I figured playing again was just a matter of getting my strength back. It wasn't like knee surgery or arm surgery, where you wonder if you'll run or throw the same. All the problems were in my head."[18]

The scholar-athlete finished his career at Washington State later that spring before getting drafted in the third round of the 1989 MLB Draft by Toronto, who saw no reason to have him dwindle in the Minor Leagues. Not even for one game. (Ironically, his father was a longtime Minor League catcher before going into medicine.) On September 3, 1989, less than a year removed from nearly succumbing to the ballooning of an artery in his brain, the sweet swinging Olerud was making his Major League debut—during a heated pennant race. Which, of course, didn't faze him after having stared down death on the operating table.

"Nobody can make him [John Olerud] lose his rhythm," says Alfredo Griffin. "He plays the game calmly. He lives his life calmly, doesn't get upset. You never see him bragging, throwing the helmet, throwing the bat. Never in 162 games. He never slammed his helmet. He never complained. Nothing bothered him. And I go, 'My God. This guy [Olerud]. To hit .300, I got

After surviving a life-threatening medical condition, John Olerud continued his spectacular collegiate career ... before going straight to the Majors (courtesy Washington State Athletics).

to do the things that this guy does? I don't think so.' I can't do that. My temper won't allow me to. But following him and watching everything he does, it was amazing. It was amazing. Great hitter. Great human being. Great teammate."[19]

"It was just incredible day in and day out, not only his preparation but the way he carried himself," recalls pitcher Woody Williams. "John was very cool, very calm, very quiet, but what a phenomenal guy, phenomenal athlete, never spent one day in the Minor Leagues. That's pretty darn good."[20]

Once the Blue Jays began snapping out of their early May funk (they finished the month going 13–5), they emerged as a serious threat to repeat. The depth of the lineup started proving immense. It wasn't just Olerud hovering around .400 or Molitor driving in runs like he had never done in Milwaukee. It was cleanup man Joe Carter being on pace for a career season. It was catcher Pat Borders being on pace for a career season. It was second baseman Roberto Alomar being a bona fide five-tool star. It was shortstop Tony Fernández, acquired mid–June from the New York Mets, hitting over .300. It was an offense that would finish the regular season with a .279 batting average while only getting shut out once. In the starting lineup, there were no automatic outs and the relatively thin bench could still provide an offensive spark on occasion, typically courtesy of utilityman Darnell Coles or backup catcher Randy Knorr.

And that was just the offense. Toronto's defense was astounding—especially up the middle.

Firstly, at second base, Alomar was a nightly highlight reel.

"Best second baseman I ever played with," says Alfredo Griffin. "I played with good second basemen. Robbie [Roberto Alomar] was a natural player. Everything he did was natural. He had the skills to do so and that's what made him so good for that position."[21]

"Robbie probably had the most raw talent. He didn't appear to have to work at it that badly," says Ken Dayley.[22]

"An exceptional talent, above and beyond just about everybody at that position at that time," recalls Dick Schofield. "There were some days he did things, I'm just like, 'How'd he do that?' It was just natural for him. He made plays offensively and defensively that were pretty exceptional. After a while, it became a norm. You kind of lose track of how great he was."[23]

(Back in the 1970s, a scout for the St. Louis Cardinals saw a *seven-year-old* Roberto Alomar playing pepper and told his father, former MLB second baseman Sandy Alomar, Sr., he was interested in signing him.)

Center fielder Devon White followed up his memorable catch of David Justice's deep liner in Game 3 of the 1992 World Series with yet another Gold Glove season. White's defensive play was astounding, so much so that he earned an All-Star nod in 1993 despite having downright pedestrian offensive numbers. Over his career, White won seven Gold Glove awards and in 1993, had twice as many outfield assists (six) as errors (three).

"I played with Gary Pettis and I thought he was outstanding, and Devo [Devon White] was equally as good," remembers Schofield. "It didn't even

In addition to being one of the greatest second basemen of all time, Roberto Alomar is also noted for his exemplary charitable work in his home of Puerto Rico. Here he is in his hometown of Salinas after Hurricane Maria. Alomar visited various communities and assisted with relief efforts by delivering water, food, and other necessities (courtesy Alomar Sports, Inc.).

look like he was running sometimes, and he'd take three steps and he'd cover half the outfield."[24]

"Devo and Robbie speak for themselves. In my mind, both are all-time greats at their positions," says Woody Williams. "They come around once in a generation, once every two generations. My job as a pitcher was to throw strikes, work ahead, work quickly, and keep the ball in the ballpark."[25]

This was no hyperbole. Particularly concerning Alomar, who, by 1993, was in the discussion for best all-around player of his generation and best defensive second baseman ever. This year, he hit .326, drove in 93 runs, and stole 55 bases. Over Toronto's two championship seasons, he accounted for only 19 errors. In truth, Alomar came into his own during the Toronto years (1991–1995), annually representing the club at the Midsummer Classic and emerging as quite possibly the most popular professional athlete in the entire province of Ontario—even though he didn't play hockey. (Alomar became such a high-profile celebrity that during an afternoon game versus the Baltimore Orioles on July 2, 1995, a maniacal female fan who had been stalking him went to the SkyDome with a loaded .22-caliber Smith and Wesson revolver, intent on killing the second baseman before turning the weapon on herself. When the gun-toting fan by the name of Tricia Miller arrived at the SkyDome hotel around 2 p.m. she asked security for medical assistance. The revolver in her purse was soon discovered, as was her intention, and Miller was subsequently arrested. While no shots were ever fired at Alomar, during his upcoming final months as a Blue Jay, he did fire some parting shots at management over the franchise's inability to re-sign core players.)

At shortstop, Fernández, though not as flashy as Alomar, showed why he had won four consecutive Gold Glove awards in the 1980s.

Aside from Iván "Pudge" Rodríguez of the Texas Rangers, Pat Borders was possibly the top defensive catcher in the American League. "Anything he [Borders] did offensively was just a bonus because he was so good at blocking balls, throwing runners out," says Williams.[26]

Although he displayed his flashiest glovework later in his career as a member of the New York Mets, John Olerud nearly always ensured his infield mates' rare errant throws didn't turn into errors.

By Father's Day, Toronto, now one of the most complete teams in baseball, was in the midst of its second seven-game winning streak. The Blue Jays grew accustomed to feasting on cellar dwellers of the American League West (California Angels, Minnesota Twins, and Oakland Athletics) and largely mediocre teams in the American League East (Boston Red Sox, New York Yankees). And on the heels of their white-hot June (19–9), the Blue Jays finished the first half with a 48–33 record. An impressive mark, but still not one commensurate with the team's exceptionally talented roster. Nevertheless, after a sluggish start, being 15 games over .500 and holding a two-game lead over the New York Yankees for first place in the AL East was at the very least, passable.

Then July reared its ugly head.

As hot as Toronto was in the second half of June (12–3), the first half of July was dreadful (the club opened the month at a 1–9 clip heading into the All-Star break).

For the lineup, the nadir occurred during July 4th weekend, when they visited the middling Kansas City Royals.

For Kansas City, baseball was not exactly a priority at this hour. All attention was on the upcoming NFL season as the Chiefs had recently acquired quarterback Joe Montana. Meanwhile, the Royals were mired in yet another so-so season while fan favorite George Brett was limping to the finish line of his outstanding career. But of more pressing concern was the biblical flooding ravaging the Midwest. By early July, intrepid Missourians were already withstanding the early effects of a cataclysmic weather phenomenon that would ultimately claim 50 lives, leave nearly 70,000 homeless, and cause approximately $12 billion in property and agricultural damage. Certainly, 1993 is a year indelibly seared into the psyches of countless Midwestern as it sparks ghastly memories of buried farmland, gutted homes, and boats trawling down roads. Yet for Kansas City, baseball proved to be a welcomed respite this holiday weekend as the Royals swept the Blue Jays, who scored only five runs over the series. The team's two biggest run producers, Joe Carter and Paul Molitor, had two hits combined in the three-game set.

The following weekend, the pitching staff was the weak link and Toronto was swept in a four-game series by the visiting Texas Rangers, a club barely treading above .500.

On the evening of Sunday, July 11, 1993, the unofficial first half of the MLB season had come to an end. Surely, Toronto had underachieved, only going 49–40. But they still held a half-game lead over the Detroit Tigers for first place in the AL East—and were sending a whopping seven players to Tuesday night's much-ballyhooed All-Star Game in Baltimore.

After the All-Star break, Toronto bounced back, closing out July by winning 11 of 16. But it was quite apparent that despite their tremendous lineup, they were not a team of burners. Aside from Roberto Alomar, Devon White, and occasionally Tony Fernández, there were virtually no other threats to swipe a bag. There weren't a lot of Rickey Henderson's on this team.

So, they acquired Rickey Henderson himself.

On July 31, 1993, Toronto GM Pat Gillick pulled off a nifty trade deadline deal, dealing a pair of prospects (reliever Steve Karsay and right fielder José Herrera) to the non-contending Oakland A's for Henderson. Though far less productive than he was while playing for the Yankees in the late eighties, or the A's in the early nineties, Henderson still posted a .356 OBP and swiped 22 bags while playing north of the border in August and September of 1993.

(Meanwhile, for the Oakland A's, it wasn't a good … or bad trade.

Henderson returned in 1994 while the returns from the trade were disappointing. The eventual journeyman Karsay only lasted a few years in Oakland and Herrera had 32 RBI over parts of two seasons for the A's.)

"We just needed that extra guy to get us over the top and I think he [Henderson] did it," says Devon White. "Throughout the years that I was in Toronto, the moves that the Blue Jays made during those years were great."[27]

(Perhaps the most impactful trade Gillick had orchestrated as Toronto's general manager was during the 1990 Winter Meetings when he dealt first baseman Fred McGriff—primarily to make John Olerud the full-time first baseman—and shortstop Tony Fernández to the San Diego Padres for Roberto Alomar and Joe Carter. Fortuitously, the cost-cutting Padres couldn't commit long-term to Fernández, so, after the 1992 season, they traded him to the Mets, where he played 48 games before being dealt back to Toronto for underachieving Darrin Jackson on June 11, 1993.)

With the newly acquired Henderson (a.k.a. "The Man of Steal") at the top of the order, Toronto could now manufacture more runs and rely less on a three-run homer from Joe Carter or two-run double from John Olerud. With this added dimension to their lineup, the Jays were emerging as a more well-rounded squad that was getting hot heading into the final, most important weeks of the season.

Toronto finished August on an 11–6 run, and, as the calendar flipped to September, held a 2.5 game lead on the New York Yankees. On paper, the AL East race was still alive but there just wasn't much buzz surrounding the Yankees, who, after going on a 12–3 run to finish July, had been playing .500 ball during the dog days of summer while their divisional foe was heating up. The Tri-State Region was teeming with frustrated fans after the Yankees were having another disappointing year despite having acquired Jimmy Key, Wade Boggs, and Paul O'Neill the prior off-season (along with having team owner George Steinbrenner reinstated from his infamous suspension). By early September, an upcoming Labor Day weekend series between the Yankees and Cleveland Indians in the Bronx was looking like it would be a snooze fest. In fact, on the afternoon of Saturday, September 4, steamy Yankee Stadium was not even half-full when lefty Jim Abbott took the hill for a Yankees team that had just dropped the series opener.

Abbott was the most improbable of baseball success stories. Born without his right hand, Abbott had learned to pitch with his left arm while resting his mitt on the end of his right forearm. After pitching the ball, Abbott would switch the glove to his left hand. He eventually mastered the cumbersome technique. After a standout career at Flint Central High School in Michigan, Abbott was recruited to pitch for the University of Michigan. He would win a gold medal during the 1988 Olympics before establishing himself as a solid middle-of-the-rotation starter for the California Angels, for whom he had won 47 games over four seasons. Now, in 1993, his first year in pinstripes, Abbott was not having his best season, but remained on pace for double-digit wins and a respectable ERA. And on this late summer afternoon, Abbott, although far from overpowering (three strikeouts, five walks), no-hit a Cleveland Indians team that had six players batting .298 or higher. Abbott induced a whopping 17 ground outs to deliver the franchise's first no-no since Dave Righetti tossed one a decade earlier. After Cleveland's second baseman Carlos Baerga grounded out weakly to shortstop Randy Velarde for the game's final out, the Yankees mobbed Abbott as if he had just fanned the last batter to win the pennant.

(After New York's 4–0 win, when Abbott and his wife Dana met star first baseman Don Mattingly for dinner at an Upper East Side restaurant, Abbott was swamped by fans requesting his autograph on early copies of the next day's paper. For one night at least, baseball was back in the Big Apple.[28])

Less than two weeks later, MLB's other Canadian franchise, the Montreal Expos, called up outfielder Curtis Pride for his big-league debut. Pride was a gifted multi-sport athlete who played basketball at the College of William and Mary before joining the New York Mets organization and later the Expos. But the versatile athleticism (he absolutely dazzled on the soccer field) was hardly the most impressive aspect of Pride's story. On the evening of September 17, 1993, Pride, who had contracted rubella during his mother's pregnancy, which left him with severely limited residual hearing, was now the first deaf big leaguer since 1945. In his second MLB at-bat, the pride of Silver Spring, Maryland, stroked a pinch-hit double off Bobby Thigpen of the Philadelphia Phillies. When time was called, Montreal third base coach Jerry Manuel jogged over to Pride, motioning for him to remove his helmet. Initially, Pride wondered if there was a defect. Then he looked around and realized the need to acknowledge the 45,757 fans at Olympic Stadium who had erupted in a standing ovation.[29] Their enthusiasm reflected universal appreciation for how tracking down 400-foot line drives and running the bases is exponentially more difficult when one can't hear the crack of the bat or directions from a base coach. After short stints with Montreal in 1993 and 1995, Pride would go on to become a valuable bench player for several teams before being named MLB's Ambassador for Inclusion as a middle-aged man in retirement.

Other highlights of the season's spectacular ending included Mark Whiten's four-homer, 12-RBI game, the last division race before the Wild Card Era (the Atlanta Braves edged the 103-win San Francisco Giants for the NL West crown), the final days of Nolan Ryan's, George Brett's, and Robin Yount's Hall of Fame careers, and Dave Winfield's 3,000th career hit.

But first and foremost, the last month of the 1993 regular season was

5. Shot Heard 'Round North America

truly a September to remember for the feats achieved by Americans with disabilities.

September 1993 was a month of highly intriguing baseball ... unless you were a member of the Toronto Blue Jays or Chicago White Sox.

By midmonth, it was apparent that the two clubs would square off in the ALCS. Ultimately, the AL East proved to be a rather weak division. The Yankees, the only real threat to Toronto's quest to repeat as division champs, would fade quickly after Labor Day weekend, finishing seven games out. In the AL West, the White Sox toppled the second-place Texas Rangers by eight games. For both clubs, the final days of the regular season were full of virtually glorified exhibition games.

Eventually October baseball arrived, and for many folks, it was a necessary diversion from disturbing news overseas, specifically the Battle of Mogadishu, one of the deadliest engagements the United States had experienced since Vietnam. Thankfully, compelling postseason competition awaited as the Blue Jays faced a formidable opponent in the White Sox in the league championship series.

The South Siders had an excellent regular season (94–68) and certain individuals would be rewarded for their banner years. First baseman Frank Thomas would be named AL MVP. Jack McDowell, the ace of the young and promising pitching staff, would receive the AL Cy Young award. Skipper Gene Lamont would be tabbed AL Manager of the Year.

However, on paper, the White Sox didn't have the world's greatest lineup. It wasn't exactly the 1927 New York Yankees, 1953 Brooklyn Dodgers, or 1976 Cincinnati Reds. Nor was it the 1993 Toronto Blue Jays. Nevertheless, Chicago's lineup featured Thomas, a prolific slugger with a Popeye body and uncanny plate discipline. Aging leadoff man Tim Raines still wreaked havoc on the basepaths and third baseman Robin Ventura was a threat in the middle of the order. The White Sox also had home-field advantage because even though the Blue Jays had a superior record, home-field advantage in the league championship series used to alternate between divisions and this year it was the AL West's turn.

Game 1 of the ALCS was slated for October 5—what was shaping up to be a special day for Chicago sports as the White Sox were playing in their first postseason game since 1983. Oh, and MICHAEL JORDAN was slated to throw out the ceremonial first pitch.

It soon turned hideous.

Once the game got underway following Jordan's pregame toss, rumors of his premature retirement started swirling around Comiskey Park. (Supposedly, before the game, Jordan had told several White Sox players about his imminent decision.) As the evening dragged on, speculation over the

American League MVP Frank Thomas and teammate Bo Jackson celebrate Chicago's first division title in a decade (photograph provided by Ron Vesely, Chicago White Sox).

depressing possibility of life without MJ started diverting fans' attention from the diamond.

Irrespective of Jordan's career status, perhaps the worthier honoree to throw out the first pitch would have been Carlton Fisk, the erstwhile face of the franchise, whose Hall of Fame career had mercifully ended in late June when he was released by the White Sox in order to make room for rookie pitcher Rodney Bolton. The White Sox brass had no use for a 45-year-old catcher hitting .189 and there was still lingering resentment over past off-season contract haggles which ended with Fisk accepting a $650,000 Minor League contract with the guarantee of promotion (he was excluded from the White Sox 40-man roster so that the team could protect younger guys in the National League expansion draft). Fisk was not asked to be part of the pregame on-field ceremonies nor was he invited to watch the game from an executive suite. Putting aside his contentious relationship with management, Fisk wanted to wish his close friends/former teammates well so before Game 1, he and pitcher Donn Pall, who had been traded late in the season, swung by the home clubhouse.

More like the entrance to the home clubhouse.

When the players strolled through the bowels of Comiskey Park and approached the regular clubhouse security guard, he paused, fidgeted, and then mumbled that per MLB protocol, the two were barred entrance.

Pall had a ticket and watched the game from the stands while Fisk, lacking a credential or ticket, was banished from the premises as if he were a trespasser.[30]

When word got out about the disgraceful incident, the press asked David Schaeffer, director of park ops, for comment. Schaeffer subsequently explained, "He had no tickets and no credentials. I just can't let Carlton stay around."[31]

Apparently, being Chicago's all-time leader in home runs (214) and longtime team captain who had represented the club during four All-Star Games did not suffice. The response reeked of pettiness on behalf of team owner Jerry Reinsdorf and general manager Ron Schueler.

Once the public became aware of the situation, it was an utter embarrassment for the franchise. In hindsight, perhaps even more so than ace Jack McDowell's performance (seven earned runs, 13 hits) in the White Sox' 7–3 defeat to the Blue Jays.

In terms of what transpired on the field, this was one sloppy postseason game. For both teams, truthfully. Toronto starter Juan Guzmán didn't get hammered like McDowell did, but was ridiculously wild, uncorking three wild pitches, plunking a batter, and issuing eight (yes, eight!) walks. Yet it mattered not as his lineup banged out 17 hits in the 7–3 win.

It was written in the next day's *Chicago Tribune*:

> Keep the facts straight. It's Michael Jordan who's supposed to be announcing his retirement, not the White Sox.
> The Sox, however, certainly played as if they were ready to retire Tuesday night, going down meek as lambs to the slaughter with a 7–3 loss to the Toronto Blue Jays in Game 1 of the American League Championship Series.[32]

The next day, the White Sox were very happy to have the distraction of MJ's impending retirement as they continued to appear overmatched by the Blue Jays in this league championship series.

In Game 2, Toronto's veteran righty Dave Stewart, who pitched for Oakland against Toronto in the 1992 ALCS, delivered a gutsy performance, scattering four hits over six innings of one-run ball. Chicago's only real threat came in the sixth, when it loaded the bases with nobody out. Stewart worked out of the jam unscathed, upping his career postseason record to 7–0 as Toronto won 3–1 to take a commanding 2–0 lead as the series shifted to Canada.

"Dave Stewart, his presence was big not only for me, but for a lot of the pitchers, a lot of the players just because of who he was," recalls righty Woody Williams. "He was a gentle, gentle man. It all changed when you went between the lines because he wanted to rip your heart out and hand it back to you."[33]

(By the early nineties, Stewart was one of the most highly-respected players in MLB, as most had forgotten a rather unfortunate incident in 1985 when, as a member of the Texas Rangers, he was arrested in Los Angeles for engaging in lewd conduct with a prostitute, one who turned out to be a transvestite.)

As masterful as Stewart was in Game 2, the primary storyline in the early part of the series was that the White Sox' lack of lineup depth was getting exposed. If Toronto's staff could work around Frank Thomas (which it did, eventually walking the imposing slugger 10 times in the series), there were virtually no other power threats.

Certainly, Thomas, a.k.a. "The Big Hurt," deserved his AL MVP award that year.

"He [Thomas] was so gifted as a hitter," says Jason Bere, who was a rookie pitcher on the 1993 White Sox. "He had the ability to hit really good pitching, the best pitching out there, which I guess that's probably how you get to the Hall of Fame, putting up those numbers. He took pride in his offense and took pride in situations. He would make sure he got the ball to the outfield for the sac fly to do his job. When you look at his numbers through that era, too, he wasn't the guy hitting 60 [home runs] a year. He was just the epitome of consistency, hitting .300, walking 100 times, scoring 100 runs, knocking in 100. It was just so consistent and that was kind of the way he played every day."[34]

Toronto had a chance to bury Chicago in Game 3 back at the Sky-Dome, but Pat Hentgen, the young 19-game winner, struggled mightily, giving up six runs over three innings in the 6–1 loss. Toronto's 2–0 series lead was halved and suddenly, the ALCS was a series again. Especially because the Blue Jays were going with back-of-the-rotation starter Todd Stottlemyre for Game 4.

In this pivotal game, Stottlemyre performed like a pitcher coming off a regular season in which he finished 11–12 with a 4.84 ERA. The tall righty, whose father, Mel, pitched for the New York Yankees against the St. Louis Cardinals in the classic 1964 World Series, gave up five earned runs and was pulled after six frames.

Yet the Jays had a chance because their offense bounced back. Chicago's starter Jason Bere coasted through his first two innings of postseason baseball before Toronto's vaunted lineup touched him for three runs in the third on an RBI double by Alomar and two-run single by Carter.

This was the most critical juncture in the series (with a win, the White Sox would tie the series 2–2 and reclaim home-field advantage) and perhaps Gene Lamont had made a mistake by going with the rookie Bere over Tim Belcher, an established veteran with a strong postseason track record.

"It was a quick outing," recalls Bere. "I only went two and a third.

At the time they [the Blue Jays] had traded to get Rickey Henderson, so that was the first time I had ever faced him. Started off great, warmup felt great, came out and got Rickey to strike out on three pitches. Command was good, everything was fine, the nerves were in check, but I ended up in the third inning running into trouble and they went with Tim Belcher to relieve me.

"Going into the postseason we had traded for Belcher at the deadline, and down the stretch I had finished pretty strong so there was kind of a debate over whether they would go with me, being the young kid, or someone a little more established like Belcher. Gene Lamont gave the ball to me probably because of the stretch I had at the end. It didn't work out that day."[35]

Ultimately, it made no difference in the outcome. After Chicago regained the lead in the sixth courtesy of a Frank Thomas solo-shot and two-run triple by Lance Johnson, the bullpen delivered a shutdown performance down the stretch as Chicago won 7–4.

With Toronto's hurlers mostly pitching around Thomas, the spark plug for Chicago's offense was the pesky Tim Raines. In Games 3 and 4, Tim "Rock" Raines was a hit machine, going a combined 7–10 with three doubles—one of the most memorable performances of his Hall of Fame career. Raines was never a dominant player, the best player at his position, or even an All-Star after 1987. But he was, simply put, the guy you never wanted to face.

And the guy you always wanted in your clubhouse.

"Rock [Tim Raines] was probably the one who kept everybody the loosest," Bere recalls while trying to keep a straight face. "He had been around the game for so long, always joking and messing with people. This was in '93 so he probably wasn't necessarily the base stealing threat that he had been prior, but there was still the threat of speed. At the time, Rock was in left. Obviously, played a solid outfield."[36]

In addition to Raines, fellow veteran outfielder Lance Johnson had a monster Game 4 (2–4, four RBI) to help the White Sox even the series.

It was now a best-of-three series. Toronto was in trouble.

Sort of.

"It was interesting, when the series was tied 2–2, *it didn't always necessarily feel like it was tied and we were right there* because it was Toronto and [of] what they had done in the past," says Bere. "Obviously, a really good lineup. Any postseason lineup is going to be good but they [Blue Jays] were real solid top to bottom. They had speed, they had power, they hit for average, they were a pretty complete lineup."[37]

And they were also facing Jack McDowell in Game 5. A pitcher who hadn't beaten them since July 1991.

With basically a two-pitch arsenal consistent of a fastball and splitter, "Black Jack" McDowell was one of the biggest reasons why Chicago won the AL West for the first time in a decade. But, after his second false start of the ALCS (this time he got yanked in the third inning after giving up three runs), he was one of the biggest reasons why the White Sox were not going to win the AL pennant for the first time since 1959.

After the 5–3 Toronto win, when asked why Toronto was his personal kryptonite, a testy McDowell responded, "If I knew what [the problem was against Toronto] I probably would have made an adjustment by now, don't you figure?"[38]

McDowell was known for losing his cool—the most infamous incident occurring in 1995 when, in his first (and only) year in pinstripes, he flipped off a jeering Yankee Stadium upon being lifted from a mid-July game. While never a fan favorite, "Black Jack" was popular in the clubhouse, particularly among younger pitchers whom he often took out to dinner to discuss situational pitching. McDowell was the trusted leader of a young staff, the guy whom other hurlers looked to for answers. But this October, McDowell (10.00 ERA in the ALCS) had no answers for Toronto's stacked lineup, which was a huge letdown for Chicago. (Although it should be noted that Chicago's infield defense was uncharacteristically sloppy while Bo Jackson, still a key cog in the lineup despite having recently undergone major hip reconstruction surgery, went hitless in the series.)

A couple evenings later, the series moved back to Chicago where Toronto won the pennant-clinching game 6–3 behind another clutch performance from Stewart (7⅓-innings of four-hit ball) who improved his postseason record to 8–0.

In his media session following Game 6, the hard-throwing, soft-speaking veteran righty who was named ALCS MVP told reporters, "I enjoy the fact that I'm sitting here and they're in their locker room and going home."[39]

For the unfailingly polite, sometimes nondescript Blue Jays, the frank remark was like an outburst of emotion.

Especially compared to the rather colorful cast of Philadelphia Phillies characters who would capture the NL pennant the following evening.

Indeed, awaiting the Toronto Blue Jays in the 1993 World Series were the out of nowhere Phillies, a squad known for beards, bellies, and biceps.

And, well, rather unconventional behavior.

That these guys were roaming the streets of Philadelphia was a bit unsettling.

Ace Curt Schilling would warn visitors entering their clubhouse, "Be careful, the animals are out of their cages."[40]

Closer Mitch "Wild Thing" Williams would eat brick-sized burritos at 9:30 a.m. with a shirtsleeve pulled smugly over his head and Tasmanian Devil prominently tattooed on his right shoulder.[41]

First baseman John Kruk, born on the West Virginia panhandle, proudly referred to himself as a "hillbilly." The slovenly looking Kruk had copious body fat, shaggy hair, and fondness for beer hops. Kruk once had a Minor League manager who said he reminded him of an Alabama truck driver.[42]

Third baseman Dave Hollins was so intense that teammate Pete Incaviglia once remarked, "He'd cut his finger off to win a game."[43]

Center fielder Lenny Dykstra and catcher Darren Daulton were almost killed in a 1991 car crash in the Philly suburbs. With a blood alcohol level over 0.10 percent (the state limit), Dykstra slammed his freshly minted Mercedes-Benz into two trees while driving home from Kruk's bachelor party with Daulton riding shotgun. Dykstra suffered a broken right collarbone, fractured right cheekbone, and three broken ribs, Daulton a fractured left eye socket, scratched left cornea, and heart bruise.

(While both Dykstra and Daulton would recover and enjoy productive careers well into the 1990s, their post-playing days were rather bleak. In 2017, Daulton would lose his battle with brain cancer at age 55. Dykstra, meanwhile, endured years of financial and legal issues, and at one point was in such dire straits that he moved to Las Vegas where he moonlighted as a male gigolo for elderly women.)

The horrific car accident set the tone for the 1991 season as the Phillies stumbled to a 78–84 finish. The 1992 season was even worse as the Phils finished in the cellar of the NL East with a 70–92 mark. The franchise was in a tailspin.

And then 1993 occurred.

Miraculously, this year's edition won the NL East with a 97–65 record before knocking off Atlanta in the NLCS. (It didn't hurt that two new regular season opponents in 1993 were the expansion Colorado Rockies and Florida Marlins.) Indeed, the 1993 Philadelphia Phillies Macho Row team were the National League's answer to the 1967 Boston Red Sox Impossible Dream team. And at the onset of the 1993 World Series, this team of wildly inappropriate, emotionally unstable misfits posed a legitimate threat to dethrone the Toronto Blue Jays.

"As a team, we weren't supposed to do well at all," remembers Philadelphia second baseman Mickey Morandini. "We finished last in all the major publications. For the most part we had a veteran team, had made some trades, and got some guys over who had some success in the big leagues. Nothing was really expected of us from Day One. We came out and we played really well. I'm pretty sure we were in first place from the first couple days on throughout the rest of the year. Just everything clicked. Jim

Fregosi pulled all the right strings. We had guys who had career years. Just a hell of a year.

"We had the best leader [Darren Daulton] that I've ever had in the clubhouse. No question about it. He knew when to get on players. He knew when to call guys together and say, 'Let's pick it up a little bit' or 'Hey, we're going to be all right.' For a guy who had seven or eight knee surgeries, and he's out there catching every day, we had a lot of respect for him. He really brought that team together.

"We had a staff that had some veteran guys and a couple young guys. Tommy Greene was young at the time, pitched very well. Ben Revere pitched very well. Of course, we had [Curt] Schilling and Danny Jackson. It was a team that had a lot of veterans but had some young players on it. We got along really well, and we had a great coaching staff."[44] (The elder statesman of the staff was revered pitching coach Johnny Podres, a former World Series MVP for the Brooklyn Dodgers.)

It was, in fact, Morandini who provided one of the timeliest hits in the NLCS. Given no chance to beat an immensely talented Braves team, one that had acquired slugger Fred McGriff in a lopsided mid-season trade, the Phillies built a 3–2 series lead with the NLCS moving back to Philadelphia for Game 6. On this evening, Atlanta's ace Greg Maddux was not himself, yet Maddux and the Braves were one out away from getting out of the sixth inning, only trailing 4–1. Then, if Atlanta could crack into Philadelphia's shaky bullpen and launch a comeback, it had Tom Glavine slated for Game 7 ... and, thus, a likely World Series rematch against the Blue Jays.

However, the Baseball Gods were still smiling on the Phillies, as Atlanta skipper Bobby Cox left Maddux in for one batter too long. With two runners on, Morandini stroked a two-out, bases-clearing triple, upping Philadelphia's lead to 6–1, effectively ending the series.

"I had a lot of success off [Greg] Maddux throughout my career," recalls Morandini. "He walked Lenny [Dykstra] to get to me and I swung at a couple pitches out of the zone early in that at-bat and he hung a changeup to me that I rifled down the right field line for a triple. It was a big hit for us, expanded the lead, gave us a little bit of a cushion late in the game, and I think we ended up winning 6–3."[45]

They did. And by upsetting the heavily favored Braves, the Phillies were on their way to the club's first World Series since Ronald Reagan was in office. Which was particularly meaningful to Philadelphia, given that its two most celebrated athletes, Charles Barkley and Reggie White, had recently left town.

"[There's] nothing better than playing in front of fifty, sixty thousand screaming Philly fans. It was a tremendous year and the fans really supported us," says Morandini.[46]

While the Philly fanatics went nuts around the concrete donut that was the Vet, Mitch Williams ripped off his shirt on the mound. Moments later in the clubhouse, John Kruk told reporters, "The Braves are the most arrogant people in the world. But we didn't care who they were or what they thought. Our feeling was they could just kiss our asses."[47]

As the 1993 World Series dawned, the contrast between pennant winners was astounding. The Phillies were brash. The Blue Jays were mild-mannered. The Phillies had a roster largely comprised of overachievers with not one surefire Hall of Famer. The Blue Jays had a star-studded roster with multiple guys headed to Cooperstown.

Unsurprisingly, the Toronto media and fans were dismissive of the scrappy underdogs. The *Toronto Star* described the Phillies as "a motley crew of hairy, beer-soused brutes who haven't a hope of beating our beloved Boys of Summer."[48]

The prediction was all but vindicated in Toronto's 8–5 triumph in Game 1. Eight Blue Jays recorded at least one hit, and six drove in at least one run. Meanwhile, the Phillies blew leads of 2–0, 3–2, and 4–3 as Schilling (eight hits, six earned runs) scuffled.

The following evening, Game 2 loomed as a mismatch ... at least on paper.

Dave Stewart, the hottest pitcher on the planet, was set to duel Philadelphia's Terry Mulholland, who, after an All-Star first half, had tailed off considerably over the past few months. While both pitchers were far from effective, Stewart was particularly disappointing (four walks, five earned runs) given how utterly dominant he had been in the ALCS. Instead, the night belonged to Philadelphia outfielder Jim Eisenreich, who capped a five-run third with a three-run blast off Stewart. Eisenreich paced a Philly offense that bailed out Mulholland with a 12-hit barrage on the way to the 6–4 series-tying victory.

With 32 career regular season homers to his name, Eisenreich was an unlikely hero to deliver the clutch home run in a World Series game—especially while representing the Phillies. Certainly, Eisenreich was not your typical 1993 Philadelphia Phillie as he was subdued and clean-shaven. More importantly, he was also not your typical professional athlete. He was one of the precious few who suffered from Tourette Syndrome, a neurological disorder that can trigger uncontrollable muscle movements. In his twenties, his condition had grown so burdensome that he had to sit out the 1985 and 1986 seasons. But with medication, he battled back to have a very respectable career in Kansas City before signing with Philadelphia as a free agent in January 1993. With reporters swarming his locker following the Game 2 heroics, Eisenreich acknowledged, "Sure, [Tourette] has been something I don't like to think about. But it's part of life, and I deal with it."[49]

As the midnight hour approached, the baseball scribes scurried back to the press box to file another inspirational story about a ballplayer who overcame his disabilities to thrive in the 1993 season.

The buzz surrounding the World Series returning to Philadelphia for the first time in over a decade was tempered by the windswept rain swirling around Veterans Stadium in the hours leading up to Game 3. Not exactly a setting of autumnal bliss befitting a World Series game. That afternoon, as sheets of rain continued to blanket the Vet's carpet field, Cito Gaston sat inside the visiting clubhouse filling out his lineup card.

One that did not include the American League's leading hitter in John Olerud.

It didn't take long for Gaston to feel justified for having benched Olerud to get Paul Molitor's bat in the lineup. Following a 70-minute rain delay, in the top of the first inning, Molitor tripled home two runs and two innings later blasted a solo shot. The Toronto offense went on a 13-hit spree, highlighted by not only Molitor's performance but also Roberto Alomar's (4–5, 2 RBI) and Tony Fernández's (2–3, 2 RBI). Following his miserable ALCS outing, starter Pat Hentgen was dynamite, scattering five hits over six innings of one-run ball. At 12:40 a.m., Toronto closer Duane Ward fanned John Kruk for the final out of his team's 10–3 victory.

But what transpired in Game 3 would soon get overlooked, because later that day, one of the most maddening, bizarre, and memorable games in World Series history would ensue.

Traditionally, classic World Series games are pitching duels, not sloppily played affairs resembling slo-pitch softball games.

Not so much for Game 4 of the 1993 World Series.

With John Olerud back in the lineup (Paul Molitor replaced Ed Sprague at third base), Toronto's lineup overcame deficits of 6–3, 12–7, and 14–9 before earning the 15–14 win, marking the highest-scoring game in postseason history. It was four hours and fourteen minutes of offensive fireworks, rancid pitching, and, oddly, given the misty and drizzly conditions, errorless baseball. This was a game in which there were more runs scored (29) than strikes thrown (26) by ultra-intense Toronto starter Todd Stottlemyre (who had been cited by Philadelphia Mayor/fanboy Ed Rendell as the reason why the Blue Jays could not sweep the Phillies); the losing team scored 14 runs; the winning team didn't homer despite scoring 15 runs; there were 367 pitches tossed.

And while for the Blue Jays, Tony Fernández (five RBI), Devon White (four RBI), and Paul Molitor (two RBI) all had great nights, it was Philadelphia's make-it-happen center fielder Lenny Dykstra who delivered one of the most remarkable offensive performances in World Series history. The final stat line for arguably the team's most valuable player read: two HR, four RBI, four runs scored.

"He [Dykstra] was a special player that year," says Mickey Morandini. "Just from Day One on, [he was] a grinder, a guy who knew how to play the game, played hard, knew how to work the count, knew what pitches to look for, knew the strike zone real well, played a good center field, could steal a base. He was just an all-around beast that year. He got on base consistently every game. You know who those special players are when you're in big situations."[50]

But unfortunately for the Phillies, Dykstra was unable to pitch.

"Well, we started out the game pretty hot," recalls Devon White. "I think we scored in the first inning, we scored in the second inning. Philadelphia kept coming back. I think they took the lead, and we took back the lead. We thought [with] us scoring that many runs, we were like, 'OK, we've got it.' But they just kept coming back. Lenny Dykstra had a great series. We would battle, we outlasted them, and we outpitched them."[51]

"That game in Philadelphia [Game 4], I can't describe that game. It's unbelievable. Oh my God, what a game. I don't think I ever saw a game like that in my career," recalls Alfredo Griffin.[52]

Never had a World Series game taken so long to complete, and afterward, in the home clubhouse, the Phillies appeared finished. The Blue Jays, up 3–1 in the series, were now one win from their second consecutive championship and the Phillies' pitching staff, particularly closer Mitch Williams, didn't instill any confidence in Philly fans that Toronto's lineup could be silenced in three consecutive games.

Naturally, the Phillies provided some amusing postgame sound bites.

Mitch Williams: "I stunk. I've stunk before except tonight it was on national TV in front of the whole country instead of our little cable TV station here in Philadelphia. That was the only difference."[53]

Lenny Dykstra: "You don't have to be a baseball genius to figure out that we should have won that game."[54]

Less than 24 hours after his fellow staff members were brutalized for 15 runs and 18 hits, Curt Schilling delivered a godsend performance in Game 5, one that catapulted Philadelphia to a 2–0 win and served as a harbinger of personal greatness in future Octobers. The burly right-hander, virtue of his five-hit, complete game shutout (in which he threw 147 pitches), nearly single-handedly prevented Toronto from holding a series-clinching party on the Veterans Stadium turf. (In the eighth inning, a beleaguered Schilling glanced over to his team's bullpen, one that was inactive. Unsurprisingly, with the relief corps taxed from the prior night's marathon game, Game 5 was Schilling's to finish.)

"He [Schilling] obviously was a big-game pitcher," says Morandini. "He thrived in that situation. Anytime there was a big game to be won, he wanted to be on that mound. He took a lot of pride in what he did. He studied film. He was always watching film and jotting stuff down. He knew exactly what he wanted to throw before the game even started, how he wanted to pitch each batter in certain situations, who he wasn't going to let beat him. He was a big-game pitcher and he came through for us obviously in those playoffs."[55]

With its formidable lineup getting shut out for the first time since June, Toronto, clinging to a 3–2 series lead, now breathed life into a Philadelphia team that was emotionally spent after a heartbreaking Game 4.

As Canada was preparing for one of its most significant nationwide elections ever on Monday, October 25, the World Series returned to Toronto on the evening of Saturday, October 23.

In the bottom of the fifth inning of Game 6, Toronto built a comfortable 5–1 lead after Paul Molitor took Phillies starter Terry Mulholland deep. Clearly, Mulholland was not long for the evening. Which meant that Toronto would get another opportunity to feast on the Philly bullpen, one that John Kruk had described as "shell-shocked" earlier in the series. The likely scenario was that Toronto starter Dave Stewart would continue cruising and the Jays lineup would plate insurance runs against Philly's battered middle relievers. Meanwhile, closer Mitch Williams, who was now an emotional wreck after his Game 4 implosion amid a recent string of subpar outings, would be spared further agony.

However, the Phillies didn't go quietly as they scored five runs in the top of the seventh inning to take a 6–5 lead. After a trio of Philadelphia relievers (Roger Mason, David West, and Larry Andersen) shut down Toronto in the sixth, seventh, and eighth innings, Game 6 entered the final frame with Philadelphia clinging to the one-run lead … and suddenly in need of Mitch Williams' services.

If the embattled closer could somehow regain his 43-save regular season form, the 90th edition of the Fall Classic would reach Game 7.

In the bottom of the ninth inning, Alfredo Griffin was praying.

His Jays were down 6–5 and there were two runners on, one out. He had been called on to pinch-run for the lead-footed Olerud in the eighth. Then he went into play third in the top of the ninth. Which meant he was now on deck, praying for Joe Carter to deliver, praying for the 1993 World Series not to hinge on *his* at-bat.

Griffin had enjoyed a highly productive career in the Majors ever since he was named co–AL Rookie of the Year in 1979. While glovework was his forte, he would finish his career batting a respectable .249. But now, at 36,

Griffin couldn't run very well, and had finished what would be his final season with a .211 batting average. Olerud was one of the game's most feared hitters and it appeared that Gaston had goofed by sacrificing Olerud's bat just so the speedier Griffin could represent the tying run in the eighth. And now, Gaston had no intention of pinch-hitting for the veteran infielder.

"I went to play third and then I was behind him [Carter]," says Griffin. "I was supposed to hit after him. And Cito [Gaston] pulled me back. He goes, 'Listen, you're going to hit.' I go, 'Me? Why?' But he goes, 'Yeah, you've got a good record against him [Mitch Williams]. You hit him good in the past.'

"So, I go, 'Please Joe. Please Joe, come through.' I didn't want to hit in that situation. I was at the end of my career. And I wasn't a good hitter. I had never been a good hitter."[56]

He was praying to be a spectator of, not a participant in, this momentous juncture.

His prayers would soon be answered.

With Paul Molitor on first, Rickey Henderson on second, Joe Carter stepped to the plate with one goal: do anything but hit into a 6–4–3 double play.

First pitch, ball.

Second pitch, ball.

Taking all the way, he watched a fastball into catcher Darren Daulton's mitt.

It was 2–1 and Joe Carter was now ready to make history.

Knowing Carter's tendency to pull everything, Philadelphia second baseman Mickey Morandini slid behind the second base bag. As Carter was blinded by a blur of grey and red, the curveball danced in and out of the shadows. He took a hellacious hack, missing the ball by a half-foot.[57]

Up in the press box, renowned *Toronto Sun* scribe Bob Elliott listened to a fellow writer predict that Carter would bounce into a game-ending double play.[58]

In the Toronto dugout, a young Pat Hentgen was a bundle of emotions as he was slated to start Game 7 of the World Series, now a very likely scenario.

On the mound, Philadelphia's wild man closer Mitch Williams, knowing that Carter was 0–4 lifetime against him, figured he could blow a fastball by him, high and outside.

Yet in the batter's box, with the count 2–2, Joe Carter was expecting Williams to try to embarrass him again with another hook. Carter knew that he shouldn't be looking curveball, but he couldn't help it. With two strikes, Morandini shifted back toward the first base side and Carter was ready for the deuce. Carter saw Williams shake off the sign, but he still prepared to wait for the breaking ball.[59]

Thankfully, for Carter, the Blue Jays, the province of Ontario, and baseball history, he guessed wrong.

Williams tossed a 2-2 heater down and in and because the dead-pull hitter was waiting back, he was just a tick behind and able to keep the ball fair down the left field line for a walk-off three-run homer that gave Toronto a series-clinching 8-6 win.

The shot heard around North America provided baseball with one of its most indelible moments and Toronto with its second consecutive world championship.

As Carter was jumping around the bases like he had matched all six winning Powerball numbers, Blue Jays television broadcaster Tom Cheek delivered his iconic line: "Touch 'em all Joe, you'll never hit a bigger home run!"[60]

In fact, only one player had ever hit a bigger home run. Not since Pittsburgh Pirates second baseman Bill Mazeroski's walk-off homer in the bottom of the ninth inning of Game 7 of the 1960 World Series had a championship been won in such dramatic fashion.

"It was kind of like an out-of-body experience where it happened so quickly and so unexpectedly," recalls Williams. "Here we are behind and the next thing you know he [Carter] hits a long drive to left field. We wondered if it was just even high enough to get out of the ballpark because it was hit so hard. And the next thing you know, everyone was just going crazy at home plate.

"I remember I was sitting there with Pat Hentgen. We were just talking about the next game, because if we hadn't won that game, he was pitching the next one. And one swing of the bat, the whole thing is over. You like to think you were ready for it or think it was going to happen but in history that stuff just doesn't happen. Just an exclamation point on a phenomenal season for a phenomenal team."[61]

"When he [Carter] hit that ball, I just went, 'Thank you Lord.' It was a tough pitch and it was a tough at-bat for him to keep the ball in play," says Griffin, who, standing in the on deck circle, was one of the closest spectators to the historic shot.[62]

"Of course, it was heroic," recalls Devon White. "But at the same time, we were a team that always battled until the last out. When he [Carter] hit that home run, it saved us the stress for the next game we had to play because we were up in the series, of course. He did that off of Mitch Williams, who was an ex-roommate of mine back in winter ball, but it was a great feeling."[63]

Toronto reserve infielder Dick Schofield didn't play an inning in the 1993 World Series ("I felt like I was in my living room watching it")[64] but made hardball history simply by partaking in the pile-up celebration at home plate. Back on October 13, 1960, days after the debut of *The Andy Griffith Show* and hours before John Kennedy and Richard Nixon would conduct their third presidential debate, Bill Mazeroski won the World Series for the Pittsburgh Pirates virtue of his walk-off home run off New York Yankees pitcher Ralph Terry in the bottom of the 9th inning in Game 7. Schofield's father, John "Ducky" Schofield, was in the mob scene celebrating the Pirates' 10–9 series-clinching win over the vaunted Yankees. Thirty-three years later, Schofield and his dad could say they were the only relatives to have participated in World Series-clinching walk-off home run celebrations.

To this day, they still can.

"I see my dad's thing all the time when they show the 1960 World Series," says Schofield, whose family tree contains a record four consecutive generations of professional ballplayers. "He's Number 11 bouncing around home plate. I get to relive that so it's pretty cool."[65]

When the players' celebration subsided, Carter was greeted not by his wife or parents, but by eccentric New York Mets PR Director Jay Horwitz, who was fulfilling his annual MLB postseason duty of arranging interviews at the conclusion of World Series games.

"I was in the Phillies dugout and I was working for MLB Radio. It was my job to get the star of the game," explains Horwitz, who was coming off a rather trying season in Flushing. (In July 1993 he had to clean up such PR messes as Vince Coleman tossing a firecracker into a crowd of fans and Bret Saberhagen spraying bleach on reporters.)

"When he hit the home run, I ran toward the plate because I was doing my job. I said, 'Joe, Jay Horwitz from the Mets, I need you to tune into CBS Radio.' He was very accommodating. I just happened to get to him before everybody else did. They like to get the star of the game right away through the affiliates at MLB. I didn't even really stop to think because once he hit the home run I was trying to get to him as soon as I could. I took that job seriously. You lose him in the beginning, you don't get him, he wanders."[66]

Carter would never forget that Horwitz, with his size 8¾ head and crooked glasses, effectively photobombed his career-defining moment.

"I decorated the walls in his house," says Horwitz.[67]

Shortly after Carter finished the interview with CBS Radio, a crush of reporters was itching for the Phillies clubhouse doors to swing open, so as to descend on Mitch Williams' locker.

For Williams, the home run marked a depressing, yet merciful end to a personally dreadful postseason. There had been death threats following the Game 4 fiasco and those would now surely intensify. Yet in Philadelphia's postgame locker room, Williams was ever the stand-up guy, facing the firing squad of reporters and saying, "I didn't do the job for two games in the

World Series.... I'm not going to sit here and make excuses. I threw the pitch that cost us the World Series. That's tough to deal with, but I'm going to deal with it."[68]

When a reporter asked about the decision to use Williams, Philadelphia manager Jim Fregosi snapped, "If you could tell me who else I was going to use, I'd be very happy."[69]

In the giddy Toronto clubhouse, Carter acknowledged to a swarming crowd of reporters, "With Mitch out there, we knew something good was going to happen. And it did."[70]

This obnoxious comment was uncharacteristic of Carter. He was, by all accounts, a pretty decent human being. (Carter would decline going on the late-night talk show circuit because he did not want to embarrass Williams.) Teammates loved him. Relatives adored him. Opponents respected him. The media even liked him. It was hard to make a big deal of this slight or begrudge Carter for becoming an instantaneous hero whose moment would be remembered as long as baseball is played.

Especially considering he was not particularly egotistical and money-grubbing—a stigma associated with 1990s star athletes such as himself.

By 1993, Joe Carter had been playing in Major League Baseball for a decade, virtue of his brief 23-game stint with the Chicago Cubs in 1983. Breaking into the big leagues in the mid–1980s did not translate into hefty paychecks. But emerging as an MLB star in the early 1990s did translate into hefty paychecks, and by 1993, Carter was one of the highest-paid players in the game. However, Carter always tried to honor his highly-esteemed father, Joe D. Carter, Sr., a man who defied mid–20th century segregationist America to become one of the first African Americans to run his own Conoco fuel station franchise, one situated at NW 6th and Robinson in Oklahoma City. So, after Joe Carter inked a 3-year, $9.2 million pact with the San Diego Padres in 1990, it surprised no one that his 10 siblings and 38 nieces and nephews suddenly had an easier time paying their bills.[71] As Carter became an established star in the early nineties, he stayed grounded, and on this evening, no one was complaining that he was getting all the attention and glory.

The other Blue Jay who was holding court with the media was the even more seasoned star, Paul Molitor. He was not just delivering terse, cliché-laden comments. After each question, a champagne drenched Molitor paused and provided an insightful response. He wanted to properly conclude this perfect evening, one in which he not only captured his first world championship, but also became the second-oldest player (37) to be named World Series MVP.

And in between the pauses and responses were tears and embraces from teammates. And then more tears. And then more hugs and handshakes. One of the most underappreciated Hall of Famers in the game's history was anything but overlooked in his own clubhouse.

"I was up roughly four and a half, five months of the season that year and when it came down to making the playoff travel roster, I wasn't going to be able to travel," recalls Woody Williams. "Paul Molitor went into Cito Gaston's office and stuck up for me and said he felt that I deserved to travel. He didn't tell me he was going to do that. He just did it and he didn't have to do that."[72]

(Ironically, the only Hall of Fame pitcher on Toronto's roster, Jack Morris, was also left off the postseason roster as he was coming off a poor regular season.)

Teammates, both grizzled and green, past and present, were ecstatic for Molitor because they knew his story. After all, he was one drug overdose away from dying and one injury away from truncating a career that, by all measures, ranks as one of the greatest ever.

"It seemed like everybody was just so surprised during the World Series and the playoffs how good a player he [Molitor] was, but those of us in the league already knew," says B.J. Surhoff. "You look at his World Series in '82, Game 1 he made an out and then he got five hits. If he doesn't get hurt four years, he's got 4,000 hits. I mean he got 200 something hits when he was 40-years-old. Had he played his whole career in New York or L.A. or Chicago, I think his name would get thrown around with the likes of a lot of other people. Just because he played in a smaller market, I don't think he's really been talked about in light of how good he actually was."[73]

Molitor's World Series performance (.500 BA, eight RBI) was even more impressive considering he was in his late thirties. At an age when most players are contemplating retirement or faltering, Molitor, armed with an acute understanding of baseball's physics and feline-like reflexes, was able to beautifully synchronize mind, eyes, and limbs to buy every available nanosecond for assessing a pitch and calculating its trajectory. Just as he had done throughout the regular season, Molitor put on a hitting clinic in the World Series, looking very much like a first-ballot Hall of Famer who was approaching 3,000 career hits. And to the voters' credit, they didn't fall in love with Carter's one magical swing, instead realizing that Molitor's weeklong performance warranted Series MVP honors.

Off the diamond, Molitor, with his veteran clubhouse presence, was most valuable to the Blue Jays in fostering improved team chemistry. For a team with such a star-studded and geographically diverse roster (players hailed from England, Canada, Venezuela, Jamaica, Dominican Republic, Puerto Rico, Oklahoma, Montana, and New Mexico among other locations), the 1993 Blue Jays maintained an effervescent sense of comity throughout the trials and tribulations that comprise a Major League Baseball season. Certainly, not every World Series winning team has such an identity seared into its legacy.

"That was a wonderful year," exclaims Alfredo Griffin. "Never in my life had I played with a team with the preparation that those guys had that year. It was a pleasure to play with all those beautiful human beings."[74]

The Blue Jays' dramatic finish in the 1993 World Series was only more meaningful given what transpired the following season.

Or rather, what didn't transpire.

In 1994, for the first time since Theodore Roosevelt was in the Oval Office, there was no World Series. The MLB Players Association strike, one that dragged from August 11, 1994, to April 2, 1995, did what world wars, an economic depression, and earthquake could not: prematurely end the baseball season.

This was devastating for seamheads, who automatically associate October with the World Series—even more so than the sun setting incrementally earlier, nights growing refreshingly cooler, and Halloween candy appearing on the shelves of CVS. If 1993 was one of baseball's most spectacular seasons (the addition of two expansion teams in the Florida Marlins and Colorado Rockies, a momentous All-Star Game, many feel-good personal stories, down-to-the wire pennant races, a highly eventful World Series), the 1994 campaign had to be one of its most dreadful. By October 1994, a largely disillusioned fan base, one also growing resentful over the players' increasingly bloated salaries, only had memories.

Memories of one of baseball's premier sluggers hooking a low fastball down the left field line and dancing around the bases as his Canadian team had successfully defended its title behind one of the most talented lineups to ever grace a baseball diamond.

6

How 'Bout Them Cowboys?

Tom Landry loved the enchiladas at Mia's.

The man who had coached the Dallas Cowboys to two Super Bowl titles, five NFC titles, and thirteen divisional titles was one of the most loyal customers at the city's most famous Tex-Mex restaurant. Situated at heavily congested Lemmon Avenue in North Dallas, Mia's was the go-to place for the Landry family for decades. Butch and Ana Enriquez's family-run restaurant was famous throughout the state of Texas for its scrumptious brisket tacos, but Landry was constantly indulging in the enchiladas, whether it was during lunch, dinner, or one of the many times Mia's would cater an event hosted by the Landry family.[1] So, when the *Dallas Morning News* published a front page story on the morning of February 25, 1989, claiming Landry was likely to be fired by new Dallas Cowboys owner Jerry Jones, accompanied by an image of Jones and Landry's successor, Jimmy Johnson, *celebrating at Mia's*, it was, for Landry, a former World War II bomber copilot, brutally humiliating.

The shamefulness unfolded, when, during the prior evening, the *Dallas Morning News* learned that Jones and Johnson were rendezvousing at Mia's and subsequently dispatched an intern from the photography department to the restaurant. After making a beeline over to Mia's, twenty-four-year-old J. Mark Kegans spotted the gentlemen and received their permission to snap what would become an iconic photo: Jones, the Arkansan who had made millions in the oil industry and was preparing to purchase the Cowboys, sitting across from Johnson, the legendary college coach who had recently led the Miami Hurricanes to a national championship. A day later, Jones' introductory press conference as the Cowboys' new owner confirmed the newspaper's report: Tom Landry was out, Jimmy Johnson was in.[2]

While teammates on the University of Arkansas football team in the 1960s, Johnson and Jones roomed together during road trips, due to the alphabetical proximity of their last names.[3] However, contrary to widely held beliefs, they had always been acquaintances more so than close friends.

After college, the two went their separate ways: Jerry, the financial wizard turned lucrative wildcatter, and Jimmy, the psychology major turned college football guru. What they did have in common was their Texas-sized egos and a relentless passion for all things football. Now, they would be operating at the highest levels of their beloved sport.

To his credit, during his introductory press conference, Jones, who had just returned from Austin, where he had delivered the news to Landry in-person, acknowledged that in regards to Landry, "This man is like Bear Bryant to me, like Vince Lombardi to me." Yet in that very same session, Jones made it clear he had no regrets in moving on from Landry when he referred to his new hire as "the best coach in America."[4]

As would be evident in the ensuing months, maybe that was true in college, but not so much in the pros.

Jimmy Johnson's initial season at the helm of America's Team was, by far, the most dreadful in the franchise's history. After going 3–13 in 1988, Dallas regressed under Johnson in 1989. They went 1–15, were shut out three times, and finished with the league's lowest scoring offense. Troy Aikman, the rookie quarterback recently selected with the No. 1 pick, posted twice as many interceptions (18) as touchdown passes (nine). The defense wasn't much better, with the nadir occurring during Week 7 when a very mediocre Kansas City Chiefs team torched Johnson's for 36 points.

Perhaps Jerry Jones had made a mistake.

"Jimmy [Johnson] comes in with a college kind of persona and frankly, in my opinion, didn't know a lot," recalls offensive lineman Crawford Ker, who played for Dallas from 1985 to 1990. "When Jimmy first got there, we were alternating guards. We were moving from left to right. It was chaos there on those 1–15 and 7–9 teams [Dallas would improve to 7–9 in 1990]—a lot of revolving doors, high turnover."[5]

(For example, defensive lineman Kevin Lilly, who, during the 1989 season, tried out on a Tuesday, was signed on Wednesday, got in the team photo on Thursday, played on Sunday, and cut on Monday.)

As a rookie NFL head coach, Johnson came across as not only clueless, but also disloyal. For this downtrodden team, *no one* had job security. Not even long-tenured veterans and captains.

"Did I really trust him as a player? Not so much," says Ker, who was one of Johnson's highest-paid players. "The rumor was they were trying to trade me to Green Bay in October of my second year [with Jimmy Johnson]. So, it's one thing being a captain and almost getting traded. So, I wouldn't say I was the greatest Jimmy Johnson fan."[6]

Johnson didn't make many fans within the organization, when, early in his inaugural year, he famously declared himself open to trading anyone

6. How 'Bout Them Cowboys?

Jimmy Johnson led the Miami Hurricanes to the 1987 national championship, but he was not exactly successful right away in his NFL rookie campaign in 1989 (courtesy Miami Athletics).

on his roster—which meant even the team's only established offensive threat—Herschel Walker.

On Tuesday, October 10, a couple days after Dallas fell to the Green Bay Packers 31–13, Johnson went on a 1.5-mile lunchtime jog with several assistants. As the heavily maligned staffers trotted through an unfinished development constructed around the Cowboys' training complex, past vacant lots and unsold residences, Johnson proposed the idea of trading Herschel Walker, the former Heisman Trophy winner who had rushed for 1,514 yards the prior season. The assistants were incredulous. They knew Walker was the only Cowboy currently justifying the star on the team's shells. Johnson didn't care. From his perspective, the Cowboys were 0–5 with Walker and the team was essentially 47 players from winning the Super Bowl. (He also preferred shifty backs to power backs like Herschel Walker.) All he needed was a trading partner that felt it was one player away from a Lombardi Trophy.

On October 12, 1989, in one of the most complex, multifaceted trades in NFL history, the Dallas Cowboys' front office, spearheaded by a very hesitant Jerry Jones, agreed to send Walker, their third and tenth picks in 1990, and third pick in 1991 to the Minnesota Vikings for linebackers Jesse Solomon and David Howard, defensive end Alex Stewart, running back Darrin Nelson, cornerback Issiac Holt, and the Vikings' first-, second-, and sixth-round picks in 1990. The only reason Johnson was interested in acquiring the veterans was because of the conditional draft picks attached to them—if they were cut before February 1, 1990. Johnson dealt Darrin Nelson to the San Diego Chargers after he refused to report for a sixth-rounder in 1990 and a second-rounder in 1991 and then cut Stewart to receive the second-round pick attached to him. However, after initially planning to trade Solomon, Howard, and Holt, Johnson opted to retain the trio and worked out a pact with Minnesota Vikings GM Mike Lynn that allowed him to do so in exchange for lowering the draft cost for Minnesota. In the end, the return haul for Walker was an aggregate total of 13 players/draft picks; in the next couple years, Johnson would leverage the draft capital toward positioning the franchise to select top prospects, many of whom would serve as cornerstones for the ensuing dynasty. (However, it should be noted that Walker had initially threatened to retire before going to Minnesota. In fact, none of this wheeling and dealing would have happened if Johnson did not cajole Jerry Jones into offering Walker a $1.25 million exit bonus, funds for a new house, and Mercedes-Benz in exchange for signing off.)

"The Vikings got Herschel Walker," Randy Galloway wrote in the *Dallas Morning News*. "The Cowboys got nothing more than a huge handful of Minnesota smoke. And who knows if there'll ever be another fire."[7]

While thinking in the future tense, Johnson made his team even worse in the present. Several days after the blockbuster trade, Walker's replacement, Darryl Clack, rushed for a paltry 32 yards as Dallas got pulverized by the visiting San Francisco 49ers. During the traditional Thanksgiving Day game, the Philadelphia Eagles humiliated Dallas, 27–0, on national television. The hideousness continued into the holiday season when, following a 20–10 loss at Philadelphia's Veterans Stadium on December 10, the Philadelphia Police Department escorted Johnson off the field as beer bottles and shards of ice rained down on his notoriously coiffed hair. On Christmas Eve, Johnson's inaugural season in Dallas ended with another 20–10 loss, merely hours after he was awoken at 4 a.m. to learn that an ice storm had frozen plumbing at Texas Stadium, causing pipes to burst and restrooms to malfunction. Meanwhile, that afternoon in the Meadowlands, Tom Landry was luxuriating in the private suite of New York Giants owner Wellington Mara during the New York Giants–Los Angeles Raiders game.[8]

It was hard to fathom that only a decade earlier the Cowboys had won a championship while having legends such as Roger Staubach and Tony Dorsett in their backfield.

6. How 'Bout Them Cowboys?

But just over three years later, on the evening of January 31, 1993, the Cowboys would once again celebrate with the Vince Lombardi Trophy, and in doing so, usher in the franchise's first dynastic era.

The Dallas Cowboys team that routed the Buffalo Bills by a score of 52–17 in Super Bowl XXVII less than two weeks after Bill Clinton's inauguration bore scant resemblance to the 1989 squad. Only several players remained from Johnson's first year. By the early nineties, the newly established offensive trio of quarterback Troy Aikman, wideout Michael Irvin, and running back Emmitt Smith was deadly. The team had acquired ferocious pass rusher Charles Haley from the San Francisco 49ers in August 1992. The return from the Herschel Walker deal was proving to be immense: defensive tackle Russell Maryland, defensive backs Kevin Smith and Darren Woodson, and most importantly, Emmitt Smith, who would lead the league in rushing during the 1992 season. And Jimmy Johnson, a man once viewed by many as a traitorous fool, was now revered as a brilliant tactician for pulling off the bold deal, one that would later be dubbed "The Great Trade Robbery."

"The story starts probably after that 1–15 year when Jimmy [Johnson] made a conscious decision to be very active once he had traded Herschel Walker," recalls safety James Washington. "And then Plan B came along and he made a conscious decision to pick certain kind of guys. Jimmy Johnson built a team to get back to the Super Bowl. I just remember being a free agent in Plan B and Jimmy told me in '90, my first year there, 'We are going to go to the Super Bowl.' And the crazy piece about that is they were 1–15 in '89. And I did everything in my power to kind of hold it in."[9]

(Before the NFL adopted a system of unrestricted free agency in 1993, there was Plan B free agency from 1989 to 1992. Under this system, teams could protect 37 players on their 47-man rosters, leaving the rest free to sign with other teams without compensation. A protected player whose contract had expired could accept an offer from another team, but the team that protected the player could match the offer and retain him. If the player's former team elected not to match the contract offer, the new team had to provide compensation via draft choices.)

America's Team would not be a laughingstock for much longer. From 1989–1992 there were incremental improvements each season (1–15, 7–9, 11–5, 13–3) as the franchise underwent a massive roster overhaul. Still, in January 1993, the feeling around the league was that Dallas was a year away from being a real powerhouse. Despite coming off an outstanding regular season and defeating the Philadelphia Eagles 34–10 in the Divisional Round, the Cowboys were underdogs going into the 1992 NFC Championship Game against the hated 49ers on January 17 at soggy Candlestick Park.

The same Candlestick Park that was the site of the 1981 NFC Championship Game ... between the Cowboys and 49ers.

On January 10, 1982, with less than a minute remaining in the conference title game, San Francisco quarterback Joe Montana, pressured by three Dallas defenders, faded backwards and heaved a spiral to the back of the end zone, where he found receiver Dwight Clark for the go-ahead score (following the successful extra-point attempt by Ray Wersching that gave the Niners a 28–27 win). The Catch was one of the most famous plays in NFL history and it punched the 49ers' ticket to Super Bowl XVI and jump-started their dynastic run throughout the 1980s. Meanwhile, Tom Landry's Cowboys never recovered and sagged through years of mediocrity and later, humiliation in the decade. But now, Jimmy Johnson's Cowboys had a chance to make the 1990s their decade. They were young, hungry, and remarkably audacious.

In the fourth quarter of the conference title game, Dallas had a 24–13 lead and was facing a 4th-and-1 from the San Francisco seven-yard line. Rather than kick the chip shot field goal for a commanding two-touchdown lead, Jimmy Johnson called for an Emmitt Smith run over right tackle. Smith was stuffed by linebacker Mike Walter. Turnover on downs. After San Francisco scored a touchdown to cut Dallas' lead to 24–20 with 4:22 remaining, simple logic now dictated handoffs to Smith. But again, Dallas flouted convention, refusing to kill time with run plays. The call was for a square-in pass to wideout Alvin Harper, who, after making the catch in front of cornerback Don Griffin, angled 70 yards across the gridiron to San Francisco's nine-yard line. After Troy Aikman connected with wide receiver Kelvin Martin on a six-yard TD pass on third down (the extra-point attempt was blocked), Dallas held a 10-point lead with 3:43 remaining. The 30–20 score would remain intact through the final whistle thanks to James Washington picking off a Steve Young pass on a last-gasp drive.

The momentous win meant that San Francisco's decade-long dominance over Dallas ended on the same turf where it started. Meanwhile, Dallas was headed to its first Super Bowl since the 1970s.

After the game, one that would ultimately alter the history of America's most important sports franchise, star wideout Michael Irvin declared in the uproarious locker room, "One more win and the big man upstairs can call me home. I've served my purpose here."[10]

While Irvin's remark captured the raw, ebullient emotions streaming through the locker room, the most memorable postgame sound bite came from Jimmy Johnson, when he famously hollered, "How 'Bout Them Cowboys?"

A slang, ungrammatical phrase that would become the team's universally recognized rallying cry for eternity.

6. How 'Bout Them Cowboys?

On the day after the NFC Championship Game, Jimmy Johnson put his psychology degree to use. He knew this was no ordinary Super Bowl. There would be nearly 100,000 spectators on hand at the Rose Bowl for Super Bowl XXVII; hundreds of millions of people around the globe would be watching; Michael Jackson was slated to perform at halftime; pregame festivities included a performance by the Rockettes and a Star-Spangled Banner rendition by country legend Garth Brooks; a Los Angeles setting meant many distractions and temptations, including a not-to-be-missed Playboy Mansion party. (The game was originally supposed to be played at Sun Devil Stadium in Tempe, Arizona, however once the state balked at observing the newly created Martin Luther King holiday, the NFL changed the destination to Pasadena.) And Johnson's Cowboys were already being written off ... against a Buffalo Bills team that had choked in the previous two Super Bowls. Not to mention, the two-week layoff between the conference championship and Super Bowl presented further opportunities to get sidetracked.

The coach's message:

> Look guys, we're the NFC Champions, but we're the youngest team in the league. The Bills have all the big names and they have two years' worth of Super Bowl experience under their belts from the last two years.
>
> But let me tell you something that I think everyone in this room already knows. If we went out on the practice field out here at Valley Ranch, right here in the backyard, and we scrimmaged the Buffalo Bills for three hours, we would kick their ass up and down the field. I know it, and everyone in this room knows that we would do that.
>
> We're clearly the better team, and we all know that. But we're not going to play them on the practice field. We're going to play them in the Super Bowl. And the Super Bowl is the biggest stage in the world. Millions of people watching in countries all over the world—everyone who has ever known you or has helped you get to where you are today—watching this one game. The biggest game you've ever played in your life.
>
> But our approach to this game is going to be very simple.
>
> Let me ask you this, if I took a 20-foot, 2-by-4 piece of wood and set it down on top of two concrete blocks at the front of this meeting room, would anyone in this room have any problem with walking across that 2-by-4 from one end to the other?
>
> Kenny Norton, could you walk across that 2-by-4 without losing your balance right here in front of me?
>
> *(Don't think it would be a problem Coach.)*
>
> Okay, if I took that same 2-by-4 and stretched it across the twin towers at the World Trade Center in New York City, 100 stories up in the air above New York City. Would you feel as confident, or as comfortable? Would it be a different deal for any of you?
>
> Well that's what this whole Super Bowl thing is all about. The piece of wood is exactly the same—doesn't matter if it is stretched across two concrete blocks or across two large buildings. We're playing a football game. That's all it is. The field is a 100 yards long and the outcome will be the same if we play it on the practice field or at the Rose Bowl.
>
> If you know how to perform the job that is right in front of your face, and you have

confidence in your ability, then the task in front of you is simple. You just do what you know how to do.

That's what we're going to do when we play Buffalo. We're better than they are, and we have confidence in what we are doing. Doesn't matter if we play them in the parking lot here at Valley Ranch or in the middle of Times Square in New York City.

The setting doesn't mean a thing. The field is 100 yards long. It's the same 2-by-4. Regardless of the stakes, or the height of the drop, it's a football game. You know how to do it, and you're going to win.[11]

A week later, the most colorful and polarizing team in football touched down in Southern California, brimming with cockiness and poised for the most star-studded spectacle in the game's history.

"At that time, we were the youngest team to ever go to the Super Bowl in Super Bowl XXVII," says James Washington. "Nobody gave us a chance. No one gave us a chance. All the media, everybody was talking about how Buffalo was going to do this, how they were going to do that. That group of guys going into our first Super Bowl, we all believed that we belonged there."[12]

Largely due to their cerebral coach.

"He [Jimmy Johnson] was a perfect fit [for Dallas]," recalls Butch Davis, who was the Cowboys' defensive line coach this season. "I mean Jimmy was brilliant, not just necessarily as a football coach. His ability to think outside the box as far as the culture that he wanted to create."[13]

It was one of arrogance, for sure, but not one of recklessness that would allow L.A.'s glitz and glamour to take focus away from the monumental task at hand.

"A lot of it was how we practiced," recalls Dallas defensive end Jim Jeffcoat. "We didn't change our practice habits. We practiced fast and we practiced physical. Even though we had been through the full season, those were some of the best practices that we had all year. We were very focused."[14]

Once the actual game started, however, the opening minutes suggested otherwise.

While the Dallas Cowboys ultimately walloped the Buffalo Bills by five touchdowns, in the early going Dallas was staying afloat *despite* its offensive unit. Indeed, it was the unsung heroes of the defense who bailed out the offense's sluggish start—and special teams unit's hiccup.

On its first possession, Dallas' offense went three-and-out before punter Mike Saxon was stuffed by Buffalo special teams standout Steve Tasker and the AFC champs took over on the Cowboys' 16. Just over a minute later, Thurman Thomas rushed in for a two-yard touchdown, giving Buffalo an early 7–0 lead.

"Buffalo came and they hit us in the mouth, they hit us in the mouth early. We were back on our heels and they were driving," says James Washington.[15]

On the next drive, Troy Aikman, looking like a quarterback playing in his first Super Bowl, misfired passes to Jay Novacek and Kelvin Martin on second and third down, respectively. Buffalo's two-deep zone was taking away Aikman's outside reads and Dallas struggled to establish a running game as Emmitt Smith only rushed for four yards on his first three carries.

As the first quarter reached the midway point, Buffalo had the early lead and was driving again when quarterback Jim Kelly connected with wideout Andre Reed for 21 yards to give Buffalo the ball at midfield. However, on the ensuing play, Washington would pick off an errant Kelly pass. The momentum-changing interception marked the first of nine Dallas-forced turnovers on the evening, a Super Bowl record-breaking performance that would turn the outcome of this championship game into what the franchise was considered only three years earlier—a joke.

Certainly, Dallas had no ordinary defense. But not just because of its superlative talent. At the time, conventional wisdom in the NFL was that high-quality defensive units sprung from high draft picks maturing into Pro Bowlers over four, five, six years. Not in Dallas. During the 1992 regular season, the Dallas defense did not have a single Pro Bowler. Following a preseason scrimmage, a Los Angeles Raiders coach had dismissed the Cowboys defenders as "nothing but a bunch of little guys."[16] Around the NFL, the unit was largely considered a combination of cast-offs, rookies, and renegades. There was some truth to that sentiment. The defense was a no-name group largely comprised of Plan B free agents, late-round draft picks, and journeymen that would account for the most dominant defensive performance in Super Bowl history.

After Washington's interception set up Aikman's 23-yard touchdown pass to Novacek that erased Buffalo's early (and only) lead, tying the game at 7, Dallas would go ahead for good on Buffalo's ensuing possession when speed rusher Charles Haley whipped around Buffalo tackle Howard Ballard and sacked Jim Kelly at the two, forcing a fumble recovered by defensive tackle Jimmie Jones, who subsequently rumbled into the end zone. Following the extra-point, Dallas was now up 14–7. Buffalo was in for a long night.

"To say that you're in the Super Bowl, but then you start setting records," says James Washington. "I had the first turnover to stop the bleeding. It was on and cracking once the energy got going and the flow got going and then our offense got going. It was one of those moments like being at Disneyland and getting on the Matterhorn for the first time. Your stomach was just so jittery and shaky. But also, [you were] excited about it. Watching the guys make play after play after play was just so fun to be a part of that. Sometimes we say winning is everything, but sometimes it's how you win also."[17]

With a ruthless barrage of blind side hits and incessant pressure, the Dallas defense won in style. Two of the nine turnovers were returned for touchdowns; three others set up touchdowns. Exploiting blazing speed, zipping through small gaps before they closed, forcing opponents to mistime their blocks. The unit came as advertised this evening.

"We were fortunate, we had a lot of very, very good defensive linemen—Russell Maryland, Jimmie Jones, Charles Haley, Leon Lett, Jim Jeffcoat, Chad Hennings," recalls Butch Davis, who would transition from defensive line coach to defensive coordinator in the ensuing days. "It was remarkable the talent that we had in the defensive line."[18]

(The current defensive coordinator Dave Wannstedt had agreed to become head coach of the Chicago Bears right before Super Bowl practices began, but apparently, it wasn't too much of a distraction.)

The brutal evening for Buffalo came to a merciful end when Dallas' turnover palooza was bookended by linebacker Ken Norton, Jr.'s fourth quarter fumble recovery and nine-yard return for the game's final touchdown that capped off the 52–17 win.

While Dallas' defense was glorified as a unit, there was extra attention paid to Ken Norton, Jr., a former second-round pick out of UCLA, now playing on his old stomping grounds. No Dallas defender was more impactful than the nonstop motoring linebacker, who, in addition to scoring the aforementioned touchdown, also had delivered a vicious hit on quarterback Jim Kelly in the second quarter that caved in his right knee, knocking him out of the game and deflating the entire Buffalo team.

Unfortunately, Norton Jr.'s father, boxer Ken Norton, Sr., who was famous himself for knocking out opponents, had no interest in making the one-hour drive to see his son play in-person.

This was a bizarre story. The father-son duo was one of the most prolific in the history of American sports. Ken Norton, Sr., once decisioned Muhammad Ali and sported the WBC heavyweight championship belt for three months in 1978. The son was a gifted athlete with breathtaking speed who was finally living up to the immense potential he showed in college. When the world-class boxer got into a debilitating car accident in 1986, the son, then a star linebacker at UCLA, was there to help him shower and get around in his wheelchair. It was the least he could do. Junior remembered how his father, before emerging as a prominent professional boxer, would come home after long days on the Ford assembly line and grueling training sessions at the gym to feed him dinner. When the Senior Norton went out on weekends to cut his teeth in the boxing world, he prioritized leaving his son with neighbors who could provide substantive meals. For Norton, Jr., growing up, there wasn't a lot of money, but a lot of laughs over Jackie Gleason shows and motorcycle rides around the neighborhood.[19] They were close. Exceptionally close.

Until spring of 1992, when they had a heated argument shortly before Norton Jr., was to be married. They soon became estranged, Norton Jr., not inviting his father to the wedding at Lake Tahoe or to the wedding party held later in Dallas. Norton Sr., who credited his son with helping him walk and talk again after the accident and had been a regular at his high school, collegiate, and professional games, didn't attend a single contest during the 1992 NFL season. No longer best buddies, the two hadn't spoken a word since the blowup.

So even though the son was now coming into his own on the professional gridiron (a fumble recovery and forced fumble in the Divisional Round win followed 88 tackles over the last 10 regular season games), the father refused to come to the Rose Bowl, a stadium where he had seen his son play many college games. And in doing so, he turned down a front-row seat to see his boy become what he, himself, had been years earlier … a world champion.

The Super Bowl MVP trophy, appearance on *The Tonight Show with Jay Leno*, and feature on the cover of *Sports Illustrated* were not for Ken Norton, Jr., or one of the other Dallas defensive studs. Those honors would be bestowed upon Troy Aikman. (James Washington: "Regardless of what the defense has, it's always going to be about the offense. We had the Big Three [Aikman, Irvin, Smith] and no matter what we could do on defense, it was always going to be about them.")[20] Aikman, the sandy-haired golden boy quarterback, who by now was quite possibly the most famous man in Texas, finished with four touchdowns and 273 passing yards in the signature game of his young career. Decades later, Michael Irvin would proclaim he never saw a quarterback throw the way Aikman did on this day.

For anyone who had been following Aikman's career, the clutch performance wasn't a shocker. He was a cerebral signal caller who, while never having gaudy regular season stats, consistently delivered in the big postseason moments. Offensive coordinator Norv Turner would later remark, "If you look at Troy's greatest plays, they came in the most critical situations. If you look at his greatest games, they came against the best teams and in the playoffs."[21]

The only thing that came as a surprise, however, was when he waived his index finger in the SoCal air after throwing his fourth and final touchdown, a 45-yard bomb to hotshot wideout Alvin Harper early in the fourth quarter.

There was a reason for this uncharacteristic gesture. *Never* one to showboat, Aikman knew this game was over once Harper crossed the end zone, giving Dallas a three-touchdown lead. Now, he knew that he wasn't going to be the next Dan Marino—an iconic franchise quarterback who could never win a Super Bowl. (A couple weeks earlier, Marino's Miami Dolphins had lost to the Buffalo Bills in the AFC Championship Game.)

This last week of January 1993 had been intense for Aikman. Naturally, the star quarterback of America's Team was going to deal with a whirlwind of media attention during Super Bowl week. But the hubbub was exponentially higher because Aikman was returning to his collegiate home of Los Angeles. The Cowboys were even practicing this week at Aikman's alma mater, UCLA. The Aikman angle was *the* storyline heading into Super Bowl XXVII and by early in the week, Aikman told *Fort Worth Star-Telegram* reporter Richie Whitt that he needed to get away from the media circus buzzing around his every move, whether it was at the team hotel in Santa Monica or at the UCLA football facilities.[22]

Even if it didn't mean going far.

So, one day after practice, the two ducked out of the Cowboys' adopted facilities and went on a stroll around the non-football related sites of the gorgeous UCLA campus.

"We [Troy and I] developed a pretty good friendship back at the start of that season," explains Richie Whitt. "I did a weekly diary with him in the *Star-Telegram* so I got to know him kind of personally. He's a really guarded guy. But that week was really interesting because basically from Jimmy [Johnson] on down, the Cowboys were extremely loose, extremely confident, because they were kind of playing with house money. They beat the Niners who were heavily favored in that NFC Championship Game at Candlestick. For most of the organization, they had achieved their goal. They had taken a big next step, and even if they didn't win the Super Bowl, they had established themselves as the team to beat for next year and the years to come. They kind of put their stamp on the NFL, and it wasn't as though they were satisfied, but there wasn't any pressure. Whereas Troy felt an enormous amount of pressure because he knew even then how Super Bowls define quarterbacks' careers. While Jimmy [Johnson] and Michael Irvin were kind of loose and playing around, Troy was really uptight and really nervous about the game."[23]

As Aikman and Whitt walked around the sun-splashed grounds and dined in the lunchroom, the former was constantly recognized, but people mostly respected his privacy. As quarterback and reporter strolled around the dormitories and Pauley Pavilion, there were very few requests for autographs and pictures. The UCLA community knew it was a big week for Aikman, and he was trying to decompress.

6. How 'Bout Them Cowboys?   183

"Even though he [Aikman] was relaxing, he still talked about [how] 'This is a huge game for me, a huge moment for me,'" says Whitt. "He realized there are no guarantees he'll ever be back here. And he talked about Dan Marino never winning one. He understood the gravity of the moment, and although he tried to have moments of relaxation, it was a big deal for him. I think he was maybe more prepared, more focused than anybody else on the team, maybe even the organization."[24]

Winning the Super Bowl brought a tremendous amount of relief, but the heroic way he did so promised to put even greater strains on his privacy and demands on his time. Hours after the final whistle an already bright limelight intensified.

There was the initial postgame press conference attended by hundreds of reporters; several TV interviews on the Rose Bowl field; a small private victory party in his Santa Monica hotel room; a stop at the Cowboys' private party at the Santa Monica Civic Auditorium (his presence caused so much chaos that he bolted within 30 minutes); at 3:30 a.m. PST he started taping interviews for *CBS This Morning* and *Good Morning America*; at 4:09 a.m. PST, he went on *Today*, live; then, several more TV and radio interviews with Dallas stations; a 90-minute nap followed by the Super Bowl MVP press conference; five hours of interviews with radio talk shows around the country; and finally, he was whisked off to the NBC studios in Burbank, where he was a guest on *The Tonight Show with Jay Leno*.[25]

Aikman, the son of a pipeline construction worker who moved his family to Henryetta, Oklahoma (pop. 6,000), in 1979, was now one of the most marketable celebrities in North America. After the media blitz, dozens of requests for public appearances and endorsements kept streaming in. It was the reward for/price of delivering a historic Super Bowl performance that crowned an immaculate postseason run: in three contests he threw 89 passes without a pick, with eight of them going for touchdowns.

No longer simply perceived as a laid-back country boy in Levi's and cowboy boots, Troy Aikman was now a bona fide All-American hero with universal appeal, quarterbacking America's Team in its resurgence to glory.

After the Aikman-to-Harper game-sealing touchdown, the Cowboys, as a team, were ready to pop the corks. For the balance of the fourth quarter, they were celebrating in a flamboyant manner—both on and off the field.

With just over four minutes remaining, the NBC camera caught Alvin Harper waving a Super Bowl champions hat and Michael Irvin trying one on. (Traditionally, the victors sport the championship garb *after* the game.) Then, Charles Haley and Emmitt Smith were shown giving noogies to Jimmy Johnson, who by this point was barely paying any attention to the game.

"Not until years later did they realize, 'Not only did we win the Super Bowl, we got to dance and prance and have fun basically for the entire fourth quarter and just make it garbage time,'" says Richie Whitt. "I mean that doesn't happen very often, especially to a team that wasn't picked to win and even go to the Super Bowl."[26]

"Nobody expected them [to do so well] especially in the first Super Bowl in Pasadena where they just wiped the table with us," says Buffalo backup tight end Rob Awalt, who had previously played a couple seasons in Dallas. "Three years from being the worst team in the NFL to being the machine they became. We and everybody thought that Buffalo probably had the upper hand that year just because maybe they [the Cowboys] were one year away."[27]

For veterans such as fullback Daryl "Moose" Johnston, who was a rookie in 1989, the win was career-defining.

"We worked really hard in 1990, and there wasn't a lot to show for it," recalls Johnston. "It finally started to pay off in 1992. That core group of guys that started in 1989, I think we appreciated it a lot more than the guys that came after that season who were key guys, like an Emmitt Smith or a Darren Woodson or a Kevin Smith. They were key guys for our Super Bowl teams, but I don't think they ever had the appreciation like the guys that suffered through 1989."[28]

It was only fitting that there was such unabashed celebration at the end of Super Bowl XXVII, truly a spectacle unprecedented in the history of North American professional sports—simply virtue of the halftime extravaganza. Once the domain of college marching bands and clumsy cartoon characters, this halftime show featured Michael Jackson, in his first live performance in America since 1989, articulating his "Heal the World" message of unity and equality to millions of viewers worldwide. Approximately one ton of pyrotechnics comprised the finale to this show that also featured over 3,000 children from Los Angeles, those of disparate racial and cultural backgrounds. (More than a few Cowboys, including Michael Irvin, had snuck out of the locker room to watch the halftime extravaganza.) And it all took place at the historic Rose Bowl, backdropped with a stunning mountainous landscape.

"I don't know if you could have added more panache and more glitz and glamour inside that one setting," says Whitt. "If you were to look back and rank all the Super Bowls for star power and just for glitz and glamour, [Super Bowl] XXVII has got to be right up there, probably at the top."[29]

In the waning moments, as the celebratory mood pervaded the Dallas sidelines, the most conspicuous showboating display happened on the field, when defensive tackle Leon Lett, who had never before been to Los

6. How 'Bout Them Cowboys?

With his "Heal the World" message, Michael Jackson put on a halftime show for the ages during Super Bowl XXVII (photograph provided by Bill Frakes).

Angeles, ("Before that first Super Bowl, L.A. to me was Lower Alabama")[30] made his notorious gaffe. After scooping up backup quarterback Frank Reich's fumble and rumbling 64 yards toward the end zone, Lett started celebrating prematurely, showing off the pigskin once he got inside the 10-yard line. Despite the lopsided score, Buffalo's speedy wideout Don Beebe had hustled across the field in pursuit of Lett and was rewarded by stripping the ball from Lett's grasp inches before the goal line.

Touchback.

(Had there been instant replay in the NFL, the referees likely would have overturned the call on the field and ruled a touchdown, as television replays showed the nose of the ball crossing the goal line.)

Lett went from elation to humiliation. He had a chance to score a touchdown in the Super Bowl, but instead made an iconic blooper. On media day, Lett hadn't been asked a single question. After the game, he had his own podium, politely answering the same question over and over. In no celebratory mood now, the crestfallen lineman just went to his hotel room after the interminable media session, feeling terrible for weeks.

The same couldn't be said for team owner Jerry Jones, who, along with his minions, were busy handing out party invitations to the glitterati sprinkled across the Cowboys' postgame locker room. The bubbly flowed until the early morning hours as Jones strutted around the lavish parties with his chest puffed out, finally vindicated for having moved on from Tom Landry four short years ago.[31]

There was reason for celebration: his young team was already being considered the heir apparent to the San Francisco 49ers of the 1980s as the NFL's next dynasty. With a third championship in tow (Dallas had won the Super Bowl in 1972 and 1978), America's Team was indeed justifying its esteemed title.

As the Cowboys were in party mode late in the fourth quarter, NBC color man Bob Trumpy had reminded America, "By the way, do you realize that Emmitt Smith is yet to be signed by the Dallas Cowboys? Now Jerry Jones doesn't think that is a big problem."[32]

At the time, it seemed like a comment to kill a few seconds during the meaningless final minutes of game time. (Play-by-play man Dick Enberg didn't even bother responding.) However, as the ensuing off-season dragged on, the contract situation did not get resolved: Emmitt Smith had played out his rookie contract and had not agreed to a new pact with the Cowboys. Jones offered Smith a four-year deal worth $11 million; Smith wanted a contract that would pay an average of $4 million per year, so he would be one of the top ten paid players in the NFL. And as the 1993 season approached, Emmitt Smith's absence, not the team's quest for a second consecutive title, was the issue hovering over America's Team.

Most NFL fans couldn't fathom how Jerry Jones was going to play hardball with a guy who had led the league in rushing for a second straight season and was just entering his prime. Without Smith, the Cowboys had barely won a single game in 1989. With Smith, they were the best team in football by the mid–'90s, not to mention one of the most lucrative franchises in professional sports. Uncomfortable questions hit the airwaves. Was Jones prioritizing his profit margin over the team's winning percentage while dwelling on the NFL's first ever salary cap that was set for the 1994 season? Was he really content with just one Super Bowl title?

As late July turned into mid–August, which soon turned into early September, Jones and Smith remained locked in a staredown. With neither side willing to blink, the Cowboys prepared to open their title-defending season against the Washington Redskins on "Monday Night Football" … with rookie Derrick Lassic as their starting running back.

Six days after they rushed for only 91 yards in a 35–16 loss to their NFC East rivals on Labor Day night, the Cowboys fell to 0–2 by dropping their home opener to the Buffalo Bills, virtually the same team they had humiliated in the Super Bowl. The final score (13–10) belied the significant flaws of a Dallas team that was clearly distracted and short-handed this afternoon. Lassic ran for only 52 yards. Troy Aikman (two interceptions) had one of his worst games since he was a rookie. After kicker Lin Elliott missed two

At the Dallas Cowboys World Headquarters in Frisco, Texas, the franchise's resurgence to glory during Super Bowl XXVII is commemorated for posterity (author's photograph).

field goals, including a 30-yard attempt late in the third quarter, a seething Jimmy Johnson remarked in his postgame news conference, "We'll bring in as many kickers as necessary before Wednesday's practice."[33]

(Veteran kicker Eddie Murray was soon brought in to replace Elliott.)

That midweek practice, like those of the prior six weeks, was torturous. Ever the browbeating taskmaster, Johnson ordered his players to run an excessive number of sprints, given the torrid late summer conditions in Texas.

"Coach Johnson at the time, he was a man to keep everybody together. He was a big disciplinarian," says Dallas rookie punter and holder John Jett.[34]

To drive home the point that winning last year's Super Bowl was now worth nothing and not having Emmitt Smith was no justification for the team's poor play, Johnson was holding some of his most brutal practices ever during August and September of 1993. And that's saying something.

"The practices and the preparation were way more physical, way more challenging than even the games," says Butch Davis, a longtime member of Johnson's collegiate and professional coaching staffs, who, at this point, was in his early days as Dallas' defensive coordinator.[35]

"The games became a piece of cake just because of how hard the training camps were, and the practices were. On Friday's practices, we always ended practice with a two-minute drill, and you would have thought the Super Bowl was on the line.

"One of the things that you learn with him is how much he absolutely loved competition. And it showed up in almost everything in his life—the way he competed when he played golf from the way he competed if he was doing anything outside of football and inside of football. It was off the charts and he loved football players who liked to compete in practice. And at Miami and even at Oklahoma State, he wanted the One's to go against the One's. He wanted them to push each other to become better."

(One of Johnson's favorite sayings was "Treat a person as he is and he will remain as he is. Treat him as he could be, and he will become what he should be."[36])

With the disappointing start, Johnson loved seeing players competing for starting nods and roster spots ... at practice. He was an angry man who saw wasted talent around him. Johnson knew that Dallas was a better team than what its 0-2 record indicated, a message clearly articulated at his grueling weekday practices.

Meanwhile, the fans only cared about what happened on Sundays. On offense at least, the Cowboys were half the team that they had been a season ago. It wasn't just the 0-2 start (and the fact that no team had ever made it to the Super Bowl after dropping the first two games). It was the fact that during the 1992 regular season, the Cowboys had averaged nearly 26 points per game. Without their all-world running back, they totaled 26 points over their first two games in 1993.

Sports fans across America couldn't grasp how the Cowboys, a franchise now worth hundreds of millions of dollars, were in danger of not making the playoffs, let alone the Super Bowl, over a contractual impasse involving several hundred thousand dollars. With Smith staying home and Jones remaining adamant that his team could repeat as world champs with the current roster, the entire franchise was humiliated.

Once again.

"After winning the previous Super Bowl and then coming out 0–2, things got kind of ugly, a lot of people [were] upset and stuff," recalls punter John Jett, who grew up in a one-stoplight county in backwoods Virginia and thus experienced a culture shock in observing a multi-million-dollar contract dispute between world-class celebrities.

"I'm always the person who sits back and watches everything happen. From a player's perspective, about giving us the money, we need it here to win. And then of course you have the management perspective—'We don't want to pay any guy any more than he's worth.'"[37]

While the public perceived this fiasco as strictly a monetary matter, the reality was far more complicated. Defensive lineman Charles Haley was one of several Cowboys who perceived this contract dispute as a matter of racial injustice. Serious tension started seeping into a locker room that was associated with jubilation and unity only months earlier.

In *Boys Will Be Boys: The Glory Days and Party Nights of the Dallas Cowboys Dynasty*, author Jeff Pearlman described the toxic environment:

> The snap judgment was that Dallas without Smith was only a so-so operation. Yet the truth ran deeper. The real issue here was shattered team morale. As Smith stayed away, Jones spoke openly—and, it seemed, eagerly—about renegotiating Aikman's contract, which still had two years remaining. Led by Haley, a number of the African-American Cowboys wondered aloud why a black man like Smith had to beg for the money he deserved while the white, sandy-haired quarterback could have riches thrown at his feet. As far as Haley was concerned, it was business as usual in the NFL, a league without an owner or general manager of color and only two black starting quarterbacks (Houston's Warren Moon and Detroit's Rodney Peete).[38]

While the locker room was a house divided, Cowboys' fans were united in their animosity toward Jerry Jones.

The morning after the home opener, Israeli Prime Minister Yitzhak Rabin and PLO Chairman Yasser Arafat shook hands on the South Lawn of the White House after signing an agreement that granted limited autonomy to Palestine. It was the most compelling news story everywhere on the planet, except for North Texas where rumors of an imminent contract resolution for Smith were gaining traction. For many Texans, the prospect of an egomaniacal Jones caving into Smith's demands was more attention-grabbing than peace in the Middle East.

Finally, three days later, on Thursday, September 16, Smith signed a four-year, $13.6 million contract, making him the league's highest-paid running back and Dallas a prohibitive favorite to repeat as Super Bowl champs.

"Once he got back on the team, it was like everybody was together now," says John Jett. "And that's what everybody was waiting for. Then the pressure is kind of on you because you start out 0–2. I'm thinking [at] that point nobody has ever gone to the Super Bowl before starting out 0–2."[39]

The 'Boys would not lose again until late November, reeling off a seven-game win streak in which they outscored opponents by an aggregate margin of 180–78. It was a run that included a dismantling of the Indianapolis Colts (27–3) and yet another win over the Niners (26–17). But perhaps the most memorable win was on Halloween at miserably rain-drenched Veterans Stadium, which had historically been a house of horrors for Dallas.

The visitors won relatively easily, 23–10, but the real story was Emmitt Smith, who ran roughshod over an overmatched Philadelphia defense, compiling 237 rushing yards in a maestro performance capped by a 62-yard touchdown romp that sealed the win. During a contest that began in a 47-degree drizzle and ended in a bone-chilling downpour with 25 mph winds zipping through the Vet, Smith shattered Tony Dorsett's franchise single-game rushing record of 206 yards, also set against Philadelphia, in 1977.

On this splish splash day, Troy Aikman struggled to grip the pigskin, only completing nine passes. Dallas was going to have to beat Philly on the ground and, single-handedly, it did. Smith had more yards rushing than the Eagles' entire offensive output (228 yards). After the game, Smith was asked how he was able to withstand the stormy weather. He didn't go into his low running style or ability to keep his feet under him. Ever the opportunist, Smith seized a chance to plug a product he endorsed, telling the media scrum, "I had a decent pair of shoes on. Reebok shoes are great shoes. It was the shoes, man."[40]

On the other side of the ball, for the sixth consecutive game, Jimmy Johnson's patchwork defense prevented the opponent from scoring multiple touchdowns. Meanwhile, the coach took great pleasure in seeing Herschel Walker, playing for his third team in five years, run for a pedestrian 65 yards.

"The biggest thing is by that time we had a lot of confidence, especially on defense," says Jim Jeffcoat. "We knew that there weren't very many offenses that we couldn't play with. At that time, we were starting to really get our confidence and we were rolling. I mean we were playing at a high level as a defense and we knew we could physically dominate people because we had eight guys that could play, and a lot of teams didn't have that at that time. We had eight defensive linemen that could rotate in and never got tired. As the season progressed, we got stronger because we were fresher."[41]

6. How 'Bout Them Cowboys?

Dallas entered November with a 5–2 record, tied atop the NFC East with the New York Giants—the team they would be hosting Sunday. On November 7, a day when the Cowboys cruised past their NFC East rival and took sole possession of first place in the division, the team finally, and rightfully, gave their only former head coach, Tom Landry, formal recognition. Several years removed from the awkward and unceremonious ending to his run in Dallas, Landry entered the Cowboys Ring of Honor at halftime. Sort of a belated public apology from Jerry Jones for his heavy-handedness back in 1989.

As the elderly former coach walked from the Texas Stadium tunnel toward midfield, he received an ovation like he was Charles Lindbergh returning from Europe. When Jones got on stage, he was met with some jeers, but such cacophony largely subsided when he turned to Landry and said, "We honor you here today. Our Ring of Honor stands for the men who built this franchise and had it called 'America's Team.' This would not be the Ring of Honor without you, Coach Landry."[42]

This ceremony could have happened in 1989, but Landry wanted nothing to do with Jones and the Cowboys, for at least a little while. Days before this ceremony, in an interview with Ken Sins of the *Dallas Cowboys Official Weekly*, Landry said, "I divorced myself complete from football and haven't missed it at all.... This [coming to Texas Stadium] is a one-shot deal."[43]

Good timing. In a defensive performance even more impressive than the prior week's showing at the Vet, Dallas held New York to a field goal after the halftime ceremony. Pro Bowl quarterback Phil Simms was limited to 155 yards passing. And Emmitt Smith followed up his dominant Halloween performance by rushing for two fourth quarter touchdowns as Dallas rolled, 31–9. (It is worth pointing out that Jimmy Johnson obnoxiously called for a gadget play, downfield pass from Alvin Harper to Michael Irvin, when Dallas was comfortably ahead by 18 points late in the second half.)

The only imperfection to the feel-good afternoon was a strained left hamstring suffered by Troy Aikman in the third quarter. With Aikman sidelined until Turkey Day, Dallas would turn to Cleveland Browns castoff Bernie Kosar (who played for Jimmy Johnson at the University of Miami) and split the next two games. Still, the defending champs stood at 7–3 going into the annual late afternoon Thanksgiving Day game—with their first-string signal caller due back.

Thankfully, by November 25, Aikman's hamstring was better.

Unfortunately, the same could not be said about Leon Lett's mind.

The lowest point in Leon Lett's career had been the fumble during garbage time in Super Bowl XXVII. Until Thanksgiving 1993. This time, Lett had a brain freeze when the game's outcome was very much in question.

In town were the 8–2 Miami Dolphins, a team whose head coach, Don Shula, had won his record-setting 325th career game earlier in November. Even with future Hall of Fame quarterback Dan Marino out for the year with a ruptured Achilles tendon, Miami was still one of the top teams in the AFC. The game was billed as a Super Bowl preview … and a classic Snow Bowl. During this unseasonably cold late November day for the Dallas/Fort Worth area, several inches of sleet and snow had blanketed the region, making for treacherous playing conditions. Traction was at a premium and visibility was, at times, non-existent.

"I was actually in that game excited about playing in the snow. I had never played in the snow before," says John Jett. "But it never hit me that was like ice. In old Texas Stadium, the old turf was like worn out carpet and it was almost [like] you needed ice skates to play that game."[44]

There were moments during the first three quarters when the Cowboys were Ice Capades on a gridiron. Rookie running back Lincoln Coleman, who was discovered while playing arena football, rampaged through the Dolphins defense for 57 yards on only 10 carries, after Emmitt Smith left early with an injury. Fellow rookie, wideout Kevin Williams, scored two touchdowns, including one on a 64-yard punt return. Yet another rookie, safety Brock Marion, made a leaping interception when the Dolphins were deep in Cowboys territory.

Going into the fourth period, Dallas held a 14–10 lead and up to this point, aside from a Keith Byars 77-yard rushing touchdown, Miami had done virtually nothing on offense. However, the Dolphins made it a 14–13 game on Pete Stoyanovich's 31-yard kick midway through the quarter. After Stoyanovich's counterpart, Eddie Murray, botched a field goal attempt that would have given Dallas a four-point lead with a couple minutes remaining, backup quarterback Steve DeBerg came through on the final drive, marching the Dolphins down to the 26-yard line with 15 seconds left.

Dallas still had a solid chance to escape with a win as Stoyanovich lined up for a 41-yard field goal, certainly a tall order given the slippery conditions. The Macedonian-American kicker, accustomed to splitting the uprights in South Florida, struggled to secure solid footing in the wintry weather before Dallas defensive lineman Jimmie Jones bulldozed his way into block the attempt. Which should have meant game over, had it not been for Lett losing his mind, once again on national television.

Seconds after the blocked kick, the deflected ball slithered to a near halt at the seven-yard line with a couple alert Cowboys screaming for everyone to stay clear. All any Cowboy had to do was pick it up cleanly and the offense would brace for victory formation. Yet instead of waiting for the ball to stop spinning and then scooping it up, Lett made a hasty attempt to corral the ball by literally skidding into it. And because a member of the receiving team (Dallas) touched the ball downfield, it was now live for the kicking team (Miami) to recover. Miami offensive lineman Jeff Dellenbach did just that by pouncing on the loose pigskin at the 1-yard line and sliding into the end zone. However, Dellenbach's dream of scoring a touchdown on Thanksgiving was crushed when referee Ed Hochuli correctly awarded the ball to the Dolphins at the 1-yard line, per the rule that the instant the kicking team recovers the ball, it becomes dead at that spot of possession.

Simply put, if Leon had just let the ball drift harmlessly in the mounds of snow, he wouldn't have been a turkey on this day. Instead, Lett's snowy slide into further infamy had allowed Dellenbach to gobble up the ball and position Stoyanovich for a far easier 19-yard attempt with three ticks remaining. The All-Pro kicker converted, and Miami secured a last-second 16–14 win in a wildly entertaining game on the sport's trademark holiday showcase. So, as Americans were bracing for Black Friday and/or making plans to see the recently released blockbuster *Mrs. Doubtfire* over the upcoming long weekend, they enjoyed arguably the most memorable Thanksgiving Day game in NFL history.

A quarter-century later, the sequence remains fresh in Dellenbach's memory.

"There were snowy, icy conditions, which I don't think anybody really expected in Dallas at that time," recalls Dellenbach. "We were lined up to kick a field goal and I was the long snapper at the time. We snapped and put the ball down. Pete Stoyanovich's plant foot slipped so he kicked the ball low, [it] got tipped at the line of scrimmage, and was rolling on the ground, which for us there was not much we could do unless they [the Cowboys] touched the ball and it so happened that they did. The ball became live. We got the ball back, went out there and kicked the field goal and won the game. Their blunder gave us a second chance to win it."[45]

Lett would rebound from these early career gaffes. (While the team was mostly supportive afterward, special teams coach Joe Avezzano did comment to reporters, "We had 11 men on the field. Ten of them knew what to do.")[46] In fact, Lett was a very important player for the Cowboys throughout the rest of the nineties, and, after serving as an anchor on their defensive line, became a staple of their coaching staff. He was good-natured and always held himself accountable for his blunders. Still, this one was hard to stomach. For portions of the game, the snow had neutralized the Cowboys' greatest asset, their blazing speed, yet the game was clearly theirs for the taking up until the end.

"I think it [snow] definitely slowed the game down for everybody involved," says Dellenbach. "It was a relatively low scoring game that day. Our run game actually was decent, and we managed to stay in the game. Anytime you play a team like Dallas at the time who was on top of their game, those are the games that you love playing in and you get excited about. Going there and playing on Thanksgiving Day and there's a national audience, things that just nobody expected really led to a completely different type of game. Those games are special, those moments are special, and when you come out on top, those are the things that you always remember. I love seeing it Thanksgiving Day when they replay."[47]

Within five days, Dallas' record had dropped from 7–2 to 7–4. (On Sunday, November 21, Dallas had lost at Atlanta, 27–14.) During Thanksgiving week, they went from Super Bowl favorites to a team jockeying for position in a cramped NFC playoff race. Still, in the home locker room afterward, Johnson reminded his guys that they knew how to handle a two-game losing streak, as the season began in such a manner. And most importantly, if they won out, the division was theirs.

Indeed, Dallas would not lose a game the rest of the season. Meanwhile, Miami didn't win another game this season and failed to even qualify for the playoffs.

December began with a showdown against Philadelphia on "Monday Night Football." Dallas squeaked out a 23–17 win behind a rested and healthier Emmitt Smith rushing for 172 yards and a smothering defense containing the Eagles to 59 yards on the ground.

The Cowboys got rolling when Troy Aikman found wide receiver Michael Irvin for an 11-yard touchdown pass in the first quarter. Dallas had the early lead, one that it would never relinquish. Truthfully, however, Aikman had an unspectacular night, getting sacked four times and throwing for only 178 yards. The aerial standout was Irvin, who was accountable for over half of the passing yards total, just as he would be the next week in a 37–20 win over the Minnesota Vikings.

Irvin continued to torch NFL secondaries in December, hauling in two more touchdowns against the New York Jets during Week 16, and snagging one more against the Washington Redskins in the penultimate game of the year. It was a December to remember for one of the most prolific wideouts of the 1990s: 25 receptions, 359 receiving yards, five touchdowns.

These were heady days for Irvin, both on and off the field. After signing a three-year, $3.75 million contract with the Cowboys in 1992, Irvin was now living large. He cruised around North Texas in his black Mercedes convertible, diamond-encrusted Rolex on one wrist, diamond bracelet on the other. A necklace of inch-thick gold bars would round out the ensemble. Four-figure Versace suits and clams casino were a couple of Irvin's other favorite indulgences.[48] Perhaps his most glaring form of ostentatiousness was his fancy shoes with feathers from exotic animals pinned at the top.[49]

How much life had changed for Irvin. A couple decades earlier, growing up on 27th Avenue in Fort Lauderdale, he became accustomed to wearing toeless sneakers. There were 17 Irvin children to provide for and his parents couldn't afford new shoes when his size changed. Nor could they afford milk. Breakfast often consisted of stale Corn Flakes and tap water. A tiny brick house only had one fan for many sweltering days. Now, he was a multi-millionaire who acted the part.[50]

An October 1993 *Sports Illustrated* cover story on Irvin included comments from Irvin's wife, Sandy, about how her husband would often lie in bed at night, giggling for no apparent reason. Other than, of course, the fact that football turned his life from misery to elation.[51]

The transformation didn't happen without a terrifying scare along the way, however. Irvin missed most of the dreadful 1989 season, after tearing the anterior cruciate ligament in his left knee six games in. Irvin's career could have been over in his mid-twenties and he never would have made millions doing something he loved. Haunted by memories of sharing a bedroom with six brothers, Irvin was steadfast in rehabilitating his knee, regularly incorporating 30-mile bike rides into his nearly year-long recovery plan. The first-round pick out of the University of Miami, whom he helped lead to a national title in 1987, wasn't going to leave professional football after two seasons.

"When I was there, he got hurt and blew out his knee and I think he made a miraculous recovery to have a Hall of Fame career because when a wide receiver blows out his knee, it's a big 'if' [in regards to] how far they are going to go in the future. He became a great player after that knee injury," recalls Crawford Ker. "Michael [Irvin] was one of my best teammates. Michael and I didn't really hang out a lot, but he was that type of guy that would ignite. Even when we had some losing seasons, he hated to lose so he was more that emotional leader that all teams need."[52]

Irvin contributed during the 1990 season (20 catches, five touchdowns) while recovering his health. The next year was his breakout year (93 catches, eight touchdowns, 1,523 receiving yards), which earned Irvin a first-team All-Pro nod—and the aforementioned multi-million-dollar contract as Dallas embarked on its 1992 renaissance season, one in which The Playmaker also dazzled. Irvin's sweet run continued into the 1993 calendar year, when, late in the first half of Super Bowl XXVII, minutes before Michael Jackson would take the stage, he snagged a pair of touchdown receptions when the whole world was watching.

But making millions of dollars instead of hundreds of thousands of dollars and emerging as a superstar didn't change Irvin's work ethic. He could act like a temperamental diva away from the field, but when it came time to strap on the pads, Irvin trained and practiced like he was fighting for one of the club's final roster spots. During early summer off-season workouts in the sizzling Texas heat, Irvin would grind out exercises with a weighted vest and girdle—strapped below his shoulder pads and helmet. When training camp got underway in late July, a common sight at the team's Valley Ranch practice facility was Irvin finishing his wind sprints with vomit dripping down his pads.

"He [Michael Irvin] was one of the hardest working guys. First guy on the practice field, last guy to leave. People can talk about all his antics and ethics off the field, but when it came to putting in work, he never fell short. He never backed away from work," says longtime teammate James Washington. "He's one of those guys that I would walk through a dark alley with when I was on the Cowboys and I would not have to worry about anyone touching me because he had my back like that."[53]

Still, it was undeniable that Irvin's fiery competitive spirit could turn into brashness that, at times, rubbed opponents, and even teammates, the wrong way.

"There were guys who had to keep Michael Irvin in check, guys like myself, guys like Charles Haley and Nate Newton and Ken Norton," acknowledges Washington. "Mike [Irvin] was a loud person, but there were so many other leaders on the team. It kind of blows me away sometimes, because the person who is the most vocal has a tendency to be recognized."[54]

The Cowboys went 4–0 in December, but they weren't the only NFC East team that caught fire down the stretch. The New York Giants entered January having won six of their past seven games. The two teams were both 11–4, tied atop the division and set to square off at Giants Stadium during the final game of the 1993 regular season, on the second day of 1994. At stake was a first-round bye and home-field advantage throughout the playoffs. For good measure, it would also be linebacker Lawrence Taylor's last regular season home game.

No ordinary Sunday afternoon in the Meadowlands.

"A lot of things didn't faze us. We were in New York and we were playing at a hostile environment. But things never fazed us," says Jim Jeffcoat. "We just continued to play and knew that things would turn our way if we just continued to play. That shows you what type of team it was and the mentality we had—a tough mentality."[55]

Judging by his team's dominant first half performance, the 77,356 raucous fans packing Giants Stadium were a non-factor: as time expired in the first half, an Eddie Murray 38-yard field goal gave Dallas a commanding 13–0 lead.

But that was not the story heading into halftime.

In the second quarter, following a 46-yard run, Emmitt Smith was slammed to the unforgiving Giants Stadium turf by New York safety Greg Jackson. The resulting damage was a first-degree separation of the right shoulder, an injury that would have jettisoned many players to the ER. But not Smith. He missed *two* snaps. This was the most important regular season finale in the franchise's long history, and he wasn't going to let Lincoln Coleman assume his workload.

During halftime, Smith popped a couple of Vicodins and had a thigh pad taped to his shoulder pad for absorbing further shock. Still, the latter precaution could only do so much. When Smith's right shoulder should have been resting in a sling, it was now poised to absorb more violent jolts.

The rest of the afternoon was one of triumph and torture. While shouldering the load for the Dallas offense, Smith found his range of motion was so limited that Troy Aikman had to lower his handoffs. But it wasn't just being unable to raise his right arm for handoffs. Each block, fall, and collision intensified the torture. Smith's horrifying shrieks from the bottom of piles were audible to players and officials. And the second half workload (13 carries for 59 yards and four receptions for 19 yards) wasn't the end of his day. New York scored 13 unanswered points after halftime to force overtime.

With one functioning arm, the courageous Smith took over in OT, touching the ball nine times for 41 yards, a performance that set up Eddie Murray's game-winning field goal for the 16–13 division-clinching win.

Given the excruciating injury, it was remarkable how the football was Smith's a franchise-record 42 times (32 carries, 10 receptions) as he accounted for 229 of the Cowboys' 339 total yards.

In the Dallas locker room afterward, massive offensive lineman Nate Newton told reporters, "He told us in the huddle to make sure we ran behind him so someone could pick him up. Coach [Jimmy] Johnson asked him if he would be ready and there wasn't a doubt or hesitation. He said he was going. That really touched me because you could see how hurt he was. After we made our blocks, the main thing was to get to him and get him up."[56]

The physical torment didn't cease when the game did. And it wasn't just the shoulder. It was severely bruised sternum and ribs stemming from other collisions. While getting dressed in the postgame locker room, Smith was afflicted with chest spasms that intensified to the point he could hardly move. Eventually, the pain would subside, enough so that he boarded the team's charter out of Newark. But while the plane was still on the tarmac, distressing palpitations returned to Smith's chest, now closer to his heart. Upon landing in Dallas, Smith was taken to a local hospital where he spent the night, one that was a blur of medicated IV and pain pills, before being released the following day.[57]

"Well that was gutsy," recalls Dallas defensive coordinator Butch Davis. "I mean that was remarkable because everybody on the team knew that Emmitt was in pain. He had the courage of a lion and he wasn't coming out. It was very typical and not unexpected coming from him in that game."[58]

"It was cold and windy of course in New York, last game of the season," recalls John Jett. "With Emmitt's shoulder, you don't want the guy to hurt himself and Emmitt's a smart man. But to see him go out and do what he did with basically one shoulder, you take your hat off to the guy."[59]

With 168 yards on the ground, Smith finished the season with 1,486 rushing yards, becoming the first player to capture the rushing title after missing two games and the fourth in history to win three consecutive times.

However, was it all for altruistic purposes? Certainly, Smith didn't want his team to finish runner-up to the Giants for the division title. However, he *really* didn't want to finish runner-up to Los Angeles Rams rookie Jerome Bettis for the rushing title. And he acknowledged as much months later in his autobiography *The Emmitt Zone* when he wrote, "It wasn't all about playing hurt. At that point at least, it wasn't even all about helping us win; with a 13-point lead, I felt we already had the game in hand. So the main reason I kept playing was to win my third consecutive rushing title."[60]

Which could have meant jeopardizing his health for the postseason.

Even as a *rookie*, before the rushing titles and Pro Bowl nods and Reebok endorsements, Smith was not exactly an ideal teammate. Traditionally, rookies are supposed to be seen, not heard from, yet Smith, as an NFL newbie, complained that he wasn't getting enough touches. Decades later, veterans from that 1990 Cowboys team don't forget Smith's self-serving tendencies.

"Emmitt was his own guy," reflects Crawford Ker, who, like Smith, played football at the University of Florida before going pro. "I would probably say he is just a cocky, confident type of guy. I mean, I don't know if he's the greatest human being going in my opinion."[61]

His self-centeredness aside, no one could downplay the remarkable courage Smith displayed in New Jersey ... or the fact that by the mid–1990s, he was the best running back in the NFL.

Emmitt Smith reaped immense benefits from the bye week that he had worked so hard to secure. By mid–January, he was now considerably healthier and ready to attack the NFL playoffs. His team's opponent in the NFC Divisional Round was the upstart Green Bay Packers, led by young gunslinging quarterback Brett Favre and prolific receiver Sterling Sharpe. Still, per everyone's expectations, the Packers didn't give their hosts much of a game (Vegas had Dallas as a 14-point favorite). Dallas held a 24–3 lead

6. How 'Bout Them Cowboys?

Emmitt Smith—simply put, the most important member of the Dallas Cowboys' 1990s dynasty and arguably the greatest running back to ever play the game (photograph provided by Bill Frakes).

midway through the third quarter and never looked back on the way to a 27–17 win.

Sound bites from the postgame locker room suggested the Cowboys had been looking past the overmatched Packers and ahead toward an NFC title game rematch with the San Francisco 49ers.

Emmitt Smith: "The way we played today, there was no possible way we could have beat San Francisco."[62]

Michael Irvin: "There's nothing like a swift kick in the mouth to get your concentration back. It's always great to play at home. When you play a team as hot as the Niners, you need all the help you can get."[63]

From the 1981 NFC Championship Game (The Catch) to the early nineties, the Dallas–San Francisco matchup really hadn't been much of a rivalry. San Francisco won four Super Bowls and Dallas never made it to one. By the late 1980s, the disparity grew even more gaping: San Francisco was at the height of its dynasty, winning Super Bowl XXIII and Super Bowl XXIV, while Dallas remained one of the worst teams of the NFC. San Francisco's offense was paced by Joe Montana, Jerry Rice, and Roger Craig. The defense was loaded with stars such as Ronnie Lott, Bill Romanowski, and most importantly, pass rusher Charles Haley, who was a constant menace charging in from the blind side to assault quarterbacks.

One of the major storylines leading up to the 1993 NFC Championship Game was that since the 49ers had jettisoned Haley to the Cowboys prior to the 1992 season, the pendulum had shifted back toward the Cowboys. Big time. Since the lopsided trade, the Cowboys had won the only Super Bowl played and had defeated San Francisco twice in two tries, and now were favored to do so again in a few days.

Of course, it would be an oversimplification, an outright falsity to say that one player was the difference maker. But Haley's presence alone was an unmistakably large factor in the rivalry becoming more balanced.

Even if he, himself, was not.

When the 49ers traded Haley to the Cowboys for a future second-round and third-round draft pick in August 1992, they knew they were getting pennies on the dollar. They were that desperate. By the end of his time in San Fran, Haley was exhibiting grossly inappropriate sexual behavior (masturbating during team meetings, rubbing his genitalia in teammates' faces) and struggled with severe anger management issues (urinating in the car of teammate whom he considered a threat to his job). In his last year as a 49er, Haley became so furious following a loss to the Los Angeles Raiders that he threatened to assault quarterback Steve Young in the post-game locker room. San Francisco had to call on Haley's former teammate and close friend Ronnie Lott—clad only in a towel—to come out of the Los Angeles locker room to calm him down.[64] Yet after the 1991 season, Dallas, a team longing for an elite pass rusher, was willing to look past Haley's stormy episodes in the Bay Area. Especially if it meant not giving up any established veterans or first-round draft picks.

When Haley landed in Dallas in August 1992, he got along well enough with the right people. His two Super Bowl rings commanded respect from not just rookies, but from seasoned vets such as Jim Jeffcoat as well.

"Well, the biggest thing was that he [Haley] had Super Bowl experience and that helped," says Jeffcoat. "Anytime you can have a player that has Super Bowl experience and understands the preparation to get to the Super Bowl, that's important."[65]

For the most part, the organization was able to tolerate Haley's ongoing salacious behavior, brashness, and occasional outbursts. Everyone knew he was troubled—but few, if any, knew that he was suffering from bipolar disorder. It wasn't until years later, in retirement, that Haley fully acknowledged his lifelong demons—and finally decided to undergo therapy and take medication. During his 2015 enshrinement speech for the Pro Football Hall of Fame, Haley said, "I walked into the league a 22-year-old man with a 16-year-old inside of me screaming for help, and I would not ask for it."[66]

Once Haley became established on the Cowboys' defensive line (he made a seamless transition from playing outside linebacker in the 49ers' 3–4 scheme to serving as a defensive end in the Cowboys' 4–3 scheme), Dallas was able to overlook the off-field behavior. Meanwhile, it soon became painfully clear to San Francisco that not being able to tolerate Haley was a mistake. Although Haley would never post eye-popping statistics for the Cowboys, he was a force on the defensive line, his sole presence drawing double-teams, much to the delight of onrushing linebackers. In fact, Dallas' sack total skyrocketed from 23 in 1991 to 44 in 1992. And he played his best football against the team that gave up on him. During the 1992 NFC Championship Game, Haley's relentless pressure on Steve Young resulted in Tony Casillas racking up three sacks. During the 1993 regular season matchup against the Niners, Haley had two sacks, one of which forced Young to fumble. (Haley's production and playing time dipped in the 1993 season, largely due to a nagging off-season back injury that never fully healed.)

Prior to this upcoming conference championship game, Young even acknowledged, "In retrospect, I wish Charles Haley was still on our team."[67]

If you were an offensive teammate of Young's preparing for the NFC Championship Game, one widely considered to be the real Super Bowl, it was hard to argue otherwise.

As if there weren't enough build-up for Sunday's conference championship game, on Thursday evening, Jimmy Johnson decided to make his own headlines when he telephoned a Fort Worth radio station from his car and declared in no uncertain terms that the Cowboys would win the game: "We will win the ballgame. And you can put it in three-inch headlines. We will win the ballgame." The *Dallas Morning News* didn't quite oblige, putting Johnson's guarantee in only half-inch type at the top of the front page of the newspaper Friday morning, right next to the headline: "Whitewater Case Counsel Expects to Grill Clintons."[68]

(When told of Johnson's prediction, the normally understated 49ers head coach George Seifert said, "Well the man has balls, I'll tell you that. I don't know if they're brass or papier-mâché. We'll find out here pretty soon."[69])

Ever the brainy tactician, Johnson was undoubtedly focused on tweaking San Francisco. Success. A few days later, his radio rant fresh in their minds, several 49ers took exception to a couple Dallas players bumping Jerry Rice during pregame warmups. Minutes before the introductions, a brouhaha broke out in the end zone.

When he published his autobiography *QB: My Life Behind the Spiral*, San Francisco quarterback Steve Young recalled the significance of Johnson's ploy: "The problem is that all of this distracts us from what we need to do to win the game. It plays right into Jimmy Johnson's hands. Our team is so emotionally charged at the start of the game that we don't execute well."[70]

But the Cowboys certainly did as they went into halftime ahead 28–7. Although his shoulder was still not one hundred percent, Emmitt Smith was flashing signs of his regular season dominance, scoring two touchdowns (five-yard rush, 11-yard reception). Safety Thomas Everett made a pivotal interception, picking off a Young pass when San Francisco was driving in the second quarter, only down 14–7. The turnover set up a quick 24-yard touchdown drive that extended Dallas' lead to 21–7. But the first half belonged to Troy Aikman, who engineered four scoring drives that covered 251 yards before halftime. His first half was nearly flawless: 14 of 18, 177 yards, two touchdowns, zero turnovers. He even ran for 25 yards. This was shaping up to be perhaps the best game of Aikman's career—even better than Super Bowl XXVII.

Until the opening seconds of the second half.

Then it became one of the worst days of the quarterback's life.

On Dallas' second play after halftime, San Francisco defensive lineman Dennis Brown inadvertently struck Aikman's helmet with his right knee while dropping him for a seven-yard loss. Aikman haltingly rose from the turf, clutching his helmet with both hands. After handing off to Emmitt Smith on third down, Aikman jogged to the sidelines, where he inhaled ammonia from capsules. In lieu of a formal concussion protocol, team doctor J.R. Zamorano asked Aikman where the upcoming Super Bowl was to be played. When a dazed and confused Aikman responded by saying the name of his hometown "Henryetta, Oklahoma" (and not the actual site, Atlanta) Zamorano suggested Aikman be admitted to Baylor Medical Center, where he would end up spending the entire night.

This would be the first major concussion of Aikman's professional career. Hours later, in his hospital room, he struggled to recall even a couple plays from the game he had just played in, and kept asking his agent, Leigh Steinberg, the same questions repeatedly. At one point, he couldn't remember his own phone number.

However, toward the end of this long and scary night, Aikman, starting to regain his mental faculties, found out he was indeed headed for Atlanta as his Cowboys held on in the second half to defeat the 49ers, 38–21, winning the NFC title for the second consecutive year.

There would be more skull-crushing football in a week.

The next day, during a press conference at the team's hotel in Atlanta, it was apparent that the severe head injuries inflicted on the franchise's other legendary quarterback, Roger Staubach, were not lost on Aikman.

"I've had concussions in the past, but this is the first one where I actually lost recall of what took place," Aikman said. "I'm not overly concerned because it was the first one. But I realize what happened to Roger Staubach and how it cut his career short."[71]

(Staubach had over 20 concussions, and by the time Aikman retired following the 2000 season he would have 10 concussions. Ironically, for a guy such as Aikman who was notorious for being terrified of death, he left himself vulnerable to severe head trauma throughout his professional life.)

In the upcoming week, there were signs that Aikman wasn't one hundred percent. He was held out of contact drills. As practices dragged on, Aikman was starting to complain of headaches. Backup Bernie Kosar was getting more than his usual number of practice reps. It was hard not to question whether the Cowboys were being responsible in planning to start Aikman. In boxing, when a fighter takes a 10 count, he is not allowed to get back into the ring for as long as 90 days in some states. In 20th century football, it was simply called "getting your bell rung," and a week later, the quarterback is back—if the contest is important enough. And this one certainly was. Had this been an early October game against the Tampa Bay Buccaneers, perhaps Aikman would have been shelved. But Dallas was on the verge of becoming only the sixth team to win consecutive Super Bowls and the third to capture four Lombardi Trophies.

Troy Aikman was going to be under center Sunday evening in the Georgia Dome.

For the second consecutive January, the Dallas Cowboys would battle the Buffalo Bills for a Lombardi Trophy. However, Super Bowl XXVIII did not have the cachet of the previous year's edition. Atlanta may have recently been called "a city on a definite '90s high"[72] by talk show host Larry King, but it was no Hollywood setting. Tens of millions of Americans would be watching, whereas the prior year hundreds of millions of people worldwide had been tuned in. In large part because the halftime show was not going to be a breathtaking spectacle: this year's headlining act was The Judds, a very talented country music duo, but nonetheless one that was far more subdued and less popular than the King of Pop.

But, for the Cowboys, all that mattered was that the halftime show featuring The Judds still lasted over 30 minutes.

The Cowboys needed time to make adjustments from a disappointing first half performance that left them trailing 13–6 at intermission. Understandably, Troy Aikman started slowly, slightly off on his reads and deliveries. While Aikman and the offense had to settle for a pair of field goals, the most pressing issues concerned Dallas' defense, a unit that was not exactly personifying the home city's nickname, "Big D." Dallas was lucky that Buffalo only had scored 13 points before halftime. It was a first half marred by blown assignments, missed open field tackles, and dearth of sacks. On multiple plays, the defense was caught off guard when Buffalo quarterback Jim Kelly came out with a three-step drop and connected with receivers on lightning-quick throws underneath.

The Cowboys didn't look or act like a team that had routed the Bills in the previous Super Bowl. As the first half ended, a team full of high-flying playmakers was dumbfounded as to how they came out so flat in the sequel to last year's romp.

"I remember walking into the tunnel, and I was talking to Leon Lett," recalls Dallas safety James Washington. "I was on him and I said, 'I need you to make a play. I need you to make a play to turn this game around.' When we went into the locker room we were down."[73]

Those present in the Dallas locker room recall that, much to their surprise at the time, Jimmy Johnson, while certainly disappointed, did not give a fire-and-brimstone speech. In fact, he didn't say much of anything, but instead allowed his veterans and assistant coaches to engage in cerebral discussions about how to improve.

Jim Jeffcoat: "It was ironic. We were worried that Jimmy [Johnson] was going to get on us about the first half but all he said was 'Hey, let's go win this game.' That was it."[74]

James Washington: "Jimmy Johnson didn't say anything out of the ordinary. He allowed the leaders of our team to talk and all you heard was 'We need to just make our plays and we will be OK.'"[75]

Defensive coordinator Butch Davis: "One of the things that was great about the Super Bowl was how long the halftimes were. Because Super Bowls have longer time, you don't have the 12 to 15 minutes during the regular season, I think we had maybe like 30, 35 minutes, and it helped us be able to fix some of those things and add in some things to do in the second half.

"At halftime we looked at a lot of the things that we had called in the first half and said, 'You know what, this isn't working. This isn't good.' Because of the veteran experience, veteran defensive team, we were able to say, 'OK, you remember the pressure that we ran against the Phoenix Cardinals. We're going to put that in.' Even though we had hardly practiced it, they knew it. And we made some adjustments for Thurman Thomas, where he was lined up and those kinds of things.

"Because we had beaten them so bad in the Super Bowl previously and we almost beat them without Emmitt [Smith] in the second game of the season, I'm not going to say that the players were lackadaisical, but I don't know if there was as sharp of an edge."[76]

In other words, Dallas knew it was the superior team.

"There was no panic in the locker room," remembers Washington. "And all we said was 'What we do best, we just need to do that in the second half.' And the two things that we did best in Dallas were we played defense and we ran the football."[77]

And for the rest of the evening, Dallas excelled in both those areas.

And it all started with, per Washington's request, Leon Lett making a play to turn the game around.

On the third play from scrimmage after halftime, Lett knocked the ball loose from Thurman Thomas, and it was recovered by Washington. The veteran defensive back returned the fumble recovery 46 yards for a touchdown that tied the game at 13. Knowing that Don Beebe, who had forced Lett's infamous Super Bowl XXVII fumble, was in his rearview mirror, Washington kept the ball tucked firmly against his shoulder pads as he soared across the Georgia Dome carpet.

"Second half comes out, Leon Lett causes the fumble and I scoop it up," recalls Washington. "And we practiced this drill a hundred times— scoop and score. All I could think about when I had the ball was 'Where's [Don] Beebe?' If you look at how everybody was blocking, and still all I could think about was 'Where's Beebe?' because I was thinking about Leon Lett. I saw him [Beebe] from the corner of my eye. He ran right by me, Thomas Everett blocked him, and I rode all the way into the end zone."[78]

Whereas Leon Lett left Super Bowl XXVII a year earlier feeling humiliated, James Washington left his collegiate home turf feeling unsatisfied. Washington had a personal connection to the game's location, Pasadena, having won two Rose Bowls as a member of the UCLA Bruins in the 1980s. But following the Cowboys' five-touchdown win last January, Washington's story was not even a sidebar. Something he never forgot. It didn't matter that his Cowboys had won their first Super Bowl in 15 years. He was the forgotten man on a heretofore unsung defensive unit that was finally getting due recognition.

"I left Super Bowl XXVII a little upset because even though I had the first turnover, it kind of went unnoticed," recalls Washington. "I had the first turnover, interception. Eight turnovers later, which made nine, nobody remembered the first turnover because nobody remembered what was happening before that. I told Michael Irvin and Ken Norton in the locker room at Super Bowl XXVII, 'When we come back to the Super Bowl next year, they are never forgetting me.'"[79]

A couple days before Super Bowl XXVIII, Washington was told by Jimmy Johnson that he would be starting at free safety. Bold move by Johnson to believe that a rusty Washington could effectively neutralize Buffalo's fleet-footed receivers. After all, Washington had been phased out of Dallas' defense this season largely due to the emergence of hard-hitting second-year defensive back Darren Woodson. Woodson, who had passed

Washington on the depth chart going into the 1993 regular season, proved to be incredibly versatile, covering speedy slot receivers like a corner and taking on tight ends like a linebacker.

"People don't realize he [Woodson] was unbelievably talented," says Butch Davis.[80]

But Washington knew that he, too, was talented. As a freshman at UCLA, watching Los Angeles Raiders cornerback Lester Hayes play in Super Bowl XVIII, Washington knew that he, too, was capable of one day excelling on the NFL's grand stage. After graduating from UCLA with a degree in history, Washington stayed in Los Angeles when the Rams selected him in the fifth round of the 1988 NFL Draft. He wasn't a Ram for long. On the morning of February 1, 1990, Washington was awakened by a phone call. It was the Phoenix Cardinals and they wanted Washington to work out for them, which meant that the Rams had designated Washington a Plan B free agent without even giving him advance notice.

Washington was crushed that his hometown team had lost interest in him. Soon, it became apparent that his best opportunity to continue playing pro football was not in Phoenix, but in Dallas, where the team was rebuilding its defense by acquiring promising yet overlooked players who were hungry for a second chance.

For Washington, earning his keep in the NFL was a breeze compared to surviving his hellacious upbringing in crime-ridden South Central Los Angeles. One day in high school, Washington's best friend, Keith Solomon, was shot in the head and murdered following a vicious argument while another day, a football teammate who got involved with drug-related gang activity went missing ... only to be found beheaded later.[81] But Washington was able to eschew drugs and violence largely because he took his studies seriously and spent his free time on the gridiron, where he eventually caught UCLA's attention.

Now, a decade later, he was drawing the country's attention.

At least for one evening, that of January 30, 1994, anyway.

"There's Christmas and then there are Super Bowls," says Washington. "Super Bowl day is kind of like Christmas for everyone. As long as they're showing the Super Bowls, people will never forget what happened in Super Bowl XXVIII. It was a day to remember on the biggest stage and I shined as bright as a star can shine on defense."[82]

Before the pivotal touchdown after halftime, Washington had forced Thurman Thomas to cough up the football near midfield in the first quarter, leading to a Dallas field goal. On the opening play of the fourth quarter, with Dallas clinging to a 20–13 lead, Washington picked off an errant Jim Kelly pass and returned it 12 yards to the Bills' 34, allowing Emmitt Smith to take over on the ensuing drive, one in which he sealed the game (and secured MVP honors) with his second rushing touchdown of the evening.

"Eleven solo tackles, three turnovers, a touchdown, and then I get an interception late in the game, and I was just exhausted, so I went to the turf," reflects Washington. "But the thing that you never do, you don't give the best player on the team [Emmitt Smith] an opportunity to outshine you. Emmitt Smith is a good friend of mine, he's my fraternity brother, and what I did was give him the ball to solidify him being the MVP of the game when he had 132 yards. I truly think he deserved it, [but] if nothing else a Co-MVP for James Washington."[83]

It didn't take Washington long to realize he had one of the most impressive defensive performances in Super Bowl history. In the postgame locker room, Washington declared to reporters, "It was like I was Michael Jordan out there."[84]

On sabbatical from the NBA, Michael Jordan was one of 72,817 fans who saw Washington's career-defining performance at the Georgia Dome that evening.

While Dallas' defense was largely a one-man show with Washington's heroics, the offense delivered a sterling teamwide performance after halftime. It was 30 minutes of football in which Dallas steamrolled Buffalo 24–0 en route to the 30–13 win.

No longer hampered with the residual effects of the harrowing shoulder injury, Emmitt Smith had a hefty workload—30 carries, including six on consecutive plays to begin the Cowboys' first drive of the second half, one that culminated with Smith's first touchdown run, which erased Buffalo's 13–6 halftime lead.

Throughout the second half, Dallas was dominating time of possession as Troy Aikman was brilliantly engineering clock-chewing drives, only throwing four incompletions after halftime. After a rocky start, Aikman, only a week removed from a potentially life-altering concussion, was precise and efficient when it mattered most.

In the locker room afterward, when a reporter suggested that Aikman was "off" in the early going, tight end Jay Novacek got defensive. The fact that his recently concussed teammate even played was impressive; that Aikman finished with over 200 yards passing was nearly heroic.

"Off? What do you mean, off? We won the damn game, didn't we? What kind of stupid question is that? Troy was Troy."[85]

In a sense, the trajectory of this game mirrored that of the team's season: A poor start eventually gave way to a brilliant performance down the stretch.

"That half it always amazed me with Norv Turner being the offensive coordinator and Troy [Aikman] at quarterback and the receiving group we had with Jay Novacek," says John Jett. "It was impossible for the DBs to cover because they were timing the routes and the ball was there when the receiver turned around. And then when you've got Emmitt [Smith] in the backfield, I mean they can't cover everything. Again, to see it click like that and all, it's something to watch when it clicks like that."[86]

For the nationwide Cowboys fan base, the back-to-back Super Bowls amid this resurgence in the nineties rekindled memories of the glory days of the seventies. Meanwhile, the lost decade of the eighties started fading from memory.

"Dallas is one of the best organizations in the history of the league," says former Detroit Lions center Kevin Glover. "You can really go down their roster and look at all the great players and the Hall of Famers they've had and the Pro Bowlers. There were times on any given year they may have seven, eight, nine Pro Bowlers on just the offense alone, not to mention great players on the defensive side."[87]

Now, people who thought after the Pasadena Super Bowl that a dynasty was brewing in Dallas felt justified. Indeed, as Super Bowl XXVIII concluded, the dominant narrative was whether Dallas was already the team of the nineties—after only the conclusion of the 1993 season. They were the odds-on favorite to return to the Super Bowl at Joe Robbie Stadium the following January, and win. Emmitt Smith, Michael Irvin, and Troy Aikman were on the right side of 30. The defense was deep, and, for the most part, not terribly old, either. And Jimmy Johnson, only 50 years old and under contract for five more years, presumably would be the team's head coach for the foreseeable future.

Less than two months after Super Bowl XXVIII, on March 21, at a party during the NFL meetings in Orlando, Jimmy Johnson was having drinks with former coordinators Norv Turner (recently named the Washington Redskins head coach) and Dave Wannstedt and executive Bob Ackles and their spouses. Notably missing was Jerry Jones, whose absence presented Johnson with the perfect opportunity to say how he really felt about his boss.

Despite the team's recent success, Johnson had found it very difficult/nearly impossible to co-exist peacefully with Jones over the past couple years. The public may have seen Jones and Johnson embracing in champagne-soaked hugs the past two Januaries, but there was significant underlying tension. Johnson had grown tired of Jones' meddlesome nature; Jones felt that Johnson had lost sight of who was boss. (Johnson had many issues with Jones' brazen approach to ownership, perhaps most notably Jones' insistence that Saudi Arabia's Prince Bandar bin Sultan and his cadre of bodyguards be allowed to visit the sidelines and locker room on game day.) Now, a well-hydrated Johnson had a captive audience to hear his grievances. At one moment, while gossiping like middle school students in a cafeteria, the staff began rehashing a story that occurred in the Dallas war room minutes before the 1992 NFL Draft ensued. It was discussed how Jones, feeling resentful that he was not notified when a trade the day before had been finalized, told Johnson, "You know the ESPN camera is in the draft room today. So whenever we're about to make a pick, you look at me, like we're talking about it."[88] For Johnson, it didn't matter that he was still employed by Jones. He couldn't turn down an opportunity to vent his lingering frustrations with his power-hungry, publicity-hogging boss.

During the storytelling, who walks over and asks to make a toast? A jovial Jerry Jones. Naturally, Jimmy Johnson and friends declined his invitation. Jones was irate. How could any employee, past or present, so blatantly disrespect him? Later that evening, in a face-to-face meeting, the still bitter owner threatened to fire Johnson, claiming that the team was so talented that "500 coaches" could have led Dallas to consecutive Super Bowl wins.[89] (Jones also believed that Johnson was not only an average coach but also had taken a disproportionate amount of credit for putting together the Cowboys rosters.)

This was the breaking point for the former college teammates whose already fragile relationship had deteriorated during this past championship season. Case in point: four days before the regular season finale in the Meadowlands, Johnson had told ESPN that he was intrigued by the possibility of coaching the expansion Jacksonville Jaguars, whose inaugural season was slated for 1995. Subsequently, Jones, peeved over the ill-timed remark, told the press he would be the one deciding Johnson's future. Johnson responded with a personal retort, walking up to his boss on the charter flight home after the division-clinching win and saying, "By the way, I'm the one who's going to decide how long I coach here."[90]

And on the morning of March 29, 1994, Johnson did just that. Tired of exchanging barbs in the press and still stewing over the incident in Orlando, Johnson stopped toying with the idea of coaching one more year in Dallas and walked into Jones' office to say it was time. Jones concurred and voided the last five years of Johnson's contract, while giving him a $2 million severance pay.[91] The strong-willed Johnson, who, after all, had won an NCAA championship and Super Bowl, now had free will to go wherever he pleased.

The official explanation for the termination of Johnson's contract was a "mutually agreed upon divorce."[92] That way the public would not be under the impression that Johnson was fired ... or felt compelled to resign.

During his final press conference in Dallas, Johnson said:

Anyone who knows me knows I have to go 100 percent totally focused, totally into it or else I'm not going to be as good as I need to be. I think Jerry was starting to understand that I was starting to lose that focus, and when I looked at myself I knew I was losing that focus. That's why I think it's in the best interests of the Dallas Cowboys that I am no longer head football coach.[93]

While Jones certainly caught flak from Dallas fans (including multiple death threats), several players questioned Johnson's character and judgment. Was it really that Johnson lost focus when he had a chance to be the first NFL head coach to lead a team to three consecutive Super Bowl victories? Perhaps his massive ego was the true culprit.

Michael Irvin remarked afterward, "When you do what's best for yourself, it isn't always best for everybody."[94]

Even Troy Aikman, the mild-mannered, cliché-spewing superstar, weighed in when he told *Sports Illustrated*'s Peter King, "Jimmy orchestrated the thing brilliantly. He wanted out, he saw a crack, and he took it. He got a ton of money, and he got everyone to feel sorry for him."[95]

Emmitt Smith publicly announced he would consider retirement without Johnson at the helm.

(He would play well into the next century.)

Truthfully, Irvin, Aikman, Smith, and the rest of the Cowboys would be just fine.

So would Johnson, who soon moved down to the Florida Keys for a life of boating, scuba diving, and sunbathing.

On March 30, 1994, Barry Switzer was named the head coach of the Dallas Cowboys.

The signing made about as much sense as parting ways with a coach who had just led your team to two straight Super Bowl titles.

Switzer, the son of a bootlegger who grew up in a shack without plumbing and electricity in Crossett, Arkansas, was an immensely successful college coach who had led the University of Oklahoma Sooners to three national titles and 157 victories in 16 seasons. However, a succession of scandals—including charges that some of his players raped a young woman—prompted his forced resignation in 1989. By the time Jerry Jones offered him the Cowboys gig, Switzer hadn't coached a football game since the late 1980s. (Switzer was a particularly dubious choice to coach Dallas given that when he was coaching at Oklahoma, he had slept with the wife of one of his assistant coaches, Larry Lacewell. The same Larry Lacewell who was now Dallas' director of college and professional scouting.)

Despite alienating many players (none more so than Troy Aikman) with his trademark insouciance, Switzer had some initial success in Dallas. Following a 1994 season (12–4 record) that ended with a loss to San

Francisco in the NFC Championship Game, the Cowboys defeated the Pittsburgh Steelers 27–17 in Super Bowl XXX on January 28, 1996, becoming the first team to win three Super Bowls in four seasons. It was, however, a team largely comprised of players who had been drafted and acquired by Jimmy Johnson. (Switzer would last a couple more years in Dallas before Jones hired and fired numerous head coaches, none of whom led the team past the second round of the playoffs.)

The following NFL season, Johnson became head coach of the Miami Dolphins, a post he would hold for the balance of the decade. Johnson would coach his last football game during the 1999 AFC Divisional Round (a 62–7 loss to the Jacksonville Jaguars).

Less than a month later, on February 12, 2000, his predecessor in Dallas, Tom Landry, succumbed to leukemia.

In the final decade of his life, Landry stayed in the Dallas area, enjoying many enchilada meals at Mia's, the site of the secret rendezvous between Johnson and Jones that spelled the end of the Tom Landry regime.

Out of respect, the restaurant owners would take the photo of Johnson and Jones down when he came in.

One day, the good-natured Landry told his friends not to bother unhooking it anymore.

To this day, the photo remains hanging above a corner booth, reminding patrons how the greatest era of America's most popular/controversial team unfolded.

7

The Comeback Game

On the morning of January 3, 1993, Buffalo Bills wide receiver Don Beebe awoke and couldn't find his roommate, Frank Reich, anywhere in his house. Beebe searched the bedroom, bathroom, and kitchen.

No Reich.

This was odd. Beebe hadn't overslept his alarm and, even if he had, his roommate/teammate surely wouldn't have bolted to work without him.

So where exactly was Frank Reich, the veteran backup quarterback recently thrust into the starting role for today's AFC Wild Card Game?

At a place where he could be in perfect solitude—the front seat of his truck.

"I go out to his truck and his truck is running and it's all fogged up because it was really cold that morning," Beebe remembers. "And I knocked on his window and I said, 'Dude, what are you doing?' He goes, 'Beebs, I've got to write these words down to this song "In Christ Alone" by Michael English.'"[1]

Beebe was incredulous. Hours before playing the biggest game of his life, Reich, set to supplant starter Jim Kelly (recently shelved with a knee injury), was not studying the Houston Oilers' blitz packages, but instead busy scribbling down a song's lyrics.

Less than 12 hours later, after orchestrating the most improbable comeback in NFL history, a 41–38 OT win following a 32-point second half deficit, one perhaps fueled by some divine intervention, Reich stood at the podium for his postgame presser, and politely told the roomful of reporters he would be happy to answer any questions, so long as he could first recite a verse he had jotted down earlier:

> "In every victory let it be said of me
> My source of strength, my source of hope
> Is Christ alone"[2]

The Buffalo Bills owned the AFC during the early 1990s. In January 1993, they were on the brink of their third consecutive run to the Super Bowl. Their K-Gun offense was a juggernaut, spearheaded by a trio of

7. The Comeback Game

future Hall of Famers (quarterback Jim Kelly, wideout Andre Reed, and running back Thurman Thomas). Defensive end Bruce Smith was considered one of the best pass rushers in NFL history while linebacker Cornelius Bennett was a perennial Pro Bowler. The team had stable ownership (Ralph Wilson) and a head coach (Marv Levy) whom players revered.

And, truthfully, the Bills had emerged as the saving grace for this Western New York city that, by the late 20th century, was getting accustomed to the shuttering of steel mills (only a decade earlier Bethlehem Steel had cut thousands of local jobs) and absence of Great Lakes freighters on railroad tracks. The devastating Blizzard of '77 froze Americans' image of this once flourishing port city along Lake Erie into one of a godforsaken wintry outpost. Oh, and Buffalo's defining historical moment (the 1901 assassination of President William McKinley) was not only tragic but becoming lost in the annals of history. The Buffalo Bills were the lasting source of pride for a city that had become the punchline of one too many jokes.

So, it would take a lot for Bills' fans to turn their backs on their gridiron heroes.

But by mid-afternoon on January 3, 1993, when the Bills were facing a 35–3 deficit early in the third quarter, the masses fled Rich Stadium prematurely, unable to watch their team continue getting humiliated.

The first half of this opening round playoff game seemingly confirmed that the Houston Oilers, with their run and shoot offense, had the Buffalo Bills' number. A week earlier, during the 1992 regular season finale, Houston had obliterated the two-time defending AFC champs, 27–3. And now, on Wild Card Weekend, the Oilers were again embarrassing the host Bills, building a 28–3 lead before intermission behind a near-flawless half of football from quarterback Warren Moon (19–22, four touchdowns).

"We did feel like we were sort of embarrassing our fans, we were embarrassing ourselves. It really wasn't much of a playoff game," remembers Buffalo kicker Steve Christie.[3]

"Little things that I remember are just kind of how we hit the tsunami early in the game and you're just like 'Holy heck,'" recalls Buffalo second-string tight end Rob Awalt. "You took their heavy punches and we went into halftime obviously shocked. We're at home. It's a blustery winter day and they [Houston Oilers] are used to playing in a dome and they throw the ball, don't run it much even though they had a good back in Lorenzo White."[4]

At halftime, Buffalo's locker room was a strange mixture of hopelessness, fury, and calmness.

There were the not-so-inspiring "Let's make this respectable" and "Let's not embarrass ourselves" comments.

Special teams ace Steve Tasker (formerly of the Houston Oilers), whose locker was adjacent to Don Beebe's, cracked to the wideout, "Well Beebs, we'll be playing golf next week. Let's go south. Let's get out of here."[5]

(Apparently, Tasker was not the only Bill pondering off-season plans at the half.)

There were other players, such as linebacker Darryl Talley, who were not in such a lighthearted mood.

"Darryl was our leader, no doubt," recalls Beebe. "He was our leader that everybody looked to. He was friends with everybody. Everybody listened to him. And he was adamant. He was yelling at us, 'What are we doing?!' with a few choice words."[6]

Defensive coordinator Walt Corey, perceiving a timid unit, also unleashed a fiery diatribe infused with R-rated words—words that had rained down on the players' hanging heads as they trudged off the field only minutes earlier.

Across the room sat the seemingly unruffled head coach Marv Levy ... busy slicing an orange and matter-of-factly rationalizing to his guys that they, too, could easily score 28 points in a half. No surprise here. Marv Levy was not one to holler vitriolic phrases. He was highly methodical, not inclined to be overblown with emotion. Levy was the rare NFL head coach who didn't believe a football game was akin to triage in the emergency department. When a reporter once asked Levy if an upcoming big game was a "must-win," Levy put things into perspective, explaining that a football game is not a must-win, but rather, World War II was a must-win. (Levy enlisted in the Army Air Corps during World War II while his father was a World War I veteran, wounded and gassed at the Battle of Belleau Wood in France, for which he was awarded the Purple Heart.)

On this day, the longtime, mild-mannered coach was able to collect himself, telling his guys, "You are two-time defending AFC champions. When you walk off that field after 30 more minutes of football, don't let anyone ever be able to say that you laid down, that you quit. Be able to walk off with your heads held high, knowing that you fought until the final tick has gone off the game clock."[7]

Recalls Rob Awalt: "You go into the locker room and I just remember going in and Coach Levy is always such a positive person, his cup is always half-full. Everybody is kind of trying to do that false enthusiasm—it's 28–3 at the time. Everybody's in there [saying], 'All right we've just got to get the ball coming out, we've got to do this, do that.' You hear all that and everybody settles down and gets re-taped. Normal stuff that happens in a locker room."[8]

Any semblance of such faux enthusiasm dissipated on the fifth play of the second half when, on third down, Frank Reich threw a pass that banged off the hands of tight end Keith McKeller and into the arms of strong safety Bubba McDowell. Fifty-eight yards later, McDowell was high-stepping into the end zone. The ensuing extra-point gave Houston a 35–3 advantage and the Bills' deficit (32) was now greater than the number of minutes remaining (28).

"It's just one of those things where the first half was not what we were expecting and certainly everything seemed to go wrong," remembers Steve Christie. "And then we came out in the second half with an interception, a turnover, except as Marv puts it, 'It was theirs.' They intercepted Frank [Reich] and ran it in for a touchdown—it was the last thing that we wanted to happen. And it did."[9]

On Buffalo's sidelines, Awalt had some advice for teammates Shane Conlan and Chris Hale: "Don't go out there and get yourself hurt and fuck up your off-season."[10]

This was not the time for Marv Levy's favorite "There is No I in TEAM" mantra. This moment called for a reminder of Bill Parcells' acronym for the NFL—"Not For Long." For Buffalo's backups and special teamers who were always one torn Achilles tendon away from never seeing another NFL paycheck, personal safety was their top priority as what lay ahead was nearly an entire half of meaningless, yet still jarringly violent football.

"You've got to know what's going on in the world," says Awalt. "You go out in the second half of that game and blow out a shoulder or blow out a knee, all you're doing is rehabbing all off-season. It's kind of a smart-ass comment but there's some truth to that. There's a little bit of an underlying truth. It's like, OK this game is out of control, now it's just a matter of self-preservation.

"What I remember is that flow—coming out, chest all pumped up at beginning of game, get punched around, try to puff your chest out again, immediately get it taken away on the pick-6, and then all of a sudden you're making plans for the off-season and trying not to get hurt."[11]

Further compounding matters was that Buffalo, already missing starting quarterback Jim Kelly (sprained knee) and All-Pro linebacker Cornelius Bennett (hamstring), was now without 1991 NFL MVP Thurman Thomas, who had checked out of the game with a sore hip pointer.

In the press box, a Houston TV station employee approached *Sports Illustrated* scribe Peter King, asking to use King's phone. The visiting Texan called his travel agent to make a non-refundable airline reservation for Pittsburgh, the site of the following week's AFC Divisional Round Game, in which, surely, the Oilers would be participating.

King, perhaps the most esteemed football voice in America at the time, told him it was a good move.[12]

As the 3 o'clock hour approached, the Rich Stadium employees, unlike the Bills players, were just doing their job.

Or at least trying to.

When the Houston lead ballooned to 32 points, hundreds, if not thousands, of Buffalo fans got an early jump on beating the New York State Thruway traffic. They did not want to bear witness to history. It was only two years ago, during the 1990 AFC Championship Game, when their Bills had accounted for the largest margin of victory in an NFL playoff game (post-merger era) virtue of their 51–3 shellacking of the Los Angeles Raiders. And now, the Bills appeared headed toward being on the flip side of breaking that record.

As the disheartened fans warmed up their cars, a quick turn to the radio broadcast indicated it was now 35–10 as backup tailback Kenneth Davis rambled into the end zone from a yard out after Buffalo recovered Houston's failed squib kickoff attempt at the 50-yard line and speedily drove downfield.

"Wasn't like Kenny Davis sat over and collected dust," remarks Rob Awalt. "Nobody [on Buffalo] was afraid when Kenny walked into the game to tag out Thurman [Thomas]. Thurman's special, he's in the Hall of Fame, but Kenny Davis was a damn good running back."[13]

Certainly, but he wasn't Thurman Thomas and Frank Reich wasn't Jim Kelly. At this point, those who had exited early had few regrets, if any. Not only was Buffalo shorthanded, but there was 8:54 remaining in the third quarter and the deficit was still 25—the number of degrees Fahrenheit to which the temperature was approaching.

However, what the fans didn't know was that during halftime, Marv Levy had instructed special teams coach Bruce DeHaven to have Steve Christie attempt an onside kick if Buffalo could ever score. On the ensuing kickoff, Christie executed the play perfectly, bouncing the football the requisite 10-plus yards. Houston linebacker Rick Graf fielded the ball for a split second before Buffalo's Mark Pike delivered a crushing blow. The ball squirted free and Christie pounced on it at the Buffalo 48.

"I had Mark Maddox and Mark Pike on either side of me, two pretty big guys," recalls Christie. "They sort of spearheaded a slot for me to slide in there and grab the ball. They really did the work. I just had to tap it about 10 yards and go get it. That certainly helped get things rolling and we certainly needed to make turnover type plays and that was certainly one of them.

"We always practiced that. We practiced that every week. We practiced a number of different onside kicks, but that seemed to be the one that both Bruce DeHaven and Marv Levy thought was our best shot. Certainly turned the tables a little bit because that's a big special teams play to have. It's like a turnover. At that point, it was certainly worth the risk."[14]

7. The Comeback Game

"When Kenny [Davis] scored his touchdown, it was basically a feeling of 'Okay, let's just kind of make it look not as bad as it really is.' And then we get the onside kick and yeah, it was momentum," says Don Beebe.[15]

Once the outcome of the desperation play hit the airwaves, a mass exodus of inebriated, intrigued fans rushed back toward Rich Stadium, only to be reminded that, of course, not one of the 75,141 tickets sold for this game allowed for re-entry. With the game being blacked out on local television, virtually the only way to lay eyes on the impending comeback was to hop over the chain fence encircling the concourses. Perhaps swept up in the emotion of the moment, stadium ops, after some initial hesitation, eventually allowed the fence hopping to ensue (even though some of the trespassers may never have had tickets initially).

"The grounds were actually shaking it was so loud," remembers Beebe. "It was quite the experience of feeling the crowd and then not feeling anything and then feeling it again toward the end of the game. When people were jumping the 12-foot linked fence by the hundreds, they basically just opened the gates back up and let them back in.

"I have many, many memories. I think the one that stands out probably the most is seeing a stadium jam-packed at the beginning of the game, basically empty in the beginning of the third quarter after the Bubba McDowell interception for a touchdown, and then by the end of the game be packed again."[16]

"I think when the half ended, we were so distraught, we went into the locker room," recalls Christie. "So when we came back out for the second half, I personally can't remember if I noticed fans were gone or not, but that was certainly what we had heard afterward—that a lot of fans had had enough and they had left. A lot of fans told me that after the game over the years that they had left. And then so many of them also said they tried to get back in when they realized that something was happening. We were so concerned about saving face, at first I really didn't notice, but certainly by the end of the game, a lot of the fans had made it back in."[17]

"I remember the fans and how resilient they were, even though a lot of them left," says Hall of Fame wideout Andre Reed. "This was before Twitter and Instagram and all the social media stuff that is going on now. And the game was blacked out, so other than going to a place where it wasn't blacked out, that was the only ticket in town to see the game. Every time I do go up there [Buffalo], I do get that 'I was at The Comeback Game' or 'I was in Buffalo during that time.' You get a lot of joy from it when people remember it in that manner."[18]

What did this development mean for the game itself?

At this juncture in which the Bills were embarking on their second scoring drive, they were playing with actual home-field advantage for the first time all afternoon.

Frank Reich had been here before.

It was November 10, 1984, and Reich, as University of Maryland's backup quarterback, was watching from the sidelines as his Terps were trailing the University of Miami Hurricanes 31–0 at the half. Maryland head coach Bobby Ross had seen more than enough of starter Stan Gelbaugh; Reich was tabbed the replacement at halftime and went on to toss three second half touchdown passes to engineer the historic 42–40 comeback win—at the time, the most prolific come-from-behind triumph in college football history.

In the Terps' postgame locker room, Reich was everyone's new favorite teammate.

"When we went into halftime, we were down 31–0, and Coach Ross said that we were going to go back and practice when we got back to College Park," recalls Kevin Glover, who was an offensive lineman for the 1984 Maryland Terps. "For every point we lost by, we were going to run 100-yard sprints. At that point, we owed him and the staff thirty-one 100-yard sprints. Some other choice words were said in the locker room by the coaches."[19]

Now, the situation nearly a decade later in which the Bills were trying to erase a 32-point deficit during Wild Card Weekend was eerily similar. Perhaps Reich could work his magic again—and restore some sense of pride in a franchise that had lost the past two Super Bowls and was on the verge of being embarrassed in its own building.

"I was watching the game [Bills vs. Oilers] and I definitely had déjà vu and for some reason I kind of felt it coming," recalls Glover. "The trust that the players on the team had in Frank, their body language, and their expressions—you could just all see them coming together to get the victory."[20]

"That was my first season there in Buffalo," says Steve Christie. "I came up from Tampa. Nobody really talked about it [Reich's comeback in college] until afterward and then I was amazed that he was able to do it twice. That's really incredible, to do it in college like that and then come back and do it in the pros, certainly in a playoff game, too. He [Reich] knows more than anybody that it's not over until it's over."[21]

"Very intelligent. Extremely hard worker, all-for-the-team guy," remarks Glover. "No hidden agendas, just a very, very strong leader. We never doubted that we could be successful."[22]

By 1993, the always steady and composed Reich, now an established NFL veteran, remained one of the most respected figures in the locker room—even given his sparse playing time.

"When Jim [Kelly] came out, obviously there was a drop-off between

Jim and Frank, but Frank found magic that day," says Rob Awalt. "Frank was always prepared. Frank was just like he is today, a coach in the NFL. He was a coach back then as well. He was always prepared."[23]

(In February 2018, Frank Reich would win a Super Bowl ring as the offensive coordinator of the Philadelphia Eagles before becoming head coach of the Indianapolis Colts the next season, one in which his team rebounded from a 1–5 start to make the playoffs.)

Today's postseason starting nod was a life-defining moment for Reich, and he was too restless to freeze his buttocks on an icy bench in Western New York. Even when the deficit had expanded to 32, Reich was still walking up and down the sidelines. And as said deficit shrank, the afternoon-long nervous pacing only intensified.

No one who ever played with Frank Reich is surprised that he enjoyed a successful career as an NFL offensive coordinator before becoming head coach of the Indianapolis Colts in 2018 (courtesy Indianapolis Colts).

"After he threw the interception for a touchdown, Frank came to the sidelines, you could watch him, he was always pacing," recalls Don Beebe. "He never sat down. He was always pacing. And he would keep saying, 'Hey, let's keep doing what we're doing.' You get to the point, it's 35–3, you're like, 'Shut up. This thing's over.' But Frank just kept going, kept pacing."[24]

And praying, too.

"From his standpoint, I don't think he [Reich] ever really gave in or gave up because he felt something spiritual going on," says Beebe.[25]

As the third quarter progressed following Christie's onside kick recovery, the football gods did indeed seem to smile down on the Buffalo Bills.

The University of Maryland is a legit football school but Kutztown University and Chadron State, the respective alma maters of Andre Reed and Don Beebe, the other offensive heroes on this day, are certainly not. Not exactly football factories on par with Ohio State University and USC, Kutztown University and Chadron State are Division II schools whose aggregate enrollment on a good year barely eclipses 10,000 students. Kutztown University lies on the outskirts of Pennsylvania's Amish Country (Kutztown is probably more well-known for its annual summer folk festival) while the nearest major city to Chadron State, nestled in the pine-covered hills of Northwest Nebraska, is Denver, which lies nearly 300 miles away. In other words, it takes a lot for their scholar-athletes to get on the radar screens of pro sports teams.

Back in the 1980s, even as Reed was establishing himself as one of the most prolific wideouts in small college football history, the Kutztown coaching staff had to badger NFL scouts into watching the phenom in-person. Eventually, Buffalo scout Elbert Dubenion made the trip down to Eastern Pennsylvania and saw Reed's potential. After a stellar career at Kutztown in which he amassed over 2,000 receiving yards on 142 receptions, Reed was selected in the fourth round of the 1985 NFL Draft by Buffalo. One of the best draft selections in franchise history, Reed was eventually enshrined in the Pro Football Hall of Fame in 2014.

Beebe, even more so, was a highly improbable NFL success story. In media guides, he was generously listed at 5'11". He began his college career at Western Illinois University, then went to Aurora College before dropping out of school to become a construction worker. After taking some classes at Waubonsee Community College, Beebe returned to Western Illinois, where he was the team's top receiver in 1987. However, due to NCAA eligibility rules, that was his final year there, so he transferred to Chadron State for his senior year and finally caught the attention of NFL scouts. Months after getting drafted by the Buffalo Bills in the third round of the 1989 NFL Draft, Beebe was nearly paralyzed as a rookie when, during a playoff game versus the Cleveland Browns, he was going across the middle and was upended by safety Felix Wright. Thankfully, Beebe was not significantly injured by the scary hit and persevered to emerge as a bona fide downfield threat for the Bills.

Certainly, by the mid–1990s, as Buffalo was winning four straight AFC titles, Reed and Beebe, long since passed over by a litany of Division I schools, were Buffalo's best receivers. And Frank Reich understood that what Reed lacked in quickness, he made up for with Velcro hands and what

7. The Comeback Game

Don Beebe posing with an NFL regulation ball on the hood of his car after becoming the first Chadron State College player drafted into the league (courtesy Con Marshall).

Beebe lacked in size, he made up for with breathtaking speed (he registered an insane 4.2 in the 40). For both Reed and Beebe, having less than 30 minutes to erase a 32-point margin was not so daunting given their respective paths to the NFL.

On the very first play after Christie had recovered his own onside kick, the Bills' streak of good fortune continued when Reich hit Beebe for a nine-yard completion. Replay reviews clearly showed that the diminutive wideout had fumbled (the ball was immediately scooped up by corner Jerry Gray), yet the official ruled that Beebe was down by contact, keeping Buffalo's drive alive. On the next set of downs, Reich once again hooked up with Beebe, this time for a 38-yard touchdown pass that, following the Christie extra-point, sliced Houston's lead down to 35–17 midway through the third quarter.

In truth, however, Beebe's touchdown should have been called off—and would have been overturned had there been instant replay in 1993. As Beebe was darting down the sideline to break free from the secondary, his right cleat brushed the white out-of-bounds paint, meaning he was now an ineligible receiver. Miraculously, the linesman's head was turned away from Beebe and the violation went unnoticed.

A couple officiating gaffes merely a few plays apart were keeping Buffalo on life support.

Perhaps Reich's prayers were being answered.

"It was a pre-snap read with a Cover 2 zone," remembers Beebe when asked to relive his touchdown. "Jerry Gray was the corner and when I got off the line of scrimmage, I was just running a go route down the sideline. And Jerry, all he did was just kind of jam me and push me. And when he pushed me, my momentum took me out-of-bounds. I didn't know it, to be honest with you. I didn't know it at the time. You don't know those things in the heat of the moment. And obviously my foot went and touched the out-of-bounds line and the safety didn't get over far enough. And Frank, as soon as he stepped back and set up, he saw that, and he hit me for an easy touchdown.

"I didn't feel the exhilaration and the feelings that I normally felt when I scored a touchdown. I was still upset that we were getting our tails kicked and so that was kind of my feeling. You watch my reaction when Ken Davis and Keith McKeller try giving me high-fives or something like that. Not that I was being rude, I was just like, 'We're getting our tails whipped. There's no time for celebration here.' When I scored the touchdown, you could see my reaction—I'm still upset. I'm still mad. I don't even want to high-five anybody. I just get to the sidelines. But, you kind of started to feel once you got to the sidelines, 'OK, it's 35–17. We got the whole half pretty much left. Let's see what we can do.'"[26]

After Houston went three-and-out on its next drive, Reich, upon marching Buffalo deep into Houston territory, hooked up with a wide-open Andre Reed, who backpedaled into the end zone for the first of three second half touchdown scores. The 26-yard TD pass and extra-point trimmed Houston's lead to 35–24.

For the highly talented slot receiver, this afternoon was sweet redemption, as the 1992 calendar year had been a trying one. Back on January 26, 1992, during the second quarter of Super Bowl XXVI, Reed, held to five catches on the evening, let his fiery temper get the best of him when he was hit by a defender before the ball got to him and pass interference wasn't called. In disgust, he slammed his helmet into the turf of the Metrodome and the resultant 15-yard unsportsmanlike conduct penalty took the Bills out of field goal range. The outburst set a dour tone for a Buffalo team that fell to the Washington Redskins, 37–24. Reed was largely phased out of the final 10 games of the 1992 regular season and finished with one of his least productive years ever (these three second half touchdowns matched his 1992 regular season total). But during this wildest of Wild Card Games, when Buffalo was without its other offensive leaders in Jim Kelly and Thurman Thomas, Reed showed why he is widely considered to be one of the top wide receivers to ever play the game.

"I think he [Andre Reed] was underrated," says Don Beebe. "I think Andre Reed is one of the top five, definitely ten wideouts of all time. He absolutely had no weakness at all. He could get off the jam. He had great hands. He had great field awareness. Tough as nails. Sure, he might not have been a 4.4, 4.3 guy, but I never saw him get caught so he was certainly fast enough. I would say personally of all the guys I ever played with and played against outside of Jerry Rice, Andre Reed was as good as I've ever seen."[27]

"It was amazing the hits that he [Reed] took over the middle, time and time again, game after game," says Steve Christie. "He was hurt every once in a while, but that is only because of the role that he played. He had a bull's-eye on him. That was definitely one of the most impressive games I've ever seen from a wide receiver."[28]

With 4:21 remaining in the third period, Houston was suddenly clinging to an 11-point lead. On first down, Warren Moon was intercepted by defensive back Henry Jones, who returned it to Houston's 23-yard line. After three unproductive plays, Buffalo faced a 4th-and-5 from the Houston 18-yard line. Bucking conventional wisdom, Marv Levy chose not to kick a field goal. And, once again, Reich delivered, as he threaded a pass through a trio of Houston defensive backs and into the arms of a sliding Reed for Buffalo's fourth touchdown in less than seven minutes.

There was exactly 2:00 left in the third period, Buffalo now only trailed 35–31, and unless you grew up in Texas rooting for the baby blue uniformed Oilers, this was one of the most exhilarating sporting events you had ever witnessed.

Sparkplugged by inspired play from linebackers Darryl Talley and Carlton Bailey, the Buffalo defense held its own on the next two Houston possessions, forcing their now bewildered opponents to punt and then settle for a chip shot field goal attempt, which was botched on a poor hold. With 6:53 remaining in regulation, Buffalo took over on its own 26-yard line. Seven plays later, Reich connected with Reed from 17 yards out for the go-ahead score.

With 3:08 remaining, Buffalo was *winning* 38–35.

Thanks to the three consecutive Reich-to-Reed hookups following Beebe's charmed touchdown, a demoralized Houston team now had to mount its own comeback to avoid pulling off the biggest choke job in NFL history.

As Buffalo's second half rally roared on, what agonized Houston wasn't so much that starters such as Andre Reed and Don Beebe were beating them, it was that sparsely used players were also.

Certainly, Frank Reich was having a career day but not to be forgotten was Kenneth Davis (93 all-purpose yards). With Cornelius Bennett sidelined and Bruce Smith kept in check, nose tackle Jeff Wright contributed with two sacks. Buffalo had started six defensive backs against Houston's high-octane aerial attack, but after getting negligible pressure on Warren Moon throughout much of the first half, swapped in linebackers Shane Conlan and Marvcus Patton, who beefed up the pass rush. However, no Buffalo defender had a more active role than linebacker Carlton Bailey, who at the time had three career regular season sacks to his name. And, unlike Houston, Buffalo was executing each special teams play perfectly.

"All the games that we played that year, we won games because guys, when it was time for them to perform, they did," recalls Andre Reed. "They didn't waver from that. They prepared like they were going to be the one to make the play. That's really what stands out to me the most. It's those guys like the Kenny Davises who had a great game and Frank Reich came in relief of Jim [Kelly] and did so many great things that game and all the variables that happened that game just because these guys really prepared the way they should.

"That's what I remember the most—the guys that didn't get all the paper, didn't get the accolades. Those were the guys that won that game for us and won a lot of games for us.

"It was one of those seasons where we had kind of an up-and-down year, just like a lot of teams have. You go through times during a year where things aren't going your way and you've got to rely on backups. There were six, seven Hall of Famers on that team, a Hall of Fame coach, an owner, so many different variables that made it the way we were."[29]

Throughout the second half, Houston's mindlessness was also winning the game for Buffalo. Although he was armed with such a commanding lead, Houston head coach Jack Pardee was not opting to run the ball—a conventional move in this situation to kill game clock and reduce the likelihood of a turnover. On both sides of the ball, Houston was committing skull-imploding penalties. Once outside the pocket, Moon, instead of chucking the ball out-of-bounds, was allowing himself to get sacked.

The Oilers' clueless expressions on the sidelines mirrored the on-field chaos.

"You're starting to look across the field and you saw Warren Moon arguing with the receivers because on one interception it looked like they had a miscommunication," remembers Rob Awalt. "You see them barking at each other. You just start to see the body language change across the field, and you're kind of like, 'OK, we get one more turnover or score or something positive that happens to us, this is on.' Those things start happening and at that point all you're doing is looking at the clock. Because if there is enough time, we've got this."[30]

The Oilers' frustration was only exacerbated by haunting memories of prior playoff collapses, including last January's fold against the Denver Broncos in which they blew a 21–6 lead in the Divisional Round. And in this January playoff game, while Houston's roster was superior to Buffalo's decimated corps, the latter group had a steelier resolve as far as not dwelling on past postseason meltdowns of their own.

For Marv Levy, having such a star-studded roster laden with Hall of Famers was, of course, a blessing. But it could also be a curse. After all, being an NFL star in the early 1990s often translated into a seven-figure yearly salary, endorsement deals ... and, naturally, a bloated ego. Of which there were many on the Buffalo Bills, a franchise long associated with excessive infighting.

Perhaps the situation resulted from the fact that Buffalo's stars played in a city nestled in the Rust Belt and were never guests on post–Super Bowl late-night shows, and thus craved opportunities for self-promotion. Regardless, the faces of the franchise didn't always make Levy's life easier off the field. The three most recognizable stars (Bruce Smith, Jim Kelly, Thurman Thomas) had big-time egos with Kelly having notoriously once called out his offensive line in public during the 1989 season. Neither Cornelius Bennett nor Darryl Talley was ever accused of lacking self-confidence. During his 2014 NFL Hall of Fame induction speech, Andre Reed, when paying homage to his former head coach, acknowledged, "You had to deal with so many egos, I don't know how in the heck you did it."[31]

Somehow, Levy did so masterfully. Accustomed to coaching collegiate players and low-paid professionals (he was a longtime college coach who also had a stint in the CFL), Levy, upon being named Buffalo's head coach in 1986, made a seamless transition toward managing the modern day rich celebrity athlete—while not marginalizing the special teamers and second-string offensive linemen. A Phi Beta Kappa member while at Coe College and recipient of a master's degree in English History from Harvard, Levy was a master communicator who could connect with everyone. (There were times when he would use words like "inculcate" and "extrapolate" in team meetings and Northwestern's Steve Tasker and Stanford's James Lofton were appointed translators.)[32]

And now, on January 3, 1993, as the Bills were mounting a 32-point comeback, it became apparent that, irrespective of whether or not he would ever win a Super Bowl ring, this day was going to be an integral part of Marv Levy's Hall of Fame legacy.

In fact, over a quarter-century later, a 93-year-old Marv Levy was attending a homecoming game at William & Mary College, where he had coached in the 1960s. One of his former W&M players, quarterback Jimmye Laycock, was being honored this afternoon for coaching the final game of his 39-year career as William & Mary's head football coach. While watching part of the game sitting next to another one of his former players, Steve Christie, also a William & Mary College alum, Levy reflected on his 70-plus year run in football—a period that began when the game's marquee stars were the likes of Bart Starr and George Halas.

No memory brought a bigger smile to Levy's face than that of a dreary winter afternoon in Western New York when his team shocked the world.[33]

For the past two years, the Buffalo Bills had been haunted by memories of their former kicker Scott Norwood.

Ever since January 27, 1991, to be precise.

At this moment in time, Norwood's eventual successor in Buffalo, Steve Christie, had recently finished his rookie season for the 6–10 Tampa Bay Buccaneers. There were no big games that season at Tampa Stadium—except this evening's all-New York Super Bowl, pitting the Buffalo Bills against the New York Giants. Days after the United States had engaged in war in the Persian Gulf, Super Bowl XXV was now being played along the shores of West Florida. The country got a much-needed diversion via this instant classic Super Bowl. In the final minute of regulation, the Giants were ahead 20–19 while the Bills were driving. Like tens of millions of people around the globe, Christie was watching on television when, with eight ticks remaining, Buffalo kicker Scott Norwood lined up for the game-winning 47-yard field goal attempt—and missed wide right. The Giants won 20–19, denying Buffalo its first ever Super Bowl title. Norwood would go down in infamy as Buffalo's version of Bill Buckner, the scapegoated individual receiving a disproportionate amount of blame for his team's devastating loss.

Now, less than two years later, on January 3, 1993, Christie, kicking in his first really meaningful pro game, found himself at the epicenter of the football universe. Following a snooze fest of a first half after which the NBC executives could hear the remotes clicking off, millions of Americans tuned in to see if Buffalo could pull off the miraculous feat. After Buffalo had gone ahead 38–35 late in the fourth, Houston responded with a 26-yard field goal with 12 seconds remaining to send the game into sudden death overtime. After winning the OT coin toss and electing to receive, Houston committed another turnover when Warren Moon was picked off by Buffalo defensive back Nate Odomes, who returned it to Houston's 35-yard line. In corralling Odomes to the ground, Houston's Haywood Jeffires was charged with a facemask penalty, which meant the Bills would start their drive at their opponent's 20-yard line. After a couple short runs inched Buffalo closer to the goal line, it became apparent that the outcome of one of the most bizarre games in football history would rest on Christie's right foot.

In the present moment, at stake for the Bills was a trip to the Divisional Round and a chance to get one game closer to returning to the Super Bowl for the third consecutive winter. Having played his first two seasons for a Tampa team that never had playoff aspirations, Christie was starting to feel overwhelmed by the pressure of January football. He was also trying to block out the disturbing memories of the now infamous miscue committed by Scott Norwood, the kicker whom he was brought into replace prior to this season. Ever the loyalist, Marv Levy had stuck with Norwood for one season (1991) after Super Bowl XXV. However, Norwood had his worst statistical season that year, converting on only 62.1 percent of his field goal attempts. Once Christie became a free agent in spring of 1992, the Buffalo front office, and ultimately Levy, deemed a change necessary and parted ways with the veteran Norwood.

Christie, who would emerge as one of the NFL's top kickers in the 1990s, was a perfect match for Marv Levy, with whom he shared the William & Mary connection, and the Buffalo Bills. Christie hailed from Oakville, a town in Southern Ontario that was a less than two-hour-drive from Buffalo. Christie wanted to play for a head coach who paid close attention to the kicking game. After serving as William & Mary's head coach, Marv Levy had enjoyed multiple stints as a special teams coach in the NFL and, even decades later as an established NFL head coach, he continued to place a premium on placekicking.

Most importantly, the entire Buffalo Bills organization believed that Christie could handle the region's inclement weather and team's high stakes moments.

And on this day, Christie proved capable of delivering in the pressure cooker of the postseason, even amidst Lake Erie-induced winds wreaking havoc on a flying pigskin's trajectory. As darkness was moments from settling on blustery Rich Stadium and Buffalo had a third down at the Houston 14, Levy sent out Christie for the 32-yard field goal attempt in case the play went awry.

It did not.

After Houston took a timeout to try to ice Christie, holder Frank Reich fielded Adam Lingner's low snap cleanly and Christie split the uprights.

FINAL SCORE: Buffalo 41, Houston 38.

The greatest comeback in NFL history was complete.

As the Bills' theme song "Shout" blared through Rich Stadium and thousands of mittens clapped in applause, the relieved kicker ("Even if I watch replays of this game, I still get nervous for Number 2," admits Steve Christie)[34] and ecstatic backup quarterback embraced. The ebullient hug between non-prominent players would be the game's lasting image, one that encapsulates the underdog spirit of the day.

A couple minutes after a pack of Bills mobbed Christie, Frank Reich did an on-field interview with NBC, in which he declared, "This is the greatest moment of my life besides having my daughters and marrying my wife."[35]

Levy would remark in his postgame news conference that coming back from 32 down was like winning the New York Lottery.

During halftime, there had been a few mild smirks floating through the Oilers' locker room. Not now. In the now-moribund visiting locker room, with many of his teammates turtling upon the media's ascendance, cornerback Cris Dishman told reporters, "It was the biggest choke job in history. Everyone on the team, everyone in the organization, choked."[36]

(On the plane ride back to Houston, Warren Moon decided he would not send his four children, ranging in age from five to 11, to school the next day as he feared they would be bullied.)

Aside from Dishman and a few others, the Houston front was silent. Simply put, it was impossible to articulate how this epic fold occurred.

Meanwhile, the Bills' locker room was one of exuberant, talkative players.

With boombox music blaring in the background and grown men leaping into the air, an emotional, half-naked Darryl Talley was trying to explain what just transpired to reporters when team owner Ralph Wilson came over to personally congratulate him.

Steve Christie was asking veteran teammates if all playoff games were this thrilling.

(No.)

In other corners of the locker room, stars Andre Reed and Jim Kelly, even though he didn't play a snap, gracefully handled the onslaught of questions.

Down the hall, as he was about to meet the crush of reporters, Reich stayed true to his narrative. Before responding to a single question that would force him to talk about himself, Reich read Michael English's words, ones that he had recited over 100 times that week—and transcribed on paper earlier that morning.

"What most people don't know that I do know because I was his roommate, was the spiritual sentence that Frank talked about at the end of the game that was really going on inside of him," recalls Don Beebe. "He never let that go because he had that feeling that morning. The end result—obviously it all unfolded right before all of our eyes and for Frank. It was really a cool thing to witness it as his friend first-hand and see the inside story that was truly taking place in Frank's life."[37]

"That was a big game for Frank, and so was the following week against Pittsburgh," says Christie. "Marv [Levy] always talked about resilience anyway, but that was the epitome of it if you ask me. Never giving up regardless of the scoreline, and that's a lesson to everybody really at any level, in any sport. It doesn't always go your way, but if you keep plugging away and you keep fighting, things may turn around for you as they did for us."[38]

From Albany to Rochester, Upstate New Yorkers rejoiced, basking in the glory of quite possibly the greatest sports moment in their hardy region's history. This game was especially meaningful for those residing in Buffalo, a city whose football team got teasingly close to winning a championship two years earlier and only had one other major sports franchise in the Buffalo Sabres.

"To just get back in that fashion was huge for the city," says Steve Christie. "The whole city was behind us. Really important for Buffalo. Still incredible to be part of that. Just grateful to be a part of it. That game kept us in everything."[39]

Indeed, the miraculous second half did keep the Bills alive in the NFL postseason tournament—and in the running for their third consecutive AFC crown. Behind another strong performance from Frank Reich, Buffalo would upset the Pittsburgh Steelers 24–3, the following weekend at hostile Three Rivers Stadium. A week later, with Jim Kelly back under center, the Bills would punch their Super Bowl ticket virtue of another convincing road win (a 29–10 defeat of the Miami Dolphins). However, two weeks later, the Bills' magical January 1993 run ended with a 52–17 loss to the Dallas Cowboys in Pasadena during Super Bowl XXVII.

During Week 1 of the 2017 NFL season, the Buffalo Bills hosted the New York Jets. At halftime, the Bills celebrated the 25th anniversary of a game that, over the years, became so steeped in NFL lore that it acquired its own name: "The Comeback Game." (The commemoration was held on September 10, 2017, several months shy of the actual 25th anniversary.) While some of those players who had suited up for Buffalo in The Comeback Game had either passed on or were suffering from grave illnesses or had found themselves on the wrong side of the law, many of the game's participants did reunite in Western New York to commemorate their feat, one against which all comebacks would be forever measured.

"You look at all the great games—sure it [Bills-Oilers game] ranks up there, but it ranks up there for different reasons," says Rob Awalt. "The dramatic swings of what happened. How does somebody dominate us, and you're dominated—where do you find the courage to chip away? It's got to rank up there in the greatest but for a different reason. Not because it was such a great game to watch. So, it wasn't like two teams going toe-to-toe the whole game in that back-and-forth type scenario."[40]

"It's a pretty special game when people are still talking about it 25 years later and the impact that it had not only on the league but on the two teams that were playing and guys that are playing the game now in high schools and colleges," reflects Andre Reed, a few months after the aforementioned celebration. "I'm sure a lot of coaches and a lot of people use that as a metaphor, use that as a teaching tool for their team. We were part of history, but we were part of something special too at the time, and I think we didn't realize 25 years later that it would stand for more than just a game. The guys that played in that game, it will be a part of their lives forever. In sports, there are only a certain number of things that really stand out and things that when people hear it and say it, or they see it, they all have a certain way they feel about it. That game definitely does [get] put in a category like that.

"I think we capitalized on a lot of things that went our way, took advantage of them. I didn't know that it was going to be like that until maybe end of the third quarter where we started getting a little momentum. Being on the sidelines, [it] was pretty special to watch something like that and see the fans and coaches and players just being one. That's how you win games. Marv [Levy] always said, 'There is no I in TEAM' and that's how we played that '92–'93 season. We fought for each other, and we relied on each other to make plays and we made them there."[41]

Unlike Andre Reed, who played virtually his entire career in Buffalo—and thus never won a Super Bowl—Don Beebe would eventually hoist the Lombardi Trophy. Beebe's time came in January 1997 when his Green Bay Packers defeated the New England Patriots in Super Bowl XXXI. But of course, Green Bay had already won multiple Super Bowls. In contrast, The Comeback Game, while only a Wild Card Game, was unprecedented. Which means, at least for Beebe, it is more special than your one and only Super Bowl victory.

"It would be Number One," says Beebe, when asked to rank where The Comeback Game stands among the most meaningful games in which he played. "When you're the only one to do something [having the greatest comeback], that's in a special class. That team holds the record for the greatest comeback in history. Until somebody beats that, it's the greatest game I've ever been a part of. And, I will also say, the greatest team I've ever been a part of when you're the only one to go to four Super Bowls in a row. Nobody's ever done that either. Many people have won back-to-back Super Bowls. So, when you're the only one to do something, that's pretty special."[42]

Epilogue

Many of the organizations chronicled in this book probably wished 1993, or at least the mid-1990s, never ended.

The Dallas Cowboys became known as the team of the 1990s because of what they did from January 1993–January 1994. After winning Super Bowl XXX in January 1996, America's Team soon became one of the league's most dysfunctional franchises, largely due to off-field issues (hello, Michael Irvin), frequent head coaching changes, frequent starting quarterback changes, and a host of other issues. The Cowboys haven't even been back to the NFC Conference Championship Game since January 14, 1996.

After winning six titles in the 1990s, the Chicago Bulls entered the 21st century as one of the NBA's most inept franchises. The post–MJ era would be a long, painful rebuilding process. It would be years before the franchise returned to the playoffs. While Chicago's baseball teams have each won World Series titles in the current century, the Bulls have not been crowned NBA champs since the night of June 14, 1998—Michael Jordan's last game as a Chicago Bull.

Ironically, the Lamar Hunt Trophy, hoisted by the winner of the AFC Championship Game, is named after the founder of the Kansas City Chiefs, Lamar Hunt. After the 1993 season, the Chiefs did not make it back to the AFC Championship Game until January 2019. It wasn't until the following year that the Chiefs actually won the conference title game, before going on to win the Super Bowl.

By the conclusion of the 1993 season, the Buffalo Bills had established themselves as the masters of the AFC Championship Game. No franchise—not even the New England Patriots nor Pittsburgh Steelers—has won four consecutive Lamar Hunt Trophies, which Buffalo did from 1990 to 1993. However, the Bills have not returned to the AFC Championship Game since the mid-1990s.

Since spring of 1993, the Montreal Canadiens have been back to the Stanley Cup playoffs several times, but have yet to return to the Stanley Cup Finals. The closest the Habs came was during the 2013–14 season when they fell to the New York Rangers in the Eastern Conference Finals. Canada's most popular team remains one of the chief culprits responsible for extending the hockey-crazed country's title drought.

Following the 1993 season, the Toronto Blue Jays underwent a precipitous decline. In the 1994 campaign, the Jays finished a mediocre 55–60; in 1995, a dismal 56–88. As the nineties progressed and the New York Yankees and Boston Red Sox annually dueled for AL East supremacy, the Blue Jays faded into hardball oblivion. By 2005, the Blue Jays were Canada's only baseball team (the Montreal Expos had morphed into the Washington Nationals), yet they remained as irrelevant as ever. To date, Toronto has not been back to the World Series since October 1993.

Since the late 1990s, the Baltimore Orioles and Camden Yards have simply not hosted many big games. Or many fans for that matter. Sadly, with the charm of the old-timey ballpark having dimmed and the club annually out of contention by Labor Day, attendance has been dreadful. The park remains a hot tourist destination—for tours given hours before the first pitch, that is. Perhaps one of these years Camden Yards will host an All-Star Game and the entire nation can be reminded of its trendsetting significance.

Will all of these great sports cities, ones that lie across wide swaths of North America, ever return to their late 20th century glory days?

Eventually.

Will they all do so within the same 12 months, though?

Perhaps, but it would have to be a special year.

One like 1993.

Chapter Notes

Chapter 1

1. Interview with author, December 15, 2017.
2. Steve Young, with Jeff Benedict, *QB: My Life Behind the Spiral* (New York: Houghton Mifflin Harcourt, 2016), p. 138.
3. Peter King, "QB or Not QB?," *Sports Illustrated*, July 27, 1992.
4. Adam Lazarus, *Best of Rivals: Joe Montana, Steve Young, and the Inside Story Behind the NFL's Greatest Quarterback Controversy* (Boston: Da Capo Press, 2012), p. 80.
5. Tom Friend, "It's Decision Time for Well-Armed 49ers," *New York Times*, December 22, 1992.
6. Keith Dunnavant, *Montana: The Biography of Football's Joe Cool* (New York: St. Martin's Press, 2015), p. 258.
7. Lazarus, p. 191.
8. *Ibid.*, p. 186.
9. Interview with author, October 1, 2018.
10. Interview with author, September 17, 2018.
11. Interview with author, December 11, 2017.
12. Tom Friend, "By Popular Demand, Montana Reconsiders," *New York Times*, April 19, 1993.
13. Interview with author, March 22, 2018.
14. Interview with author, October 1, 2018.
15. Interview with author, December 15, 2017.
16. Interview with author, December 11, 2017.
17. Interview with author, December 15, 2017.
18. *Ibid.*
19. *Ibid.*
20. *Ibid.*
21. Rick Reilly, "Joe's a Go," *Sports Illustrated*, September 13, 1993.
22. Interview with author, September 17, 2018.
23. Interview with author, March 22, 2018.
24. Interview with author, December 11, 2017.
25. Interview with author, September 17, 2018.
26. Interview with author, March 22, 2018.
27. Interview with author, September 17, 2018.
28. Lazarus, p. 196.
29. Bob Gretz, *Hail to the Chiefs* (Champaign, Illinois: Sagamore Publishing, 1994), p. 73.
30. Interview with author, March 22, 2018.
31. Interview with author, December 11, 2017.
32. Interview with author, October 1, 2018.
33. Interview with author, March 22, 2018.
34. Interview with author, October 1, 2018.
35. Interview with author, December 15, 2017.
36. Richard Hoffer, "The Old Montana Mystique," *Sports Illustrated*, January 24, 1994.
37. Interview with author, September 17, 2018.
38. Interview with author, October 1, 2018.
39. Interview with author, March 2, 2018.
40. Interview with author, October 1, 2018.
41. Richard Hoffer, "The Old Montana Mystique," *Sports Illustrated*, January 24, 1994.
42. Interview with author, March 22, 2018.
43. Interview with author, September 17, 2018.
44. Interview with author, December 15, 2017.
45. Interview with author, October 1, 2018.
46. Lazarus, p. 208.

47. Leonard Shapiro, "Montana Goes Down for the Count, and So Does Kansas City," *Washington Post*, January 24, 1994.
48. Interview with author, December 11, 2017.
49. Interview with author, September 17, 2018.
50. Bob Verdi, "Montana's Blessing: He Can't Remember What Happened," *Chicago Tribune*, January 24, 1994.
51. Interview with author, September 17, 2018.
52. Interview with author, October 1, 2018.
53. Randy Kovitz, "Joe Montana Brought Something Special to the Chiefs," *Kansas City Star*, August 26, 2013.
54. Interview with author, September 17, 2018.

Chapter 2

1. Interview with author, September 29, 2017.
2. *Ibid.*
3. *Ibid.*
4. *Ibid.*
5. Interview with author, August 31, 2017.
6. Interview with author, August 31, 2017.
7. Peter Richmond, *Ballpark: Camden Yards and the Building of an American Dream* (New York: Simon & Schuster, 1993), p. 183.
8. *Ibid.*, p. 184.
9. *Ibid.*, p. 184.
10. Interview with author, September 29, 2017.
11. Interview with author, August 1, 2017.
12. *Ibid.*
13. Richard Justice, "Orioles Inaugurate Camden Yards, Defeat Mets," *Washington Post*, April 4, 1992.
14. James Dodson, "Attention to Detail," *1993 All-Star Game Official Major League Baseball Program*, New York: Sports Publishing Group, July 13, 1993.
15. Interview with author, September 29, 2017.
16. *Ibid.*
17. James Dodson, "Attention to Detail," *1993 All-Star Game Official Major League Baseball Program*, New York: Sports Publishing Group, July 13, 1993.
18. *Ibid.*
19. *Ibid.*
20. *Ibid.*
21. Interview with author, May 15, 2017.
22. Milton Kent, "Longest Day for Griffey, González," *Baltimore Sun*, July 13, 1993.
23. Herbert H. Harwood, *Impossible Challenge: The Baltimore and Ohio Railroad in Maryland* (Baltimore, Maryland: Barnard Roberts & Company, 1979), p. 416.
24. Interview with author, May 26, 2017.
25. *Ibid.*
26. Interview with author, August 31, 2017.
27. Interview with author, May 8, 2017.
28. Interview with author, May 31, 2017.
29. Saul Wisnia, *Miracle at Fenway: The Inside Story of the Boston Red Sox 2004 Championship Season* (New York: St. Martin's Press, 2014), p. 34.
30. Interview with author, May 8, 2017.
31. Interview with author, May 15, 2017.
32. Interview with author, May 31, 2017.
33. Dan Shaughnessy, "Hanging Out in the Hot Corner," *Boston Globe*, July 13, 1993.
34. Interview with author, June 13, 2017.
35. "Where Today's Stars Grew Up," *1993 All-Star Game Official Major League Baseball Program*, New York: Sports Publishing Group, July 13, 1993.
36. Interview with author, July 17, 2017.
37. *Ibid.*
38. Interview with author, May 15, 2017.
39. Interview with author, May 31, 2017.
40. *Ibid.*
41. Interview with author, May 26, 2017.
42. *Ibid.*
43. Interview with author, May 15, 2017.
44. Scott Shane, "The Secret History of City Slave Trade," *Baltimore Sun*, June 20, 1999.
45. Dan Shaughnessy, *Reversing the Curse: Inside the 2004 Boston Red Sox* (New York: Houghton Mifflin Company, 2005), p. 56.
46. Interview with author, June 11, 2017.
47. William Hageman, "The Hunt for Babe Ruth's Baltimore Beginnings," *Chicago Tribune*, February 11, 2014.
48. Broadcast of 1993 MLB All-Star Game, CBS Sports, July 13, 1993.
49. *Ibid.*
50. *Ibid.*
51. Interview with author, August 31, 2017.
52. Broadcast of 1993 MLB All-Star Game, CBS Sports, July 13, 1993.

53. *Ibid.*
54. Interview with author, August 31, 2017.
55. Interview with author, May 1, 2017.
56. *Ibid.*
57. Interview with author, August 31, 2017.
58. Interview with author, May 1, 2017.
59. Interview with author, July 17, 2017.
60. Interview with author, August 1, 2017.
61. Interview with author, May 8, 2017.
62. Interview with author, September 29, 2017.
63. Interview with author, August 31, 2017.
64. Noah Trister, "The Camden Effect: At 25, Ballpark's Legacy Is Large in MLB," *Associated Press*, March 31, 2017.
65. Interview with author, September 29, 2017.

Chapter 3

1. Interview with author, February 21, 2018.
2. Interview with author, October 9, 2017.
3. Interview with author, July 22, 2019.
4. Interview with author, September 26, 2017.
5. Jack McCallum. "They're History," *Sports Illustrated*, June 28, 1993.
6. Sam Smith, *The Jordan Rules* (New York: Simon & Schuster, 1992), p. 110.
7. *Ibid.*
8. *Ibid.*
9. Interview with author, January 3, 2018.
10. Interview with author, January 12, 2018.
11. Evan F. Moore, "Craig Hodges and the Modern Activist Athlete," *Rolling Stone*, March 23, 2017.
12. Melissa Isaacson, "Bulls Veterans Accept Roles, but...," *Chicago Tribune*, October 22, 1992.
13. *Ibid.*
14. *Ibid.*
15. Interview with author, February 21, 2018.
16. Steve Nidetz, "As Jordan Soared, So Did TV Revenues," *Chicago Tribune*, October 13, 1993.
17. Nancy Goldberger, "Off the Court," *A Tribute to Michael Jordan: Commemorative Edition*, 1993.
18. *Ibid.*
19. Interview with author, October 9, 2017.
20. Interview with author, January 3, 2018.
21. Interview with author, July 22, 2019.
22. Interview with author, November 13, 2017.
23. Interview with author, January 3, 2018.
24. *Ibid.*
25. *Three-Peat: The Chicago Bulls' Historic Third Championship Season*, audio-visual, executive producer Don Sperling.
26. Interview with author, September 26, 2017.
27. Melissa Isaacson, "Perdue Fears He's Bulls' Insurance," *Chicago Tribune*, January 5, 1993.
28. Jack McCallum, "Eye of the Storm," *Sports Illustrated*, June 14, 1993.
29. Interview with author, November 13, 2017.
30. Interview with author, October 9, 2017.
31. Interview with author, January 12, 2018.
32. Interview with author, March 29, 2017.
33. Interview with author, March 29, 2017.
34. Interview with author, March 29, 2017.
35. Interview with author, January 3, 2018.
36. Mike Mulligan, "Bulls 'Level' Hawks," *Chicago Sun-Times*, May 1, 1993.
37. Interview with author, March 29, 2017.
38. Sam Smith, "Bring on the Bulls, Cry Knicks, Cavaliers," *Chicago Tribune*, October 11, 1992.
39. "Same Player, Same Place, Same Result: Bulls Win," *Associated Press*, May 18, 1993.
40. Interview with author, October 9, 2017.
41. Mark Heisler, "Starks Gives Bulls One to Remember," *Los Angeles Times*, May 24, 1993.
42. Dave Anderson, "Jordan's Atlantic City Caper," *New York Times*, May 27, 1993.
43. Melissa Isaacson, "Angry Jordan Denies Charge," *Chicago Tribune*, May 28, 1993.
44. Interview with author, October 9, 2017.
45. Sam Smith, *The Jordan Rules* (New York: Simon & Schuster, 1992), p. 96.
46. Jack McCallum, "The Lips Were Zipped," *Sports Illustrated*, June 7, 1993.
47. Melissa Isaacson, "Angry Jordan Denies Charge," *Chicago Tribune*, May 28, 1993.
48. Interview with author, February 21, 2018.
49. Melissa Isaacson, "Angry Jordan Denies Charge," *Chicago Tribune*, May 28, 1993.

Notes—Chapter 3

50. Ibid.
51. Mark Heisler, "Bulls Bullied, Leave New York in Sorry State," *Los Angeles Times*, May 26, 1993.
52. Jack McCallum, "Friends and Foes Together," *Sports Illustrated*, May 31, 1993.
53. Jack McCallum, "The Lips Were Zipped," *Sports Illustrated*, June 7, 1993.
54. Melissa Isaacson, "Game 3 Follows Pattern of Eastern Finals to a 'T,'" *Chicago Tribune*, May 30, 1993.
55. Ibid.
56. Melissa Isaacson, "Father Knows Best about Jordan's Frustrations," *Chicago Tribune*, May 31, 1993.
57. Interview with author, January 12, 2018.
58. David Moore, "Grant-Oakley Matchup Key to Bulls, Knicks," *Dallas Morning News*, June 2, 1993.
59. Interview with author, January 3, 2018.
60. Jay Mariotti, "In Crunch, Bulls Deliver Like Champs," *Chicago Sun Times*, June 3, 1993.
61. Ibid.
62. David Moore, "Bulls Knock Off Knicks to Return to Finals," *Dallas Morning News*, June 5, 1993
63. John Diamond, "The Drive for Three," *World Champion Chicago Bulls 1993 Official Yearbook*, 1993.
64. Interview with author, January 3, 2018.
65. David Moore, "Suns Will Pose Substantial Problems for Favored Bulls," *Dallas Morning News*, June 6, 1993.
66. Interview with author, April 20, 2017.
67. Interview with author, July 22, 2019.
68. Interview with author, February 21, 2018.
69. Interview with author, January 3, 2018.
70. Interview with author, February 21, 2018.
71. Wire reports, "76ers Send Barkley to Suns," *Los Angeles Times*, June 18, 1992.
72. Interview with author, April 20, 2017.
73. Jack McCallum, *Dream Team: How Michael, Magic, Larry, Charles, and the Greatest Team of All Time Conquered the World and Changed the Game of Basketball Forever* (New York: Ballantine Books, 2012), p. 75.
74. Mark Heisler, "Barkley Spoils His Best Shots," *Los Angeles Times*, July 27, 1992.
75. Interview with author, March 29, 2017.
76. Mike Mulligan, "NBA Finals Series in Review," *Chicago Sun-Times*, June 21, 1993.
77. Ibid.
78. Interview with author, April 7, 2017.
79. Ibid.
80. Ibid.
81. Terry Armour, "Bulls Wilt from Suns' Overtime Heat," *Chicago Tribune*, June 14, 1993.
82. David Casstevens, "There's Lots of Bite—and Sheer Determination—Left Behind This Team's Bark," *Chicago Tribune*, June 15, 1993.
83. Terry Armour, "Bulls Wilt from Suns' Overtime Heat," *Chicago Tribune*, June 14, 1993.
84. David Casstevens, "There's Lots of Bite—and Sheer Determination—Left Behind This Team's Bark," *Chicago Tribune*, June 15, 1993.
85. Melissa Isaacson, "Bulls Vow to Regain Their Fire," *Chicago Tribune*, June 15, 1993.
86. Melissa Isaacson and Terry Armour, "Lack of Playing Time Frustrates Perdue," *Chicago Tribune*, June 16, 1993.
87. Broadcast of 1993 NBA Finals Game 4, NBC Sports, June 16, 1993.
88. Paul Sullivan and Terry Armour, "Barkley Balks at Three-Peat," *Chicago Tribune*, June 19, 1993.
89. Interview with author, January 12, 2018.
90. Sam Smith, "Ainge: We Know We're Better Team," *Chicago Tribune*, June 20, 1993.
91. Interview with author, November 13, 2017.
92. Broadcast of 1993 NBA Finals Game 6, NBC Sports, June 20, 1993.
93. Interview with author, October 9, 2017.
94. Broadcast of 1993 NBA Finals Game 6, NBC Sports, June 20, 1993.
95. Melissa Isaacson. "Bulls Seal Legacy with Dramatic Finish," *Chicago Tribune*, June 21, 1993.
96. Phil Jackson and Hugh Delehanty, *Eleven Rings: The Soul of Success* (New York: Penguin Press 2013), p. 131.
97. Jay Mariotti, "3-Peat Assures Bulls' Place in History," *Chicago Sun-Times*, June 21, 1993.
98. Ibid.
99. Interview with author, October 9, 2017.

100. Interview with author, September 26, 2017.
101. Interview with author, March 29, 2017.
102. Interview with author, January 12, 2018.
103. Interview with author, November 13, 2017.
104. Dan Wiederer, "The James Jordan Murder—Absence of Answers," *Chicago Tribune*, August 9, 2018.
105. Interview with author, February 21, 2018.
106. Jack McCallum, "'The Desire Isn't There,'" *Sports Illustrated*, October 18, 1993.
107. *Ibid.*
108. *Ibid.*
109. *Ibid.*
110. Christian Red and Peter Botte, "Michael Jordan's Baseball Foray: The Inside Story, 25 Years Later," *New York Post*, March 16, 2019.
111. Jon Solomon, "20 Years Ago, Michael Jordan Came to Birmingham," www.al.com, April 8, 2014.
112. Interview with author, March 29, 2017.
113. Sam Smith, *Second Coming: The Strange Odyssey of Michael Jordan—from Courtside to Home Plate and Back Again* (New York: HarperCollins, 1995), p. 2.
114. *Ibid.*

Chapter 4

1. Interview with author, March 8, 2017.
2. Scott Burnside, "Demers' Secret Struggle with Pain, Shame of Illiteracy," espn.com, November 3, 2005.
3. *Ibid.*
4. *Ibid.*
5. Todd Denault, *A Season in Time: Super Mario, Killer St. Patrick, The Great One, and the Unforgettable 1992-93 NHL Season* (Mississauga, Ontario: Wiley, 2012), p. 68.
6. Interview with author, January 11, 2017.
7. Pat Hickey, "Coach Demers Lays Down the Law," *Montreal Gazette*, October 14, 1992.
8. *Ibid.*
9. Interview with author, January 11, 2017.
10. Interview with author, March 8, 2017.
11. Denault, p. 119.
12. James Bisson, "An Oral History of the 1992-93 Montreal Canadiens," thescore.com, January 26, 2018.
13. Interview with author, January 11, 2017.
14. Denault, p. 184.
15. Richard Hoffer, "Return of the King," *Sports Illustrated*, January 18, 1993.
16. Interview with author, January 21, 2017.
17. Interview with author, January 18, 2017.
18. Interview with author, January 21, 2017.
19. Wayne Gretzky, with Kirstie McLellan Day, *99: Stories of the Game* (New York: Penguin, 2016), p. 116.
20. Interview with author, January 18, 2017.
21. Interview with author, February 8, 2017.
22. Interview with author, January 18, 2017.
23. Interview with author, February 12, 2017.
24. *Ibid.*
25. Interview with author, January 11, 2017.
26. Interview with author, February 22, 2017.
27. Interview with author, February 12, 2017.
28. *Ibid.*
29. *Ibid.*
30. Jeff Jacobs, "Canadiens Deny 'Favorites' Role," *Hartford Courant*, May 22, 1993.
31. Bob McKenzie, "Gretzky Playing as if He's Got a Piano on His Back," *Toronto Star*, May 26, 1993.
32. Interview with author, February 8, 2017.
33. *Ibid.*
34. Interview with author, February 12, 2017.
35. Denault, p. 315.
36. Lisa Dillman, "NOTES: Kings' Carson Finds Cup Dream Scratched," *Los Angeles Times*, June 2, 1993.
37. Red Fisher, "Habs Brutal in Loss to Kings," *Montreal Gazette*, June 2, 1993.
38. Joe Lapointe: "Wayne's Whirl Lead Kings," *New York Times*, June 2, 1993.
39. Interview with author, January 18, 2017.
40. *Ibid.*
41. E.M. Swift, "Stick It to 'Em," *Sports Illustrated*, June 14, 1993.

42. Interview with author, January 21, 2017.
43. Interview with author, January 18, 2017.
44. Interview with author, February 8, 2017.
45. *Ibid.*
46. Michael Farber, "Vermont Made John LeClair of the Flyers Has Become a Force at Power Forward and a Hero in His Home State," *Sports Illustrated*, November 3, 1997.
47. Helene Elliott, "LeClair's New Role a Winner," *Los Angeles Times*, June 6, 1993.
48. Michael Farber, "Vermont Made John LeClair of the Flyers Has Become a Force at Power Forward and a Hero in His Home State," *Sports Illustrated*, November 3, 1997.
49. *Ibid.*
50. Interview with author, January 11, 2017.
51. Interview with author, March 8, 2017.
52. *Ibid.*
53. Interview with author, January 11, 2017.
54. Interview with author, February 12, 2017.
55. Interview with author, January 21, 2017.
56. Interview with author, January 18, 2017.
57. Interview with author, February 8, 2017.
58. "Victory Party Turns into Riot and Looting," *Associated Press*, June 11, 1993.
59. *Ibid.*
60. Interview with author, January 11, 2017.
61. "Looking back, Montreal has not won a Stanley Cup": Interview with author, January 21, 2017.

Chapter 5

1. Interview with author, June 25, 2017.
2. Interview with author, January 31, 2018.
3. Richard Hoffer, "The Importance of Being Barry," *Sports Illustrated*, May 24, 1993.
4. Joe Konte, *The Rivalry Heard 'Round the World: The Dodgers-Giants Feud from Coast to Coast* (New York: Skyhorse Publishing, 2013), p. 212.
5. Interview with author, December 7, 2017.
6. Larry Stone, "Man About Cooperstown: Molitor Takes His Place with Game's Best," *Seattle Times*, July 25, 2004.
7. Interview with author, December 7, 2017.
8. Interview with author, June 11, 2017.
9. Interview with author, February 2, 2018.
10. Interview with author, April 16, 2019.
11. Interview with author, January 31, 2018.
12. Interview with author, June 11, 2017.
13. *1993 Toronto Blue Jays Story!* Sports History Channel, 2013.
14. Interview with author, June 11, 2017.
15. Tim Kurkjian, "Birds of Prey," *Sports Illustrated*, April 5, 1993.
16. Phil Taylor, "A Swing So Sweet," *Sports Illustrated*, May 10, 1993.
17. Mike DiGiovanna, "Big Leagues No Big Deal to Him," *Los Angeles Times*, May 24, 1990.
18. *Ibid.*
19. Interview with author, June 25, 2017.
20. Interview with author, February 2, 2018.
21. Interview with author, June 25, 2017.
22. Interview with author, January 31, 2018.
23. Interview with author, April 16, 2019.
24. *Ibid.*
25. Interview with author, February 2, 2018.
26. *Ibid.*
27. Interview with author, June 11, 2017.
28. Tom Verducci, "A Special Delivery," *Sports Illustrated*, September 13, 1993.
29. Ross Newhan, "Pride of the Tigers," *Los Angeles Times*, July 23, 1996.
30. Doug Wilson, *Pudge: The Biography of Carlton Fisk* (New York: St. Martin's Press, 2015), p. 290.
31. "Caught on the Fly," *Sporting News*, October 18, 1993.
32. Joey Reaves, "Blue Jays' Hit Squad KO's McDowell in Round 1," *Chicago Tribune*, October 6, 1993.
33. Interview with author, February 2, 2018.
34. Interview with author, August 2, 2017.
35. *Ibid.*
36. *Ibid.*
37. *Ibid.*
38. Joey Reaves, "Jack of All Fades," *Chicago Tribune*, October 11, 1993.

39. Joey Reaves, "No Miracle on 35th St.," *Chicago Tribune*, October 13, 1993.
40. Tim Kurkjian, "A Flying Start," *Sports Illustrated*, May 10, 1993.
41. Ibid.
42. Ibid.
43. Ibid.
44. Interview with author, June 13, 2017.
45. Ibid.
46. Ibid.
47. William Kashatus, *Macho Row: The 1993 Phillies and Baseball's Unwritten Code* (Lincoln: University of Nebraska Press, 2019), p. 218.
48. Kashatus, p. 221.
49. Bob Nightengale, "From Odd Man Out to Phillies' Hero," *Los Angeles Times*, October 18, 1993.
50. Interview with author, June 13, 2017.
51. Interview with author, June 11, 2017.
52. Interview with author, June 25, 2017.
53. Kashatus, p. 230.
54. Jack Curry, "In REM Sleep? You Missed All the R.B.I.," *New York Times*, October 22, 1993.
55. Interview with author, June 13, 2017.
56. Interview with author, June 25, 2017.
57. Sportsnet Staff, "Touch 'Em All Joe: 21 Years Later," www.sportsnet.ca, October 21, 2013.
58. Ibid.
59. Ibid.
60. Ibid.
61. Interview with author, February 2, 2018.
62. Interview with author, June 25, 2017.
63. Interview with author, June 11, 2017.
64. Interview with author, April 16, 2019.
65. Ibid.
66. Interview with author, March 28, 2019.
67. Ibid.
68. Hal Bodley, "Williams Adds Name to Infamous List," *USA Today*, October 25, 1993.
69. Ibid.
70. Ibid.
71. Kevin Kernan, "Say It's So Joe," *San Diego Union-Tribune*, March 22, 1990.
72. Interview with author, February 2, 2018.
73. Interview with author, December 7, 2017.
74. Interview with author, June 25, 2017.

Chapter 6

1. Interview with author, November 20, 2017.
2. Jeff Pearlman, *Boys Will Be Boys: The Glory Days and Party Nights of the Dallas Cowboys Dynasty* (New York: HarperCollins, 2008), p. 20.
3. Ibid., p. 28.
4. William Oscar Johnson, "A Chapter Closed," *Sports Illustrated*, March 6, 1989.
5. Interview with author, August 25, 2017.
6. Ibid.
7. Randy Galloway, "Take Wool from Cowboys' Eyes, Vikings Flat Out Fleeced Them," *Dallas Morning News*, October 14, 1989.
8. Pearlman, p. 75.
9. Interview with author, October 23, 2017.
10. Tim Kawakami, "Irvin Cowboy: He Was Landry's Last First-Round Pick and Choicest of a New Generation," *Los Angeles Times*, January 22, 1993.
11. Kurt Daniels, "Super Bowl XXVII: The First of a Dynasty," *Cowboys Star Gameday*, November 19, 2017.
12. Interview with author, October 23, 2017.
13. Interview with author, October 18, 2017.
14. Interview with author, October 30, 2017.
15. Interview with author, October 23, 2017.
16. Paul Zimmerman, "Big D, As in Dynasty," *Sports Illustrated*, February 8, 1993.
17. Interview with author, October 23, 2017.
18. Interview with author, October 18, 2017.
19. Kevin Sherrington, "A House Divided," *Dallas Morning News*, January 24, 1993.
20. Interview with author, October 23, 2017.
21. Interview with author, November 20, 2017.
22. Interview with author, July 10, 2017.
23. Ibid.
24. Interview with author, Ibid.
25. Jill Lieber, "Most Visible Player," *Sports Illustrated*, February 15, 1993.
26. Interview with author, July 10, 2017.

27. Interview with author, January 18, 2017.
28. Kurt Daniels, "Super Bowl XXVII: The First of a Dynasty," *Cowboys Star Gameday*, November 19, 2017.
29. Interview with author, July 10, 2017.
30. Kurt Daniels, "Super Bowl XXVII: The First of a Dynasty," *Cowboys Star Gameday*, November 19, 2017.
31. Interview with author, July 10, 2017.
32. Broadcast of Super Bowl XXVII, NBC Sports, January 31, 1993.
33. Michael Wilbon, "This Time, Bills Beat Smith-less Cowboys," *Washington Post*, September 13, 1993.
34. Interview with author, January 13, 2017.
35. Interview with author, October 18, 2017.
36. Interview with author, November 20, 2017.
37. Interview with author, January 13, 2017.
38. Pearlman, pp. 192–193.
39. Interview with author, January 13, 2017.
40. Jim Browder, "One Word Says It: Emmitt," *Dallas Cowboys Official Weekly*, November 6, 1993.
41. Interview with author, October 30, 2017.
42. Pearlman, p. 204.
43. Ken Sins, "An Interview with Tom Landry," *Dallas Cowboys Official Weekly*, November 6, 1993.
44. Interview with author, January 13, 2017.
45. Interview with author, March 14, 2017.
46. Jim Browder, "Dolphins Ice Cowboys," *Dallas Cowboys Official Weekly*, December 4, 1993.
47. Interview with author, March 14, 2017.
48. Sally Jenkins, "The Mouth that Roars," *Sports Illustrated*, October 25, 1993.
49. Pearlman, p. 150.
50. Sally Jenkins, "The Mouth that Roars," *Sports Illustrated*, October 25, 1993.
51. *Ibid*.
52. Interview with author, August 25, 2017.
53. Interview with author, October 23, 2017.
54. *Ibid*.
55. Interview with author, October 30, 2017.
56. Ed Werder, "Smith Shoulders Load, Keeps Offense Running," *Dallas Morning News*, January 3, 1994.
57. Emmitt Smith, with Steve Delsohn, *The Emmitt Zone* (New York: Crown Publishers, Inc., 1994), p. 6.
58. Interview with author, October 18, 2017.
59. Interview with author, January 13, 2017.
60. Emmitt Smith, with Steve Delsohn, *The Emmitt Zone* (New York: Crown Publishers, Inc., 1994), p. 4.
61. Interview with author, August 25, 2017.
62. Tim Cowlishaw, "Recovering for a Rematch," *Dallas Morning News*, January 17, 1994.
63. *Ibid*.
64. Pearlman, p. 112.
65. Interview with author, October 30, 2017.
66. Bob Glauber, "Charles Haley, Bipolar Issues Long Behind Him, Eager to Give Back," *Newsday*, August 8, 2015.
67. Tim Cowlishaw, "Teams Find It's Always Good to Have Haley on Their Side," *Dallas Morning News*, January 22, 1994.
68. T.J. Simers, "Johnson Puts It All on the Line," *Los Angeles Times*, January 22, 1994.
69. *Ibid*.
70. Steve Young, with Jeff Benedict, *QB: My Life Behind the Spiral* (New York: Houghton Mifflin Harcourt, 2016), p. 225.
71. Ed Werder, "Aikman Recalls Little of NFC Title Game," *Dallas Morning News*, January 25, 1994.
72. David Jackson, "Atlanta's Winning Ways," *Dallas Morning News*, January 25, 1994.
73. Interview with author, October 23, 2017.
74. Interview with author, October 30, 2017.
75. Interview with author, October 23, 2017.
76. Interview with author, October 18, 2017.
77. Interview with author, October 23, 2017.
78. *Ibid*.
79. *Ibid*.
80. Interview with author, October 18, 2017.
81. Peter King, "A Puzzle of Many Pieces," *Sports Illustrated*, February 1, 1993.
82. Interview with author, October 23, 2017.

83. *Ibid.*
84. Scott Fowler, "Washington Monumental in Sparking the Cowboys' Turnaround," *Miami Herald*, January 31, 1994.
85. Paul Zimmerman, "The Fumble!," *Sports Illustrated*, February 7, 1994.
86. Interview with author, January 13, 2017.
87. Interview with author, February 27, 2017.
88. Peter King, "Bad Blood," *Sports Illustrated*, April 11, 1994.
89. *Ibid.*
90. *Ibid.*
91. *Ibid.*
92. *Ibid.*
93. William C. Rhoden, "2 Titles but Now No Coach for Cowboys," *New York Times*, March 30, 1994.
94. *Ibid.*
95. Peter King, "Bad Blood," *Sports Illustrated*, April 11, 1994.

Chapter 7

1. Interview with author, November 10, 2017.
2. Joel A. Erickson, "Toughest Call Frank Reich Ever Made: Leaving Preaching for Coaching," *Indianapolis Star*, August 4, 2019.
3. Interview with author, November 20, 2018.
4. Interview with author, January 18, 2017.
5. Interview with author November 10, 2017.
6. *Ibid.*
7. Marv Levy, *Marv Levy: Where Else Would You Rather Be?* (New York: Sports Publishing, 2004), p. 370.
8. Interview with author, January 18, 2017.
9. Interview with author, November 20, 2018.
10. Interview with author, January 18, 2017.
11. *Ibid.*
12. *Sports Illustrated: 1993—The Year in Sports*, Produced by Ross Greenburg.
13. Interview with author, January 18, 2017.
14. Interview with author, November 20, 2018.
15. Interview with author, November 10, 2017.
16. *Ibid.*
17. Interview with author, November 20, 2018.
18. Interview with author, December 1, 2017.
19. Interview with author, February 27, 2017.
20. *Ibid.*
21. Interview with author, November 20, 2018.
22. Interview with author, February 27, 2017.
23. Interview with author, January 18, 2017.
24. Interview with author, November 10, 2017.
25. *Ibid.*
26. *Ibid.*
27. *Ibid.*
28. Interview with author, November 20, 2018.
29. Interview with author, December 1, 2017.
30. Interview with author, January 18, 2017.
31. Matthew Fairburn, "Andre Reed Hall of Fame Speech: 10 Best Quotes from Former Bills Receiver," www.syracuse.com, August 3, 2014.
32. Adam Lazarus, *Super Bowl Monday: From the Persian Gulf to the Shores of West Florida: The New York Giants, the Buffalo Bills, and Super Bowl XXV* (Lanham, Maryland: Taylor Trade Publishing, 2011), p. 194.
33. Interview with author, November 20, 2018.
34. Interview with author, January 3, 2017.
35. *Frank Reich: The Man Behind the Comeback Beard*, NFL Films, 2019.
36. Steve Tasker, with Scott Pitoniak, *Steve Tasker's Tales from the Buffalo Bills* (Champaign, Illinois: Sports Publishing L.L.C., 2006), p. 83.
37. Interview with author, November 10, 2017.
38. Interview with author, November 20, 2018.
39. *Ibid.*
40. Interview with author, January 18, 2017.
41. Interview with author, December 1, 2017.
42. Interview with author, November 10, 2017.

Bibliography

Newspaper Articles

Anderson, Dave. "Jordan's Atlantic City Caper." *New York Times*, May 27, 1993.
Antonen, Mel. "Molitor Lives Dream and Is Named MVP." *USA Today*, October 24, 1993.
Antonen, Mel. "Olerud Family Shares Joy." *USA Today*, October 15, 1993.
Armour, Terry, and Melissa Isaacson. "Lack of Playing Time Frustrates Perdue." *Chicago Tribune*, June 16, 1993.
Armour, Terry, and Paul Sullivan. "Barkley Balks at Three-Peat." *Chicago Tribune*, June 19, 1993.
Baker, Chris. "One Goaltender Is a Hometown Product; the Other Talks to Goalposts." *Los Angeles Times*, May 20, 1986.
Bernstein, Viv. "Kings Must Work Overtime to Stay with Canadiens Now." *Baltimore Sun*, June 8, 1993.
Bodley, Hal. "Williams Adds Name to Infamous List." *USA Today*, October 25, 1993.
Botte, Peter, and Christian Red. "Michael Jordan's Baseball Foray: The Inside Story, 25 Years Later." *New York Post*, March 16, 2019.
Bowen, Les. "Jackson Says Eight-Day Layoff Did Him In." *Philadelphia Daily News*, October 20, 1993.
Browder, Jim. "Dolphins Ice Cowboys." *Dallas Cowboys Official Weekly*, December 4, 1993.
Browder, Jim. "One Word Says It: Emmitt." *Dallas Cowboys Official Weekly*, November 6, 1993.
Brown, Clifton. "Bright Day for Suns: They Get Barkley." *New York Times*, June 18, 1992.
Casstevens, David. "There's Lots of Bite—and Sheer Determination—Left Behind This Team's Bark." *Chicago Tribune*, June 15, 1993.
Covitz, Randy. "Joe Montana Brought Something Special to the Chiefs." *Kansas City Star*, August 26, 2013.
Cowlishaw, Tim. "'How 'Bout Them Cowboys!' Cowboys Stand Atop NFC, 30–20." *Dallas Morning News*, January 18, 1993.
Cowlishaw, Tim. "Recovering for a Rematch." *Dallas Morning News*, January 17, 1994.
Cowlishaw, Tim. "Teams Find It's Always Good to Have Haley on Their Side." *Dallas Morning News*, January 22, 1994.
Curry, Jack. "In REM Sleep? You Missed All the R.B.I." *New York Times*, October 22, 1993.
DiGiovanna, Mike. "Big Leagues No Big Deal to Him." *Los Angeles Times*, May 24, 1990.
Dillman, Lisa. "It's Canadiens Who Are Kings." *Los Angeles Times*, June 10, 1993.
Dillman, Lisa. "NOTES: Kings' Carson Finds Cup Dream Scratched." *Los Angeles Times*, June 2, 1993.
"Dykstra and Daulton Injured in Car Accident." *New York Times*, May 7, 1991.

Elliott, Helene. "LeClair's New Role a Winner." *Los Angeles Times*, June 6, 1993.
Erickson, Joel A. "Toughest Call Frank Reich Ever Made: Leaving Preaching for Coaching." *Indianapolis Star*, August 4, 2019.
"Fan Planned to Kill Jays' Alomar." *Associated Press*, July 3, 1995.
Finn, Robin. "Life in the Fast Lane." *New York Times*, May 2, 1993.
Fisher, Red. "Habs Brutal in Loss to Kings." *Montreal Gazette*, June 2, 1993.
Fitzpatrick, Frank. "Bounty Bowl Legacy Recalled 25 Years Later." *Philadelphia Inquirer*, November 21, 2014.
Fitzpatrick, Frank. "Phils Never Really Get Started." *Philadelphia Inquirer*, October 20, 1993.
Fowler, Scott. "Washington Monumental in Sparking the Cowboys' Turnaround." *Miami Herald*, January 31, 1994.
Friend, Tom. "By Popular Demand, Montana Reconsiders." *New York Times*, April 19, 1993.
Friend, Tom. "Chiefs and 49ers Come to Terms on Montana Trade at Last." *New York Times*, April 21, 1993.
Friend, Tom. "It's Decision Time for Well-Armed 49ers." *New York Times*, December 22, 1992.
Galloway, Randy. "Take Wool from Cowboys' Eyes, Vikings Flat Out Fleeced Them." *Dallas Morning News*, October 14, 1989.
George, Thomas. "Montana, the Chiefs, and the Dream: At 37, the Legend Continues." *New York Times*, September 5, 1993.
Glauber, Bob. "Charles Haley, Bipolar Issues Long Behind Him, Eager to Give Back." *Newsday*, August 8, 2015.
Hageman, William. "The Hunt for Babe Ruth's Baltimore Beginnings." *Chicago Tribune*, February 11, 2014.
Hagen, Paul. "Save: Schilling Back at You, Toronto." *Philadelphia Daily News*, October 22, 1993.
Heisler, Mark. "Barkley Spoils His Best Shots." *Los Angeles Times*, July 27, 1992.
Heisler, Mark. "Bulls Bullied, Leave New York in Sorry State." *Los Angeles Times*, May 26, 1993.
Heisler, Mark. "Starks Gives Bulls One to Remember." *Los Angeles Times*, May 24, 1993.
Hickey, Pat. "Coach Demers Lays Down the Law." *Montreal Gazette*, October 14, 1992.
Hunter, Paul. "Kings See Game 7 as Stop on Cup Road to Montreal." *Toronto Star*, May 29, 1993.
Isaacson, Melissa. "Angry Jordan Denies Charge." *Chicago Tribune*, May 28, 1993.
Isaacson, Melissa. "Bulls Seal Legacy with Dramatic Finish." *Chicago Tribune*, June 21, 1993.
Isaacson, Melissa. "Bulls Veterans Accept Roles, but…" *Chicago Tribune*, October 22, 1992.
Isaacson, Melissa. "Bulls Vow to Regain Their Fire." *Chicago Tribune*, June 15, 1993.
Isaacson, Melissa. "Father Knows Best about Jordan's Frustrations." *Chicago Tribune*, May 31, 1993.
Isaacson, Melissa. "Game 3 Follows Pattern of Eastern Finals to a 'T.'" *Chicago Tribune*, May 30, 1993.
Isaacson, Melissa. "Perdue Fears He's Bulls' Insurance." *Chicago Tribune*, January 5, 1993.
Jackson, David. "Atlanta's Winning Ways." *Dallas Morning News*, January 25, 1994.
Jacobs, Jeff. "Canadiens Deny Favorite Role." *Hartford Courant*, May 22, 1993.
Johnston, David. "Gretzky Not Looking Past Next Season." *Montreal Gazette*, June 1, 1993.
Justice, Richard. "Orioles Inaugurate Camden Yards, Defeat Mets." *Washington Post*, April 4, 1992.
Kawakami, Tim. "Irvin Cowboy: He Was Landry's Last First-Round Pick and Choicest of a New Generation." *Los Angeles Times*, January 22, 1993.

Kent, Milton. "Longest Day for Griffey, González." *Baltimore Sun,* July 13, 1993.
Kernan, Kevin. "Say It's So Joe." *San Diego Union-Tribune,* March 22, 1990.
Lapointe, Joe. "Wayne's Whirl Lead Kings." *New York Times,* June 2, 1993.
Luksa, Frank. "Young Going into Game with Weight of Montana on His Back." *Dallas Morning News,* January 17, 1993.
Mariotti, Jay. "In Crunch, Bulls Deliver Like Champs." *Chicago Sun-Times,* June 3, 1993.
Mariotti, Jay. "3-Peat Assures Bulls' Place in History." *Chicago Sun-Times,* June 21, 1993.
McKenzie, Bob. "Gretzky Playing as if He's Got a Piano on His Back." *Toronto Star,* May 26, 1993.
Moore, David. "Grant-Oakley Matchup Key to Bulls, Knicks." *Dallas Morning News,* June 2, 1993.
Mulligan, Mike. "Bulls 'Level' Hawks." *Chicago Sun-Times,* May 1, 1993.
Mulligan, Mike. "NBA Finals Series in Review." *Chicago Sun-Times,* June 21, 1993.
Newhan, Ross. "Pride of the Tigers." *Los Angeles Times,* July 23, 1996.
Nidetz, Steve. "As Jordan Soared, So Did TV Revenues." *Chicago Tribune,* October 13, 1993.
Nightengale, Bob. "From Odd Man Out to Phillies' Hero." *Los Angeles Times,* October 18, 1993
Plaschke, Bill. "A Broken Bond." *Los Angeles Times,* January 16, 1993.
Plaschke, Bill. "Montana's Magic Makes Oilers Disappear." *Los Angeles Times,* January 17, 1994.
Reaves, Joey. "Blue Jays Hit Squad KO's McDowell in Round 1, Sox Let Guzmán off Hook." *Chicago Tribune,* October 6, 1993.
Reaves, Joey. "Jack of All Fades." *Chicago Tribune,* October 11, 1993.
Reaves, Joey. "No Miracle on 35th Street: MVP Stewart Helps Jays Eliminate Sox." *Chicago Tribune,* October 13, 1993.
Rhoden, William C. "2 Titles but Now No Coach for Cowboys." *New York Times,* March 30, 1994.
"Same Player, Same Place, Same Result: Bulls Win." *Associated Press,* May 18, 1993.
Schmuck, Peter. "Camden Yards, the Stadium that Changed Baseball and Baltimore, Turns 20." *Baltimore Sun,* March 31, 2012.
Shane, Scott. "The Secret History of City Slave Trade." *Baltimore Sun,* June 20, 1999.
Shapiro, Leonard. "Montana Goes Down for the Count, and So Does Kansas City." *Washington Post,* January 24, 1994.
Shaughnessy, Dan. "Hanging Out in the Hot Corner." *Boston Globe,* July 13, 1993.
Sherrington, Kevin. "A House Divided." *Dallas Morning News,* January 24, 1993.
Simers, T.J. "Johnson Puts It All on the Line." *Los Angeles Times,* January 22, 1994.
Sins, Ken. "An Interview with Tom Landry." *Dallas Cowboys Official Weekly,* November 6, 1993.
Smith, Sam. "Ainge: We Know We're Better Team." *Chicago Tribune,* June 20, 1993.
Smith, Sam. "Bring on the Bulls, Cry Knicks, Cavaliers." *Chicago Tribune,* October 11, 1992.
Stellino, Vito. "Cowboys' Haley Has Score to Settle in San Francisco." *Baltimore Sun,* January 16, 1993.
Stone, Larry. "Man about Cooperstown: Molitor Takes His Place with Game's Best." *Seattle Times,* July 25, 2004.
Trister, Noah. "The Camden Effect: At 25, Ballpark's Legacy Is Large in MLB." *Associated Press,* March 31, 2017.
Verdi, Bob. "Montana's Blessing: He Can't Remember What Happened." *Chicago Tribune,* January 24, 1994.
"Victory Party Turns into Riot and Looting." *Associated Press,* June 11, 1993.
Weir, Tom. "Game 4: So Many Hits and Too Many Records." *USA Today,* October 21, 1993.
Werder, Ed. "Aikman Recalls Little of NFC Title Game." *Dallas Morning News,* January 25, 1994.

Werder, Ed. "Cowboys Crush Buffalo, 52–17 in Super Bowl." *Dallas Morning News,* February 1, 1993.

Werder, Ed. "Smith Shoulders Load, Keeps Offense Running." *Dallas Morning News,* January 3, 1994.

Wiederer, Dan. "The James Jordan Murder—Absence of Answers." *Chicago Tribune,* August 9, 2018.

Wilbon, Michael. "This Time Bills Beat Smith-less Cowboys." *Washington Post,* September 13, 1993.

Zurkowsky, Herb. "Canadiens Head Coach Jacques Demers Is Living His Dream." *Montreal Gazette,* May 28, 1993.

Magazine Articles

"Caught on the Fly." *Sporting News,* October 18, 1993.

Daniels, Kurt. "Super Bowl XXVII: The First of a Dynasty." *Cowboys Star Gameday,* November 19, 2017.

Diamond, John. "The Drive for Three." *World Champion Chicago Bulls 1993 Official Yearbook,* 1993.

Dodson, James. "Attention to Detail." *1993 All-Star Game Official Major League Baseball Program,* New York: Sports Publishing Group, July 13, 1993.

Farber, Michael. "Vermont Made John LeClair of the Flyers Has Become a Force at Power Forward and a Hero in His Home State." *Sports Illustrated,* November 3, 1997.

Goldberger, Nancy. "Off the Court." *A Tribute to Michael Jordan: Commemorative Edition,* 1993.

Hoffer, Richard. "The Importance of Being Barry." *Sports Illustrated,* May 24, 1993.

Hoffer, Richard. "The Old Montana Mystique." *Sports Illustrated,* January 24, 1994.

Hoffer, Richard. "Return of the King." *Sports Illustrated,* January 18, 1993.

Jenkins, Sally. "The Mouth that Roars." *Sports Illustrated,* October 25, 1993.

Johnson, William Oscar. "A Chapter Closed." *Sports Illustrated,* March 6, 1989.

King, Peter. "Bad Blood." *Sports Illustrated,* April 11, 1994.

King, Peter. "A Puzzle of Many Pieces." *Sports Illustrated,* February 1, 1993.

King, Peter. "QB or Not QB?" *Sports Illustrated,* July 27, 1992.

Kurkjian, Tim. "A Flying Start." *Sports Illustrated,* May 10, 1993.

Lieber, Jill. "Most Visible Player." *Sports Illustrated,* February 15, 1993.

McCallum, Jack. "'The Desire Isn't There.'" *Sports Illustrated,* October 18, 1993.

McCallum, Jack. "Eye of the Storm." *Sports Illustrated,* June 14, 1993.

McCallum, Jack. "Friends and Foes Together." *Sports Illustrated,* May 31, 1993.

McCallum, Jack. "The Lips Were Zipped." *Sports Illustrated,* June 7, 1993.

McCallum, Jack. "They're History." *Sports Illustrated,* June 28, 1993.

McCallum, Jack. "Triple Play." *Sports Illustrated,* June 21, 1993.

Montville, Leigh. "Bitter Ending." *Sports Illustrated,* May 31, 1993.

Moore, Evan F. "Craig Hodges and the Modern Activist Athlete." *Rolling Stone,* March 23, 2017.

Nightengale, Bob. "He's Not Just Your Average Joe." *Baseball America,* April 25, 1990.

Swift, E.M. "Saving Grace." *Sports Illustrated,* June 21, 1993.

Swift, E.M. "Stick It To 'Em." *Sports Illustrated,* June 14, 1993.

Taylor, Phil. "A Swing So Sweet." *Sports Illustrated,* May 10, 1993.

Verducci, Tom. "A Special Delivery." *Sports Illustrated,* September 13, 1993.

"Where Today's Stars Grew Up." *1993 All-Star Game Official Major League Baseball Program,* July 13, 1993.

Zimmerman, Paul. "Big D, As in Dynasty." *Sports Illustrated,* February 8, 1993.

Zimmerman, Paul. "Cure for a Headache." *Sports Illustrated,* February 7, 1994.
Zimmerman, Paul. "The Fumble!" *Sports Illustrated,* February 7, 1994.
Zimmerman, Paul. "Joe Goes." *Sports Illustrated,* April 26, 1993.
Zimmerman, Paul. "Soaring to the Top." *Sports Illustrated,* February 8, 1993.
Zimmerman, Paul. "Youth over Young." *Sports Illustrated,* January 25, 1993.

Website Articles

Burnside, Scott. "Demers' Secret Struggle with Pain, Shame of Illiteracy." www.espn.com, November 7, 2005.
Carucci, Vic. "Bills—Greatest Comeback." www.profootballhof.com, January 1, 2005.
Chesterton, Eric. "25 Years Ago, Barry Bonds Signed with the Giants—and Got Even Better." www.mlb.com, December 6, 2017.
Fairburn, Matthew. "Andre Reed Hall of Fame Speech: 10 Best Quotes from Former Bills Receiver." www.syracuse.com, August 3, 2014.
Markazi, Arash. "In 1993, They Were Kings of Los Angeles." www.espn.com, June 1, 2012.
Solomon, Jon. "20 Years Ago, Michael Jordan Came to Birmingham." www.al.com, April 8, 2014.
Sportsnet Staff. "Touch 'Em All Joe: 20 Years Later." www.sportsnet.ca, October 21, 2013.
Wulf, Steve. "The Run that Birthed Dallas' Dynasty." www.espn.com, October 8, 2014.

Books

Burgoyne, Tom, and Robert Gordon. *More Than Beards, Bellies, and Biceps: The Story of the 1993 Phillies (And the Phillie Phanatic Too).* New York: Sports Publishing, 2002.
Denault, Todd. *A Season in Time: Super Mario, Killer, St. Patrick, the Great One, and the Unforgettable 1992-93 NHL Season.* Mississauga, Ontario: John Wiley & Sons, Ltd., 2012.
Dunnavant, Keith. *Montana: The Biography of Football's Joe Cool.* New York: St. Martin's Press, 2015.
Gretz, Bob. *Hail to the Chiefs.* Champaign, Illinois: Sagamore Publishing, 1994.
Gretzky, Wayne, with Kirstie McLellan. *99: Stories of the Game.* New York: Penguin Random House, 2016.
Halberstam, David. *Playing for Keeps: Michael Jordan and the World He Made.* New York: Random House, 1999.
Harwood, Herbert, Jr. *Impossible Challenge: The Baltimore and Ohio Railroad in Maryland.* Baltimore, Maryland: Barnard Roberts & Company, 1979.
Jackson, Phil, with Hugh Delehanty. *Eleven Rings: The Soul of Success.* New York: Penguin Press, 2013.
Jenish, D'Arcy. *The Montreal Canadiens: 100 Years of Glory.* Toronto: Doubleday Canada, 2008.
Kashatus, William. *Macho Row: The 1993 Phillies and Baseball's Unwritten Code.* Lincoln: University of Nebraska Press, 2017.
Konte, Joe. *The Rivalry Heard 'Round the World: The Dodgers-Giants Feud from Coast to Coast.* New York: Skyhorse Publishing, 2013.
Lazarus, Adam. *Best of Rivals: Joe Montana, Steve Young, and the Inside Story Behind the NFL's Greatest Quarterback Controversy.* Boston: Da Capo Press, 2012.
Lazarus, Adam. *Super Bowl Monday: From the Persian Gulf to the Shores of West Florida: The New York Giants, the Buffalo Bills, and Super Bowl XXV.* Lanham, Maryland: Taylor Trade Publishing, 2011.

Lazenby, Roland. *Michael Jordan: The Life.* Boston: Little, Brown, 2014.
Levy, Marv. *Marv Levy: Where Else Would You Rather Be?* New York: Sports Publishing, 2004.
McCallum, Jack. *Dream Team: How Michael, Magic, Larry, Charles, and the Greatest Team of All Time Conquered the World and Changed the Game of Basketball Forever.* New York: Ballantine Books, 2012.
Patoski, Joe Nick. *The Dallas Cowboys: The Outrageous History of the Biggest, Loudest, Most Hated, Best Loved Football Team in America.* New York: Little, Brown, 2012.
Pearlman, Jeff. *Boys Will Be Boys: The Glory Days and Party Nights of the Dallas Cowboys Dynasty.* New York: HarperCollins, 2008.
Richmond, Peter. *Ballpark: Camden Yards and the Building of an American Dream.* New York: Simon & Schuster, 1993.
Shaughnessy, Dan. *Reversing the Curse: Inside the 2004 Boston Red Sox.* New York: Houghton Mifflin Company, 2005.
Simon, Ron. *The Game Behind the Game: Negotiating in the Big Leagues.* Stillwater, Minnesota: Voyageur Press, 1993.
Smith, Emmitt, with Steve Delsohn. *The Emmitt Zone.* New York: Crown Publishers, 1994.
Smith, Sam. *The Jordan Rules.* New York: Simon & Schuster, 1992.
Smith, Sam. *Second Coming: The Strange Odyssey of Michael Jordan—from Courtside to Home Plate and Back Again.* New York: HarperCollins, 1995.
Tasker, Steve, with Scott Pitoniak. *Steve Tasker's Tales from the Buffalo Bills.* New York: Sports Publishing, 2006.
Wilson, Doug. *Pudge: The Biography of Carlton Fisk.* New York: St. Martin's Press, 2015.
Wisnia, Saul. *Miracle at Fenway: The Inside Story of the Boston Red Sox 2004 Championship Season.* New York: St. Martin's Press, 2014.
Young, Steve, with Jeff Benedict. *QB: My Life Behind the Spiral.* New York: Houghton Mifflin Harcourt, 2016.

Videos

ABC Sports Game Broadcast of 1993 AFC Wild Card Game, January 8, 1994.
CBS Sports Game Broadcast of 1990 NFC Championship Game, January 20, 1991.
CBS Sports Game Broadcast of 1993 MLB All-Star Game, July 13, 1993.
CBS Sports Game Broadcast of 1993 World Series Game 6, October 23, 1993.
ESPN 30 for 30: *The Great Trade Robbery.*
Frank Reich: The Man Behind the Comeback Beard, NFL Films, 2019.
NBC Sports Game Broadcast of 1992 AFC Wild Card Game, January 3, 1993.
NBC Sports Game Broadcast of 1993 AFC Championship Game, January 23, 1994.
NBC Sports Game Broadcast of 1993 NBA Finals Game 6, June 20, 1993.
NBC Sports Game Broadcast of 1993 NFL Divisional Round, January 16, 1994.
NBC Sports Game Broadcast of Super Bowl XXVII, January 31, 1993.
NBC Sports Game Broadcast of Super Bowl XXVIII, January 30, 1994.
1993 Toronto Blue Jays Story! Sports History Channel, 2013.
Sports Illustrated: 1993—The Year in Sports, Executive Producer Ross Greenburg.
Three-Peat: The Chicago Bulls' Historic Third Championship Season, Executive Producer Don Sperling.

Index

Numbers in *bold* italics indicate pages with illustrations

Abbott, Jim 1, 151–152
Abdul, Paula 68
Abdul-Jabbar, Kareem 34, 93
Ackles, Bob 208
Adams, Alvan 94
Agassi, Andre 129
Aikman, Troy 68, 172, 175–176, 179, 181–183, 186, 189–191, 194, 197, 202–203, 207–208, 210
Ainge, Danny 88
Air Jordan 63, 109
A.J.'s 107
Alabama 159
Albany 229
Alberta 118
Alcindor, Lew 34
Ali, Muhammad 180
Allen, Marcus 14, 19–23, 28–29
Alm, Jeff 27
Alomar, Roberto 48–49, 51, 139, 147–151, 156, 162
Alomar, Sandy, Sr. 147
America West Arena 62, 92
American Airlines Arena xii
America's Team 172, 175, 182–183, 186, 191, 231
Amish Country 220
Anaheim 137
Anaheim Ducks 137
Anders, Kimble 30
Andersen, Larry 164
Anderson, Dave 79–80
Andy Griffith Show 167
Angola 91
Anthony, Greg 82
Arafat, Yasser 189
Arbour, Al 123
Armstrong, B.J. 71–72, 76, 82, 84–85, 88, 105
Arrowhead 19–20, 29
Arsenio Hall Show 67
Arthur, Chester 130
Associated Press 61
Astrodome 19, 26, 34
Atlanta 35, 76, 137, 194, 202–203

Atlanta Braves 1, 140, 143, 152, 160–161
Atlanta Hawks 70, 75–76
Atlantic City 62, 79, 81, 83
Auerbach, Red 100
Augmon, Stacey ix, 75–76, 92
Aurora College 220
Avery, Steve 52
Awalt, Rob ix, 184, 213–216, 219, 224, 229
Awtrey, Dennis ix, 93–94

B&O Railroad 37, 39
B&O Warehouse 37–39, 43, 58
Baby Barkley 91
Bach, Johnny 73
Baerga, Carlos 152
Bahr, Matt 7
Bailey, Carlton 223–224
Ballard, Howard 179
Bally's Grand Casino 62, 79, 81
Baltimore 3, 35–37, 39–42, 44, 46–47, 49, 51–53, 55–56, 58–61
Baltimore Colts 32, 36, 41
Baltimore Orioles 35–36, 40, 53–56, 149, 232
Baltimore Sun 39
Barcelona 64, 69, 92
Barker, Bryan x, 12, 17–19, 26, 29, 31, 33
Barkley, Charles 62, 64, 87–97, 160
Barnett, Tim 25
Barney the Dinosaur 26
Barry, Rick 96
Barton, Harris 9
Baseball America 145
Battle of Belleau Wood 214
Battle of Mogadishu 153
Battle of Quebec 120
Battle of the Sexes 34
Bay Area 8, 11, 18, 23, 35, 200
Beebe, Don ix, 185, 205, 212, 214, 217, 219–224, 228, 230
Beeston, Paul 144
Belcher, Tim 156–157
Béliveau, Jean 138

Index

Bell, Jay ix, 45–46, 59
Belle, Albert 52–53
Bellows, Brian ix, 110, 113, 116, 131, 133
Bench, Johnny 34
Benes, Andy ix, 46–47, 51
Bennett, Cornelius 213, 215, 224–225
Bere, Jason ix, 156–157
Bergeron, Michel 111, 123
Berto Center 105
Bethlehem Steel 213
Bettis, Jerome 198
Bettman, Gary 134
Big Apple 82, 152
"Big D" 203
"Big Hurt" 156
Binder, Art 104
Bird, Larry 63–64, 85, 106, 117
Birden, J.J. x, 12, 14, 23, 25, 27–29, 32
Birmingham Barons 47, 107
Blackman, Rolando 78
Blaylock, Mookie 75
Bledsoe, Drew 2
Blizzard of '77 213
Blundin, Matt ix, 12, 15, 18, 22, 31
BMW 8
Bodger, Doug 122
Boggs, Wade 48, 51, 151
Bolton, Rodney 154
Bonds, Barry 48, 53, 140–141
Bono, Steve 10
Borders, Pat 147, 149
Boston Bruins x, 110, 122–123, 135–136
Boston Celtics x, 63, 93–94, 98, 100, 104
Boston Garden 93
Boston Globe 47, 65
Boston Red Sox x, xi, 1, 54, 107, 112, 149, 159, 232
Bouler, James "Slim" 80, 105
Bowie, Sam 70
Boys Will Be Boys: The Glory Days and Party Nights of the Dallas Cowboys 189
Bradley, Bill 71
Bradley University 49
Bradshaw, Terry 7
Brandeis University 104
Brett, George 26, 150, 152
Brisebois, Patrice 115
British Columbia 125
Broad Street Bullies 123
Brokaw, Tom 105
Brooklyn Dodgers 34, 153, 160
Brooks, Garth 177
Brown, Dennis 202
Brunet, Benoît 123, 128
Bryant, Bear 172
Buckner, Bill 226
Buechler, Jud 102
Buffalo 3, 31, 121, 213, 217–218, 226–227, 229–230
Buffalo Bills 2, 13, 24, 30–32, 175, 177–178, 182, 186, 203–204, 206, 212–213, 215–218, 220–222, 225–229, 231

Buffalo Sabres 112, 116, 122, 229
Burbank 183
Burkett, John ix, 44, 52
Burlington, Vermont 10
Burns, Pat 110, 112, 124
Bush, George H.W. 66
BYU 6, 12

Caffey, Jason 102
Calgary Flames 110, 114, 124, 136
California 125, 127, 129–130
California Angels 57, 149, 151
Camden Station 39, 48
Camden Yards 35–48, 52–53, 57–61, 232
Candlestick Park 6, 9, 44, 175–176, 182
Candy, John 125, 130
Carbonneau, Guy 123, 127–128, 134
Carlson, Scott 145
Carney, Keith 122
Carson, Jimmy ix, 117, 128, 135, 138
Carter, Joe xi, 140, 144, 147, 150–151, 156, 164–169
Carter, Joe D., Sr. 168
Cartwright, Bill x, 65–67, 71, 73, 75, 78, 82, 84, 97–98, 102, 105
Cash, Keith 25, 28, 31
Casillas, Tony 201
The Catch 176, 199
CBS Radio 167
CBS This Morning 183
Ceballos, Cedric 94
CFL 225
Chadron State 220, **221**
Chambers, Tom 88
Charlotte 91, 103
Charlotte Hornets x, 72, 78
Charm City 41
Cheek, Tom 166
Chesapeake Region 38
Chicago 3, 30, 36, 46, 49–50, 63–64, 68, 74, 80, 82, 85–86, 95, 97, 102–103, 108, 231
Chicago Bears 6, 102, 180
Chicago Blackhawks 134, 137
Chicago Bulls 1–2, 47, 62–66, 68–79, 81–89, 92–102, 106–109, 231
Chicago Cubs 54, 102, 168
Chicago Stadium 70, 93, 95, 97
Chicago Sun-Times 100, 105
Chicago Tribune 67, 155
Chrétien, Jean 2
Christie, Steve ix, 213, 215–218, 220–221, 223, 226–229
Christmas 6, 13, 141–142, 174, 206
Cincinnati 34, 36, 59
Cincinnati Bengals 21
Cincinnati Reds 153
Civil War 53, 130
Clack, Darryl 174
Clark, Dwight 11, 176
Clemens, Roger xi
Cleveland 41, 61, 68, 77

Cleveland Browns 191, 220
Cleveland Cavaliers 70, 76
Cleveland Indians 41, 46, 54, 151–152
Clinton, Bill 2, 47, 68, 175
Coe College 225
Coffey, Paul 117
Coimbra, Herlander 91–92
Cold War 37
Coleman, Lincoln 192, 197
Coleman, Vince 167
Coles, Darnell 147
Colisée Pepsi 120
College Park 218
Collins, Doug 73
Collins, Phil 68
Colorado Rockies 144, 159, 170
The Comeback Game 217, 229–230
Comiskey Park 2, 46, 153–154
Conacher, Pat ix, 118, 120, 127, 129, 135
Cone, David 144
Conlan, Shane 215, 224
Conn Smythe Trophy 114, 120, 133
Converse 88
Cool Runnings 125
Coolidge, Calvin 130
Corey, Walt 214
Corliss High 102
Corvette 8
Costas, Bob 99–100
Cotton Bowl 30
Country Club of Birmingham 107
Cowens, Dave 93
Cowher, Bill 24–25
Cox, Bobby 160
Craig, Roger 21, 199
Crosley Field 35
Crossett, Arkansas 210
Cruise, Tom 68
Cumberland County (N.C.) 104
CVS 170
Cyrus, Billy Ray 124

Dailey, Quintin 102
Dalgarno, Brad 123
Dallas 3, 137, 174, 179, 183–184, 192–193, 197, 200, 206, 209–211
Dallas Cowboys 2, 9, 30, 171, 173–179, 182–189, 191–194, 196–205, 207–211, 229, 231
Dallas Cowboys Official Weekly 191
Dallas Morning News 171, 174, 201
Daly, Chuck 73
Damphousse, Vincent 116, 128, 133
Daulton, Darren 159, 160, 165
Davis, Al 21
Davis, Butch x, 178, 180, 188, 198, 204, 206
Davis, Kenneth 216–217, 224
Davis, Willie 19, 25, 27–28
Day, Leon 54
Dayley, Ken x, 140, 143, 147
DeBartolo, Eddie, Jr. 10–11
Deerfield, Illinois 105

DeHaven, Bruce 216
Dele, Bison 102
Del Greco, Al 26, 28
Dellenbach, Jeff ix, 193
Demers, Jacques 110–113, 115–116, 126–128, 131, 133
Demery, Larry 103–104
Dempsey's Brew Pub & Restaurant 58
Denver Broncos 13, 19, 225
Desjardins, Éric 115, 128
Detroit 68, 118
Detroit Lions 9, 208
Detroit Pistons 65, 82, 88, 102
Detroit Red Wings 110, 117, 136–137
Detroit Tigers 160
Dickerson, Eric 21
DiPietro, Paul 133
Dishman, Cris 28, 228
Disneyland 179
Dodson, James 42
Dominican Republic 169
Dorsett, Tony 174, 190
Douglas, Michael 78
Dream Team 63–64, 67, 69, 89, 102
Dream Team 104
Drew, Larry x, 68, 70, 88
Drexler, Clyde 63, 70, 89
Dubenion, Elbert 220
Duke 69
Dyer, Don 86
Dykstra, Lenny 159–160, 162–163

Ebbets Field 35, 42
Eden Prairie, Minnesota 50
Edmonton 118, 125
Edmonton Oilers 117, 136–137
Edwards, Edwin 11
Edwards, Herm x, 14, 18, 22–23, 27, 29
Ehlo, Craig 76–77
Eisenreich, Jim 161
Eleven Rings: The Soul of Success 100
Elliott, Bob 165
Elliott, Lin 186–187
Elway, John 19, 32
Emerson, Richard 95
The Emmitt Zone 198
Empire State Building 58
Emsley A. Laney High School 69
Enberg, Dick 186
England 169
English, Michael 212, 228
Enriquez, Ana 171
Enriquez, Butch 171
ESPN 209
Europe 108, 191
Eutaw Street 37, 43, 58, 59
Evans, Donald 25
Everett, Thomas 202, 205
Ewing, Patrick 48, 64, 78, 82–87

Fall Classic 164
Favre, Brett 199

Index

Fayetteville, N.C 104
Fells Point 53
Fenway Park xi, 1, 36, 42
Fernández, Tony 147, 149–151, 162
Ferrari Testarossa 8
Ferrari 308 8
Field of Dreams 53
Fielder, Cecil 52–53
Fisher, Red 126
Fisherman's Wharf 8
Fisk, Carlton 154–155
Flint Central High School 151
Florida 129
Florida Marlins 48, 159, 170
Flushing 167
Forbes Field 36
Ford 180
Fort Lauderdale 195
Fort Worth Star-Telegram 182
Foster, Greg ix, 74–75, 102, 108
Francona, Terry 107
Fraser, Kerry 123, 128
Fregosi, Jim 160, 168
Fryman, Travis 56
Fuller, William 28

Galarraga, Andrés 144
Galloway, Randy 174
The Game Behind the Game: Negotiating in the Big Leagues 141
"Game of the Century" 34
Gammons, Peter 42
Gant, Ron 1
Gaston, Cito 52, 54, 56–57, 139–140, 162, 165, 169
Gehrig, Lou 61
Gelbaugh, Stan 218
Georgia Dome 203, 205, 207
Germany 67, 104
Gettysburg 48
Giants Stadium 196–197
Gibbs, Alex 5
Gilbride, Kevin 27
Gillick, Pat 150
Gilmour, Doug 124
Givins, Ernest 28
Gleason, Jackie 181
Glover, Kevin ix, 208, 218
Goldberger, Paul 43
Golden Gate Park 8
González, Juan 44
Good Morning America 183
Graf, Rick 216
Granato, Tony ix, 118, 124–125, 129–130, 135
Grant, Horace 64, 82, 84, 93, 97–99, 101, 105
Grapefruit League 107
Grateful Dead 97
Gray, Jerry 221–222
The Great One 116, 124, 126
"Great Trade Robbery" 175
Great Western Forum 129–130, 137

Great White North 136
Green, Daniel 103
Green, Sidney 102
Green Bay 172
Green Bay Packers 173, 198–199, 230
Gretzky, Wayne 68, 110, 116–120, 124–130, 132–133, 135, 137
Greystone 107
Griffey, Ken, Jr. 43–44, 47–49, 51–53, 68
Griffin, Alfredo ix, 139, 145, 147, 163–166, 170
Griffin, Don 176
Gulf War 91
Gum Swamp 103
Gusarov, Alexei 121
Guzmán, Juan 155
Gwynn, Tony 48, 51, 53, 56

Hackett, Paul 10, 12, 14, 28
Halas, George 226
Hale, Chris 215
Haley, Charles 175, 179–180, 183, 189, 196, 199, 200–201
Haller, Kevin 115
Halloween 170, 190–191
Hardaway, Penny ix, 64, 69, 89
Harper, Alvin 176, 181–183, 191
Hartford Whalers 114–115
Harvard 225
Harwood, Herbert H. 43
Havlicek, John 93
Hawn, Goldie 129
Hayes, Elvin 34
Hayes, Lester 206
"Heal the World" 184–**185**
Heard, Gar 94
Heisman 6, 173
Helland, Erik x, 64, 71, 101
Henderson, Rickey 150–151, 157
Hennings, Chad 180
Henryetta, Oklahoma 183, 202
Hentgen, Pat 156, 162, 165–166
Herrera, José 150–151
Hextall, Ron 121
Highsmith, Alonzo 107
Hochuli, Ed 193
Hockey Night in Canada 116
Hodges, Craig 66
HOK Sports 37, 55
Hollingbery Fieldhouse 145
Hollins, Dave 159
Hollywood 135, 203
Holt, Issiac 174
Hoover Metropolitan Stadium 107
Hornacek, Jeff 90
Horwitz, Jay 167
House of Pain 26, 29
Houston 29, 34, 80, 215, 228
Houston Oilers 13, 19, 26–29, 212–215, 218, 223–225, 228–229
Houston Rockets 70, 71, 80
Howard, David 174

Hriniak, Walt 107
Hrudey, Kelly 126, 128, 131
Huffman, Kerry ix, 121
Hurricane Isabel 44
Hussein, Saddam 30

The Icarus Agenda 144
Impossible Dream 160
Incaviglia, Pete 159
Indiana Pacers 75, 78, 108
Indianapolis 36, 41, 108
Indianapolis Colts 190, 219
Inner Harbor 35, 40, 55
Inside Sports 72
Instagram 217
Inverness 107
Irvin, Michael 175–176, 181–184, 191, 194–196, 199, 205, 208, 210, 231

Jackson, Bo 21, **154**, 158
Jackson, Danny 160
Jackson, Darrin 151
Jackson, Greg 197
Jackson, Michael 68, 177, 184, **185**, 195
Jackson, Phil 64–66, 70–74, 81–82, 84, 86, 88, 95–98, 100, 102, 105, 108
Jackson, Reggie 48, 129
Jacksonville Jaguars 209, 211
Jacobs, Eli 37
Jamaica 169
James, LeBron 89
Jeffcoat, Jim ix, 178, 180, 190, 196, 200, 204
Jefferies, Gregg 56
Jeffires, Haywood 227
Jett, John ix, 188–190, 192, 198, 208
Joe Cool 7, 19, 25, 30
Joe Robbie Stadium 24, 208
Johnson, Dennis 85
Johnson, Jimmy 171–178, 183, 187–188, 190–191, 194, 197, 201, 204–205, 208–211
Johnson, Kevin 88, 92, 95–99
Johnson, Lance 157
Johnson, Magic 64, 106, 117
Johnson, Randy 57
Johnston, Daryl "Moose" 184
Jones, Fred 25
Jones, Henry 30, 223
Jones, James Earl 53
Jones, Jerry 171–174, 185–186, 189, 191, 208–211
Jones, Jimmie 179–180, 192
Jordan, James 62–63, 83, 103–104
Jordan, Michael 2, 47, 62–85, 89–93, 95–109, 153–155, 207, 231
The Jordan Rules 65, 105
Le Journal de Montréal 115
The Judds 203
Justice, David 147

Kansas City 3, 10–11, 16, **20**, **22**, 25–26, 30, 32, 40, 59, 70, 150, 161

Kansas City Chiefs 5, 10, 12–13, 17–21, 24, 26–30, 32–33, 150, 172, 231
Kansas City Royals 1, 144, 150
Karsay, Steve 150–151
Katz, Harold 90
Kauffman Stadium 40
Keenan, Mike 134
Kegans, J. Mark 171
Kelly, Jim 13, 179–180, 204–206, 212–213, 215–216, 223, 225, 228–229
Kemp, Jeff 6
Kennedy, John 167
Kentucky 44
Kentucky Derby 8
Ker, Crawford ix, 172, 195, 198
Kerrigan, Nancy 26
Key, Jimmy 144, 151
King, Billy Jean 34
King, Larry 203
King, Martin Luther 177
King, Peter 8, 210, 215
King, Rodney 53
King, Stacey 65, 73, 78, 83
Knorr, Randy 147
Kobe 73
Korean War 28
Kosar, Bernie 191, 203
Krause, Jerry 72
Krieg, Dave 13, 19, 21, 23–25, 31–32
Kruk, John 57, 159, 161–162, 164
Kukoč, Toni 72
Kutztown University 220
Kuwait 30

Labor Day 1, 151, 153, 186, 232
Lacewell, Larry 210
Laettner, Christian 69
LaFontaine, Pat 122
Lake Erie 213, 227
Lake Michigan 30
Lakeshore Hospital 127
Lamar Hunt Trophy 231
Lamont, Gene 153, 156–157
Landry, Tom 171–172, 174, 176, 186, 191, 211
Lane, Jerome 77
Langston, Mark 48
Larkin, Barry 48
Las Vegas 108, 137, 159
Lassic, Derrick 186
Laycock, Jimmye 226
Lazarus, Adam 8
LeClair, John 110, 116, 130–133
Lemieux, Mario 122
Lett, Leon 180, 184, 191–193, 204–205
Levy, Marv 213–216, 223, 225–230
Lewis, Albert 27
Lewis, Reggie 104
Lexus 103–104
Lilly, Kevin 172
Lincoln, Abraham 48
Lincoln High School 22

Index

Lofton, James 225
Lofton, Kenny 54
Lombardi, Vince 172
Longley, Luc 102
Los Angeles 21, 53, 74, 117–118, 125, 129, 156, 177, 182, 184, 206
Los Angeles Kings 110, 116–120, 124–129, 131–133, 135–138
Los Angeles Lakers 63, 68, 72–73, 78, 80, 87–88, 100, 109, 130
Los Angeles Memorial Coliseum 35
Los Angeles Raiders 10, 13, 15, 19–22, 174, 179, 200, 206, 216
Los Angeles Rams 6, 32, 198, 206
Lott, Ronnie 199, 200
Lowery, Nick 26, 30
Lucchino, Larry 36–37, 39, 42, 54, 58, 60–61
Ludlum, Robert 144
Lynn, Mike 174

Macho Row 159
MacMullan, Jackie 65, 75, 85, 89
Maddox, Mark 216
Maddux, Greg 160
Madhouse on Madison 97
Madison Square Garden 78
Madonna 68, 90
Magowan, Peter 141
Majerle, Dan 88, 92–93, 95–96, 98
Major League Baseball 34–35, 47, 49, 53–54, 61, 168, 170
Malone, Karl 64
Manfred, Rob 61
Manning, Peyton 32
Manuel, Jerry 152
Maple Leaf Gardens 124–125
Mara, Wellington 174
March Madness 74
Marciano, Rocky 16
Marino, Dan 13, 23, 182–183, 192
Marion, Brock 192
Mariotti, Jay 100
Marshall, Leonard 7
Martin, Kelvin 176, 179
Maryland, Russell 175, 180
Maryland Lottery 39
Maryland Stadium Authority 37
Maryland Terps 218
Mason, Anthony 83
Mason, Roger 164
Material Girl 90
Matterhorn 179
Mattingly, Don 152
Mazeroski, Bill 166
McCallum, Jack 67, 81, 89, 104
McCarver, Tim 56–57
McColl, South Carolina 104
McCray, Rodney 82
McDonough, Sean 56–57
McDowell, Bubba 215
McDowell, Jack ix, 43, 46, 50, 52, 153, 155, 157

McGriff, Fred 151, 160
McHale, Kevin 85
McKeller, Keith 215, 222
McKenzie, Bob 124
McKinley, William 213
McSorley, Marty 127–130, 133
Meadowlands 174, 196, 209
Melrose, Barry 118, 120, 124–125
Memorial Day 1, 82–83, 124
Memorial Stadium 36, 39–40, 46, 59–60
Mercedes-Benz 500 SEC 8
MetLife Stadium xii
Metrodome 59, 222
Miami xii
Miami Dolphins 2, 13, 21, 24, 32, 182, 192–193, 211, 229
Miami Heat 104
Miami Hurricanes 171, *173*, 218
Mia's 171, 211
Michaels, Al 21
Michigan 151
Middle East 189
Midsummer Classic 35, 149
Midtown Manhattan 79
Milacki, Bob ix, 40–41, 59
Miller, Oliver 96
Miller, Tricia 149
Mills, Alan ix, 58
Milwaukee 141–142, 147
Minneapolis Lakers 98
Minnesota North Stars 113
Minnesota Twins 49, 59, 144, 149
Minnesota Vikings 6–7, 10, 174, 194
Mississippi River 49
Mlakar, Roy 125
MLB Radio 167
Mogilny, Alexander 122
Molitor, Paul 139–144, 147, 150, 162, 164–165, 168–169
Monaco 79
Monday Night Football 6, 9, 19, 21, 186, 194
Monongahela, Pennsylvania 24
Montana 169
Montana, Joe 2, 5–32
Monte Carlo Casino 79
Montreal 3, 44, 51, 111–116, 123, 125, 128, 130, 134–138
Montreal Canadiens 110, 112–114, 116, 120–121, 123, 125–128, 130–132, 134–137, 231
Montreal Expos 152, 232
Montreal Forum 110, 115, 120, 123, 128, 132, 137–138
Montreal Gazette 126
Moog, Andy 114
Moon, Warren 13, 27–28, 189, 213, 223–224, 226, 228
Morandini, Mickey ix, 48, 159–160, 163–165
Morgan State University 53
Moroski, Mike 6
Morris, Jack 144, 169
Mrs. Doubtfire 193

Index   255

Mulholland, Terry 48–49, 51, 161, 164
Muller, Kirk ix, 110, 116, 120–122, 125, 127–128, 131, 133–134
Murray, Eddie (Baltimore Orioles) 41, 60
Murray, Eddie (Dallas Cowboys) 187, 192, 196–197
Mussina, Mike 56–57

Nagasaki 73
Naismith College Player of the Year 70
Namath, Joe 32
Nassau Veterans Memorial Coliseum 123
National Guard 71
NBC 62, 84, 92, 99–100, 105, 108, 183, 186, 226, 228
Nealy, Ed 99
Negro Leagues 53–54
Nelson, Darrin 174
New England 131–132
New England Patriots 2, 230–231
New Jersey 91, 198
New Jersey Devils 122
New Jersey Nets 104
New Mexico 169
New Orleans 53
New Orleans Saints 10
New York City 79, 177–178
New York Giants 7, 174, 191, 196, 226
New York Islanders 115, 122, 135–136
New York Jets 194, 229
New York Knicks 1, 65, 71, 75, 78–79, 82–87, 98, 108–109
New York Lottery 228
New York Mets 41, 152, 167
New York Post 80
New York Rangers 135–136, 232
New York Times 43, 79, 83, 106
New York Yankees 1, 55, 58, 144, 149–153, 156, 167, 232

Nidetz, Steve 67
Nike 67, 88
99: Stories of the Game 118
Nixon, Richard 167
North Carolina 99
North Texas 189, 194
Northwestern 225
Norton, Ken, Jr. 177, 180–181, 196, 205
Norton, Ken, Sr. 180–181
Norwood, Scott 226–227
Notre Dame 20
Novacek, Jay 179, 207–208

Oakland 151
Oakland Athletics 143, 149, 150
Oakland Coliseum 35
Oakley, Charles 65, 84
Oakville 227
Odomes, Nate 227
O'Donnell, Neil 25
Ohio State University 220

Oklahoma 169
Oklahoma City 168
Oklahoma State 188
Olajuwon, Hakeem 70
Old Overton 107
Oldsmobile Cutless 8
Olerud, John 51–52, 139–140, 144–147, 149, 151, 162, 164–165
Olympic Saddledome 114
Olympic Stadium 44, 152
O'Neal, Shaquille 72
O'Neill, Paul 151
Ontario 149, 166
Oriole Park 35, 39, 42, 47
Orlando 208–209
Orlando Magic 72, 89
Ortiz, David xi
Ottawa Senators 112
Otto, Joel 124
Oxmoor Valley 107

Palestine 189
Pall, Donn 154
Palmer, Jim 60
Parcells, Bill xi, 2, 215
Pardee, Jack 224
Parish, Robert 85
Pasadena 177, 184, 205, 208, 229
Patton, Marvcus 224
Pauley Pavilion 182
Paxson, John 66–67, 71–72, 82, 88, 98–100, 105
Pea Bridge 103
Pearlman, Jeff 189
Peete, Rodney 189
Perdue, Will 72–73, 78, 96, 98
Persian Gulf 226
Petco Park 61
Peters, Tony 141
Peterson, Carl 15
Petrović, Dražen 104
Pettis, Gary 147
Pfeiffer, Michelle 130
Phi Beta Kappa 225
Philadelphia 34–35, 52, 59, 89–91, 123, 139, 158, 160, 162–163, 174
Philadelphia Eagles 174–175, 190, 194, 219
Philadelphia Flyers 113
Philadelphia Phillies 48, 52, 139, 152, 158–164, 167
Philadelphia Police Department 174
Philadelphia 76ers 88, 90–91
Phoenix 10, 62, 90–91, 93, 97, 109, 137, 206
Phoenix Cardinals 10, 204, 206
Phoenix Suns 62, 71, 87–88, 90, 92–98, 101
Piazza, Mike 1, 48, 57
Pierce, Paul xi
Pike, Mark 216
Pippen, Scottie 63–64, 66, 70, 72, 76–77, 81–82, 84–87, 92–93, 95, 97–98, 100, 102, 105, 108
Pittsburgh 34, 36, 59, 61, 122, 215

Index

Pittsburgh Penguins 113, 122, 135, 137
Pittsburgh Pirates 46, 166–167
Pittsburgh Steelers 7, 24–25, 29, 211, 229, 231
Plan B 175, 179, 206
The Playmaker 195
The Plaza 79
Podres, Johnny 160
Policy, Carmen 9–11
Polo Grounds 35, 42
Polynice, Olden 86
Porsche 928 8
Powell, Boog 59
Powerball 166
Powers, Richie 93
Pratt Street 53
Prince Bandar bin Sultan 208
Princess Diana 68
Princeton 36
Pro Football Hall of Fame 200, 220
Prohibition Era 38
Provo, Utah 12
Puckett, Kirby 48–53
Puerto Rico **148**, 169

QB: My Life Behind the Spiral 6, 201
Quality Inn 104
Quebec City 121
Quebec Nordiques 110–111, 115–116, 120–121, 123, 133
Queens, New York 35

Rabin, Yitzhak 189
Raines, Tim 153, 157
Raleigh 137
Rashad, Ahmad 92, 108
Reagan, Nancy 129
Reagan, Ronald 129
Reebok 190, 198
Reed, Andre ix, 179, 213, 217, 220–225, 228, 230
Reich, Frank 185, 212, 214–216, 218–224, 227–229
Reinsdorf, Jerry 86, 105, 107, 155
Renaissance Center 117–118
Rendell, Ed 162
Revere, Ben 160
Reversing the Curse: Inside the 2004 Boston Red Sox 54
Rice, Jerry 15, 199, 201, 223
Rich Stadium 32, 213, 216–217, 227–228
Richard, Maurice 138
Riggs, Bobby 34
Righetti, Dave 152
Riley, Pat 78, 82, 108
Ring of Honor 191
Ripken, Cal, Jr. 41, 48–49, 51, 56, 60–61
River Falls, Wisconsin 5, 13, 17–18
Riverfront Stadium 34, 44, 59
Rivers, Doc 78
Robert Taylor Homes 49
Robinson, Brooks 60

Robinson, David 64, 92
Robinson, Frank 60
Robitaille, Luc 130–131
Rochester 229
Rodríguez, Iván "Pudge" 48, 52, 149
Romanowski, Bill 199
Ronald McDonald House Charities 66
Ronan, Ed ix, 112–113, 115, 121, 132, 134, 137
Roosevelt, Theodore 170
Rose Bowl 177, 181, 183–184, 205
Ross, Bobby 218
Roy, Jana 127
Roy, Michele 127
Roy, Patrick 110, 113–114, 121, 126–127, 129, 134
Russell, Bill 65, 100
Rust Belt 225
Ruth, Babe 55
Ruth, George, Sr. 55
Ryan, Buddy 26–29
Ryan, Nolan 152

Saberhagen, Bret 167
Sacramento 26
St. Albans, Vermont 130, 132
St. Louis Blues 110, 135
St. Louis Cardinals 140, 142, 147, 156
St. Paul 142, 144
St. Petersburg 141
Sammy's 107
San Diego 21–22, 51, 58, 61, 69
San Diego Chargers 24, 32, 174
San Diego Padres 46, 54, 151, 168
San Francisco Examiner 13
San Francisco 49ers 5–11, 19, 30, 174–176, 186, 199–202
San Francisco Giants 44, 52, 140, 152
Sandberg, Ryan 48
Sandstrom, Tomas 131
Santa Clara 11
Santa Clara University 17
Santa Monica 182–183
Santa Monica Civic Auditorium 183
Saturday Night Live 67
Savard, Denis 116, 134
Savard, Serge 111, 121, 123
Saxon, Mike 178
Schaefer, William Donald 36
Schaeffer, David 155
Schilling, Curt 52, 158, 160–161, 163–164
Schmidt, Mike 34
Schneider, Mathieu 115, 128
Schofield, Dick x, 143–144, 147, 166–167
Schofield, John "Ducky" 167
Schottenheimer, Marty 10, 13, 19, 23, 25, 28, 30
Schueler, Ron 155
Schwarzenegger, Arnold 68
Seattle Seahawks 6, 24
Seattle SuperSonics 71, 86–87
Seifert, George 7, 9–11, 201
Selleck, Tom 48
Sharpe, Sterling 198

Index

Shaughnessy, Dan 47, 54
Shaw, Brian 104
Sheffield, Gary 48, 53
Sherwin-Williams 132
Shibe Park 35
Shoal Creek 107
The Shot 77
Showtime Lakers 63, 78, 130
Shue, Gene 90
Silver Spring, Maryland 152
Simms, Phil 191
Sinden, Harry 114, 123
Sins, Ken 191
SkyDome 125, 139, 149, 156
Smith, Bruce 31, 213, 224–225
Smith, Charles 78, 82, 85
Smith, Dean 99
Smith, Emmitt 175–176, 179, 181, 183–184, 186, 188–192, 194, 196–199, 202, 204, 206–208, 210
Smith, Janet Marie x, 36–37, 39–40, 42, 60–61
Smith, Kevin 175, 184
Smith, LaBradford 74
Smith, Neil 27
Smith, Sam 65
Smoltz, John 55
Soldier Field 30
Solomon, Jesse 174
Solomon, Keith 206
South Carolina 63, 103–104
South Central Los Angeles 206
South Chicago 49
South Lawn 189
South Side 49, 102, 153
Soviet Union 64
Spanish American War 37
Special Olympics 66
Spokane 145
Sports Illustrated 1, 8, 65, 67, 107, 127, 132, 144, 181, 195, 210, 215
Sprague, Ed 162
Stanford 225
Stargell, Willie 34
Starks, John 78–79, 82–84
Starlight Children's Foundation 66
Starr, Bart 226
Staubach, Roger 174, 202–203
Steadman, John 39
Steel City 36, 122
Steinbach, Terry 55
Steinberg, Charles 53–54
Steinberg, Leigh 202
Steinbrenner, George 151
Stern, David 106
Stetka, Bill x, 56–58, 60
Steve's Pizza 17
Stewart, Alex 174
Stewart, Dave 155–156, 158, 161, 164
"Storm of the Century" 74
Stottlemyre, Todd 156, 162
Stoyanovich, Pete 192–193
Sun Belt 129, 137

Sun Devil Stadium 177
Sunrise 137
Super Bowl IX 5
Super Bowl XVI 6, 176
Super Bowl XIX 6
Super Bowl XXIII 7, 24, 199
Super Bowl XXIV 7, 199
Super Bowl XXV 226–227
Super Bowl XXVI 222
Super Bowl XXVII 175, 177–178, 182, 184, **185**, **187**, 191, 195, 202, 205, 229
Super Bowl XXVIII 30, 203, 205–206, 208
Super Bowl XXX 211, 231
Surhoff, B.J. ix, 141–142, 169
Sutcliffe, Rick 41
Swift, E.M. 127
Switzer, Barry 210–211
Sydor, Darryl 131–132

Talley, Darryl 214, 223, 225, 228
Tampa Bay 137
Tampa Bay Buccaneers 5, 17, 203, 226
Tampa Bay Lightning 117, 137
Tampa Stadium 226
Tasker, Steve 178, 214, 225
Tasmanian Devil 159
Taylor, Lawrence 7, 196
Tempe, Arizona 177
Terry, Ralph 167
Testaverde, Vinny 5–6
Texas 41, 99, 171–172, 181, 188, 196, 223
Texas Rangers 44, 52, 149–150, 153, 156
Texas Stadium 174, 191–192
Thanksgiving xi, 2, 24, 117, 174, 192–194
Thigpen, Bobby 152
Thomas, Derrick 27
Thomas, Frank 48, 53, 153–**154**, 156–157
Thomas, Thurman 32, 178, 204–206, 213, 215–216, 223, 225
Three Rivers Stadium 34, 44, 59, 229
Times Square 178
Today 183
The Tonight Show with Jay Leno 181, 183
Toronto 3, 124, 130, 139, 151, 161, 164, 166
Toronto Blue Jays xi, 51, 54, 56, 139, 141, 143, 147, 149–151, 153, 155–163, 166, 169–170, 232
Toronto Maple Leafs 120, 124, 136
Toronto Star 124, 161
Triton Junior College 49
Trombley, Mike 49–50, 59
Trumpy, Bob 186
Turkey Day 191
Turner, Norv 181, 207–208
Twitter 217

Unitas, Johnny 32
United Negro College Fund 66
United States Football League 6
University of Arkansas 171
University of California, Los Angeles x, 180, 182, 205–206

Index

University of California, San Diego 64
University of Central Arkansas 86
University of Florida 198
University of Iowa 84
University of Maryland 218, 220
University of Miami 5, 191, 195, 218
University of Michigan 151
University of Nevada, Las Vegas 76
University of North Carolina Tar Heels 69, 74
University of North Dakota 73
University of Oklahoma Sooners 210
University of Pennsylvania 16
University of Pittsburgh 36
University of San Francisco 65
University of Southern California 20, 22, 220
University of Vermont 130
University of Virginia 86
University of Washington Medical Center 145
University of Wisconsin-River Falls 5
Upper Manhattan 35
USA Basketball 63
USA Today 12

Valerio, Joe ix, 14–17, 25, 29
Valley Avenue 107
Valley Ranch 177–178, 196
Vancouver Canucks 115, 124
Vaughn, Mo xi
Velarde, Randy 152
Venezuela 169
Ventura, Robin 153
Vermont 10, 130, 132
Versace 194
Veterans Stadium 34, 52, 59, 139, 162–163, 174, 190
Vietnam War 71
Vincent, Fay 41
Virginia 189

Waco Siege 75
Walcott, Jersey Joe 16
Wales Conference Finals 123
Walker, Darrell 69, 73, 99, 102
Walker, Herschel 173–175, 190
Wallace, Aaron 20
Wallace, North Carolina 104
Walsh, Bill 6–7
Walter, Mike 176
Walter Payton NFL Man of the Year Award 16
Walton, Bill 85
Wannstedt, Dave 180, 208
Ward, Duane 55–56, 162
Washington, James ix, 175–176, 178–179, 181, 196, 204–207
Washington Nationals 232
Washington Post 41
Washington Redskins 9, 21, 186, 194, 208, 223
Washington State 145-**146**
Washington State Cougars 145
Washington Wizards 69
Waubonsee Community College 220

WBC 180
Weatherspoon, Clarence ix, 88, 91
Weaver, Earl 60
Wersching, Ray 176
West, David 164
West Camden Street 41
West Coast Offense 10, 14
Western Illinois University 220
Western New York 2, 30, 213, 216, 226, 229
Westphal, Paul 88, 93–95
White, Devon ix, xi, 54–55, 143, 147, 150–151, 162–163, 166
White, Jo Jo 93–94
White, Lorenzo 27, 213
White, Reggie 10, 160
Whiten, Mark 152
Whitmore, David 5, 11
Whitt, Richie x, 182–184
Wilkins, Dominique 75–76
Wilkins, Gerald 77
Will, George 42
William & Mary College 226–227
Williams, Corey 99
Williams, David 27
Williams, Edward Bennett 36
Williams, Harvey 21, 29
Williams, Kevin 192
Williams, Mitch 161, 163–167
Williams, Scott ix, 63, 68, 71, 73, 78, 80, 82, 95, 99, 101, 105
Williams, Ted 144
Williams, Woody x, 143, 146, 148–149, 155, 169
Willis, Kevin 75–76
Wilmington, North Carolina 69, 103
Wilson, Ralph 213, 228
Windy City 102
Winfield, Dave 140, 144, 152
Winnipeg 117
Winnipeg Arena 117
Winnipeg Jets 117
Winter, Tex 65, 73
Woodson, Darren 175, 184, 205–206
World Trade Center 177
World War I 214
World War II 34, 36, 53, 73, 171, 214
Worthy, James 80
Wright, Felix 220
Wright, Jeff 224
Wrigley Field 36, 42
Wyche, Sam 19

Yale University 53
Yankee Stadium 151, 158
Yonkers 8
Young, Cy 52, 153
Young, Steve x, 6–8, 10–12, 20, 23, 30, 176, 200–201
Youngstown, Ohio 11

Zamorano, J.R. 202
Zen Buddhism 74

www.ingramcontent.com/pod-product-compliance
Ingram Content Group UK Ltd.
Pitfield, Milton Keynes, MK11 3LW, UK
UKHW041932140426
5217IPUK00014B/444